D0850088

The Garland Library
of Medieval Literature

General Editors
James J. Wilhelm, Rutgers University
Lowry Nelson, Jr., Yale University

Literary Advisors
Ingeborg Glier, Yale University
William W. Kibler, University of Texas
Norris J. Lacy, University of Kansas
Fred C. Robinson, Yale University
Aldo Scaglione, University of North Carolina

Art Advisor
Elizabeth Parker McLachlan, Rutgers University

Music Advisor
Hendrik van der Werf, Eastman School of Music

Hunting scene, possibly Arthur in pursuit of the white stag. Paris, B.N., f.fr. 1376, fol. 95r (Phot. Bibl. nat. Paris).

Chrétien de Troyes

Erec and Enide

edited and translated by
CARLETON W. CARROLL

with an Introduction by
WILLIAM W. KIBLER

Volume 25
Series A
GARLAND LIBRARY OF MEDIEVAL LITERATURE

Garland Publishing, Inc.
New York & London
1987

Library of Congress Cataloging-in-Publication Data
Chrétien, de Troyes, 12th cent.
 Erec and Enide.

 (The Garland library of medieval literature ; v. 25.
Series A)
 Translation of: Erec et Enide.
 Bibliography: p.
 Includes index.
  1. Arthurian romances. I. Carroll, Carleton W.
II. Title. III. Series: Garland library of medieval
literature ; v. 25.
 PQ1445.E6A33 1987   841'.1   84-48060
 ISBN 0-8240-8957-X (alk. paper)

Printed on acid-free, 250-year-life paper
Manufactured in the United States of America

Por ma fame et m'amie

Hunting scene, possibly Arthur in pursuit of the white stag. Paris, B.N., f.fr. 24403, fol. 119r (Phot. Bibl. nat. Paris).

Preface of the General Editors

The Garland Library of Medieval Literature was established to make available to the general reader modern translations of texts in editions that conform to the highest academic standards. All of the translations are original, and were created especially for this series. The translations attempt to render the foreign works in a natural idiom that remains faithful to the originals.

The Library is divided into two sections: Series A, texts and translations; and Series B, translations alone. Those volumes containing texts have been prepared after consultation of the major previous editions and manuscripts. The aim in the editing has been to offer a reliable text with a minimum of editorial intervention. Significant variants accompany the original, and important problems are discussed in the Textual Notes. Volumes without texts contain translations based on the most scholarly texts available, which have been updated in terms of recent scholarship.

Most volumes contain Introductions with the following features: (1) a biography of the author or a discussion of the problem of authorship, with any pertinent historical or legendary information; (2) an objective discussion of the literary style of the original, emphasizing any individual features; (3) a consideration of sources for the work and its influence; and (4) a statement of the editorial policy for each edition and translation. There is also a Select Bibliography, which emphasizes recent criticism on the works. Critical writings are often accompanied by brief descriptions of their importance. Selective glossaries, indices, and footnotes are included where appropriate.

The Library covers a broad range of linguistic areas, including all of the major European languages. All of the important literary forms and genres are considered, sometimes in anthologies or selections.

The General Editors hope that these volumes will bring the general reader a closer awareness of a richly diversified area that has for too long been closed to everyone except those with precise academic training, an area that is well worth study and reflection.

James J. Wilhelm
Rutgers University

Lowry Nelson, Jr.
Yale University

Contents

Erec defeats one of the robber-knights, as Enide looks on. Paris, B.N., f.fr.
24403, fol. 142r (Phot. Bibl. nat. Paris).

Introduction

by William W. Kibler

Life of the Author

Chrétien de Troyes's first extant full-length romance, *Erec and Enide*, is also the first Arthurian romance preserved. With it Chrétien launched a vogue which was to continue uninterrupted until the very end of the Middle Ages, and which has left important vestiges even into our twentieth century. Few literate people today have not heard of the loves of Lancelot and Guinevere or of Perceval's search for the secrets of the Grail. These and many other adventures associated with the court of the legendary King Arthur were all directly or indirectly inspired by the twelfth-century romances composed by Chrétien.

Erec and Enide was one of the three great romances completed by Chrétien. The others, in order of composition, were *Cligés* and *The Knight of the Lion (Yvain)*. Two other romances, begun for specific patrons, were left uncompleted by our author. Many believe that he abandoned *The Knight of the Cart (Lancelot)*, which he dedicated to Marie de Champagne, the wife of Henry the Liberal, because of dissatisfaction with the subject matter; and most critics accept that *The Story of the Grail (Perceval)* was interrupted by Chrétien's death, or by that of his patron, Philip of Alsace, Count of Flanders. Three additional narrative poems have been ascribed to Chrétien, with varying degrees of success. Following Maurice Wilmotte,[1] a number of critics recognize him as the author of the hagiographical romance *William of England*; but D.D.R. Owen's attributions to Chrétien of *Le Chevalier à l'épée (The Knight with the Sword)* and *La Mule sans frein (The Unbridled Mule)*, two romances found in a manuscript containing his *Perceval*, have not met with widespread acceptance (Bianchini, Williams). In addition to these narrative works, Chrétien has left us two lyric poems in the courtly manner, which make him the first identifiable North French practitioner of the courtly

---

[1] All names and page references are keyed to the Select Bibliography, which follows.

lyric style begun in southern France in the early years of the twelfth century. In the opening lines of his second romance, *Cligés*, Chrétien includes a list of works that he had previously composed:

> Cil qui fist d'Erec et d'Enide,
> Et les comandemanz d'Ovide
> Et l'art d'amors an romans mist,
> Et le mors de l'espaule fist,
> Del roi Marc et d'Ysalt la blonde,
> Et de la hupe et de l'aronde
> Et del rossignol la muance,
> Un novel conte rancomance
> D'un vaslet qui an Grece fu
> Del lignage le roi Artu.   (ed. Micha, lines 1-10)

> [He who wrote of Erec and Enide, who translated Ovid's Commandments and the Art of Love, who wrote of the Shoulder Bite, of King Mark and Iseult the Blond, of the metamorphosis of the hoopoe, the swallow and the nightingale, begins here a new story about a youth who, in Greece, was of Arthur's line.]

From this list it seems established that early in his career Chrétien perfected his technique by practicing the current literary mode of translations and adaptations of tales from Latin into the vernacular. The *comandemanz d'Ovide* can be identified with Ovid's *Remedia Amoris*; the *art d'amors* is Ovid's *Ars amatoria* (*Art of Love*), and the *mors de l'espaule* is the Pelops story in the *Metamorphoses*, Book 6. These works by Chrétien have all been lost. Only the *muance de la hupe et de l'aronde et del rossignol* (the Philomela story in *Metamorphoses*, Book 6) is preserved in a version that might be by Chrétien.

Chrétien also informs us in this passage that he composed a poem *del roi Marc et d'Ysalt la blonde*. As far as we know, this was the first treatment of this famous Breton legend in French. Chrétien does not tell us whether he had written a full account of the tragic loves of Tristan and Iseult, and scholars today generally agree that most likely he treated only an episode of that legend, since Mark's name, rather than Tristan's, is linked with Iseult's. But we are nonetheless permitted to believe that he is in some measure responsible for the subsequent success of that story, as he was to be in large measure for that of King Arthur. Indeed, in his earliest romances Chrétien seems obsessed with the Tristan legend, which he mentions several times in *Erec and Enide* and against which his *Cligés* (frequently referred to an an "anti-Tristan") is seen to react.

All that we know about the dates and circumstances of Chrétien's literary production, and what little we know of his life, must be patiently pieced together from the works themselves. In the prologue to *Erec and Enide* he gives the fullest version of his name, Crestïens de Troies (v. 9), and this designation is also used by Gerbert de Montreuil in his continuation of Chrétien's unfinished *Perceval*. In the prologues to *Cligés* (v. 43), *Lancelot* (v. 25), and *Perceval* (v. 62), and in the closing lines of *Yvain* (v. 6821) he calls himself simply Crestïens. The fuller version of his name given in this romance suggests that he was born or at least spent his formative years in Troyes, which is located some hundred miles along the Seine southeast of Paris and was one of the leading cities in the region of Champagne. The language in which he composed his works, which is tinted with dialectal traits from the Champagne area, lends further credence to this supposition.

At Troyes, Chrétien most assuredly was associated with the court of Marie de Champagne, one of the daughters of Eleanor of Aquitaine by her first marriage, to Louis VII of France. Marie's marriage to Henry the Liberal, Count of Champagne, furnishes us with one of the very few dates that can be determined with any degree of certainty in Chrétien's biography. For many years it was thought to have occurred in 1164, but recent archival research by Holmes and Klenke (p. 18) and Misrahi (pp. 109-113) has pushed this date back to at least 1159. In the opening lines of *The Knight of the Cart*, Chrétien informs us that he is undertaking the composition of his romance at the behest of "my lady of Champagne," and critics are in unanimous accord today that this can only be the great literary patroness Marie. Chrétien could not have begun a romance for "my lady of Champagne" before 1159.

Another relatively certain date in Chrétien's biography is furnished by the dedication of his *Perceval* to Philip of Flanders. It appears that, sometime after the death of Henry the Liberal in 1181, Chrétien found a new patron in Philip of Alsace, a cousin to Marie de Champagne, who became count of Flanders in 1168 and to whom Chrétien dedicated his never-to-be-completed *Story of the Grail*. This romance surely was begun before Philip's death in 1191 at Acre in the Holy Land, and most likely prior to his departure for the Third Crusade in September of 1190. Chrétien may have abandoned the poem after learning of Philip's death, or he may well have been interrupted by his own death around this time.

Apart from the dates 1159 and 1191, nothing else concerning Chrétien's biography can be fixed with certainty. Allusions in *Erec and Enide* to Macrobius and the Liberal Arts, to Alexander, Solomon, Helen of Troy and others, coupled with similar allusions in his other romances, suggest that he received the standard preparation of a *clerc* in the flourishing church schools in Troyes and therefore must have entered minor orders. The style of his love monologues shows that he was formed in the dialectal method of the schools, in which opposites are juxtaposed and analyzed, as well as in the rhetorical traditions of classical and medieval Latin literature.

The elaborate descriptions of clothing and ceremonies in this first romance can be traced to contemporary works composed in French, particularly to Wace's *Roman de Brut* and the anonymous *Eneas* and *Floire et Blancheflor*.

Circumstantial evidence also strongly suggests that Chrétien spent some of his early career in England and may well have composed his first romance there. Early in this century Gaston Paris (1910) had noted the precision in the treatment of English topography in *Cligés*, and recent detailed research by Constance Bullock-Davies has shown that for all Chrétien's romances, the Britain of Arthur was the England of Henry II. Urban T. Holmes (1970: 24) has noted the special link between Troyes and England in the person of Henry of Blois, abbot of Glastonbury (1126-71) and bishop of Winchester (1129-71). This prelate was the uncle of Henry the Liberal of Champagne, at whose court we know Chrétien was engaged. Henry of Blois had important contacts with Geoffrey of Monmouth and William of Malmesbury, two Latin writers who, more than any others, popularized the legends of King Arthur that Chrétien was to seize upon.

Even more intriguing for the genesis of *Erec and Enide*, Beate Schmolke-Hasselmann has recently made an excellent case for seeing a reflection of contemporary politics in the coronation of Erec at Nantes on Christmas Day. In 1169 Henry II Plantagenet held a Christmas court in Nantes in order to force the engagement of his third son, Geoffrey, to Constance, the daughter of Conan IV of Brittany. This court had significant political ramifications, for it assured through marital politics the submission of the major Breton barons, a submission Henry had not been able to attain by successive military campaigns in 1167, 1168, and 1169. The guest list at the coronation of Erec includes barons from all corners of Henry Plantagenet's domains but, significantly, none from those of his rival Louis VII of France. Two other details from this coronation scene lend credence to such an identification: the thrones in which Arthur and Erec are seated are described as having leopards sculpted upon their arms, and the identification of the donor of these thrones as Bruianz des Illes. Leopards were the heraldic animals on Henry's royal arms, and Bruianz des Illes has been positively identified as Henry's best friend, Brian of Wallingford, named in contemporary documents as Brian Fitz Count, Brian *de Insula*, or Brian de l'Isle.

Schmolke-Hasselmann has suggested that *Erec and Enide* was composed at the behest of Henry II to help legitimize Geoffrey's claim to the throne of Brittany by underscoring the "historical" link between Geoffrey and Arthur. This would place its composition shortly after 1169, while memories of the Nantes court were still fresh. Such a dating corresponds well with what we know about the composition of Chrétien's other romances. Although earlier in this century Foerster and Holmes had placed the composition of *Cligés*, *Lancelot*, and *Yvain* in the 1160s, most other critics have placed them in the 1170s (G. Paris, Hofer, Fourrier, Frappier) or, in the case of *Lancelot* and *Yvain*, even later (Luttrell, Hunt).

Since Chrétien gave the fuller version of his name in the prologue to *Erec and Enide*, we must assume he was away from the region of Troyes at the time of its composition, and it now seems quite reasonable to speculate that he was in England at the court of Henry II, where he would have had ample opportunity to learn of the new "Matter of Britain" which was just then reaching popularity there. *Erec*, a brilliant psychological study, would be the first romance composed in a vernacular tongue to incorporate Arthurian materials. This romance posed a problem familiar to courtly circles: how can a knight, once married, sustain the prowess and glory that won him his bride? That is: can a knight serve both his honor (*armes*) and his love (*amours*)? Erec, caught up in marital bliss, neglects the pursuit of his glory until reminded by Enide, who has overheard some knights gossiping maliciously. Accompanied by her, he sets out on a series of adventures in the course of which both Erec and his bride are tested. The mixture of psychological penetration and extraordinary adventures would become a trademark of Chrétien's style and of the Arthurian romances written in imitation of his work. And the question of *armes vs. amours* would be reconsidered from a different perspective in *Yvain*.

Chrétien's second major work, *Cligés*, is in part set at Arthur's court, but is principally an adventure romance based on Greco-Byzantine material, which was exceedingly popular in the second half of the twelfth century. This romance, which exalts the pure love of Fenice for Cligés, has been seen by many as a counter-argument to the adulterous passion of Iseult for Tristan. Numerous textual parallels have been adduced to support this contention, but the poem is even more interesting to us for its use of irony, its balanced structure, and its psychological insights into the hearts of the two lovers. Here, as elsewhere, Chrétien shows the influence of Ovid, the most popular classical writer throughout the twelfth century.

The relationship between Chrétien's third and fourth romances is complex. There are several direct references in *The Knight with the Lion* to action that occurs in *The Knight of the Cart*, particularly to Meleagant's abduction of Guinevere and the subsequent quest by Lancelot (vv. 3700-13, 3918-41). Yet at the same time, the characterization of Kay in the early section of *Lancelot* seems explicable only in terms of *Yvain*. Further, the blissful conjugal scene between Arthur and Guinevere at the beginning of *Yvain* seems incomprehensible after *Lancelot*. These contradictory factors have led some recent scholars, notably Frappier, Ménard, Shirt, and Hunt, to follow and refine the reasoning of Fourrier, who first proposed in 1950 that Chrétien composed these two romances simultaneously, beginning with *Yvain*, then breaking off to *Lancelot*, which itself was perhaps completed in three stages. According to this theory as it has been eventually refined, Chrétien wrote the first part of *Lancelot*, then turned it over to Godefroy de Lagny to complete. Dissatisfied with the contrast between the two sections,

Chrétien himself would then have composed the tournament at Noauz section to harmonize the two parts. However, this whole elaborate superstructure has recently been challenged on stylistic grounds by Jan Janssens.

Lancelot tells of the adulterous relationship of its eponymous hero with Arthur's queen, Guinevere. Its central theme, the acting out in romance form of a story of *fin'amors*, has generally been attributed to a suggestion by Marie de Champagne, for it is in stark contrast to Chrétien's other romances, which extol the virtues of fidelity in marriage. For this reason many critics today find in *Lancelot* extensive irony and humor, which serve to bring its thesis in line with Chrétien's other romances. The composition of *Lancelot*, and *Yvain* with it, marks an important stage in the development of Chrétien's thought, for he turns away in these works from the couple predestined to rule to the individual who must discover his own place in society.

Chrétien's final work, begun sometime before the death of Philip of Flanders in 1191 and never completed, was and still is his most puzzling: *The Story of the Grail* (*Perceval*). Controversy continues today over whether or not Chrétien intended this romance to be read allegorically. Even those critics who agree that his intent was indeed allegorical argue over the proper nature and significance of the allegory. His immediate continuators, Robert de Boron and the anonymous author of the *Perlesvaus*, clearly assumed that the allegory was Christian. Unfortunately, death apparently overcame Chrétien before he could complete his masterwork and reveal the mysteries of the Grail Castle.

Artistic Achievement

Chrétien was the first and best writer of Arthurian romance in French. The vogue for romance began in the 1150s, with the several romances and stories composed in Old French on classical themes: *The Romance of Æneas* (*Eneas*), *The Romance of Troy*, *The Romance of Thebes*, *Piramus and Thisbe*, and *Narcissus*. These romances, composed in the octosyllabic line that would be favored in turn by Chrétien, gave new emphasis to the love interest that was often only latent in their classical sources. To the nascent love intrigue and the octosyllabic line inherited from the romances of antiquity, Chrétien added a profound interest in the psychology of love, derived in large measure from the example of troubadour love poetry, and a new source of material hitherto unexplored upon the continent: the *matière de Bretagne* (Matter of Britain). *Erec and Enide*, the first Arthurian romance, is a brilliant combination of Arthurian material found in the "histories" of Geoffrey of Monmouth and Wace, the love psychology of the troubadour lyric, and the octosyllabic line favored by Norman chroniclers and the authors of the "Romances of Antiquity."

In the prologue to *Erec and Enide*, Chrétien tells us that he *tret d'un conte d'avanture / une molt bele conjointure* ("from a tale of adventure/ he draws a beautifully ordered composition"). This *conjointure* has been variously translated "arrangement," "linking," "coherent organization," "internal unity," etc., but always implies to modern literary researchers that Chrétien has moulded and organized materials that were only inchoate before he set his artistry to them. A good discussion is that by Eugène Vinaver, who writes in *The Rise of Romance*: "the art of *composition* [is] the proper means of turning a mere tale of adventure into a romance ... [The] *conjointure* is merely a method of dealing with the material; it is not a substitute for the *conte*, but something a skilful poet can and must superimpose upon it" (p. 37).

In speaking of *un conte d'avanture* in the singular and with the article, Chrétien makes it clear that he conceived of his source as a single work, rather than as a collection of disparate themes or motifs. He goes on to inform us that other story-tellers, the professional *jongleurs* who earn their living by performing such narrative poems before the public, were wont to *depecier et corronpre* ("mangle and corrupt") these tales (vv. 20-22). Chrétien, on the other hand, clearly implies that he has provided a coherent structure for his tale, a structure that most critics today agree is that of a triptych. Like the traditional triptych altarpiece, Chrétien's work has a broad central panel flanked by two balanced side-panels. The first panel, which Chrétien refers to as *li premiers vers* ("the first movement," v. 1808), comprises lines 27-1808 and weaves together the episodes of the Hunt of the White Stag and the Joust for the Sparrow-hawk. The final episode, known as the Joy of the Court, forms an analogous panel of approximately the same length as the first, from line 5321 to 6912. The central panel of our triptych, from line 1809 to 5320, is by far the largest and most important, covering as it does the main action of the poem.

This romance, like the others that were to follow, was arranged around the motif of the quest. In each of his romances Chrétien varied the nature and organization of the central quest. In *Erec*, his first long poem, the quest is essentially linear and graduated in structure, moving from simple to increasingly more complex and meaningful encounters. But already in *Erec* he was experimenting with a technique for interrupting the linearity and varying the adventures, a technique he would employ with marked success in his later romances and which would be used extensively in the later prose romances: interlacing. In its simplest manifestations, as in the opening section of *Erec*, interlacing involves the weaving together of two distinct lines of action: beginning one action, only to interrupt it with another before returning to complete it. Here the action cuts back and forth between the hunt for the white stag and the joust for the sparrow-hawk. The initial action of the hunt, with the ensuing council, occupies lines 69-341, but the last part of this (323-41) ties in with the encounter with Yder in the forest and also foreshadows what is to come when Erec returns to court. Then the scene shifts back to Erec throughout the sparrow-hawk episode at Laluth (342-1083). Toward the end of this section Chrétien recaps the scene in the forest and sends Yder to Guinevere at Arthur's court (1084-1241). After he is welcomed, the scene returns to Laluth and the sparrow-hawk motif with the words, *Or redevons d'Erec parler* ("Now we must speak again of Erec," v.1242). We follow Erec now as he returns to court, and Chrétien fully interweaves the two motifs, as he has Arthur bestow the kiss of the white stag upon Enide, who had already won the competition for the sparrow-hawk.

The many adventures that in combination form the quest in *Erec and Enide* are varied yet symmetrical, and we can see the hero progressing from a self-centered existence to an appreciation of his role within society. In the first part of *Erec*, the hero is a single knight at Arthur's court, which is feverish with activity, but which seems to lack direction or purpose. It is filled with confusion, bickering, and bloodshed, appropriately dominated by the image of the hunt and the quarrel surrounding the bestowal of the kiss upon the fairest maiden. Erec is *in* this world, but not truly *of* it. In defeating Yder in the sparrow-hawk contest, Erec neutralizes a challenge to Arthur's supremacy and brings an alien custom under Arthur's aegis. After his wedding at the beginning of the central part of the romance, Erec settles down to a life of complacency, where his only thoughts are for his own comforts. When Enide reveals to him the court gossip about his indolence and unworthiness, his concerns are still basically self-centered as he sets out upon his quest with Enide in tow. That he still sees himself as only another knight and Enide as a courtly lady is symbolically underscored by the clothing they wear as they depart on their quest: he dressed in full armor, and she in her most beautiful dress. It is only after they have successfully achieved a series of adventures that restore Erec's individual honor and effect their reconciliation as a couple, that they are prepared to go beyond the ordinary to fulfill their higher mission. In the episode of the Joy of the Court, Erec foregoes his individual objectives to pursue action that is beneficial to the entire community. This episode forms what Norris Lacy (1969) terms a "thematic analogue" with the earlier action of the poem. In each part of the triptych we have a knight who prefers to be alone with his *amie* rather than participating fully in society. After Erec has, through his quest, achieved a proper balance of love and prowess, he is able to profit from his own experiences and open to Maboagrain and others the same possibilities for personal happiness within the bounds of society. When Erec sounds the horn and releases Maboagrain from imprisonment, he unleashes a Joy that will permeate every level of society. He has successfully transcended the individual pursuit of personal prestige to undertake personal action for a collective purpose, the liberation of the community.

Chrétien's artistry was not limited to overall structure, but extends as well into the details of composition. In *Erec*, as in his later romances, Chrétien reveals himself as a master of dialogue, which he frequently uses for dramatic effect. In spite of his rhetorical training, his dialogues are never stiff or formal, and the frequent use of stichomythia gives one the impression of a real conversation overheard, rather than of a learned discourse. He gives them a familiar tone by his choice of imagery and a generous sprinkling of proverbial expressions. In Erec's defiance of Maboagrain, he incorporates five proverbial expressions in but ten lines of dialogue (5873-82), using traditional wisdom to justify and support his current course of action. In an appendix to his edition, Mario Roques lists over thirty proverbs, maxims, and sententious sayings in the romance (pp. 281-82).

Chrétien's use of humor and irony has been frequently noted, as has his ability to incorporate keenly observed realistic details into the most fantastic adventures. Like the dialogues, the descriptions of persons and objects are not rhetorical or lengthy, but are precise, lively, and colorful. In *Erec* in particular Chrétien treats with consummate skill the activities, intrigues, passions, and color of contemporary court life. This romance is filled with lavish depictions of garments, saddles and harnessings, gems, and ceremonies that give proof of his keen attention to detail and his pleasure in description. Justly famous is the elaborate description of Erec's coronation robe (6687-6763), on which four fairies had skilfully embroidered portrayals of the four disciplines of the quadrivium: Geometry, Arithmetic, Music, and Astronomy. Also worthy of note is the detailed description of the horse and harnessings at the end of the central episode (5270-5307). Enide's chestnut steed is distinguished by having one white and one black cheek, divided by a green stripe. Its harnessings are studded with emeralds, and on its ivory saddlebows is carved the story of Æneas' departure from Troy, Dido's welcoming him with joy into her bed, his departure and her suicide, and his conquest of Laurentum and Lombardy. The symbolism of the colors and the relationship of the story of Æneas' and Dido's story to that of Erec and Enide has provoked considerable debate.

In these descriptions, as in much of what he writes, Chrétien tantalizes us with details that are precise yet mysterious in their juxtapositions. He refuses to explain, and in that refusal lies much of his interest for us today. His artistry is one of creating a tone of mystery and mystification: What is Erec's motivation? Why does Enide set off on the quest in her best dress? Did Lancelot consummate his love with Guinevere? What is the significance of Yvain's lion? What is the mystery of the Grail Castle? In his prologue to *Erec and Enide*, Chrétien hints at a greater purpose behind his story than simple entertainment, but he deliberately refuses to spell out that purpose. And at the end of the romance, as Erec is about to recount his own tale for King Arthur, Chrétien significantly refuses to repeat it, telling us in words that apply equally well to this and all of his romances:

> Mes cuidiez vos que je vos die
> quex acoisons le fist movoir?
> Naie, que bien savez le voir

> et de ice et d'autre chose,
> si con ge la vos ai esclose. . . (6432-36)

> [Do you expect me to tell you the
> reason that made him set out? No
> indeed, for you well know the truth of
> this and of other things, just as I have
> disclosed it to you.]

All the answers we may require, Chrétien assures us, are already
imbedded within the *bele conjointure* he has just spread before us with such
consummate artistry.

Among Chrétien's greatest achievements must be counted his mastery
of the octosyllabic rhymed couplet. This relatively short line with frequent
rhyme could become monotonous in untalented hands, but Chrétien handled
it with great freedom and sensitivity—varying his rhythms; adapting his
rhymes and couplets to the flow of the sentence, rather than forcing his
syntax to adhere to a rigidly repeated pattern; using repetitions and word-
play, enjambments and anaphora; combining sounds harmoniously through
the interplay of complementary vowels and consonants; using expressive
rhythms to highlight significant words. He was particularly adept at rhyming
together two words which had identical spellings but nothing whatever in
common etymologically: *prest* (verb 259 : adj. 260); *cort* (noun 312, 383,
1511, 2647, 6133 : verb 311, 384, 1512, 2648, 6134); *oste* (verb 461 : noun
462); *enuit* (verb 1267 : adv. 1268); *fust* (verb 3569, 6677 : noun 3570,
6678); etc. He likewise was fond of playing upon several forms of the same
or homonymous words, as in the following:

> Au matinet sont esvellié
> si resont tuit aparellié
> de monter et de *chevauchier*.
> Erec ot molt son *cheval chier*,
> que d'autre *chevalchier* n'ot cure. (5125-29)

Particularly impressive are the multiple effects achieved in a passage
such as the following:

> "...Enuit ferons *logier* nostre ost
> jusqu'au matin par mi ces chans,
> car grant bien vos fera, ce pans,
> enuit un petit de repos:
> ci nos *loigerons* par mon *los*."
> Erec respont: "Ce *relo gié*."
> Iluec sont remés et *logié*.
> Ne furent pas de *loigier quoi*,

> mes petit troverent de *quoi,*
> car il n'i avoit pas po *gent;*
> par ces haies se vont *loigent.* (5068-78)

Here we have the interplay of forms of *lo(i)gier* and *loer,* culminating
in the delightful rhyme of 5073-74 (*relo gié : et logié*), followed immediately
by an "identical" rhyme (*quoi : quoi*) and then, as if to cap it off, another play
on words between *gent* and the present participle of *loigier,* given the unusual
spelling in -*ent* rather than -*ant.*

Unfortunately, no translation can begin to imitate Chrétien's subtle
harmonies or hope to reproduce his unique tone, particularly not one that
aspires to provide as accurate a line-for-line rendering as possible. On the
other hand, it is hoped that the presence of the Old French opposite the
English will encourage one to examine the original more closely, to seek out
the repetitions, to observe the syntactical patterns, and to note the rhythmic
flow of the sentence over multiple couplets.

Sources and Influences

Twelfth-century France, led by the cathedral schools of Orléans and Chartres,
experienced a renaissance of classical learning that would remain unsurpassed
until the sixteenth century. Virgil, Ovid, and Statius were widely read and
translated, and their influence was more than passing. The most evident echo
of Virgil in *Erec and Enide* is in the depiction of Enide's saddle described
above, but it is more likely that this came through the Old French *Romance of
Æneas* (*Eneas*) than through direct knowledge of Virgil's text. The
immediate influence of Ovid, however, is much easier to gauge. Chrétien, as
we have noted, was well versed in the classics and spent his early career
translating Ovid, whose influence is evident throughout his romances.
Further influence of the learning acquired in the cathedral schools can be seen
in his references to Macrobius, Alexander the Great, Helen of Troy,
Constantine, and Solomon.

However, after a brief period of success as the principal source
material for vernacular literature, classical antiquity began to lose its
predominant status in the 1160s. As Marie de France tells us in the preface to
her collection of *Lais,* too many people had been translating from Latin to
French and fresh new material was wanted. Marie, Chrétien, and many
contemporaries found this in the rich folk sources of Brittany and the British
Isles, especially Ireland and Wales.

Like most of his other romances, *Erec and Enide* seems to have its
roots in the soil of the British Isles. A general parallel to the romance is
found in a story from the Welsh *Mabinogi* called *Gereint Son of Erbin,* which
includes the episodes of the stag hunt, the joust for the sparrow-hawk,

Enide's tears, the quest with Enide's repeated warnings for Gereint (= Erec), the lecherous count, the "little king" Gwiffred Petit (= Guivret le Petit), and even a "mini-Joy of the Court." This relatively late Welsh prose tale, dating probably from the thirteenth century, could not have influenced Chrétien, and marked differences in details, tone, and artistry suggest that it was not directly influenced by Chrétien's work either. Together, however, they attest to an earlier common source, which most critics now assume to have been written rather than oral.

In addition to the general parallel provided by *Gereint Son of Erbin*, there are numerous individual motifs that can be traced to Celtic influence. Foremost among these are the episodes of the White Stag Hunt and the Joy of the Court, which have distinct analogies with Celtic otherworld tales. The chase of the White Stag occurs also in the romance *Partonopeus of Blois*, the *lais* of *Graelent*, *Guingemor*, and *Guigemar*, and in the *Mabinogi* of *Manawydan Son of Llyr*. It is part of an otherworld motif in which a fairy sends a bait (here, the stag) to lure a mortal as a potential lover. The Celtic origin is even more evident in the "Joy of the Court" episode: it is the amalgam of two originally distinct motifs, the voyage to the castle of Brân son of Febal and the liberation of Mabon in *Culhwch and Olwen*. The name of Evrain's castle, Brandiganz, would be a confusion of the name of the castle for that of its owner; and Mabon certainly lent his name to Maboagrain. A number of other details in *Erec* have also been seen as having a Celtic provenance: Guivret le Petit, Evrain's horn, Gawain's horse "le Gringalet," the heads mounted on stakes, Maboagrain's fairy *amie*, etc. It is essential, however, to bear in mind that Chrétien has not just assembled a hodge-podge of Celtic motifs, but has drawn elements from this rich folklore that he has skilfully reassembled in his own *bele conjointure*. Chrétien never reproduces his source materials in their raw state, but adapts them consciously to the needs of his own composition and to the accepted mores of his own time.

In spite of many attempts at explanation, we must still wonder how this legendary material reached France and French-speaking England from its Celtic homelands. Numerous routes have been proposed, but none seems truly satisfactory. There is no doubt that the tales of Tristan and King Arthur were indeed circulating in France by the 1160s, but we cannot be certain under what form, or how widely distributed they were. William of Malmesbury asserts in his *Historia regum anglorum* (History of the English Kings, 1125), that "idle fictions" and "wild tales" were already being told in his day about the great King Arthur, whom he apparently accepts as a historical figure. At the beginning of *Erec and Enide*, Chrétien tells us that he has incorporated into his beautifully ordered composition materials of which earlier story-tellers were wont to destroy the coherence (*depecier*) or omit important episodes (*corronpre*). Evidence might be deduced from these statements to support the contention that there was no fixed Arthurian tradition at this time, or one might argue conversely that there was a true tradition that Chrétien knew and sought to restore. Or, the reference to a garbled tradition could be no more than a standard literary device designed to render acceptable modifications and inventions by Chrétien himself.

Under what circumstances did Chrétien first hear these legends? It is doubtful that he himself understood the Celtic dialects, though he may well have visited the British Isles, as noted earlier. If so, we can imagine that he visited Glastonbury, one of the great centers in the diffusion of the Arthurian legends, for the abbot of Glastonbury from 1125 to 1171, Henry of Blois, was the brother of the English king Stephen and the uncle of Marie de Champagne's husband, Henry the Liberal. Henry of Blois was extremely interested in enhancing the prestige of Glastonbury and no doubt favored the spread of the Arthurian materials that brought it fame. In 1191, some twenty years after Abbot Henry's death, the "body" of King Arthur was exhumed under mysterious conditions at the abbey.

Even had he not visited England, Chrétien could well have heard these stories and legends recounted orally on the French mainland, from Henry of Blois or members of his entourage on the occasion of one of his many trips through France to Cluny or Rome, or from wandering storytellers, many of whom were of Breton origin and who, like many modern Bretons, were bilingual. At the close of *The Knight with the Lion*, Chrétien tells us that he is ending his romance because he had *heard* no more (*onques plus conter n'en oï* , v. 6822); and in *Erec* he specifically condemns the professional *jongleurs* (*cil qui de conter vivre vuelent*, v. 22) who deformed this tale. His contemporary Marie de France, in the preface to her *Lais* already alluded to, likewise makes reference to oral sources, which she had heard (*oïz aveie*). Much similar testimony is offered by other writers to attest to the existence of such wandering storytellers in the twelfth century.

In addition to first-hand tellings of these tales and legends, Chrétien was certainly familiar with the pseudo-historical *Historia regum Britanniæ* (History of the Kings of Britain, 1136-37), by Geoffrey of Monmouth, in which the author purports to give a history of the kings of Britain from the time of their mythical ancestor Brut to the present. Modern scholars have concluded that Geoffrey relied more upon imagination than research, but his work was widely accepted as true by his contemporaries and was translated into French in 1155 for Henry II Plantagenet by the Anglo-Norman poet Wace. Though Geoffrey had given his story a courtly flavor with his inclusion of chess games, feasts, and tourneys, Wace far surpassed his predecessor. Where Geoffrey had written of fortresses, Wace substituted castles; senators became barons, and consuls became counts. Most notably, Wace significantly enhanced the role of the magician and advisor Merlin and was the first to mention the soon to be celebrated Round Table. Though both Geoffrey's *Historia* and Wace's *Brut* touched upon the matter of Arthur, both were resolutely historical in approach and neither could claim to be an Arthurian romance.

From Geoffrey and Wace, as from oral tradition, Chrétien could have taken little more than the names of characters, perhaps some rudiments of story lines and characterization, and a general tone. It was his genius alone to assemble these various fictions into a coherent form recognized today as Arthurian romance, which would guarantee them their lasting success.

Editorial Policy for This Text and Translation

by Carleton W. Carroll

TITLE

When Chrétien first announces the subject of his romance, in line 19, he names only his hero:

> D'Erec, le fil Lac, est li contes

but the Guiot MS ends: *Explycyt li romans d'Erec et d'Enide* , and two other MSS name both hero and heroine in their explicits. Similarly, the table of contents of MS *C*, written in verse and presumably dating from somewhat later than the MS itself, though still from the thirteenth century (Frank, 1952: 179, n. 6; Roques, 1952: 184-5), announces

> Erec et Enyde ert a la premiere ensoigne.[2]

Finally, it is as

> Cil qui fist d'Erec et d'Enide

that Chrétien refers to himself in announcing his previous creations at the beginning of *Cligés*, line 1. Today it is usual to include both characters in the title of the romance, though the title is often shortened to *Erec*, perhaps more for convenience than because of a deliberate desire to restrict the reference to the hero alone.[3]

LIST, DESCRIPTION, AND CLASSIFICATION OF MANUSCRIPTS

The text is preserved in more-or-less complete form in seven MSS, in addition to which there are four fragments. The seven "full" MSS and the Annonay fragment are described in detail by Micha (1939). Certain MSS,

---

[2] A transcription of this table is also given by Micha (1939: 34), but he omits the word *et*. Frank prints the verb as *ert*, whereas Micha and Roques have *est*. Although there is some room for hesitation, I believe Frank's reading is correct.

[3] For the aptness of the inclusion of Enide in the title, see Haidu (1972: 53) and Maddox (1978: 136).

containing more than one of Chrétien's works, are known by more than one siglum, frequently because Foerster, the first general editor of Chrétien, chose them to honor some prior editor. The resulting confusion is discussed—and deplored—by Micha: 28 and Roques, ed.: xxxi-xxxii (who nevertheless adopted a divergent system); it has been commented upon by various other editors. In order not to complicate matters further by the choice of still other sigla, I have adopted those used by Foerster and Micha. Essentially complete texts are found in the following seven MSS:[4]

> *A* — Chantilly, Musée Condé, 472. Picard-Walloon, late 13th century. Contains *EE*, 78r-99v; *Y*, *Ch* (incomplete). (Micha: 38-39; Roques, ed.: xxix.)
>
> *B* — Paris, Bibl. Nationale, f.fr., 1376. Perhaps of Burgundian origin. Contains only *EE* by Chrétien, 95ra-144vb. One miniature, folio 95, within the initial *L* of line 1: in a forest, a crowned figure (Micha identifies him as Erec, though Erec is never described in such a situation in the text), on horseback, carrying a bow, accompanied by a youthful attendant, also mounted, and two dogs, pursuing a stag.[5] (Micha: 42-43; Roques, ed.: xxviii.)
>
> *C* — Paris, Bibl. Nationale, f.fr., 794. Champenois, early 13th century. Contains *EE*, 1ra-27ra; *Ch*, *Cl*, *Y*, *P*. This is the "Guiot MS." (Micha: 32-34; Roques, ed.: xxviii; xxxvii-li; 1952: 177-199.) See below, xxx-xxxi.
>
> *E* — Paris, Bibl. Nationale, f.fr., 1420. Francien, tinged with Picard features, late 13th century. Contains *EE*, 1ra-28vc; *Cl* (incomplete). (Micha: 34-35; Roques, ed.: xxviii.)
>
> *H* — Paris, Bibl. Nationale, f.fr., 1450. Picard, first half of the 13th century. Contains *EE*, 140ra-158vb; *P*, *Cl*, *Y* (incomplete), *Ch*. (Micha: 35-37; Roques, ed.: xxviii-xxix.)
>
> *P* — Paris, Bibl. Nationale, f.fr., 375. Written in Arras, second half of the 13th century; Picard "coloring" introduced by scribes working from a French or Champenois model. Contains *Cl*, *EE*, 281vb-295va. (Micha: 29-32; Roques, ed.: xxviii.)
>
> V — Paris, Bibl. Nationale, f.fr., 24403. Dialect heavily tinged with Picard features, 13th-14th centuries. Contains only *EE*

---

[4] In addition to the references given, Foerster briefly described these MSS in his 1890 edition: i-iii.

[5] Micha's remark (193, n. 1), to the effect that B.N. 24403 is the only MS containing miniatures for *EE*, is obviously erroneous, and at variance with his own description of this miniature in *B*.

by Chrétien, 119*ra*-174*vb*. One leaf has been torn out, corresponding to our 6570-6683. There are two folios numbered 174: the first corresponds to our 6684-6803; the second to our 6804-96 plus seven extraneous lines. This second folio 174 has been torn, so that only part of each outer column (*rb* and *va*) remains. See Textual Notes. There are three miniatures. Folio 119*ra*, replacing the initial *L* of line 1, presents a hunting scene, in a forest: a crowned figure (identified as Erec by Micha; cf. *B*), on horseback, carrying a bow, accompanied by two men and two dogs, pursuing a white stag. Folio 142*rb* shows a combat between two mounted knights, one of whom (presumably Erec) runs the other through with his lance, as a lady (Enide?) observes (the accompanying text, corresponding to our 2744-95, includes the beginning of the encounter with the three robber-knights). Folio 155*rb*, replacing the initial *E* of our 4333, has a combat between several mounted knights (possibly intended to represent successive actions performed by Erec) and two mounted figures with clubs (probably the two giants, abductors of Cadoc). The accompanying text, corresponding to our 4287-4338, includes the damsel's plea and Erec's pursuit of the giants. (Micha: 50-51; Roques, ed.: xxix.)

The following MSS contain fragments of *EE*:

> *An* — Annonay. Champenois, late 12th or early 13th century. Contains fragments of *Cl* (about 1800 lines), *Y* (758), *EE* (302, corresponding to our 5373-5680), *P* (152); the original order is unknown. Published by Pauphilet (1937): 313-16. (Micha: 40; Misrahi: 953-6; Roques, ed.: xxx [*a*]. Roques' numbers are wrong with respect to both the total lines present and to Foerster's and his own editions: the fragment corresponds to F5419-5726 and to R5371-5676.) See Note to 5373.
>
> *G* — Paris, Bibliothèque Sainte-Geneviève, No. 1269. Francien, late 12th or early 13th century. Contains, in whole or in part, 88 lines of *EE*, corresponding to our 5313-35, 5339-60, 5366-86, and 5390-5411. Published by Misrahi (1941): 959-61. (Foerster, 1909: xxxi, n. 3; Micha: 64; Roques, ed.: xxx [*c*]. Both Misrahi and Roques state that the fragment contains 92 lines, but as printed by the former there are 86 complete lines and parts of two others.) See Note to 5313.
>
> *L* — Laigle. Thirteenth century. This fragment is so small (0.113 x 0.32 m.) that it is in fact a mere scrap. Contains 27 lines or portions of lines, corresponding to our 979-984, 1012-18,

1046-52, and 1080-86. Published by Thomas (1914): 253.
(Misrahi: 952-3 [*Th*]; Roques, ed.: xxxi [*d*].) See Note to
979-84.

M — Mons, Archives de l'Etat. Francien with Picard
"coloring", second half of the 13th century. Contains 273
lines of *EE*, corresponding to our 4343-4617. Published by
Jodogne (1950): 314-26. (Roques, ed.: xxx [*b*]. Roques'
line numbers are wrong with respect to both Foerster's edition
and his own: the fragment corresponds to F4389-4663 and to
R4363-4627.) See Note to 4343.

The manuscript tradition of the text of *EE* is "highly confused"
(Misrahi: 955). We can be sure than none of the surviving MSS was written
by Chrétien himself, and scholars agree that none seems to have been copied
directly from any of the others, at least not as its sole source. In other words,
if one of these MSS was directly copied from one of the others, the scribe
also had access to a different source, and used it as the need arose (Micha:
78).

Already in 1890 Foerster acknowledged that the task of classifying
the MSS of *EE* was no easy matter. He divided them into two families, *alpha*
(*HC*) and *beta* (*PB* and a subgroup *gamma*, *VAE*), but postulated some
secondary influences between them (iii-vi). In 1896 he modified this view to
show a closer link between *P* and *H* (xxx), reflected in the slightly revised
stemma of 1909 (xxxi). It was his contention that *H* and *P* were the best
representatives of their respective families, and that *VAE* were "worthless"
(*wertlos*) for the construction of the text (1909: xxxii). Micha discusses the
question in considerable detail (78-102; cf. also 217-221). He follows the
main lines of Foerster's classification, but postulates a larger number of lost
MSS between the original and the surviving representatives, and an *alpha* MS
somewhere in the ancestry of *E* (94).

As for the fragments, Misrahi concludes that *An* is more closely
related to *PBVAE* than to *C* (956) and that "the probability is . . . that *G* is
more closely related to *PBVA* than to *CH*" (958). Though the evidence
presented by *L* is extremely meager, Misrahi says we can "surmise that [*L*]
comes from a 'good' early MS, possibly more closely related to *C* and *H* than
to *PBVAE*, and with a marked inclination toward independent readings"
(953). Jodogne considers *M* as belonging to the *gamma* group, closer to *V*
and especially to *A* than to *E*, but influenced by the *alpha* family, particularly
H (330).

OTHER MEDIEVAL VERSIONS

- Hartmann von Aue, *Erec*, Middle High German, verse, late 12th century.
Tr. Thomas (1982).

With this work Hartmann introduced the Arthurian verse-romance to Germany. Though based on Chrétien's romance, it departs significantly from it, indicating that "Hartmann's basic plan was quite different from that of his source. . . . Hartmann starts with a younger, impulsive, and quite inexperienced Erec, stresses his development, and concludes with an account of his successful reign. His work is clearly an education novel in which the hero learns through varied experiences what one needs to know and be in order to rule a country well" (Thomas, Intro.: 9). Cf. Roques, ed.: xxxiii.

- *Erex Saga*, Old Norse, prose, probably 13th century. Tr. Blaisdell and Kalinke (1977).
    This may be considered an adaptation rather than a translation, since not only is there a difference in literary form but numerous substantive changes were introduced as well, in order to suit the needs of "a culture that was as yet unfamiliar with the courtly civilization of continental Europe and England" (Introduction, xvii; see xiii-xv for specific illustrations of this cultural adaptation). Cf. Roques, ed.: xxxiii-xxxiv.

- *Gereint Son of Erbin*, Welsh, prose, 13th century. Tr. Jones and Jones, *The Mabinogion* (1949; 1974: 229-273).
    This tale is not in fact part of the *Mabinogi* proper, but is one of three later Arthurian romances; these show "abundant evidence of Norman-French influences" (Jones and Jones, Intro.: x). It seems probable that the Welsh work was not a direct translation from Chrétien, but rather that both derived from the same Celtic tradition (xxix). Cf. Roques, ed.: xxxiv.

- *Erec*, Arthurian prose romance, late 13th or early 14th century. Ed. Pickford (1968).
    The hero of this prose romance is apparently the same Erec (identified as *le filz au roy Lac*), but he is presented at the time when he had only recently been knighted by Arthur. This work is more directly linked to other prose romances, and has little in common with Chrétien's, since Enide does not appear and there is no treatment of the basic theme: conflict and reconciliation between knighthood and marriage. Two incidents occur in both works, the dwarf with the whip and the broken sword that brings a sudden end to a combat between two knights, but these resemblances may only be due to chance. For a detailed discussion of the relationship between this *Erec* and the rest of Arthurian literature, see Pickford, Introduction, pp. 15-36.

- Burgundian prose version, mid-15th century. Ed. Foerster (1890: 253-294; *Anmerkungen*, 334-336).
    This anonymous work, presumably composed for the library of the Dukes of Burgundy, constitutes both a translation and an adaptation of Chrétien's romance. "The Burgundian adapter . . . realized that Chrétien

presented a hero who was both valorous and uxorious, and a heroine who could not be flatly condemned for criticizing her husband even though she thereby risked their common happiness" (Wallen, 1982: 194-195). Cf. Roques, ed.: xxxiii; Pickford, ed., *Erec* (1968): 17.

PREVIOUS EDITIONS

"A major problem in Chrétien studies is the lack of a good critical edition of his romances. No holographs survive. And the manuscripts themselves show sometimes remarkable divergencies. The two complete editions we have—Foerster's and Roques's—were established on editorial principles generally considered unsatisfactory today." (Kelly, 1985: 26).

An extensive description of Foerster's methods may be found in Micha (1939: 18-27). Instead of choosing a base MS, Foerster's approach was to compare the readings presented by the various MSS, as grouped into families, and to weigh them, as it were, against one another. The goal of this operation was to discover, if not what Chrétien had actually written, at least what had been in an archetype, the source of the surviving MSS. This led to what Micha calls Foerster's "eclecticism" (*éclectisme*), and sometimes produced lines which are "une véritable mosaïque", fabricated from bits and pieces found in the various MSS. An example is *Erec* 305: *"Bien (CBVA) dient tuit que (HCPAE) ja n'iert (HE) fet."* Additional examples of this in *EE*, listed by Micha (Foerster's line numbers): 938, 1134, 1569, 1727, 1891, 2748, 3219, 3783, 4983, 5192, 5528, 5750, 6005, 6341 (22-23). Though such "mosaics" may be criticized, Micha recognizes that they are at least based on the reality of surviving MSS. But Foerster was sometimes guilty of substituting his own invention, when no MS presented a reading that was to his liking. Examples from *EE*, listed by Micha, include 908, 1057, 1125, 1716, 1954, 2888, 3031, 4546, 4581, 5763, 5830 (23).

Further, Micha criticizes Foerster's inconsistency: although he did not choose a base MS, he did express—arbitrarily, according to Micha—a preference for one MS above the others. But the place of honor (given to *H* in the case of *EE*) is, for Micha, rather theoretical: Foerster frequently chooses another reading, even when it is no better, and on occasion "completely abandons logic" and relegates to the variants the readings which ought to appear in the text (Micha: 25, with examples).

Another feature of Foerster's editions was a system of normalized spelling. This had the advantage of giving the same form to a word in each of its occurrences, but the form might be unlike that of any of the MSS.

Whatever fault one may find with Foerster's critical method (and recent scholars seem generally to agree that a different approach is preferable), there is to my mind an even more serious flaw to his editions. Despite his efforts to "normalize" the text, the result would still be valuable if the critical apparatus, and in particular the variants, were what they purport to be. Unfortunately, they are not, for in a disturbing number of cases Foerster's notes and variants tell us that a MS has one reading when in fact it has another. Though I have only occasionally checked Foerster's readings against the MSS, I have found enough discrepancies between the two to render his work suspect in general. For a similar evaluation of the critical apparatus in Foerster's *Karrenritter* (*Lancelot*, 1899), see Stone (1937). As Misrahi has remarked, "Foerster's collation [in his large edition] was careless and incomplete" (1941: 951), and "Foerster's collation of the Sainte-Geneviève fragment [(of *EE*), 1909 ed.: xxxi] is incomplete and inexact as usual" (956). And Hunt: "It has long been known that Foerster's recording of variants is incomplete and unreliable and that a critical revision of his editions is indispensable" (1979: 257).

When Roques prepared his editions of Chrétien's works for the C.F.M.A. series, he adopted an approach that can be considered the other extreme from Foerster's. Instead of combining elements from several MSS (representing, in fact, the whole manuscript tradition), he adopted one MS, B.N. 794, the "Guiot MS," and remained zealously faithful to it. This would perhaps be defensible in the case of a flawless MS, but not one of the MSS of *EE* can be so described. There are many places where Guiot's text is flawed, and Roques has been criticized at considerable length for his conservative approach to editing. Reid has suggested it should be regarded as the *reductio ad absurdum* of the "non-interventionist" principle in editing (1976: 1). Hunt concurs: "it may be stressed that Roques is extremely conservative in his presentation of the Guiot text, and frequent correction is necessary if it is taken as the basis of a critical edition" (1979: 262).

THE PRESENT EDITION

A. Choice of base manuscript

"Of all the extant manuscripts of Old French texts, there is not one that anybody would maintain to be a completely faithful copy of the original" (Reid, 1984: 1). Opinions have long been divided concerning the relative value of the various MSS of *Erec et Enide*. Several scholars have spoken in favor of B.N. 794 ("Guiot"), albeit with some reservations. Micha (1939: 217, "Etude comparative des manuscrits"): "Le B.N. 794 présente un texte *alpha* incomparablement plus pur que celui de son confrère 1450 [footnote 1, statistics], mais déjà loin de l'archétype commun: si les suppressions ne sont pas en nombre très considérable (27), ses deux grandes interpolations accusent des retouches assez profondes. Malgré tout il fournit plus d'une fois le bon texte." Micha (1939: 392-3, "Conclusion"): "Pour *Erec*, c'est encore B.N. 794 qui, tout bien pesé, mériterait ce titre de ms.-base. Sans aucun doute, on devra ici resserrer le contrôle, car les divergences individuelles sont en plus grand nombre que dans *Cligès*; il en comporte moins cependant que B.N. 1450 (*H*), préféré par Foerster, sur qui plane en outre ce soupçon de double modèle. On contrôlera utilement par B.N. 375 [*P*], le meilleur représentant de *beta*, et aussi par B.N. 1420 [*E*]" (392-3). Misrahi (1941: 958): "I have long been convinced . . . that *C* is the best representative of *CH* and that *B* is the best representative of *PBVA*." Reid (1976: 1): "Guiot appears to have had a good model for most of the romances, and usually to have copied and revised with care: since he was, it seems, a native of Provins, his dialect was very similar to that of Chrétien; his copy was probably made within some forty years of the poet's death, and the linguistic system represented by his orthography (which is unusually homogeneous) corresponds closely to what is implied by Chrétien's rhyme and metre. The Guiot manuscript can therefore be reasonably considered to be the best extant copy of the corpus of Chrétien's works." Other pronouncements in favor of B.N. 794 may be found in Woledge (1978a: 589 and 1978b: 718).

On the other hand, there have been some negative views: Roach (1959: x): "C'est sans doute un manuscrit excellent, mais ce n'est certainement pas le moins arbitraire ni celui qui contient le moins de variantes individuelles et de retouches de copiste." Hunt (1979: 269, n. 6): "Micha ... certainly overestimates the value of B.N. 794 in the case of *Cligès* and *Erec*." But no one, at least in recent years, seems to have argued for, or even proposed, another candidate that might replace Guiot.

Woledge, introducing his excellent and thorough study of Chrétien's language, acknowledges a fundamental problem, that the author's usage can be known to us only through the MSS: "Nous ne possédons aucun manuscrit d'un roman de Chrétien qui remonte au XIIe siècle, et les manuscrits qui nous restent présentent des milliers de variantes. Nous ne retrouverons jamais le texte authentique tel qu'il est sorti des mains de Chrétien. Il faut s'y résigner: toute étude <<sur Chrétien>> est une étude sur Chrétien tel qu'il a été transmis par les copistes" (1979a: 7-8). After a discussion of various opinions and reservations about the value of Guiot, Woledge makes this highly pertinent remark: "La difficulté que l'on a à formuler un jugement rationnel sur le travail de ce copiste s'explique en partie par le fait que le concept <<Guiot>> n'est pas simple. <<Guiot>> est non seulement un copiste vivant à Provins au XIIIe siècle, un être humain avec sa personnalité propre, c'est aussi l'aboutissement de toute une série de copies, de modèles, de personnalités de copiste, —ou plutôt, car les choses ne sont pas aussi simples, c'est l'aboutissement de plusieurs séries de copies, etc. En effet, il ne semble pas que celui qui a écrit BN 794 ait eu devant lui un modèle unique pour les romans de Chrétien, ni même qu'il ait suivi d'un bout à l'autre de chaque roman un modèle unique" (1979a: 9).

B. Editorial approach

Recent studies of the textual problems involved have stressed the need for a different editorial approach in editing Chrétien's works: "Roques is extremely conservative in his presentation of the Guiot text, and frequent correction is necessary if it is taken as the basis of a critical edition." (Hunt, 1979: 262). In preparing the present edition, I have attempted to find a middle ground between Foerster's eclecticism and Roques' conservatism. I have chosen to adopt a base MS and adhere to it whenever it seemed adequate, i.e. whenever it presented a completely satisfactory reading. Despite the very legitimate reservations expressed by other scholars, B.N. 794 still seems the best choice. This has the further advantage of creating a certain unity within the present series, since Kibler has similarly based his editions of *Lancelot* and *Yvain* on Guiot.

     Even though virtually all of my editorial decisions were made before I saw Reid's "The Right to Emend" (1984), I find that I am fundamentally in agreement with the "interventionist" principles he sets forth. His earlier articles (1965 and, especially, 1976), and Hunt (1979) have been extremely valuable in preparing the present edition. I have frequently found myself in agreement with Foerster, and have adopted many—though by no means all—of his readings. The resulting text is therefore different from that of any previous edition. I have generally avoided purely "grammatical" emendations, i.e. corrections of Guiot's language in such matters as the declension of nouns, adjectives, and pronouns. On the other hand, I have emended Guiot in many places and in various ways:

1. Additions: I have added a total of 86 lines, in 25 passages where Guiot seems to have omitted necessary material. See Appendix B.
2. Deletions: I have deleted two passages, present only in Guiot (R2323-46 and R2349-76). See Textual Notes 2340 and 2342.
3. Interversions: I have in some cases reestablished the order of a couplet where Guiot seems to have interverted the lines. In cases where Guiot's line-order seemed acceptable, I have generally maintained it, even though it was not that of the other MSS.
4. Identical rhymes: In a number of cases I have emended Guiot's text in order to avoid rhyming a word with itself.
5. Miscellaneous: Individual words other than rhyme-words, which seemed less correct than the corresponding reading in other MSS; obvious errors (most of them mentioned by Roques) such as repeated or omitted words; etc.

I have slightly modified the spelling of some words introduced from other MSS, in order to make them fit better with the predominant spellings used by Guiot. All emendations to MS *C* are indicated in the footnotes; the footnotes also provide information about such peculiarities of the MS as the dot below a letter to indicate expunctuation, additions of letters above the line, and physical accidents such as holes, tears, and creases in the MS. Many emendations are discussed in the Textual Notes. In the footnotes, "*F*" indicates readings given by Foerster. When no year is indicated, the same reading is to be found in the 1890, 1896, and 1909 editions. When Foerster's later editions present different readings, this fact is indicated by "*F1896*" or "*F1909*." "*R*" indicates an emendation already adopted by Roques. The absence of this symbol implies that Roques retained Guiot's reading.

Besides the actual emendations, I have been able to correct a number of errors in Roques, where his text does not accurately reflect Guiot. These changes are listed in Appendix C. See Appendix A for a table comparing line numbers in this edition with those of both Foerster and Roques. Textual divisions, marked by large initials in the MS, are indicated by indentations in the text and translation. I have occasionally introduced such a division where none was present in *C*, or suppressed one that was present. All such modifications are indicated in the footnotes. Folio numbers are bracketed and in italics in the right-hand margin. When the manuscript was bound, the second sheet of the first quire was turned around, and interchanged with the third. The folio numbers indicate this fact, though the proper order of the poem has been reestablished. Cf. Roques, ed.: xxxvii-xxxviii, n. 2, and 1952: 178, n. 2

The entire text has been checked against a photocopy of the MS; all problematic readings have been verified by a personal study of the MS itself. All references to other MSS have been verified by one of these two methods, the great majority by direct examination, in Paris and in Chantilly. In a few cases I have indicated readings given by Foerster; these must, as always, be accepted with caution. (See above, xxix-xxx.) Besides the emendations and corrections already mentioned, I have modified the text in the following (customary) ways: resolving all abbreviations, including those for numbers; distinguishing *i* from *j* and *u* from *v*; providing punctuation in order to convey the meaning of the text as I understand it (Guiot introduced a rudimentary system of punctuation, but it is not adequate for a modern edition. Cf. Roques, ed.: xl-xlii; 1952: 193-196.); supplying capitalization in accordance with modern usage; adding the acute accent and the dieresis (see Foulet and Speer, 1979: 67-73, for a summary of principles in this connection); separating words according to current editorial practices rather than maintaining the divisions found in the MS.

Considerable and even extreme variations in the spelling of proper names occur from one manuscript to another; it is not rare to find that the seven MSS present seven distinct spellings of what is, nevertheless, identifiable as the "same" name, in essentially the "same" line. This is particularly true where secondary and episodic characters are concerned, and applies equally to most place-names. The Guiot manuscript itself is relatively consistent, but I have chosen, with rare exceptions, to preserve whatever spellings it presents, including such variations as *Enyde* (primary spelling, 74 occurrences) / *Enide* (variant spelling, 5 occurrences); *Ganievre* (3) / *Guenievre* (1); *Lymors* (4) / *Limors* (3); *Maboagrain(s)* (3) / *Maboagrins* (1); *Ydiers* (7) / *Yder(s)* (3). When the name appears in abbreviated form (as is usually the case for Erec, *.e.*), the expanded form is chosen to match the predominant spelling elsewhere in the text.

The Textual Notes are of essentially two types. Some, indicated by asterisks in the Old French text, explore questions of a textual and interpretive nature. Others, indicated by asterisks in the translation, relate specifically to medieval institutions or customs and are frequently essential to a proper understanding of the text. Chrétien made considerable use of proverbs and proverbial expressions—beginning immediately in lines 1-3 of *Erec et Enide*. I consider this a significant feature of his style, and the Textual Notes call attention to their presence in the text. No attempt has been made, however, to determine whether they existed prior to the composition of *Erec et Enide*, or whether it was later that they achieved proverbial "status"—only that they can be considered to have achieved that status at some point during the Middle Ages. For a detailed discussion of Chrétien's use of proverbs, see Altieri (1976), especially pages 76-92, which deal specifically with *EE*.

In discussing the problem of editing *Yvain*, Woledge concludes that "The future editor . . . must give the reader copious notes explaining how he understands the text, why he has kept such and such a reading and has emended in such and such cases. He must provide variants, and it will be difficult for him to avoid the task of giving all variants except the most trivial. . . . This means unfortunately that the edition will take a long time to prepare and will be very expensive . . ." (1984: 267). The same is true of *Erec et Enide*. Unfortunately, such an edition is beyond the scope and purpose of the present series. I hope, however, that the edited text, the partial variants, and the Textual Notes, together with the translation, will constitute a first step towards accomplishing that goal.

THE TRANSLATION

At best, one can translate only what one understands. Any honest translation must, therefore, be based on the translator's understanding of the source text, and this, of course, is a matter of interpretation. In translating *Erec et Enide* I have endeavored to be as faithful as possible to the original, while at the same time respecting the constraints of modern English. With the notable exception of specific, sometimes semi-technical vocabulary indispensable for naming certain objects, titles, and actions referred to by Chrétien (and which often contribute to the vivacity and authenticity of the text), I have chosen to avoid archaism, aiming instead for a fairly neutral contemporary style. If we can assume, as I feel we must, that Chrétien's language, apart presumably from its poetic style and occasional word-play, would not have sounded in any way odd or peculiar to the contemporary audience for whom he intended his romances, then the English of the translation should, ideally, achieve the same effect.

But of course Chrétien's medium was poetic in form, whereas the present translation, despite the arrangement in corresponding lines, is not. I have made no attempt to echo either Chrétien's rhyme or his rhythm. I have neither sought to confine my version to rhythmically regular lines, nor have I systematically avoided producing such a line when, largely by chance, what I deemed to be the most accurate rendering of Chrétien's thought turned out to be readable as an octosyllabic line in English. The effect of Chrétien's rhymes is, unfortunately, almost totally lost in translation, as is the word-play alluded to above.

In the case of personal names already well-known in English (e.g. Arthur, Guinevere, Gawain, Kay, as well as names of actual places and of historical and literary figures), I have preserved the customary forms. For unfamiliar names (many of which occur only in passing) I have retained the Old French spelling, but in the oblique case, e.g. Amauguin, Cadiolan, Girflet, Yder, if it occurs in the text, or have endeavored to create one, by analogy, where none was present. I have in all cases adopted one consistent spelling, even though variant forms occur in the Old French text.

Certain peculiarities of Chrétien's style would, I believe, have hindered comprehension, had I preserved them in translation. One of these is his use of pronouns, sometimes only implied rather than expressed, in preference to nouns. Parallel usage in English would frequently have led to confusion in the mind of the reader, particularly in the numerous battle scenes involving two male characters. Another stylistic trait favored by Chrétien is the accumulation of negatives. Though this technique can sometimes be used to good effect, present-day English is less tolerant of it than the French of Chrétien's time seems to have been, and I have frequently preferred to substitute a positive turn of phrase. Finally, Chrétien's narrative frequently alternates between past and present tenses; I have chosen to narrate the story uniformly in the past tense.

ACKNOWLEDGMENTS

It is a real pleasure to recognize in print the many organizations and individuals who have helped me in the preparation of this book. My thanks to the staff members of the libraries whose materials and services I used: Bibliothèque Nationale, Paris; Centre d'Etudes Supérieures de Civilisation Médiévale, Poitiers; Hofstra University; New York Public Library;

University of Oregon; Oregon State University; Université de Poitiers; State University of New York, Stony Brook; and the many others whose materials I consulted through the wonderful services of inter-library loan. I wish especially to thank the Curators of Manuscripts of the Bibliothèque Nationale, Paris, for permission to reproduce photographs from their collections.

Several individuals deserve particular mention. First among these is James J. Wilhelm, General Editor of the Garland Library of Medieval Literature, for his extraordinary patience, his careful reading of the translation and introduction, and for his many constructive suggestions. Glyn S. Burgess, Department of French at the University of Liverpool, read both text and translation with a critical eye and made a number of suggestions for the improvement of both. William S. Bregar, of the Department of Computer Science at Oregon State University, provided me with access to the university's computing facilities, and arranged for the collaboration of his student Gregory L. Finch, who contributed the energy and expertise needed to produce a preliminary version of a concordance to the text. Christopher Kleinhenz, Department of French and Italian at the University of Wisconsin (Madison), was extremely generous in allowing me to borrow microfilms of three of the manuscripts. Mary Speer, Department of French, Rutgers University, provided particularly valuable guidance in the difficult matter of the use of the dieresis. The late Diane Bornstein, of the Department of English, City University of New York, offered much encouragement during the initial phases of my work.

Sheila M. Cordray, Department of Sociology, and James A. Folts, Department of Journalism, both of Oregon State University, were extremely helpful in teaching me the use of the IBM PC. Phillip Brown, David Cawlfield, Richard Griffin, D. J. Rogers, and the support staff of the Milne Computer Center at Oregon State University spent many hours helping me get my text printed on the Apple LaserWriter Plus. Without these now indispensable tools, the present form of this text would never have been possible.

Special thanks go to William W. Kibler, Department of French and Italian at the University of Texas at Austin, for, first, serving as a pioneer and model in the context of this series, and, second, for agreeing to contribute the opening sections of the Introduction. I particularly wish to acknowledge the extraordinary services rendered by Lois Hawley Wilson (Independent Medievalist, Eagle Point, Oregon), who studiously compared my translation with the original and made many felicitous suggestions for improvement. Lastly, I acknowledge a great debt of gratitude to my wife, Paulette Carroll, Department of Foreign Languages and Literatures, Willamette University, who not only read the introduction, listened to the entire translation, and contributed a wealth of stylistic suggestions, but also bore with me and encouraged me during the entire course of this project.

Select Bibliography

The total number of works on Chrétien de Troyes is immense; even an exhaustive listing of studies dealing specifically with *Erec et Enide* would be quite lengthy, and completeness in such endeavors is virtually impossible to achieve. The following bibliography is therefore limited; it contains all works referred to in the introductory material and notes, as well as a number of others which have proven useful in the preparation of this edition and translation. Many of the works listed contain extensive bibliographies, e.g. Maddox (1978), Topsfield (1981), Cormier (1982), and Kelly (1985).

I. Editions of *Erec et Enide*

Christian von Troyes. *Sämtliche Werke, nach allen bekannten Handschriften, herausgegeben von Wendelin Foerster.* 4 vols. Halle: Niemeyer, 1884-99. III, *Erec und Enide*, 1890; rpt. Amsterdam: Rodopi, 1965.

Kristian von Troyes. *Erec und Enide, neue verbesserte Textausgabe mit Einleitung und Glossar, herausgegeben von Wendelin Foerster.* Romanische Bibliothek, 13. Halle: Niemeyer, 1896.

Kristian von Troyes. *Erec und Enide, Textausgabe mit Variantenauswahl, Einleitung, erklärenden Anmerkungen und vollständigem Glossar, herausgegeben von Wendelin Foerster.* Romanische Bibliothek, 13. Halle: Niemeyer, 1909 (zweite ... Auflage).

Kristian von Troyes. *Erec und Enide, Textausgabe mit Variantenauswahl, Einleitung und erklärenden Anmerkungen, herausgegeben von Wendelin Foerster.* Romanische Bibliothek, 13. Halle: Niemeyer, 1934 (dritte Auflage). [Identical to the 1909 edition, except for minor revisions in a dozen lines; there is no glossary.]

Chrétien de Troyes. *Les Romans de Chrétien de Troyes édités d'après la copie de Guiot (Bibl. nat., fr. 794)*, I, *Erec et Enide*, publié par Mario Roques. Classiques Français du Moyen Age, 80. Paris: Champion, 1952; rpt. 1955, etc.

II. Translations of *Erec et Enide* into English and Modern French

Comfort, W. W., tr. *Arthurian Romances*. Intro. and notes by D.D.R. Owen. Everyman's Library, 698 (paperback, 1698). London: J.M. Dent; New York: E.P. Dutton, 1914; revised and rpt. 1975. Prose translation into somewhat archaic-sounding English, closely following Foerster's small editions. *Erec et Enide*, pp. 1-90.

Foucher, Jean-Pierre, tr. *Romans de la Table Ronde*. Livre de Poche Classique, 1998. Paris: Gallimard, 1970; rpt. Collection Folio, 696, 1975. Rather free translation into modern French prose; of limited interest for *Erec et Enide* (pp. 38-87), since many passages are given only in summary form.

Louis, René, tr. *Erec et Enide, roman traduit de l'ancien français d'après l'édition de Mario Roques*. Paris: Champion, 1954; rpt. 1982. Fine translation into modern French prose, with a very helpful glossary (pp. 183-193).

III. Criticism, Study Guides, and Reference Works

A. *Guides to Bibliography*

Bulletin Bibliographique de la Société Internationale Arthurienne—Bibliographical Bulletin of the International Arthurian Society (BBSIA). Published annually since 1949.

Coleman, Arthur. *Epic and Romance Criticism*. 2 vols. (vol. 1, *A Checklist of Interpretations 1940-1972 of English and American Epics and Metrical Romances*; vol. 2, *A Checklist of Interpretations 1940-1973 of Classical and Continental Epics and Metrical Romances*). New York: Watermill, 1973, 1974. *EE*: 2: 126-129. Limited to studies in English; somewhat dated but a useful starting-point.

Kelly, Douglas. *Chrétien de Troyes: An Analytic Bibliography*. Research Bibliographies & Checklists, 17. London: Grant & Cutler, 1976. Lengthy and extremely useful bibliography; works are grouped under 21 headings and many sub-headings, with cross-references to the *BBSIA*, an index of romances and an index of authors.

Reiss, Edmund, et al. *Arthurian Legend and Literature: An Annotated Bibliography*. 2 vols. (vol. 1, *The Middle Ages*; vol. 2, *Renaissance to the Present*). Garland Reference Library of the Humanities, 415. New York: Garland, 1984- . Chrétien: 1: 19-23 (items 124-57); *EE*: 1: 324-27 (items 2395-2420). Selective yet very extensive; covers the entire spectrum of Arthurian literature, organized by subject; comprehensive indices.

B. *General Studies of Chrétien or* Erec et Enide

Altieri, Marcelle. *Les Romans de Chrétien de Troyes: Leur perspective proverbiale et gnomique*. Paris: Nizet, 1976.

Bruckner, Matilda Tomaryn. *Narrative Invention in Twelfth-Century French Romance: The Convention of Hospitality (1160-1200)*. French Forum Monographs, 17. Lexington, Ky.: French Forum, 1980.

Burgess, Glyn S. *Chrétien de Troyes: Erec et Enide*. Critical Guides to French Texts, No. 32. London: Grant & Cutler, 1984.

Cormier, Raymond J., tr. Jean Frappier, *Chrétien de Troyes: The Man and His Work*. Athens, Ohio: Ohio University Press, 1982.

Frappier, Jean. *Chrétien de Troyes: l'homme et l'œuvre*. Paris: Hatier, 1957; 1968.

Haidu, Peter. *Lion-queue-coupée: L'écart symbolique chez Chrétien de Troyes*. Genève: Droz, 1972.

Hofer, Stefan. *Chrétien de Troyes. Leben und Werke des altfranzösischen Epikers*. Graz-Köln: Böhlaus, 1954.

Holmes, Urban T. *Chrétien de Troyes*. Twayne's World Authors Series, 94. New York: Twayne, 1970.

———, and Sister M. Amelia Klenke. *Chrétien, Troyes, and the Grail*. Chapel Hill: University of North Carolina Press, 1959.

Kelly, Douglas, ed. *The Romances of Chrétien de Troyes, A Symposium*. Edward C. Armstrong Monographs on Medieval Literature, 3. Lexington, Ky.: French Forum, 1985.

Lacy, Norris J. *The Craft of Chrétien de Troyes: An Essay on Narrative Art.* Davis Medieval Texts and Studies, 3. Leiden: E. J. Brill, 1980.

Loomis, Roger Sherman. *Arthurian Tradition and Chrétien de Troyes.* New York: Columbia University Press, 1949; rpt. 1961.

Love, Nathan LeRoy. *Forms of Address in Old French Romances.* Ann Arbor: University Microfilms International, 1982.

Luttrell, Claude. *The Creation of the First Arthurian Romance: A Quest.* Evanston: Northwestern University Press, 1974.

Maddox, Donald. *Structure and Sacring: The Systematic Kingdom in Chrétien's* Erec et Enide. French Forum Monographs, 8. Lexington, Ky.: French Forum, 1978. [= "1978a"]

Pickens, Rupert T., ed. *The Sower and His Seed: Essays on Chrétien de Troyes.* French Forum Monographs, 44. Lexington, Ky.: French Forum, 1983.

Topsfield, L. T. *Chrétien de Troyes: A Study of the Arthurian Romances.* Cambridge: Cambridge University Press, 1981.

Woledge, Brian. *La Syntaxe des substantifs chez Chrétien de Troyes.* Genève: Droz, 1979 [= "1979a"].

Zaddy, Z. P. *Chrétien Studies: Problems of Form and Meaning in* Erec, Yvain, Cligés *and the* Charrette. Glasgow: University of Glasgow Press, 1973.

C. *Briefer Studies of Chrétien and* Erec et Enide

Adler, Alfred. "Sovereignty as the Principle of Unity in Chrétien's *Erec*." *PMLA* 60 (1945): 917-36.

————. "The Themes of 'The Handsome Coward' and of 'The Handsome Unknown' in *Meraugis de Portlesguez*." *Modern Philology* 44 (1946-7): 218-224.

Bianchini, Simonetta. "Due brevi romanzi di Chrétien de Troyes." *Cultura Neolatina* 33 (1973): 55-68.

Brogyanyi, Gabriel John. "Plot Structure and Motivation in Chrétien's Romances." *Vox Romanica* 31 (1972): 272-286.

Buckbee, Edward J. "*Erec et Enide.*" *The Romances of Chrétien de Troyes, A Symposium*, ed. Kelly (1985): 48-88.

Bullock-Davies, Constance. "Chrétien de Troyes and England." In Richard Barber, ed., *Arthurian Literature I*. Woodbridge, Suffolk: D. S. Brewer, 1981, 1-61.

Coghlan, Maura. "The Flaw in Enide's Character: A Study of Chrétien de Troyes' *Erec*." *Reading Medieval Studies* 5 (1979): 21-37.

Foulon, C. "La Fée Morgue chez Chrétien de Troyes." *Mélanges ... Frappier* (1970): I, 283-290.

Fourrier, Anthime. "Encore la chronologie des œuvres de Chrétien de Troyes." *BBSIA*, 2 (1950), 69-88.

———. "Retour au 'terminus.'" *Mélanges ... Frappier* (1970): I, 299-311.

Frappier, Jean. "Sur la versification de Chrétien de Troyes: l'enjambement dans *Erec et Enide*." *Research Studies* (Washington State University) 32 (1964): 41-49.

———. "La Brisure du couplet dans *Erec et Enide*." *Romania* 86 (1965): 1-21.

———. "Le Motif du 'don contraignant' dans la littérature du Moyen Age." *Travaux de Linguistique et de Littérature* (Strasbourg) 7,2 (1969): 7-46.

———. "Pour le commentaire d'*Erec et Enide*: Notes de lecture." *Marche Romane* 20 (1970): 15-30.

Hunt, Tony. "Redating Chrétien de Troyes." *BBSIA* 30 (1978), 209-37.

Huppé, Bernard F. "The Gothic Hero: Chrétien's *Erec*." *The Twelfth Century* (1975): 1-19.

Imbs, Paul. "*La Charrette* avant *La Charrette*: Guenièvre et le roman d'*Erec*." *Mélanges ... Frappier* (1970): I, 419-432.

Janssens, Jan. "The Simultaneous Composition of *Yvain* and *Lancelot*: Fiction or Reality?" Forthcoming in *Forum for Modern Language Studies*.

Kelly, Douglas. "The Source and Meaning of *conjointure* in Chrétien's *Erec* 14." *Viator* 1 (1970): 179-200.

―――. "La Forme et le sens de la quête dans l'*Erec et Enide* de Chrétien de Troyes." *Romania* 92 (1971): 326-358.

―――. "The Logic of the Imagination in Chrétien de Troyes." *The Sower and His Seed: Essays on Chrétien de Troyes*, ed. Pickens (1983): 9-30.

―――. "Chrétien de Troyes: The Narrator and His Art." *The Romances of Chrétien de Troyes, A Symposium*, ed. Kelly (1985): 13-47.

Lacy, Norris J. "Thematic Analogues in *Erec*." *Esprit Créateur* 9 (1969): 267-274.

―――. "Narrative Point of View and the Problem of Erec's Motivation." *Kentucky Romance Quarterly* 18 (1971): 355-362.

Le Goff, Jacques. "Quelques Remarques sur les codes vestimentaire et alimentaire dans *Erec et Enide*." *Mélanges ... Louis* (1982): 1243-1258.

Luttrell, Claude. "La Nouveauté significative dans *Erec et Enide*." *Romania* 101 (1980): 277-280.

Maddox, Donald. "Nature and Narrative in Chrétien's *Erec et Enide*." *Mediaevalia* 3 (1977): 59-82 [= "1977a"].

―――. "The Prologue to Chrétien's *Erec* and the Problem of Meaning." *Jean Misrahi Memorial Volume* (1977): 159-174. [= "1977b"]

―――. "The Structure of Content in Chrétien's *Erec et Enide*." *Mélanges ... Wathelet-Willem* (1978): 381-394. [= "1978b"]

―――. "Trois sur deux: Théories de bipartition et de tripartition des œuvres de Chrétien." *Œuvres & Critiques* 5,2 (1980-1981): 91-102.

Ménard, Philippe. "Le Temps et la durée dans les romans de Chrétien de Troyes." *Moyen Age* 73 (1967): 375-401.

―――. "Note sur la date du *Chevalier de la Charrette*." *Romania* 92 (1971): 118-26.

Misrahi, Jean. "More Light on the Chronology of Chrétien de Troyes." *BBSIA* 11 (1959): 89-120.

Niemeyer, Karina H. "The Writer's Craft: *La Joie de la Cort*." *Esprit Créateur* 9 (1969): 286-292.

Nitze, William A. "Erec's Treatment of Enide." *Romanic Review* 10 (1919): 26-37.

———. "Erec and the Joy of the Court." *Speculum* 29 (1954): 691-701.

Owen, D.D.R. "Two More Romances by Chrétien de Troyes?" *Romania* 92 (1971): 246-60.

Paris, Gaston. Review of Foerster, ed., *Cligés*; rpt. in *Gaston Paris: Mélanges de littérature française du moyen âge*, ed. Mario Roques. Paris: Champion, 1910.

Sargent, Barbara Nelson. "Petite Histoire de Maboagrain (à propos d'un article récent)." *Romania* 93 (1972): 87-96.

———. "Belle Enide, bonne Enide." *Mélanges ... Le Gentil* (1973): 767-771.

———. Review of Luttrell, *The Creation of the First Arthurian Romance*. *Speculum* 52 (1977): 394-397.

Sargent-Baur, Barbara N. "Erec's Enide: 'sa fame ou s'amie'?" *Romance Philology* 33 (1980): 373-387.

Schmolke-Hasselmann, Beate. "Henri II Plantagenêt, roi d'Angleterre, et la genèse d'*Erec et Enide*." *Cahiers de Civilisation Médiévale* 24 (1981): 241-46.

Sheldon, E. S. "Why Does Chrétien's Erec Treat Enide So Harshly?" *Romanic Review* 5 (1914): 115-126.

Shirt, David J. "Chrétien de Troyes and the Cart." In *Studies in Medieval Literature and Languages in Memory of Frederick Whitehead*. Manchester: Manchester University Press, 1973, pp. 279-301.

———. "Chrétien de Troyes et une coutume anglaise." *Romania* 94 (1973): 178-95.

———. "Godefroy de Lagny et la composition de la *Charrete*." *Romania* 96 (1975): 27-52.

————. "How Much of the Lion Can We Put Before the Cart? Further Light on the Chronological Relationship of Chrétien de Troyes' *Lancelot* and *Yvain*." *French Studies* 31 (1977): 1-17.

Titchener, Frances H. "The Romances of Chrétien de Troyes." *Romanic Review* 16 (1925): 165-173.

Uitti, Karl D. "Vernacularization and Old French Romance Mythopoesis with Emphasis on Chrétien's *Erec et Enide* ." *The Sower and His Seed: Essays on Chrétien de Troyes*, ed. Pickens (1983): 81-115.

Wallen, Martha. "Significant Variations in the Burgundian Prose Version of *Erec et Enide*." *Medium Ævum* 51 (1982): 187-196.

Williams, Harry F. "The Authorship of *Guillaume d'Angleterre*." South Atlantic Review 52 (1987): 17-24.

Wilmotte, Maurice. "Chrétien de Troyes et le conte de *Guillaume d'Angleterre*." *Romania* 46 (1920): 1-38.

Woledge, Brian. "Apostrophe et déclinaison chez Chrétien de Troyes." *Mélanges ... Lods* (1978): 588-603.

————. "*La flors* et *la flor*. La déclinaison des féminins chez Chrétien de Troyes." *Mélanges ... Wathelet-Willem* (1978): 717-740.

Zaddy, Z. P. "Pourquoi Erec se décide-t-il à partir en voyage avec Enide?" *Cahiers de Civilisation Médiévale* 7 (1964): 179-185.

————. "The Structure of Chrétien's *Erec*." *Modern Language Review* 62 (1967): 608-619.

————. "Chrétien misogyne." *Mélanges ... Foulon* (1980): 301-307.

D. *Manuscripts and Textual Questions*

Burgess, Glyn S. "Editions of Old French Texts: Some Desiderata." *Teaching Language Through Literature* 19 (1979): 44-47.

Foulet, Alfred, and Mary Blakely Speer. *On Editing Old French Texts.* Edward C. Armstrong Monographs on Medieval Literature, 1. Lawrence: The Regents Press of Kansas, 1979.

Foulet, Alfred. "On Editing Chrétien's *Lancelot*." *The Romances of Chrétien de Troyes, A Symposium*, ed. Kelly (1985): 287-304.

Frank, István. "Le Manuscrit de Guiot entre Chrétien de Troyes et Wolfram von Eschenbach." *Annales Universitatis Saraviensis* 1 (1952): 169-183.

Hunt, Tony. "Chrestien de Troyes: The Textual Problem." *French Studies* 33 (1979): 257-71.

Jodogne, Omer. "Fragments de Mons." *Lettres Romanes* 4 (1950): 311-330.

Micha, Alexandre. *La Tradition manuscrite des romans de Chrétien de Troyes*. Genève: Droz, 1966 (2e tirage, rpt. of 1939).

Misrahi, Jean. "Fragments of *Erec et Enide* and their Relation to the Manuscript Tradition." *PMLA* 46 (1941): 951-61.

Paris, Gaston. Review of Foerster, ed., *Erec und Enide. Romania* 20 (1891): 148-166.

Pauphilet, Albert. "Nouveaux Fragments manuscrits de Chrétien de Troyes." *Romania* 63 (1937): 310-323.

Reid, T.B.W. "On the Text of the *Tristan* of Béroul." *Medieval Miscellany Presented to Eugène Vinaver* (1965): 263-288; rpt. *Medieval Manuscripts and Textual Criticism* (1976): 245-271.

———. "Chrétien de Troyes and the Scribe Guiot." *Medium Ævum* 45 (1976): 1-19.

———. "The Right to Emend." *Medieval French Textual Studies in Memory of T.B.W. Reid* (1984): 1-32.

Roques, Mario. "Le Manuscrit fr. 794 de la Bibliothèque Nationale et le scribe Guiot." *Romania* 73 (1952): 177-199.

Stone, Herbert K. "Le *Karrenritter* de Foerster." *Romania* 63 (1937): 398-401.

Thomas, A. "Fragmant [sic] de l'*Erec* de Crétien de Troies [sic]." *Romania* 43 (1914): 253-4.

Vinaver, Eugène. "Principles of Textual Emendation." *Studies in French Language and Mediæval Literature Presented to Professor Mildred K.*

Pope (1939): 351-369; rpt. *Medieval Manuscripts and Textual Criticism* (1976): 139-159.

Williams, Harry F. Review of Roques, ed., *Erec et Enide. Romance Philology* 9 (1956): 457-460.

Woledge, Brian. "Traits assurés par la rime ou par la mesure: l'exemple de Guiot copiste de Chrétien." *Mélanges ... Jonin* (1979): 719-727 [= "1979b"].

————. "Les Couples *COM/CON* et *DOM/DON* chez le copiste Guiot." *Mélanges ... Foulon* (1980): 403-408.

————. "The Problem of Editing *Yvain*." *Studies ... Reid* (1984): 254-267.

E. *Other Medieval Works*

Blaisdell, Foster W., and Marianne E. Kalinke, trs. *Erex Saga and Ivens Saga, The Old Norse Versions of Chrétien de Troyes's* Erec *and* Yvain. Lincoln: University of Nebraska Press, 1977.

Geoffrey of Monmouth. *History of the Kings of Britain*, tr. Lewis Thorpe. London: Penguin, 1966; 4th ed. 1976.

Hartmann von Aue. *Erec*, tr. J. W. Thomas. Lincoln: University of Nebraska Press, 1982.

Jenkins, T. Atkinson, ed. *La Chanson de Roland, Oxford Version*. Revised ed. Boston: D. C. Heath, 1924.

Jones, Gwyn and Thomas, trs. *The Mabinogion*. London: J. M. Dent & Sons, 1974.

Kibler, William W., ed. and tr. Chrétien de Troyes, *Lancelot or, The Knight of the Cart (Le Chevalier de la Charrete)*. Garland Library of Medieval Literature, 1, Series A. New York: Garland, 1981.

————, ed. and tr. Chrétien de Troyes, *The Knight with the Lion, or Yvain (Le Chevalier au Lion)*. Garland Library of Medieval Literature, 48, Series A. New York: Garland, 1985.

Morawski, Joseph, ed. *Proverbes français antérieurs au XVe siècle*. Classiques Français du Moyen Age, 47. Paris: Champion, 1925.

Owen, D.D.R., and R. C. Johnston, eds. *Two Old French Gauvain Romances*. Edinburgh and London: Scottish Academic Press, 1972; New York: Harper & Row, 1973.

Pickford, Cedric E., ed. *Erec, roman arthurien en prose*. Genève: Droz; Paris: Minard, 2me ed., 1968.

Reid, T.B.W., ed. Chrétien de Troyes, *Yvain (Le Chevalier au lion): The Critical Text of Wendelin Foerster with Introduction, Notes and Glossary by T.B.W. Reid*. Manchester: Manchester University Press, 1942; rpt. 1984.

Roach, William, ed. *Le Roman de Perceval ou Le Conte du graal, publié d'après le ms. fr. 12576 de la Bibliothèque Nationale*. Textes Littéraires Français, 71. Genève: Droz; Paris: Minard, 1956; rpt. 1959.

Rychner, Jean, ed. *Les Lais de Marie de France*. Classiques Français du Moyen Age, 93. Paris: Champion, 1966; rpt. 1981.

Salverda de Grave, J.-J., ed. *Eneas, roman du XIIe siècle*. Classiques Français du Moyen Age, 44 (tome I, vers 1-5998); 62 (tome II, vers 5999-10156). Paris: Champion, 1925 (rpt. 1964); 1929.

William of Malmesbury. *Chronicle of the Kings of England*, tr. John Sharpe; rev. by J. A. Giles. London: George Bell, 1904.

F. Mélanges *and Other Collections*

Caluwé, Jacques de, ed. *Mélanges de philologie et de littérature romanes offerts à Jeanne Wathelet-Willem*. Liège: Cahiers de l'A. R. U. Lg. (Marche Romane), 1978.

La Chanson de geste et le mythe carolingien: Mélanges René Louis publiés par ses collègues, ses amis et ses élèves à l'occasion de son 75e anniversaire. 2 vols. Saint-Père-sous-Vézelay: Musée Archéologique Régional, 1982.

Combe, T.G.S., and P. Rickard, eds. *The French Language: Studies Presented to Lewis Charles Harmer*. London: Harrap, 1970.

Dufournet, Jean, and Daniel Poirion, eds. *Mélanges de langue et de littérature médiévales offerts à Pierre Le Gentil ... par ses collègues, ses élèves et ses amis*. Paris: S.E.D.E.S. and C.D.U. Réunis, 1973.

Fourrier, Anthime, ed. *L'Humanisme médiéval dans les littératures romanes du XIIe au XIVe siècle.* Paris: Klincksieck, 1964.

Kleinhenz, Christopher, ed. *Medieval Manuscripts and Textual Criticism (MMTC).* North Carolina Studies in the Romance Languages and Literatures, Symposia, 4. Chapel Hill: University of North Carolina Press, 1976.

Levy, Bernard, and Sandro Sticca, eds. *The Twelfth Century.* Acta 2. Binghamton: Center for Medieval and Early Renaissance Studies, State U. of N. Y. at Binghamton, 1975.

Mélanges de langue et littérature françaises du Moyen Age et de la Renaissance offerts à Monsieur Charles Foulon ... par ses collègues, ses élèves et ses amis. 2 vols. Rennes: Inst. de Fr., Univ. de Haute-Bretagne, 1980.

Mélanges de langue et littérature françaises du moyen-âge offerts à Pierre Jonin. Senefiance, 7. Aix-en-Provence: C.U.E.R. M.A.; Paris: Champion, 1979.

Mélanges de littérature: Du moyen âge au XXe siècle. Offerts à Mademoiselle Jeanne Lods ... par ses collègues, ses élèves et ses amis. 2 vols. Paris: Ecole Normale Supérieure de Jeunes Filles, 1978.

Payen, J. C., and C. Regnier, eds., *Mélanges de langue et de littérature du moyen âge et de la renaissance offerts à Jean Frappier.* 2 vols. Genève: Droz (1970).

Runte, Hans R., Henri Niedzielski, & William L. Hendrickson, eds. *Jean Misrahi Memorial Volume: Studies in Medieval Literature.* Columbia, S.C.: French Literature Publications, 1977.

Short, Ian, ed. *Medieval French Textual Studies in Memory of T.B.W. Reid.* Occasional Publications Series, 1. London: Anglo-Norman Text Society, 1984.

Studies in French Language and Mediæval Literature Presented to Professor Mildred K. Pope. Manchester: Manchester University Press, 1939; rpt. Freeport, N.Y.: Books for Libraries Press, 1969.

Sutcliffe, F. E., ed. *Medieval Miscellany Presented to Eugène Vinaver.* Manchester: Manchester University Press, 1965.

G. *Dictionaries, Glossaries, Grammars, and General Studies*

Foerster, Wendelin. *Wörterbuch zu Kristian von Troyes' Sämtlichen Werken.* Zweite veränderte Auflage von Hermann Breuer. Halle: Niemeyer, 1933.

Foulet, Lucien. *Glossary of the First Continuation* (Vol. III, Part 2 of Roach, William, ed., *The Continuations of the Old French Perceval of Chrétien de Troyes*). Philadelphia: American Philosophical Society, 1955.

Godefroy, Frédéric. *Dictionnaire de l'ancienne langue française et de tous ses dialectes, du IXe au XVe siècle.* 10 vols. Paris, F. Viewig (1-5); Emile Bouillon (6-10), 1881-1902.

Grandsaignes d'Hauterive, R. *Dictionnaire d'ancien français, moyen âge et renaissance.* Paris: Larousse, 1947.

Greimas, A. J. *Dictionnaire de l'ancien français jusqu'au milieu du XIVe siècle.* Paris: Larousse, 1980.

Jauss, Hans Robert. "La Transformation de la forme allégorique entre 1180 et 1240: d'Alain de Lille à Guillaume de Lorris." *L'Humanisme médiéval*, ed. Fourrier (1964): 107-144.

Kibler, William W. *An Introduction to Old French.* Introductions to Older Languages, 3. New York: Modern Language Association of America, 1984.

Lacy, Norris J., ed. *The Arthurian Encyclopedia.* Garland Reference Library of the Humanities, 585. New York: Garland, 1986.

Moignet, Gérard. *Grammaire de l'ancien français*, 2e éd. Paris: Klincksieck, 1973.

Morris, William, ed. *The American Heritage Dictionary of the English Language (AHD).* Boston: American Heritage Pub. Co. and Houghton Mifflin, 1969, 1970, 1971.

Raynaud de Lage, Guy. *Introduction à l'ancien français*, 7e éd. Paris: S.E.D.E.S., 1970.

Strayer, Joseph R., ed. *Dictionary of the Middle Ages (DMA)*. 6 vols. (through "Italian Literature", 1985). New York: Charles Scribner's Sons, 1982- .

Tobler, Adolf, and Ehrard Lommatzsch. *Tobler-Lommatzsch Altfranzösisches Wörterbuch. Adolf Toblers nachgelassene Materialen, bearbeitet und herausgegeben von Erhard Lommatzsch; Von der 25. Lieferung an mit Unterstützung der Akademie der Wissenschaften und der Literatur (Mainz)* (T.-L.). 10 vols. (through *T*). Berlin, 1915- ; rpt. Wiesbaden: Steiner, 1955-1976.

Vinaver, Eugène. *The Rise of Romance*. New York: Oxford University Press, 1971.

West, G. D. *An Index of Proper Names in French Arthurian Verse Romances 1150-1300*. Toronto: University of Toronto Press, 1969 (University of Toronto Romance Series, 15).

―――. *An Index of Proper Names in French Arthurian Prose Romances*. Toronto: University of Toronto Press, 1978 (University of Toronto Romance Series, 35).

Woledge, Brian. "Notes on the Syntax of Indeclinable Nouns in 12th-Century French." *The French Language*. London: Harrap, 1970: 38-52.

Zumthor, Paul. *Essai de poétique médiévale*. Paris: Seuil, 1972.

H. *Medieval Civilization*

Allen, Robert, tr. Robert Delort, *Life in the Middle Ages*. Lausanne: Edita, 1973; rpt. New York: Greenwich House, 1983.

Bottomley, Frank. *The Castle Explorer's Guide*. London: Kaye and Ward, 1979; New York: Avenel, 1983.

Cunnington, C. Willett and Phillis. *The History of Underclothes*. London: Michael Joseph, 1951.

Delort, Robert. *Le Moyen Age: Histoire illustrée de la vie quotidienne*. Lausanne: Edita, 1972.

Goddard, Eunice Rathbone. *Women's Costume in French Texts of the Eleventh and Twelfth Centuries*. Baltimore: Johns Hopkins Press, 1927; rpt. New York: Johnson Reprint Corp., 1973.

Hindley, Geoffrey. *Medieval Warfare*. New York: Putnam's, 1971.

Holmes, Urban Tigner, Jr. *Daily Living in the Twelfth Century, Based on the Observations of Alexander Neckam in London and Paris* . Madison: The University of Wisconsin Press, 1952; rpt. 1964.

Koch, Hannsjoachim Wolfgang. *Medieval Warfare*. London: Bison Books, 1978; rpt. New York: Crescent Books, 1983.

Mavrogordato, Jack. *A Hawk for the Bush: A Treatise on the Training of the Sparrow-hawk and other Short-Winged Hawks*. New York: Clarkson N. Potter, 2d ed., 1973. Illustrations by G. E. Lodge. Glossary, 197-200. Bibliography, 201-202. Index, 203-206.

Pastoureau, Michel. *La Vie quotidienne en France et en Angleterre au temps des chevaliers de la Table ronde (XIIe-XIIIe siècles)*. [Paris:] Hachette, 1976. Bibliographie, 231-236.

Planché, James Robinson. *A Cyclopædia of Costume or Dictionary of Dress* ... 2 vols. (vol. I, The Dictionary; vol. II, A General History of Costume in Europe). London: Chatto and Windus, 1876, 1879. II: Chapter III, "Twelfth Century," 48-65.

Sadie, Stanley, ed. *The New Grove Dictionary of Music and Musicians (New Grove)*. 20 vols. London: Macmillan, 1980.

Stone, George Cameron. *A Glossary of the Construction, Decoration and Use of Arms and Armor in All Countries and in All Times, Together with Some Closely Related Subjects*. Portland, Me.: Southworth Press, 1934; rpt. New York: Jack Brussel, 1961. Bibliography, 687-694.

Wood, Casey A., and F. Marjorie Fyfe, trans. and eds. *The Art of Falconry, being the De Arte Venandi cum Avibus of Frederick II of Hohenstaufen*. Stanford: Stanford U. Press, 1943; reissued 1961; rpt. 1981. Glossary, 613-629. General index, 631-637.

Combat between mounted knights. Paris, B.N., f.fr. 24403, fol. 155r (Phot. Bibl. nat. Paris).

Erec and Enide

Erec et Enide

    Li vilains dit an son respit
que tel chose a l'an an despit *
qui molt valt mialz que l'an ne cuide;
por ce fet bien qui son estuide
5   atorne a sens quel que il l'ait,
car qui son estuide antrelait,
tost i puet tel chose teisir
qui molt vandroit puis a pleisir.
Por ce dist Crestïens de Troies
10   que reisons est que totevoies
doit chascuns panser et antandre
a bien dire et a bien aprandre,
et tret d'un conte d'avanture
une molt bele conjointure,
15   par qu'an puet prover et savoir
que cil ne fet mie savoir
qui s'escïence n'abandone
tant con Dex la grasce l'an done.
D'Erec, le fil Lac, est li contes,
20   que devant rois et devant contes
depecier et corronpre suelent
cil qui de conter vivre vuelent.
Des or comancerai l'estoire
qui toz jorz mes iert an mimoire
25   tant con durra crestïantez:
de ce s'est Crestïens vantez.
    Au jor de Pasque, au tans novel,
a Quaradigan, son chastel,
ot li rois Artus cort tenue.
30   Einz si riche ne fu veüe,
que molt i ot boens chevaliers,
hardiz et conbatanz et fiers,
et riches dames et puceles,
filles de rois, gentes et beles;
35   mes einçois que la corz fausist,

5.   sens *PE* (san *F1909*)] bien *CBVA* = *F1890, 1896* (*H omits 1-26*).

Erec and Enide

The peasant says in his proverb
that one may hold in contempt something
that is worth much more than one believes;
therefore he does well who makes good use of his learning
5   according to whatever understanding he has,
for he who neglects his learning
may easily keep silent something
that would later give much pleasure.
Therefore Chrétien de Troyes says
10   that it is reasonable
that each person think and strive in every way
to speak well and to teach well,
and from a tale of adventure he draws
a beautifully ordered composition,
15   whereby one may prove and know
that he does not act intelligently
who does not give free rein to his knowledge,
as long as God gives him the grace to do so.
This is the tale of Erec, son of Lac,
20   which, before kings and before counts,
those who try to live by storytelling
customarily mangle and corrupt.
Now I shall begin the story
which evermore will be in memory
25   for as long as Christendom lasts—
of this does Chrétien boast.
    On Easter day, in springtime,
at Cardigan, his castle,
King Arthur held court.
30   So rich a one was never seen,
for there were many good knights,
brave and combative and fierce,
and rich ladies and maidens,
daughters of kings, noble and beautiful;
35   but before the court concluded

li rois a ses chevaliers dist
qu'il voloit le blanc cerf chacier
por la costume ressaucier.
Mon seignor Gauvain ne plot mie
40   quant il ot la parole oïe:
"Sire," fet il, "de ceste chace
n'avroiz vos ja ne gré ne grace.
Nos savomes bien tuit piece a
quel costume li blans cers a:
45   qui le blanc cerf ocirre puet   [1b]
par reison beisier li estuet
des puceles de vostre cort
la plus bele, a que que il tort.
Maus an puet avenir molt granz,
50   qu'ancor a il ceanz cinc cenz
dameiseles de hauz paraiges,
filles de rois, gentes et sages,
n'i a nule qui n'ait ami
chevalier vaillant et hardi,
55   don chascuns desresnier voldroit,
ou fust a tort ou fust a droit,
que cele qui li atalante
est la plus bele et la plus gente."
Li rois respont: "Ce sai ge bien,
60   mes por ce n'an lerai ge rien,
car parole que rois a dite *
ne doit puis estre contredite.
Demain matin a grant deduit
irons chacier le blanc cerf tuit
65   an la forest avantureuse:
ceste chace iert molt mervelleuse."
Ensi est la chace atornee
a l'andemain, a l'anjornee.
L'andemain, lués que il ajorne,
70   li rois se lieve et si s'atorne,
et por aler an la forest
d'une corte cote se vest.
Les chevaliers fet esvellier,
les chaceors aparellier.
75   Lor ars et lor saietes ont;
an la forest chacier s'an vont.
Aprés aus monte la reïne,
ansanble o li une meschine;
pucele estoit, fille de roi,
80   et sist sor un boen palefroi.
Aprés les siust a esperon
uns chevaliers, Erec a non.

58.   plust b. *C, with expunctuating dot under the* t.
63.   *Initial* D *in C.*

4

the king said to his knights
that he wanted to hunt the white stag
in order to revive the tradition.
My lord Gawain was not a bit pleased
40   when he heard this:
"Sire," said he, "from this hunt
you will never have either gratitude nor thanks. *
We have all known for a long time
what tradition is attached to the white stag:
45   he who can kill the white stag
by right must kiss
the most beautiful of the maidens of your court,
whatever may happen.
Great evil can come from this,
50   for there are easily five hundred
damsels of high lineage here,
daughters of kings, noble and prudent,
and there is not a one who is not the favorite
of some valiant and bold knight,
55   each of whom would want to contend,
either rightly or wrongly,
that the one who pleases him
is the most beautiful and the most noble."
The king replied: "This I know well,
60   but I will not give up my plan for all that,
for the word of a king
must not be opposed.
Tomorrow morning with great pleasure
we will all go to hunt the white stag
65   in the forest of adventures:
this hunt will be truly wondrous."
Thus was the hunt arranged
for the morrow, at daybreak.
The next day, as soon as it was light,
70   the king arose and made ready;
to go into the forest
he put on a short tunic.
He had the knights awakened,
the hunting-steeds readied.
75   They had their bows and their arrows,
and set off to hunt in the forest.
The queen mounted up after them,
accompanied by an attendant;
she was a maiden, daughter of a king,
80   and sat upon a good palfrey.
A knight came spurring after them:
his name was Erec.

De la Table Reonde estoit;
an la cort molt grant los avoit:
85 de tant com il i ot esté,
n'i ot chevalier si loé,
et fu tant biax qu'an nule terre
n'estovoit plus bel de lui querre.
Molt estoit biax et preuz et genz, [1c]
90 et n'avoit pas vint et cinc anz;
onques nus hom de son aage
ne fu de si grant vaselage.
Que diroie de ses bontez?
Sor un destrier estoit montez,
95 afublez d'un mantel hermin;
galopant vient tot le chemin,
s'ot cote d'un dïapre noble
qui fu fez an Costantinoble. *
Chauces de paile avoit chauciees,
100 molt bien fetes et bien tailliees,
et fu es estriés afichiez,
uns esperons a or chauciez;
n'ot avoec lui arme aportee
fors que tant seulemant s'espee. *
105 La reïne vint ateignant
au tor d'une rue poignant:
"Dame," fet il, "a vos seroie,
s'il vos pleisoit, an ceste voie.
Je ne ving ça por autre afere
110 fors por vos conpaignie fere."
Et la reïne l'an mercie:
"Biax amis, vostre conpaignie
aim je molt, ce saichiez de voir:
je ne puis pas meillor avoir."
115   Lors chevalchent a grant esploit;
an la forest vienent tot droit.
Cil qui devant erent alé
avoient ja le cerf levé:
li un cornent, li autre huïent;
120 li chien aprés le cerf s'esbruient,
corent, angressent et abaient;
li archier espessemant traient.
Devant ax toz chace li rois
sor un chaceor espanois.
125 La reïne Ganievre estoit
el bois, qui les chiens escotoit;
lez li Erec et sa pucele,
qui molt estoit cortoise et bele.
Mes tant d'ax esloignié estoient
130 cil qui le cerf levé avoient

106.   d'une rue *HBPVA = F*] de la rue *C*.

He was of the Round Table
and had great honor at court:
85   as long as he had been there,
there had not been a knight so highly praised,
and he was so handsome that there was no need
to seek a handsomer man anywhere.
He was very handsome and valiant and noble,
90   and he was not yet twenty-five years old;
never was any man of his age
so accomplished in knighthood.
What should I say of his virtues?
He was mounted on a charger
95   and came galloping along the road;
he was dressed in a fur-lined cloak
and a tunic of noble, patterned silk,
that had been made in Constantinople.
He had put on silken stockings,
100   very finely made and tailored;
he was well set in his stirrups,
and was wearing golden spurs;
he had brought no weapon with him
except for his sword.
105   Spurring his horse, he caught up with the queen
at a bend in the road.
"My lady," said he, "I would go with you,
should it please you, on this road.
I have come here for no other reason
110   than to keep you company."
And the queen thanked him for that:
"Fair friend, I greatly like
your company; know this truly:
I can have none better."
115   Then they rode speedily on
and came straight to the forest.
Those who had gone on ahead
had already raised the stag:
some blew on horns, others shouted;
120   the dogs went noisily after the stag,
running, rushing and barking;
the archers were shooting thick and fast.
Out in front of all of them the king was hunting,
mounted on a Spanish hunter.
125   Queen Guinevere was in the woods,
listening to the dogs;
beside her were Erec and her maiden,
who was very courtly and beautiful.
But those who had raised the stag
130   were so far off

7

que d'ax ne pueent oïr rien,
ne cor, ne chaceor, ne chien.
Por orellier et escouter [1d]
s'il orroient home parler
135   ne cri de chien de nule part,
tuit troi furent an un essart
delez le chemin aresté.
Mes molt i orent po esté
qant il virent un chevalier
140   venir armé sor un destrier,
l'escu au col, la lance el poing.
La reïne le vit de loing:
delez lui chevalchoit a destre
une pucele de bel estre;
145   devant ax, sor un grant roncin,
venoit uns nains tot le chemin,
et ot en sa main aportee
une corgiee an son noee.
La reïne Guenievre voit
150   le chevalier bel et adroit,
et de sa pucele et de lui
vialt savoir qui il sont andui.
Sa pucele comande aler
isnelemant a lui parler:
155   "Dameisele," fet la reïne
"ce chevalier qui la chemine
alez dire qu'il vaigne a moi
et amaint sa pucele o soi."
La pucele vet l'anbleüre
160   vers le chevalier a droiture.
Li nains a l'ancontre li vient,
qui sa corgiee an sa main tient.
"Dameisele, estez!" fet li nains,
qui de felenie fu plains.
165   "Qu'alez vos ceste part querant?
Ça n'avez vos que fere avant!"
"Nains," fet ele, "lesse m'aler:
a ce chevalier voel parler,
car la reïne m'i anvoie."
170   Li nains s'estut en mi la voie,
qui molt fu fel et de put' ere:
"Ça n'avez vos," fet il, "que fere.
Alez arrieres! N'est pas droiz
qu'a si boen chevalier parloiz."
175   La pucele s'est avant trete;
passer volt oltre a force fete,
que lo nain ot an grant despit [1e]
por ce qu'ele le vit petit.

137.   delez le *BVA* = *F*] anz en .i. *C*; Jouste le *P*, Les le *H* (sont areste).

8

that they could hear nothing of them—
neither horn nor horse nor hound.
In order to listen attentively
to see if they could hear a human voice
135 or the cry of a hound from any side,
all three had stopped in a clearing
beside the road.
They had not been there long
when they saw approaching
140 an armored knight on a charger,
his shield at his neck, his lance in his hand.
The queen saw him from afar:
beside him at his right was riding
a fine-looking maiden;
145 before them, on a big draft horse,
a dwarf was riding along,
and he carried in his hand
a whip with lashes knotted at one end.
Queen Guinevere saw the knight,
150 handsome and elegant,
and she wanted to know who they were,
he and his maiden.
She told her maiden to go
quickly to speak to him:
155 "Damsel," said the queen,
"go tell that knight
riding there to come to me
and to bring his maiden with him."
The maiden rode apace, *
160 straight toward the knight.
The dwarf came to meet her,
holding his whip in his hand.
"Damsel, halt!" said the dwarf,
who was full of evil.
165 "What are you looking for here?
You have no business in this direction!"
"Dwarf," said she, "let me pass:
I wish to speak to that knight,
for the queen sends me there."
170 The dwarf, who was very evil and baseborn,
stood blocking her way:
"You have no business here," said he.
"Go back! It's not right
for you to talk to such a fine knight."
175 The maiden moved forward;
she wanted to force her way past,
for she felt great contempt for the dwarf
because she saw how little he was.

Et li nains hauce la corgiee,
180   quant vers lui la vit aprochiee.
Ferir la volt par mi le vis,
mes cele a son braz devant mis;
cil recuevre, si l'a ferue
a descovert sor la main nue.
185   Si la fiert sor la main anverse
que tote an devint la mains perse.
La pucele, quant mialz ne puet,
voelle ou non, retorner l'estuet.
Retornee s'an est plorant:
190   des ialz li descendent corant
les lermes contreval la face.
La reïne ne set que face;
quant sa pucele voit bleciee,
molt est dolante et correciee:
195   "Hé! Erec, biax amis," fet ele,
"molt me poise de ma pucele
que si a bleciee cil nains.
Molt est li chevaliers vilains,
quant il sofri que tex fauture
200   feri si bele criature.
Biax amis Erec, alez i
au chevalier, et dites li
qu'il veigne a moi, et nel lest mie:
conuistre vuel lui et s'amie."
205   Erec cele part esperone,
des esperons au cheval done,
vers le chevalier vient tot droit.
Li nains cuiverz venir le voit;
a l'ancontre li est alez:
210   "Vasax," fet il, "arriers estez!
Ça ne sai ge qu'a fere aiez.
Je vos lo qu'arriers vos traiez."
"Fui!" fet Erec, "nains enuieus!
Trop es fel et contralïeus.
215   Lesse m'aler!"—"Vos n'i iroiz!"
"Je si ferai!"—"Vos nel feroiz!"
Erec bote le nain an sus.
Li nains fu fel tant con nus plus:
de la corgiee grant colee
220   li a par mi le col donee.   *[1f]*
Le col et la face ot vergiee
Erec del cop de la corgiee:
de chief an chief perent les roies
que li ont feites les corroies.
225   Il sot bien que del nain ferir

203. qu'il *HBPVAE = F*] Que il *C.* | et *HBE = F*] *CPV omit*, quil *A.* |
nel *CVA = F* (nou *B*, ne le *P*)] ne *HE.* | l. il mie *V.*

10

But the dwarf raised his whip
180 when he saw her approaching him.
He tried to strike her in the face,
but she protected herself with her arm;
then he took aim again, and struck her
openly on her bare hand.
185 He struck her on the back of her hand
so that her hand became all blue.
The maiden, since she could do no more,
was obliged to turn back, whether she wanted to or not.
She came back weeping:
190 tears were running from her eyes
down her face.
The queen knew not what to do;
when she saw her maiden wounded
she was very sad and angry:
195 "Oh! Erec, fair friend," said she,
"I am very upset about my maiden,
whom this dwarf has wounded in such a way.
The knight is very unchivalrous,
since he has allowed such a freak
200 to strike such a beautiful creature.
Fair friend Erec, go over
to the knight and tell him
to come to me without fail:
I want to meet both him and his lady."
205 Erec spurred in that direction,
put his spurs to his horse,
and came straight to the knight.
The despicable dwarf saw him coming
and went to meet him:
210 "Knight," said he, "stay back!
I don't know what business you have here.
I advise you to withdraw."
"Be gone," said Erec, "bothersome dwarf!
You're very nasty and hateful.
215 Let me pass!"—"You won't pass!"
"Yes, I will!"—"No, you won't!"
Erec gave the dwarf a shove.
The dwarf was as evil as could be:
with the whip he struck Erec
220 a great blow on the neck.
Erec's neck and face
were striped by the blow:
the welts raised by the strands of the whip
appeared from one end to the other.
225 Erec knew full well that he could not

ne porroit il mie joïr,
car le chevalier vit armé,
molt félon et desmesuré,
et crient qu'asez tost l'ocirroit
230 se devant lui son nain feroit.
Folie n'est pas vaselages; *
de ce fist molt Erec que sages:
rala s'an, que plus n'i ot fet.
"Dame," fet il, "or est plus let:
235 si m'a li nains cuiverz blecié
que tot le vis m'a depecié.
Ne l'osai ferir ne tochier,
mes nus nel me doit reprochier,
que ge toz desarmez estoie:
240 le chevalier armé dotoie,
qui vilains est et outrageus.
Et il nel tenist pas a geus:
tost m'oceïst par son orguel.
Itant bien prometre vos vuel
245 que, se ge puis, je vangerai
ma honte, ou je la crestrai!
Mes trop me sont mes armes loing:
nes avrai pas a cest besoing,
qu'a Quaradigan les lessai
250 hui matin, quant je m'an tornai.
Se je la querre les aloie,
ja mes retrover ne porroie
le chevalier par avanture,
car il s'an vet grant aleüre.
255 Sivre le me covient adés,
ou soit de loing ou soit de pres,
tant que ge puisse armes trover
ou a loier ou a prester.
Se ge truis qui armes me prest,
260 maintenant me trovera prest
li chevaliers de la bataille.
Et bien sachiez sanz nule faille
que tant nos conbatrons andui
qu'il me conquerra ou ge lui.
265 Et, se ge puis, jusqu'al tierz jor   *[3a]*
me serai ge mis el retor:
lors me reverroiz a l'ostel,
lié ou dolant, ne sai lequel.
Dame, je ne puis plus tardier:
270 sivre m'estuet le chevalier.
Je m'an vois; a Deu vos comant."
Et la reïne autresimant

251.   la *HBPVA* = *F*] ia *C.*
256.   loing *BP* = *FR* (*cf. 142, 361*)] loig *C*, loins *V*, lons *H*, lonc *A.*

12

have the satisfaction of striking the dwarf,
for he saw the armored knight,
ruthless and arrogant,
and he feared that the knight would very quickly kill him
230   if he struck his dwarf in his presence.
Folly is not prowess;
in this Erec acted very wisely:
he withdrew, without doing anything more.
"My lady," said he, "now things are even worse:
235   that despicable dwarf has injured me
so that my face is torn to bits.
⌐ I dared not touch or strike him,
but no one must blame me for that,
since I was completely unarmed: *
240   I was afraid of the armed knight;
he is uncourtly and unprincipled.
And he would have considered it no joke:
he would at once have killed me, in his pride.
But I want to promise you
245   that, if I can, I will avenge
my shame, or else I'll augment it!
But my own armor is too far away:
I won't have it for this task,
for I left it at Cardigan
250   this morning, when I set out.
If I went back there to get it,
I could probably never
find the knight again,
for he is riding off at a brisk pace.
255   I must follow him right now,
either closely or at a distance,
until I can find some armor
to rent or to borrow.
If I can find someone to lend me armor,
260   then the knight will immediately
find me ready to do battle.
And be assured, without any doubt,
that we will fight together
until he defeats me or I defeat him.
265   And, if I can, by the third day *
I shall begin my return:
then you shall see me at the castle,
joyful or sad, I know not which.
My lady, I can delay no more:
270   I must follow the knight.
I am leaving; I commend you to God."
And the queen likewise

13

a Deu, qui de mal le desfande,
plus de cinc cenz foiz le comande.
275 Erec se part de la reïne;
del chevalier sivre ne fine.
Et la reïne el bois remaint,
ou li rois ot le cerf ataint:
a la prise del cerf einçois
280 vint que nus des autres li rois.
Le blanc cerf ont desfet et pris.
Au repeirier se sont tuit mis,
le cerf an portent, si s'an vont;
a Caradigan venu sont.
285 Aprés soper, quant li baron
furent tuit lié par la meison,
li rois, si con costume estoit,
por ce que le cerf pris avoit,
dist qu'il iroit le beisier prandre
290 por la costume del cerf randre.
Par la cort an font grant murmure:
li uns a l'autre afie et jure
que ce n'iert ja fet sanz desresne
d'espee ou de lance de fresne.
295 Chascuns vialt par chevalerie
desresnier que la soe amie
est la plus bele de la sale;
molt est ceste parole male.
Quant mes sire Gauvains le sot,
300 sachiez que mie ne li plot.
a parole en a mis le roi:
"Sire," fet il, "an grant esfroi
sont ceanz vostre chevalier.
Tuit parolent de ce beisier:
305 bien dïent tuit que n'iert ja fet
que noise et bataille n'i et."
Et li rois li respont par san:
"Biax niés Gauvain, conselliez m'an,
sauve m'annor et ma droiture,   [3b]
310 que je n'ai de la noise cure."
Au consoil grant partie cort
des mellors barons de la cort:
li rois Ydiers i est alez,
que premiers i fu apelez;
315 aprés li rois Cadiolanz,
qui molt fu saiges et vaillanz;
Kex et Girflez i sont venu
et Amauguins li rois i fu,
et des autres barons asez
320 i ot avoec ax amassez.

316. fu *added above line.*

14

commended him to God, more than five hundred times,
that he might defend him from evil.
275 Erec left the queen
and followed the knight.
And the queen remained in the woods,
where the king had caught up with the stag:
at the taking of the stag
280 the king arrived before any of the others.
They killed and took the white stag.
All started back,
carrying the stag as they went;
they arrived at Cardigan.
285 After the evening meal, when the nobles *
were joyful throughout the house,
the king, according to the tradition,
since he had taken the stag,
said that he would bestow the kiss
290 in order to observe the tradition of the stag.
Throughout the court there was much muttering:
they promised and swore to one another
that this would never be done without contention
by means of sword or lance of ash-wood.
295 Each one wanted, by deeds of arms,
to contend that his lady
was the most beautiful in the hall;
these words did not bode well. *
When my lord Gawain heard this,
300 you may be sure that he was not at all pleased.
He spoke to the king about it:
"Sire," said he, "your knights here
are greatly disturbed.
They are all speaking of this kiss:
305 they all say that it will never be done
without there being arguments and fighting."
And the king replied wisely:
"Fair nephew Gawain, advise me in this,
so that my honor and justice may be preserved,
310 for I do not care for discord."
Many of the best barons of the court
hurried to the council:
King Yder went there,
who had been called there first;
315 then came King Cadiolan,
who was most wise and valiant;
Kay and Girflet came there,
and King Amauguin,
and many of the other barons
320 were gathered there with them.

15

Tant est la parole esmeüe
que la reïne i est venue.
L'avanture lor a contee
qu'an la forest avoit trovee:
325 del chevalier que armé vit
et del nain felon et petit
qui de s'escorgiee ot ferue
sa pucele sor la main nue,
et ot feru tot ansimant
330 Erec el vis molt leidemant,
qui a seü le chevalier
por sa honte croistre ou vangier,
et que il repeirier devoit
jusqu'a tierz jor, se il pooit.
335 "Sire," fet la reïne au roi,
"antandez un petit a moi!
Se cist baron loent mon dit,
metez cest beisier an respit
jusqu'a tierz jor, qu'Erec revaingne."
340 N'i a nul qu'a li ne se taigne,
et li rois meïsmes l'otroie.
    Erec va suiant tote voie
le chevalier qui armez fu
et le nain qui l'avoit feru,
345 tant qu'il vindrent a un chastel
molt bien seant et fort et bel;
par mi la porte antrent tot droit.
El chastel molt grant joie avoit
de chevaliers et de puceles,
350 car molt en i avoit de beles.
Li un peissoient par les rues
espreviers et faucons de mues,
et li autre aportoient hors   *[3c]*
terciax, ostors müez et sors;
355 li autre joent d'autre part
ou a la mine ou a hasart,
cil as eschas et cil as tables.
Li garçon devant ces estables
torchent les chevax et estrillent;
360 les dames es chanbres s'atillent.
De si loing com il venir voient
le chevalier qu'il conuissoient,
son nain et sa pucele o soi,
ancontre lui vont troi et troi:
365 tuit le conjoent et salüent,
mes contre Erec ne se remüent,

338. *A crease in C causes* te *of* metez *to appear superimposed, but all the
letters are in fact clearly present.*
342. *No large initial, C.*

16

The debate went on so long
that the queen arrived on the scene.
She recounted to them the adventure
that she had had in the forest:
325 about the armed knight she had seen
and the evil little dwarf
who had struck her maiden
on her bare hand with his whip,
and had in just the same way struck
330 Erec most horribly on the face;
and how he had then followed the knight
in order to avenge his shame or augment it,
and that he was to return,
if he could, by the third day.
335 "My lord," said the queen to the king,
"just listen to me!
If these barons approve what I say,
postpone this kiss
until the third day, so that Erec may return."
340 There was not a one who disagreed with her,
and the king himself granted it.
    Erec kept on following
the armored knight
and the dwarf who had struck him,
345 until they came to a fortified town, *
well situated and strong and fine;
they went right in through the gate.
In the town there was great joy
among the knights and damsels,
350 for there were many beautiful ones.
Some, in the streets, were feeding
sparrow-hawks and moulted falcons, *
and others were bringing out
tercels and red and moulted goshawks;
355 others, here and there, were playing
different dice games, *
or chess, or backgammon.
In front of the stables, boys
were currying horses and wiping them down;
360 ladies, in their chambers, were adorning themselves.
As soon as they saw, from afar,
the knight, whom they knew,
coming with his dwarf and his maiden,
they went to meet him, three by three:
365 all welcomed and greeted him,
but they made no move to welcome Erec,

*she postpones
disaster*

17

qu'il ne le conuissoient pas.
Erec va suiant tot le pas
par le chastel le chevalier,
370   tant que il le vit herbergier:
formant an fu joianz et liez
quant il vit qu'il fut herbergiez.
Un petit est avant passez
et vit gesir sor uns degrez
375   un vavasor auques de jorz,
mes molt estoit povre sa corz.
Biax hom estoit, chenuz et blans,
deboneres, gentix et frans;
iluec s'estoit toz seus assis:
380   bien resanbloit qu'il fust pansis.
Erec pansa que il estoit
preudom; tost le herbergeroit.
Par mi la porte antre an la cort.
Li vavasors contre lui cort;
385   einz qu'Erec li eüst dit mot,
li vavasors salüé l'ot:
"Biax sire," fet il, "bien vaingniez!
Se o moi herbergier daingniez,
vez l'ostel aparellié ci."
390   Erec respont: "Vostre merci!
Je ne sui ça venuz por el:
mestier ai enuit mes d'ostel."
Erec de son cheval descent.
Li sires meïsmes le prent;
395   par la resne aprés lui le tret.
De son oste grant joie fet.
Li vavasors sa fame apele   [3d]
et sa fille qui molt fu bele,
qui an un ovreor ovroient,
400   mes ne sai quele oevre i feisoient.
La dame s'an est hors issue
et sa fille, qui fu vestue
d'une chemise par panz lee,
delïee, blanche et ridee.
405   Un blanc cheinse ot vestu desus;
n'avoit robe ne mains ne plus.
Et tant estoit li chainses viez
que as costez estoit perciez.
Povre estoit la robe dehors,
410   mes desoz estoit biax li cors.
Molt estoit la pucele gente,
car tote i ot mise s'antante
Nature, qui fete l'avoit.
Ele meïsmes s'an estoit

352.   mues *HBPVA = FR*] mue *C*.

because they did not know him.
Erec kept on closely following
the knight, through the town,
370　until he saw him lodged:
he was very pleased and joyful
when he saw that he was lodged.
He went on a bit farther
and saw, sitting on some steps,
375　an elderly vavasor, *
whose court was very poor.
He was a handsome man, white-haired,
well-born, and noble;
he was seated there all alone:
380　he seemed to be deep in thought.
Erec thought he was a gentleman; *
he would give him lodging without delay. *
Through the gate Erec entered the courtyard.
The vavasor ran to meet him;
385　before Erec had said a word,
the vavasor had greeted him:
"Good sir," said he, "welcome!
If you deign to lodge with me,
here are your lodgings, already prepared."
390　Erec replied: "I thank you!
I had no other purpose in coming here:
I need lodgings for this very night."
Erec dismounted from his horse.
The gentleman himself took it
395　and led it after him by the reins.
He rejoiced greatly because of his guest.
The vavasor called his wife
and his daughter, who was very beautiful;
they were working in a workshop,
400　but I know not what work they were doing there.
The lady came out
as did her daughter, who was dressed
in a flowing chemise, *
of fine cloth, white and pleated.
405　Over it she wore a white dress; *
she had no other clothes.
And the dress was so old
that it was worn through at the elbows.
The clothing was poor on the outside,
410　but the body beneath was lovely.
The maiden was very beautiful,
for Nature, who had made her,
had turned all her attention to the task.
Nature herself had marveled

415 plus de cinc cenz foiz mervelliee
comant une sole foiee
tant bele chose fere sot, *
car puis tant pener ne se pot
qu'ele poïst son essanplaire
420 an nule guise contrefaire.
De ceste tesmoingne Nature
c'onques si bele criature
ne fu veüe an tot le monde.
Por voir vos di qu'Isolz la blonde
425 n'ot les crins tant sors ne luisanz,
que a cesti ne fust neanz.
Plus ot que n'est la flors de lis
cler et blanc le front et le vis;
sor la blanchor, par grant mervoille,
430 d'une fresche color vermoille,
que Nature li ot donee,
estoit sa face anluminee.
Si oel si grant clarté randoient
que deus estoiles ressanbloient;
435 onques Dex ne sot fere mialz
le nes, la boche ne les ialz.
Que diroie de sa biauté?
Ce fu cele por verité
qui fu fete por esgarder,
440 qu'an se poïst an li mirer
ausi com an un mireor.   [3e]
Issue fu de l'ovreor.
Quant ele le chevalier voit,
que onques mes veü n'avoit,
445 un petit arriere s'estut
por ce qu'ele ne le quenut;
vergoigne en ot et si rogi.
Erec d'autre part s'esbahi
quant an li si grant biauté vit.
450 Et li vavasors li a dit:
"Bele douce fille, prenez
ce cheval et si le menez
an cele estable avoec les miens.
Gardez qu'il ne li faille riens:
455 ostez li la sele et le frein,
si li donez aveinne et fein;
conreez le et estrilliez
si qu'il soit bien aparelliez."
    La pucele prant le cheval,
460 si li deslace le peitral,

411. *Initial* M *in* C.
417. sot *HPV* = *F*] pot *CB*; soit *A* (*with* sot *in following line*).
429. blanchor *BV* (-cor *HA*) = *F*] color *C* (*P omits 427-486*).

20

415   more than five hundred times
      how she had been able to make
      such a beautiful thing just once,
      for since then, strive as she might,
      she had never been able to duplicate
420   in any way her original model.
      Nature bears witness to this one:
      never was such a beautiful creature
      seen in the whole world.
      In truth I tell you that Iseult the blonde *
425   had not such shining golden hair,
      for compared to this one, she was nothing.
      Her face and forehead were fairer and brighter
      than is the lily-flower;
      contrasting marvelously with the whiteness,
430   her face was illuminated
      by a fresh, glowing color
      which Nature had given her.
      Her eyes glowed with such brightness
      that they resembled two stars;
435   never had God made finer
      nose, mouth, nor eyes.
      What should I say of her beauty?
      She was truly one
      who was made to be looked at,
440   for one might gaze at her
      just as into a mirror.
      She had come out of the workshop.
      When she saw the knight,
      whom she had never seen before,
445   she stayed back a bit
      because she did not know him;
      she was embarrassed and she blushed.
      Erec, on the other hand, was astonished
      when he saw such great beauty in her.
450   And the vavasor said to her:
      "Fair sweet daughter, take
      this horse and lead it
      into the stable with mine.
      Be sure it has everything it needs:
455   take off the saddle and the bridle
      and give it oats and hay;
      rub it down and curry it
      so that it is well taken care of."
        The maiden took the horse,
460   undid the breastplate,

le frain et la sele li oste.
Or a li chevax molt boen oste;
molt bien et bel s'an antremet.
Au cheval un chevoistre met,
465 bien l'estrille et torche et conroie,
a la mangëoire le loie
et si li met foin et aveinne
devant, assez novele et seinne. *
Puis revint a son pere arriere
470 et il li dist: "Ma fille chiere,
prenez par la main ce seignor
si li portez molt grant enor.
Par la main l'an menez leissus." *
La pucele ne tarda plus,
475 qu'ele n'estoit mie vilainne:
par la main contre mont l'an mainne.
La dame an ert devant alee,
qui la meison ot atornee;
coutes porpointes et tapiz
480 ot estanduz par sor les liz,
ou il se sont asis tuit troi:
Erec la pucele ot lez soi
et li sires de l'autre part.
Li feus molt clers devant ax art.
485 Li vavasors sergent n'avoit   [3f]
for un tot seul qui le servoit,
ne chanberiere ne meschine;
cil atornoit an la cuisine
por le soper char et oisiax.
490 De l'atorner fu molt isniax;
bien sot aparellier et tost
char cuire et an eve et an rost.
Quant ot le mangier atorné,
tel con l'an li ot comandé,
495 l'eve lor done an deus bacins;
tables et napes, pains et vins *
fu tost aparellié et mis,
et cil sont au mangier asis.
Trestot quanque mestiers lor fu
500 ont a lor volanté eü.
Quant a lor eise orent sopé
et des tables furent levé,
Erec mist son oste a reison,
qui sires ert de la meison:
505 "Dites moi, biax ostes," fet il,
"de tant povre robe et si vil

473, 474 *HBE = F] interverted CVA (P omits 427-486).*
473. menez *BE = F* (menes *H*)] mainne *C*, mana *V*, mena *A*.
496. pains et vins *HBPVA = F*] et bacins *C*.

22

and took off the saddle and bridle.
Now the horse was in good hands;
she took excellent care of it.
She put a halter on it,
465 curried it well, rubbed it down and cared for it,
tied it to the manger
and put hay and oats before it,
very fresh and wholesome.
Then she came back to her father
470 and he said to her: "My dear daughter,
take this lord by the hand
and show him very great honor.
Lead him upstairs, by the hand."
The maiden delayed no longer,
475 for she was in no way ill-bred:
by the hand she led him upstairs.
The lady had gone before
and had prepared the house;
she had spread out embroidered quilts and rugs
480 on top of the beds,
where all three of them sat down:
Erec had the maiden next to him
and the lord on the other side.
The fire burned very brightly before them.
485 The vavasor had no servant
besides the one who served him—
no chambermaid or serving-girl;
in the kitchen, the servant was preparing
meat and fowl for the evening meal.
490 He was very prompt in his preparations;
he knew well how to prepare and quickly cook
meat, both boiled and roasted.
When he had prepared the meal
as he had been ordered,
495 he gave them water in two basins;
tables and tablecloths, bread and wine
were quickly prepared and set forth,
and they sat down to eat.
They had as much as they wanted
500 of everything they needed.
When they had dined at their ease
and had arisen from the tables,
Erec questioned his host,
the lord of the house:
505 "Tell me, good host," said he,
"why is your daughter,

por qu'est vostre fille atornee,
qui tant est bele et bien senee?"
"Biax amis," fet li vavasors,
510 "Povretez fet mal as plusors
et autresi fet ele moi.
Molt me poise quant ge la voi
atornee si povremant,
ne n'ai pooir que je l'amant:
515 tant ai esté toz jorz an guerre,
tote en ai perdue ma terre,
et angagiee, et vandue.
Et ne por quant bien fust vestue,
se ge sofrisse qu'el preïst
520 ce que l'an doner li vossist.
Nes li sires de cest chastel
l'eüst vestue bien et bel
et se li feïst toz ses buens,
qu'ele est sa niece et il est cuens;
525 ne n'a an trestot cest païs
nul baron, tant soit de haut pris,
qui ne l'eüst a fame prise
volantiers tot a ma devise.
Mes j'atant ancor meillor point,   [7a]
530 que Dex greignor enor li doint,
que avanture li amaint
ou roi ou conte qui l'an maint.
A dons soz ciel ne roi ne conte
qui eüst an ma fille honte,
535 qui tant par est bele a mervoille
qu'an ne puet trover sa paroille?
Molt est bele, mes mialz asez
vaut ses savoirs que sa biautez:
onques Dex ne fist rien tant saige
540 ne qui tant soit de franc coraige.
Quant ge ai delez moi ma fille,
tot le mont ne pris une bille:
c'est mes deduiz, c'est mes deporz,
c'est mes solaz et mes conforz,
545 c'est mes avoirs et mes tresors;
je n'ain tant rien come son cors."
    Quant Erec ot tot escoté
quanque ses ostes ot conté,
puis li demande qu'il li die
550 dom estoit tex chevalerie
qu'an ce chastel estoit venue,
qu'il n'i avoit si povre rue
ne fust plainne de chevaliers
et de dames et d'escuiers,

533. *Initial* A *in* C.

who is so lovely and full of good sense,
dressed in such a poor and ugly dress?"
"Good friend," said the vavasor,

510 "Poverty ill-treats many men,
and likewise she does me.
It grieves me when I see my daughter
so poorly dressed,
yet I am powerless to change the situation:

515 I have spent so much time at war
I have lost all my land thereby,
and mortgaged it and sold it.
And yet she would be well clothed
if I allowed her to accept

520 what someone would like to give her.
The lord of this town himself
would have clothed her handsomely
and would have granted her every wish,
for she is his niece and he is a count;

525 nor is there a lord in all this land,
however grand his reputation,
who would not have taken her for his wife,
and gladly, according to my conditions.
But I am still waiting for a better opportunity,

530 for God to grant her greater honor
and for chance to bring to her
a king or a count who will take her away with him.
Is there in all the world a king or count
who would be ashamed of my daughter,

535 who is so wonderfully beautiful
that her equal cannot be found?
She is indeed beautiful, but her good sense
is worth even more than her beauty:
God never made such a wise creature

540 nor one so noble in spirit.
When I have my daughter near me,
the whole world is not worth a marble:
she is my delight, she is my diversion,
she is my solace and my comfort,

545 she is my wealth and my treasure;
I love nothing else as much as I love her."
    When Erec had listened
to all his host had told him,
he asked him to tell him

550 why there was such a gathering of knights
as had come to this town,
for there was no street so poor,
and no inn so poor or small,
that it was not full of knights

Erec recognizes her worth

father recognizes her worth

25

555 n'ostel tant povre ne petit.
Et li vavasors li a dit:
"Biax amis, ce sont li baron
de cest païs ci an viron:
trestuit li juene et li chenu
560 a une feste sont venu
qui an ce chastel iert demain;
por ce sont li ostel si plain.
Molt i avra demain grant bruit,
quant il seront assanblé tuit,
565 que devant trestote la gent
iert sor une perche d'argent
uns espreviers molt biax assis,
ou de cinc mues ou de sis,
le meillor qu'an porra savoir.
570 Qui l'esprevier voldra avoir,
avoir li covandra amie
bele et saige sanz vilenie;
s'il i a chevalier si os   [7b]
qui vuelle le pris et le los
575 de la plus bele desresnier,
s'amie fera l'esprevier
devant toz a la perche prandre,
s'autres ne li ose desfandre.
Iceste costume maintienent
580 et por ce chascun an i vienent."
    Aprés li dit Erec et prie:
"Biax ostes, ne vos enuit mie,
mes dites moi, se vos savez,
qui est uns chevaliers armez
585 d'unes armes d'azur et d'or,
qui par ci devant passa or,
lez lui une pucele cointe
qui molt pres de lui s'estoit jointe,
et devant ax un nain boçu?"
590 Lors a li ostes respondu:
"C'est cil qui avra l'esprevier
sanz contredit de chevalier:
ja n'i avra ne cop ne plaie;
ne cuit que nus avant s'an traie.
595 Par deus anz l'a il ja eü,
c'onques chalongiez ne li fu,
mes se il ancor ouan l'a,
a toz jorz desresnié l'avra:
ja mes n'iert anz que il ne l'et
600 quite, sanz bataille et sanz plet."
Erec respont en es le pas:
"Cest chevalier, je ne l'aim pas.

568. cinc *HBPVA = FR*] .ii. *C*.

555   and ladies and squires.
And the vavasor replied:
"Good friend, those are the lords
of this land hereabouts:
everyone, young and old,
560   has come for a festival
that will occur in this town tomorrow;
that is why the inns are so full.
Tomorrow there will be great excitement
when they are all assembled,
565   for in front of all the people,
seated on a silver perch,
there will be a very fine sparrow-hawk,
five or six years old,
the best that can be found.
570   Whoever wants to have the sparrow-hawk
will have to have a lady
who is beautiful and wise and free from baseness;
if there is any knight so bold
as to want to claim the reputation
575   and the honor of the most beautiful,
he will have his lady, in front of everyone,
take the sparrow-hawk from its perch,
if no one else dares oppose him.
They uphold this tradition
580   and that is why they come here each year."
Then Erec asked him:
"Good host, may it not trouble you,
but tell me, if you know,
who is the knight bearing
585   arms of azure and gold,
who passed by here a while ago,
an attractive maiden beside him,
who stayed very close to him,
and a hunchbacked dwarf in front of them?"
590   Then the host replied:
"He is the one who will have the sparrow-hawk
without being challenged by any other knight:
never will there be blow or wound,
for I believe no one else will come forward.
595   He has already had it two years in a row
without ever being challenged,
but if he gets it again this year
he will have claimed it forever:
he will retain it each year,
600   without combat and without argument."
Erec immediately replied:
"I have no love for this knight.

27

Saichiez, se je armes avoie,
l'esprevier li contrediroie.
605 Biax ostes, por vostre franchise,
por guerredon et por servise,
vos pri que vos me conselliez
tant que je soie aparelliez
d'unes armes, viez ou noveles,
610 ne me chaut quiex, leides ou beles."
Et il li respont come frans:
"Ja mar an seroiz an espans:
armes boenes et beles ai,
que volantiers vos presterai.
615 Leanz est li haubers tresliz,
qui antre cinc cenz fu esliz,
et les chauces beles et chieres,   [7c]
boenes et fresches et legieres;
li hiaumes i rest boens et biax
620 et li escuz fres et noviax.
Le cheval, l'espee et la lance,
tot vos presterai sanz dotance,
que ja riens n'an sera a dire."
"La vostre merci, biax dolz sire,
625 mes je ne quier meillor espee
de celi que j'ai aportee,
ne cheval autre que le mien:
de celui m'aiderai ge bien.
Se vos le sorplus me prestez,
630 vis m'est que c'est molt granz bontez;
mes ancor vos voel querre un don,
don ge randrai le guerredon,
se Dex done que je m'an aille
atot l'enor de la bataille."
635 Et cil li respont franchemant:
"Demandez tot seüremant
vostre pleisir, comant qu'il aut:
riens que je aie ne vos faut!"
Lors dist Erec que l'esprevier
640 vialt par sa fille desresnier,
car por voir n'i avra pucele
qui la centiesme part soit bele,
et se il avoec lui l'an mainne,
reison avra droite et certainne
645 de desresnier et de mostrer
qu'ele an doit l'esprevier porter.
Puis dist: "Sire, vos ne savez
quel oste herbergié avez,
de quel afeire et de quel gent.

624. dolz *H = FR*] *omitted C (-1); BV*: V. m. fait erec s.;
P: La v. grant m. b. s.; *A*: V. m. fait cil b. s.

Be assured that, if I had armor,
I would challenge him for the sparrow-hawk.
605   Good host, because of your generosity,
as a favor and a service,
I ask you to advise me
so that I may be equipped
with armor, old or new,
610   I care not which, ugly or beautiful."
And he replied generously:
"You need never be concerned on that account:
I have good and beautiful armor
which I will gladly lend you.
615   Inside there is the hauberk of woven mail, *
chosen from among five hundred,
and beautiful and expensive greaves,
good and new and light;
the helmet is likewise good and beautiful
620   and the shield brand new.
The horse, the sword, and the lance,
I shall lend you all, without hesitation,
so that you need ask for nothing more."
"Pray excuse me, good kind sir,
625   but I wish for no better sword
than the one I brought with me,
nor any horse besides my own:
I shall make good use of that one.
If you lend me the rest,
630   I shall deem it a very great favor;
but I wish to ask one other gift of you, *
which I shall repay,
if God grants that I may emerge
with the honor of the battle."
635   And the vavasor generously replied:
"Ask confidently for what you wish,
whatever it may be:
nothing I have will be denied you!"
Then Erec said that he wanted
640   to contend for the sparrow-hawk by means of his daughter,
for in truth no other maiden would be there
who was the hundredth part as beautiful,
and if he took her there with him,
he would be perfectly justified
645   in contending and in claiming
that she should carry off the sparrow-hawk.
Then he said: "Sir, you do not know
to what guest you have given lodging,
of what station and from what people.

650 Filz sui d'un riche roi puissant:
mes peres li rois Lac a non;
Erec m'apelent li Breton.
De la cort le roi Artus sui;
bien ai esté trois anz a lui.
655 Je ne sai s'an ceste contree
vint onques nule renomee
ne de mon pere ne de moi,
mes je vos promet et otroi,
se vos armes m'aparelliez
660 et vostre fille me bailliez
demain a l'esprevier conquerre,   [7d]
que je l'an manrai an ma terre,
se Dex la victoire m'an done;
la li ferai porter corone,
665 s'iert reïne de dis citez."
"Ha! biax sire, est ce veritez?
Erec, li filz Lac, estes vos?"
"Ce sui mon," fet il, "a estros."
Li ostes molt s'an esjoï
670 et dist: "Bien avomes oï
de vos parler an cest païs.
Or vos aim assez plus et pris,
car molt estes preuz et hardiz;
ja de moi n'iroiz escondiz:
675 tot a vostre comandemant
ma belle fille vos comant."
Lors l'a prise par mi le poing:
"Tenez," fet il, "je la vos doing."
Erec lieemant la reçut:
680 or a quanque il li estut.
Grant joie font tuit par leanz:
li peres an ert molt joianz
et la mere plore de joie.
Et la pucele ert tote coie,
685 mes molt estoit joianz et liee
qu'ele li estoit otroiee,
por ce que preuz ert et cortois,
et bien savoit qu'il seroit rois
et ele meïsme enoree,
690 riche reïne coronee.
   Molt orent cele nuit veillié.
Li lit furent apareillié
de blans dras et de costes moles.
A tant faillirent les paroles;
695 lieemant se vont couchier tuit.
Erec dormi po cele nuit.
L'andemain, lués que l'aube crieve,
isnelemant et tost se lieve,
et ses ostes ansanble o lui.

30

650 I am the son of a rich and powerful king:
     my father is named King Lac;
     the Bretons call me Erec.
     I am of the court of King Arthur;
     I have been with him for three years.
655 I do not know whether any fame, *
     either of my father or of me,
     ever came to this land,
     but I promise and grant you,
     if you equip me with armor
660 and entrust your daughter to me
     to win the sparrow-hawk tomorrow,
     that I shall take her to my land,
     if God gives me the victory;
     there I shall have her wear a crown
665 and she will be queen of ten cities."
     "Ah, good sir, is this the truth?
     Are you Erec, the son of Lac?"
     "That I am," said he, "without a doubt."
     The host rejoiced greatly at this
670 and said: "We have indeed
     heard tell of you in this land.
     Now I love and esteem you even more,
     for you are very valiant and bold;
     I shall never refuse your request:
675 just as you desire
     I entrust my beautiful daughter to you."
     Then he took her by the hand:
     "Here," said he, "I give her to you."
     Erec joyfully received her:
680 now he had everything he needed.
     Within the house all showed great joy:
     the father was very joyful
     and the mother wept for joy.
     And the maiden was very still,
685 but she was very joyful and happy
     that she was granted to him,
     because he was valiant and courtly,
     and she knew well he would be king
     and that she herself would be honored,
690 rich, and crowned a queen.
        They had stayed up late that night.
     The beds were prepared
     with white sheets and soft mattresses. *
     Then the conversation ended
695 and joyfully all went to bed.
     Erec slept little that night.
     The next day, as soon as dawn broke,
     he got up quickly,
     and his host along with him.

700 Au mostier vont orer andui
et firent del Saint Esperite
messe chanter a un hermite;
l'oferande n'oblïent mie.
Quant il orent la messe oïe,
705 andui anclinent a l'autel,
si s'an repeirent a l'ostel.
Erec tarda molt la bataille.
Les armes quiert et l'an li baille:
la pucele meïsmes l'arme;
710 n'i ot fet charaie ne charme.
Lace li les chauces de fer *
et queust a corroie de cer;
hauberc li vest de boene maille
et se li lace la vantaille;
715 le hiaume brun li met el chief:
molt l'arme bien de chief an chief.
Au costé l'espee li ceint.
Puis comande qu'an li amaint
son cheval, et l'an li amainne;
720 sus est sailliz de terre plainne.
La pucele aporte l'escu
et la lance qui roide fu:
l'escu li baille, et il le prant;
par la guige a son col le pant.
725 La lance li ra el poing mise;
cil l'a devers l'arestuel prise.
Puis dist au vavasor gentil:
"Biax sire, s'il vos plest," fet il,
"feites vostre fille atorner,
730 qu'a l'esprevier la voel mener
si con vos m'avez covenant."
Li vavasors fist maintenant
anseler un palefroi bai;
onques ne le mist an delai.
735 Del hernois a parler ne fet,
car la granz povretez ne let,
don li vavasors estoit plains.
La sele fu mise et li frains.
Deslïee et desafublee
740 est la pucele sus montee,
qui de rien ne s'an fist proier.
Erec ne volt plus delaier:
or s'an va, delez lui an coste
an mainne la fille son oste;
745 aprés les sivent amedui
li sires et la dame o lui.
    Erec chevalche lance droite,

701. int of saint missing due to a hole, C (saint HBVA = FR).

700 They went together to pray at the church
and had a hermit sing
a mass of the Holy Spirit;
they did not forget the offering.
When they had heard the mass,
705 they both bowed down before the altar,
and then went back to the house.
Erec was impatient for the battle.
He asked for the armor and it was brought to him:
the maiden herself armed him;
710 she used neither spell nor charm in doing so. *
She laced on the iron greaves
and attached them solidly with deer-hide thongs;
she dressed him in the hauberk of good chain mail
and laced on the ventail; *
715 she put the burnished helmet on his head:
she armed him well from head to foot.
She girded his sword at his side.
Then he ordered someone to bring him
his horse, and it was brought to him;
720 he jumped directly on it from the ground.
The maiden brought him the shield
and the sturdy lance:
she gave him the shield, and he took it;
he slung it round his neck by the guige. *
725 In turn she put the lance into his hand;
he grasped it near the base. *
Then he said to the noble vavasor:
"Good sir, if it please you," said he,
"have your daughter get ready,
730 for I wish to take her to the sparrow-hawk,
as you have agreed that I should."
The vavasor straightaway
had a bay palfrey saddled; *
he lost no time in doing so.
735 The harness does not deserve mention
because of the great poverty
of the vavasor.
The saddle was put on and the bridle.
Her hair loose and wearing no cloak,
740 the maiden mounted;
she needed no bidding.
Erec wished to delay no longer:
he rode off, taking at his side
the daughter of his host;
745 behind them followed both
the vavasor and the lady.
      Erec rode with lance upright,

delez lui la pucele adroite.
Tuit l'esgardent par mi les rues,
750   et les granz genz et les menues.
Trestoz li pueples s'an mervoille;
li uns dit a l'autre et consoille:
"Qui est, qui est cil chevaliers?
Molt doit estre hardiz et fiers,
755   quant la bele pucele an mainne.
Cist anploiera bien sa painne!
Cist doit bien desresnier par droit
que ceste la plus bele soit!"
Li uns dit a l'autre: "Por voir,
760   ceste doit l'esprevier avoir!"
Li un la pucele looient,
et mainz en i ot qui disoient:
"Dex! qui puet cil chevaliers estre
qui la bele pucele adestre?"
765   "Ne sai, ne sai," ce dit chascuns,
"mes molt li siet li hiaumes bruns
et cil haubers et cil escuz
et cil branz d'acier esmoluz.
Molt est adroiz sor ce cheval;
770   bien resanble vaillant vassal:
molt est bien fez et bien tailliez
de braz, de janbes et de piez."
Tuit a aus esgarder antandent,
et il ne tardent ne atandent
775   tant que devant l'esprevier furent.
Iluec de l'une part s'esturent
ou le chevalier atandoient.
Estes vos que venir le voient,
lez lui son nain et sa pucele.
780   Ja avoit oï la novele
c'uns chevaliers venuz estoit
qui l'esprevier avoir voloit,
mes ne cuidoit qu'el siegle eüst
chevalier qui si hardiz fust
785   qui contre lui s'osast conbatre:
bien le cuidoit vaintre et abatre.
Totes les genz le conuissoient;
tuit le salüent et convoient.
Aprés lui ot grant bruit de gent:
790   li chevalier et li sergent
et les dames corent aprés,
et les puceles a eslés.
Li chevaliers va devant toz,
lez lui sa pucele et son goz.
795   Molt chevalche orguilleusemant

763.   s *of* chevaliers (ch'rs) *added above line.*

the comely maiden beside him.
In the streets everyone looked at him,
750 the great folk and the small.
All the people marveled;
they said to one another:
"Who is this, who is this knight?
He must be very brave and proud
755 to lead the beautiful maiden.
He will make good use of his efforts!
He must very rightfully contend
that she is the most beautiful!"
One said to the other: "Truly,
760 she must have the sparrow-hawk!"
Some praised the maiden,
and there were many there who said:
"God! Who can this knight be
who accompanies the beautiful maiden?"
765 "I don't know, I don't know," said each,
"but the burnished helmet suits him well,
as do that hauberk and that shield,
and that blade of sharpened steel.
He rides that horse extremely well;
770 he certainly looks like a valiant knight:
he's very well built and well proportioned
in his arms, his legs, and his feet."
Everyone was intent on looking at them,
but they neither tarried nor hesitated
775 until they were in front of the sparrow-hawk.
There they stood to one side
where they waited for the knight.
Then they saw him coming,
his dwarf and his maiden beside him.
780 He had already heard the news
that a knight had come
who wanted to have the sparrow-hawk,
but he did not believe there was in all the world
a knight who was so bold
785 as to dare to fight against him:
he thought he would easily subdue and vanquish him.
All the people knew him;
everyone greeted and escorted him.
Following him there was a great noise of people:
790 the knights and the men-at-arms
and the ladies ran behind him,
and the maidens, as fast as they could go.
The knight went on ahead of them all,
his maiden and his dwarf beside him.
795 He rode most haughtily and fast

35

vers l'esprevier isnelemant,
mes an tor avoit si grant presse
de la vilainne gent angresse
que l'an n'i pooit aprochier
800 del trait a un arbalestier.
    Li cuens est venuz an la place;
as vilains vient, si les menace:
une verge tient an sa main;
arriers se traient li vilain.
805 Li chevaliers s'est avant trez;
a sa pucele dist an pez:
"Ma dameisele, cist oisiax,
qui tant bien est müez et biax,
doit vostre estre par droite rante,
810 que molt par estes bele et gente,
et si iert il tote ma vie.
Alez avant, ma dolce amie,
l'esprevier a la perche prandre."
La pucele i vost la main tandre,
815 mes Erec li cort chalongier,
qui rien ne prise son dongier:
"Dameisele," fet il, "fuiez!
A autre oisel vos deduiez,
car vos n'avez droit an cestui.
820 Cui qu'an doie venir enui,
ja cist esprevier vostres n'iert,
que miaudre de vos le requiert,
plus bele asez et plus cortoise."
A l'autre chevalier an poise,
825 mes Erec ne le prise guere.
Sa pucele fet avant trere:
"Bele," fet il, "avant venez!
L'oisel a la perche prenez,
car bien est droiz que vos l'aiez.
830 Dameisele, avant vos traiez!
Del desresnier tres bien me vant,
se nus s'an ose trere avant,
que a vos ne s'an prant nes une,
ne que au soloil fet la lune,
835 ne de biauté, ne de valor,
ne de franchise, ne d'enor."
Li autres nel pot plus sofrir,   [4b]
quant il si l'oï porofrir
de la bataille a tel vertu:
840 "Cui?" fet il, "vassax, qui es tu,
qui l'esprevier m'as contredit?"
Erec hardïemant li dit:
"Uns chevaliers sui d'autre terre.
Cest esprevier sui venuz querre,
845 et bien est droiz, cui qu'il soit let,

36

toward the sparrow-hawk,
but around it there was such a press
of the eager common-folk
that one could get no closer to it
800   than the length of a crossbow shot.
      The count came into the field;
he came toward the commoners and threatened them:
he held a switch in his hand;
the commoners drew back.
805   The knight advanced;
he said tranquilly to his maiden:
My damsel, this bird,
which is so well moulted and so beautiful,
is to be rightfully yours,
810   for you are very beautiful and noble,
and thus it shall be all my life.
Go ahead, my sweet friend,
take the sparrow-hawk from the perch."
The maiden started to reach for it,
815   but Erec ran to challenge her,
caring nothing for the other's haughtiness:
"Damsel," said he, "begone!
Take some other bird for your pleasure,
for you have no right to this one.
820   Whoever may be displeased by it,
this sparrow-hawk will never be yours,
for a better one than you claims it,
much more beautiful and more courtly."
This displeased the other knight,
825   but Erec esteemed him little.
He had his damsel come forward:
"Fair one," said he, "come forward!
Take the bird from the perch,
for it is right that you should have it!
830   Damsel, come forward!
I make bold to uphold the contest,
if anyone dares come forth against me,
for not one can compare with you,
no more than the moon compares with the sun,
835   neither in beauty, nor in worth,
nor in nobility, nor in honor."
The other could stand it no more,
when he heard Erec so boldly
propose battle:
840   "What?" said he, "vassal, who are you,
who have challenged me for the sparrow-hawk?"
Erec boldly answered him:
"I am a knight from another land.
I have come to seek this sparrow-hawk,
845   and it is right, whoever may find it unpleasant,

37

que ceste dameisele l'et."
"Fui!" fet li autres, "ce n'iert ja;
folie t'a amené ça!
Se tu viax avoir l'esprevier,
850 molt le t'estuet conparer chier."
"Conparer, vassax? Et de quoi?"
"Conbatre t'an covient a moi,
se tu ne le me clainmes quite."
"Or avez vos folie dite,"
855 fet Erec; "au mien escïant
ce sont menaces de neant,
que tot par mesure vos dot."
"Donc te desfi ge tot de bot,
car ne puet estre sanz bataille."
860 Erec respont: "Or Dex i vaille,
c'onques riens nule tant ne vos!"
Des or mes an orroiz les cos.
    La place fu delivre et granz;
de totes parz furent les genz.
865 Cil plus d'un arpant s'antr'esloingnent;
por assanbler les chevax poignent;
as fers des lances se requierent.
Par si grant vertu s'antre fierent
que li escu piercent et croissent,
870 les lances esclicent et froissent,
depiecent li arçon derriers: *
guerpir lor estuet les estriés.
Contre terre amedui se ruient;
li cheval par le chanp s'an fuient.
875 Cil resont tost an piez sailli.
Des lances n'orent pas failli;
les espees des fuerres traient,
felenessemant s'antre essaient
des tranchanz; granz cos s'antre donent:
880 li hiaume cassent et resonent.
Fiers est li chaples des espees: [4c]
molt s'antre donent granz colees,
que de rien nule ne se faignent;
tot deronpent quanqu'il ataignent,
885 tranchent escuz, faussent haubers.
Del sanc vermoil rogist li fers.
Li chaples dure longuemant;
tant se fierent menüemant
que molt se lassent et recroient.
890 Andeus les puceles ploroient;
chascuns voit la soe plorer,
les mains tandre a Deu et orer
qu'il doint l'enor de la bataille

857. dot *BA* (dout *PV*, dolt *H*) = *FR*] doit *C*.

that this maiden should have it."
"Begone!" said the other, "that will never be;
it was madness that brought you here!
If you want to have the sparrow-hawk,
850   you'll have to pay dearly for it."
"Pay for it, vassal? And with what?"
"You'll have to do battle with me
if you don't relinquish it to me."
"Now you've said something unwise,"
855   said Erec; "in my opinion
these are empty threats,
for I fear you very little."
"Then I defy you immediately,
for this cannot be without a battle."
860   Erec replied: "Then may God grant it,
for I never desired anything so much!"
Now you will hear the blows.
    The field was clear and open;
there were people on all sides.
865   The two knights drew well apart from one another; *
they spurred their steeds to begin the battle;
they sought each other with the heads of their lances.
They struck each other with such power
that the shields were pierced and broke,
870   the lances shattered and splintered,
and the cantles broke into pieces behind them: *
they could no longer stay in their stirrups.
Both of them were thrown to the ground;
the horses ran off across the field.
875   At once they jumped back to their feet.
They had not missed with their lances;
they drew their swords from their scabbards,
savagely went at each other
with the cutting edges, and gave each other great blows:
880   their helmets resounded and broke.
The combat with the swords was intense:
they gave each other great blows,
for they in no way held themselves back;
they split apart whatever they hit,
885   slicing shields and deforming hauberks.
The iron reddened with their blood.
The combat lasted a long time;
they struck each other so intensely
that they grew very tired and discouraged.
890   Both the maidens were weeping;
each of the knights saw his damsel weep,
raise her hands to God and pray
that he might grant the victory

celui qui por li se travaille.
895 "Vassax," ce dit li chevaliers,
     "car nos traions un po arriers,
     s'estons un petit an repos,
     car trop feromes foibles cos;
     miaudres cos nos covient ferir,
900 car trop est pres de l'anserir.
     Molt est grant honte et grant leidure
     quant ceste bataille tant dure.
     Voi la cele gente pucele *
     qui por toi plore et Deu apele!
905 Molt prie dolcemant por toi
     et la moie autresi por moi,
     si nos devons as branz d'acier
     por noz amies resforcier."
     Erec respont: "Bien avez dit."
910 Lors se reposent un petit.
     Erec regarde vers s'amie,
     qui molt dolcemant por lui prie.
     Tot maintenant qu'il l'ot veüe,
     se li est sa force creüe;
915 por s'amor et por sa biauté
     a reprise molt grant fierté.
     Remanbre li de la reïne,
     qu'il avoit dit an la gaudine
     que il sa honte vangeroit
920 ou il ancore la crestroit.
     "Hé! mauvés," fet il, "qu'atant gié?
     Ancores n'ai ge pas vangié
     le let que cil vasax sofri,
     quant ses nains el bois me feri!"
925 Ses mautalanz li renovele;
     le chevalier par ire apele:
     "Vassax," fet il, "tot de novel
     a la bataille vos rapel:
     trop avons fet grant reposee;   [4d]
930 recomançons nostre meslee."
     Cil li respont: "Ce ne m'est grief!"
     Lors s'antre vienent de rechief.
     Andui sorent de l'escremie:
     a cele premiere anvaïe,
935 s'Erec bien coverz ne se fust,
     li chevaliers blecié l'eüst;

903-06 HBPA = F] omitted CV.
903. Voi B = F] Vois HP, Ves A.
904. plore BPA = F] prie H.
905. H] M. d. prie BP = F, M. pr. bonemant A.
906. autresi B (al- H) = F] ensement PA.
933. deles repeated, C.

40

to the one who was striving for her.
895   "Vassal," said the knight,
"let us draw back a bit,
and rest a while,
for our blows have become too weak;
we should strike better blows,
900 for it is very near evening.
It is a very shameful and humiliating thing
that this battle is taking so long.
See there that gracious maiden
who weeps for you and calls upon God!
905 She is praying very softly for you
and mine is doing likewise for me,
and we must renew our efforts,
on behalf of our ladies, with our steel blades."
Erec replied: "You have spoken well."
910 Then they rested for a bit.
Erec looked toward his lady,
who was very softly praying for him.
As soon as he saw her,
his strength was renewed;
915 because of her love and her beauty
he regained his great courage.
He remembered the queen,
to whom he had said in the woods
that he would avenge his shame
920 or else augment it further.
"Well, what am I waiting for, like a coward?" said he.
"I haven't yet avenged
the outrage that this vassal allowed,
when his dwarf struck me in the woods!"
925 His wrath renewed itself within him;
he called out angrily to the knight:
"Vassal," he cried, "I call upon you
to begin our battle anew:
we have rested too long;
930 let us resume our combat."
The other replied: "I agree."
Then they went at each other anew.
Both of them knew about fighting:
at that first attack,
935 if Erec had not covered himself,
the knight would have wounded him;

si l'a li chevaliers feru
a descovert, desor l'escu,
c'une piece del hiaume tranche.
940   Res a res de la coisfe blanche
l'espee contre val descent,
l'escu jusqu'a la bocle fant,
et del hauberc lez le costé
li a plus d'un espan osté.
945   Bien dut estre Erec afolez:
jusqu'a la char li est colez
sor la hanche li aciers froiz.
Dex le gari a cele foiz:
se li fers ne tornast dehors,
950   tranchié l'eüst par mi le cors.
Mes Erec de rien ne s'esmaie;
se cil li preste, bien li paie.
Molt hardïemant le requiert;
par selonc l'espaule le fiert.
955   Tele anpointe li a donee
que li escuz n'i a duree,
ne li haubers rien ne li vaut
que jusqu'a l'os l'espee n'aut:
tot contre val jusqu'au braier
960   a fet le sanc vermoil raier.
Molt sont fier andui li vasal:
si se conbatent par igal
que ne puet pas un pié de terre
li uns desor l'autre conquerre.
965   Molt ont lor haubers desmailliez
et les escuz si detailliez
qu'il n'ont tant d'antier, sanz mantir,
dont il se puissent recovrir:
tuit se fierent a descovert.
970   Chascuns del sanc grant masse i pert;
molt afeblissent anbedui.
Cil fiert Erec, et Erec lui:
tel cop a delivre li done   *[4e]*
sor le hiaume que tot l'estone.
975   Fiert et refiert tot a bandon:
trois cos li done de randon,
li hiaumes escartele toz
et la coisfe tranche desoz.
Jusqu'au test l'espee n'areste: *
980   un os li tranche de la teste,
mes nel tocha an la cervele.
Cil anbrunche toz et chancele;
que qu'il chancele Erec le bote,
et cil chiet sor le destre cote.
985   Erec par le hiaume le sache,
a force del chief li arache

42

the knight struck him such a blow
above the shield, where he was unprotected,
that he sliced off a piece of his helmet.
940 Just even with the white coif *
the sword came down,
split the shield down to the boss, *
and from the hauberk, along the side,
took off more than a hand's breadth.
945 Erec should have been badly injured:
the cold steel, on his hip,
sank right to his flesh.
God protected him that time:
if the blade had not turned outward,
950 it would have sliced right through his body.
But Erec was not at all dismayed;
he truly repaid whatever the other lent him.
Very boldly he returned the attack;
he struck him along the shoulder.
955 Erec gave him such an attack
that his shield could not resist,
and his hauberk was worthless
as the sword went right to the bone:
it made the crimson blood stream downward
960 all the way to his belt.
Both knights were very bold:
they were so evenly matched
that not one foot of ground
could one gain over the other.
965 Their hauberks were badly broken
and their shields were so hacked up
that they had nothing left whole—it is no lie—
with which to cover themselves:
they were striking one another openly.
970 Each of them was losing a lot of blood;
both were growing very weak.
The other struck Erec, and Erec struck him:
he gave him such a blow, unimpeded,
on his helmet, that he quite stunned him.
975 He struck him freely, again and again:
he gave him three blows in quick succession,
broke the helmet completely apart
and sliced the coif beneath.
The sword went all the way to his skull:
980 it sliced through one of the bones in his head,
but did not touch his brain.
He slumped down and staggered;
while he was staggering Erec shoved him,
and he fell onto his right side.
985 Erec pulled him by the helmet,
forcibly tore it from his head

43

et la vantaille li deslace;
le chief li desarme et la face.
Quant li remanbre de l'outrage
990 que ses nains li fist el boschage,
la teste li eüst colpee
se il n'eüst merci criee:
"Ha! vasax," fet il, "conquis m'as.
Merci! Ne m'ocirre tu pas!
995 Des que tu m'as oltré et pris,
ja n'an avroies los ne pris
se tu des or mes m'ocioies:
trop grant vilenie feroies.
Tien m'espee; je la te rant."
1000 Mes Erec mie ne la prant,
einz dit: "Bien va, je ne t'oci."
"Ha! gentix chevaliers, merci!
Por quel forfet ne por quel tort
me doiz tu donc haïr de mort?
1005 Einz mes ne te vi, que je sache, *
n'onques ne fui an ton domage
ne ne te fis honte ne let."
Erec respont: "Si avez fet."
"Hé! sire, car le dites donques!
1010 Ne vos vi mes, que je saiche, onques,
et se ge rien mesfet vos ai,
an vostre merci an serai."
Lors dist Erec: "Vasax, je sui
cil qui an la forest hier fui
1015 avoec la reïne Ganievre,
ou tu sofris ton nain anrievre
ferir la pucele ma dame.   [4f]
Granz viltance est de ferir fame!
Et moi aprés referi il;
1020 molt me tenis lors anpor vil:
trop grant orguel asez feïs, *
quant tu tel oltrage veïs,
si le sofris et si te plot
d'une tel fauture et d'un bot,
1025 qui feri la pucele et moi.
Por ce forfet haïr te doi,
car trop feïs grant mesprison.
Fïancier t'an estuet prison,
et sanz nul respit or androit
1030 iras a ma dame tot droit,

989. li *HPVA* = *F* (il li membre *B*)] lui *C*.
991. colpee *repeated, C*.
1021. orguel *B* = *F*] oltrage *C* (*P*), laidure *VA*; *H*: Qant tu tel oltrage feis /
Qui ton nain ferir me sofrir [*sic, presumably for* sofris];
P: Trop grant outrage voir fesis / Et asses grant orgoel offris.

and untied his ventail;
he removed the armor from his face and head.
When he remembered the outrage
990 that his dwarf had committed in the wood,
Erec would have cut off his head
had the other not cried out for mercy:
"Ah! Vassal," said he, "you have vanquished me.
Mercy! Do not kill me!
995 Since you have defeated me and taken me prisoner,
you would gain no glory nor esteem
if you went on to kill me:
you would commit a very unknightly act.
Take my sword; I surrender it to you."
1000 But Erec did not take it,
and said: "All right, I won't kill you."
"Ah, noble knight, mercy!
For what injury or what wrong
must you bear me this deadly hatred?
1005 I have never seen you before, to my knowledge,
nor was I ever responsible for wronging you,
nor did I cause you shame or outrage."
Erec replied: "Yes, you did."
"Ah, sir, then do tell me!
1010 I have never seen you before, to my knowledge,
and if I have wronged you,
I shall place myself at your mercy."
Then said Erec: "Vassal, I am
he who was in the forest yesterday
1015 with Queen Guinevere,
when you allowed your ignoble dwarf
to strike my lady's maiden.
It is a vile thing to strike a woman!
And he struck me in turn afterwards;
1020 you held me in very low esteem:
your action was far too haughty,
when you saw such an outrage,
and yet allowed it and were not displeased
on the part of such a freak and a dwarf,
1025 who struck the maiden and me.
For this injury I must hate you,
for you committed too great an offense.
You must constitute yourself my prisoner,
and without delay, immediately,
1030 you will go directly to my lady,

car sanz faille la troveras
a Caradigan, se la vas.
Bien i vandras ancor enuit:
n'i a pas set liues, ce cuit.
1035 Toi et ta pucele et ton nain
li deliverras an sa main
por fere son comandemant,
et se li di que ge li mant
que demain a joie vanrai
1040 et une pucele amanrai,
tant bele et tant saige et tant preu
que sa paroille n'est nul leu:
bien li porras dire por voir.
Et ton non revoel ge savoir."
1045 Lors li dist cil, ou voelle ou non:
"Sire, Ydiers, li filz Nut, ai non.
Hui matin ne cuidoie mie
c'uns seus hom par chevalerie
me poïst vaintre; or ai trové
1050 meillor de moi et esprové:
molt estes chevaliers vaillanz.
Tenez: ma foi je vos fïanz
que or androit, sanz plus atandre,
m'irai a la reïne randre.
1055 Mes dites moi, nel me celez,
par quel non estes apelez?
Qui dirai ge qui m'i anvoie?
Aparelliez sui de la voie."
Et cil respont: "Jel te dirai;
1060 ja mon non ne te celerai.
Erec ai non; va, se li di   [5a]
que je t'ai anvoié a li."
"Et je m'an vois, jel vos otroi;
mon nain et ma pucele o moi
1065 metrai an sa merci del tot:
ja mar an seroiz an redot.
Et si li dirai la novele
de vos et de vostre pucele."
Lors en a Erec la foi prise.
1070 Tuit sont venu a la devise,
li cuens et les genz an viron,
les puceles et li baron.
De maz et de liez en i ot:
a l'un pesa, a l'autre plot.
1075 Por la pucele au cheinse blanc, *
qui le cuer ot gentil et franc,
qui estoit fille au vavasor,

1040. amanrai *HVA = F*] an manrai *CB*, i menrai *P*.
1052. je *BPVA* (io *H*) = *F*] iel *C*.

46

for you will find her without fail
at Cardigan, if you go there.
You will easily reach there before nightfall:
it is less than seven leagues, I believe.
1035 Into her hands you will deliver
yourself and your maiden and your dwarf,
to do her bidding,
and tell her that I send this message:
that I shall joyfully arrive tomorrow,
1040 and shall bring along a maiden,
so beautiful and so wise and so prudent
that her equal is nowhere to be found:
you can tell her so in truth.
And now I want to know your name."
1045 Then the other was forced to reveal it:
"Sir, my name is Yder, son of Nut.
This morning I did not believe
that a single man could best me
by his knighthood; now I have found
1050 and encountered a better man than I:
you are a very valiant knight.
Here: I solemnly promise you
that straightaway, without further delay,
I shall go deliver myself to the queen.
1055 But tell me, do not conceal it,
by what name are you called?
Whom shall I say sends me there?
I am all ready to set on my way."
And he replied: "I shall tell you;
1060 I shall never conceal my name from you.
My name is Erec; go, and tell her
that I have sent you to her."
"I am on my way, I agree to your terms;
my dwarf and my maiden and myself
1065 I shall place completely at her mercy:
you need have no fear on that account.
And I shall tell her the news
of you and your maiden."
Then Erec took his solemn pledge.
1070 Everyone came to witness their settlement,
the count and the people around him,
the maidens and the nobles.
Some were grieved, but others were joyful:
it pleased some; it displeased others.
1075 For the maiden in the white dress
with the noble and generous heart,
the daughter of the vavasor,

47

s'esjoïssent tuit li plusor;
et por Yder dolant estoient
1080 et por s'amie qui l'amoient.
Yders n'i volt plus arester:
sa foi li covint aquiter.
Maintenant sor son cheval monte.
Por coi vos feroie lonc conte?
1085 Son nain et sa pucele an mainne.
Le bois trespassent et la plainne;
tote la droite voie tindrent
tant que a Caradigan vindrent.
Es loiges de la sale hors
1090 estoit mes sire Gauvains lors
et Kex li senechax ansanble;
des barons i ot, ce me sanble,
avoec ax grant masse venuz.
Cez qui vienent ont bien veüz.
1095 Li senechax premiers les vit;
a mon seignor Gauvain a dit:
"Sire," fet il, "mes cuers devine
que cil vasax qui la chemine,
c'est cil que la reïne dist
1100 qui hier si grant enui li fist.
Ce m'est avis que il sont troi:
le nain et la pucele voi."
"Voirs est," fet mes sire Gauvains,
"c'est une pucele et uns nains
1105 qui avoec le chevalier vienent;   [5b]
vers nos la droite voie tienent.
Toz armez est li chevaliers,
mes ses escuz n'est pas antiers;
se la reïne le veoit,
1110 je cuit qu'ele le conuistroit.
Hé! senechax, car l'apelez!"
Cil i est maintenant alez;
trovee l'a en une chanbre.
"Dame," fet il, "s'il vos remanbre
1115 del nain qui hier vos correça
et vostre pucele bleça?"
"Oïl, molt m'an sovient il bien,
seneschax; savez an vos rien?
Por coi l'avez ramanteü?"
1120 "Dame, por ce que j'ai veü
venir un chevalier errant,
armé sor un destrier ferrant,
et, se mi oel ne m'ont manti,
une pucele a avoec li,

1095. les *BP* (*V*) = *F*] le *CHA*. *V*: a mon segnor .G. a dit /
Keux qui premerains les vit (*-1*).

48

many were joyful;
and those who loved Yder and his lady
1080 were saddened on their account.
Yder wished to stay no longer:
he had to honor his pledge.
At once he got onto his horse.
Why should I tell you a long tale?
1085 He took his dwarf and his maiden with him.
They traversed the wood and the plain;
they kept to the most direct route
until they came to Cardigan.
My lord Gawain and Kay the seneschal *
1090 were together then
in the galleries outside the hall;
a great number of barons, I believe,
had come there with them.
They saw clearly those who were arriving.
1095 The seneschal saw them first;
he spoke to my lord Gawain:
"My lord," said he, "it is my guess
that that knight riding there
is the one of whom the queen spoke,
1100 who caused her so much distress yesterday.
I believe there are three of them:
I see the dwarf and the maiden."
"It's true," said my lord Gawain,
"there's a maiden and a dwarf
1105 coming with the knight;
they're heading directly toward us.
The knight is fully armed,
but his shield is far from whole;
if the queen saw him,
1110 I believe she would recognize him.
I say, seneschal, go call her!"
Kay immediately went to do so;
he found her in a chamber.
"My lady," said he, "do you remember
1115 the dwarf who angered you yesterday
and wounded your maiden?"
"Yes, I remember him very well,
seneschal; do you know anything of this?
Why have you reminded me of it?"
1120 "My lady, because I have seen
a traveling knight in armor, *
coming on an iron-gray charger,
and, if my eyes have not deceived me,
he has a maiden with him,

49

1125   et si m'est vis qu'avoec ax vient
       li nains qui l'escorgiee tient,
       dom Erec reçut la colee."
       Lors s'est la reïne levee
       et dist: "Alons i, seneschax,
1130   veoir se ce est li vasax.
       Se c'est il, bien pöez savoir
       que je vos an dirai le voir
       maintenant que je le verrai."
       Et Kex dist: "Je vos i manrai;
1135   or venez as loiges a mont,
       la ou nostre conpaignon sont;
       d'ilueques venir le veïsmes,
       et mes sire Gauvains meïsmes
       vos i atant. Dame, alons i,
1140   que trop avons demoré ci."
       Lors s'est la reïne esmeüe;
       as fenestres s'an est venue.
       Lez mon seignor Gauvain s'estut;
       le chevalier molt bien conut:
1145   "Haï!" fet ele, "ce est il!
       Molt a esté an grant peril;
       conbatuz s'est. Ce ne sai gié,
       se Erec a son duel vangié
       ou se cist a Erec vaincu,   [5c]
1150   mes molt a cos an son escu;
       ses haubers est coverz de sanc:
       del roge i a plus que del blanc."
       "Voirs est," fet mes sire Gauvains;
       "dame, je sui trestoz certains
1155   que de rien nule ne mantez:
       ses haubers est ansanglantez;
       molt est hurtez et debatuz.
       Bien pert que il s'est conbatuz;
       savoir poons, sanz nule faille,
1160   que forz a esté la bataille.
       Ja li orrons tel chose dire
       don nos avrons ou joie ou ire:
       ou Erec l'anvoie a vos ci
       an prison, an vostre merci,
1165   ou cil se vient par hardemant *
       vanter antre nos folemant
       qu'il a Erec vaincu ou mort.
       Ne cuit qu'autre novele aport."
       Fet la reïne: "Je le cuit."
1170   "Bien puet estre," ce dïent tuit.
          A tant Yders antre an la porte,
       qui la novele lor aporte:

1165. cil *E*] se il *C* (*+1*), il *HBPVA = F*. | se *CPV*] s<u>en</u> *HBEA = F*.

1125 and I believe the dwarf is coming with them,
holding the whip
with which Erec was struck on the neck."
Then the queen rose
and said: "Seneschal, let us go
1130 and see whether it is that vassal.
If it is he, you may be sure
that I will tell you the truth of the matter
as soon as I see him."
And Kay said: "I shall take you there;
1135 now come up to the galleries,
where our companions are;
from there we saw him coming,
and my lord Gawain himself
awaits you there. My lady, let us go there,
1140 for we have tarried too long here."
Then the queen went forth;
she came to the windows.
She stood by my lord Gawain;
she clearly recognized the knight:
1145 "Aha!" said she, "it is he!
He has been in very great danger;
he has seen combat. I do not know
whether Erec has avenged his injury,
or whether this knight has beaten Erec,
1150 but he has many blows on his shield;
his hauberk is covered with blood:
there is more red on it than white."
"That is true," said my lord Gawain;
"my lady, I am quite certain
1155 that you are absolutely right:
his hauberk is bloodied;
it has been much struck and bruised.
It is clear that he has been in combat;
we may be sure, without any doubt,
1160 that the battle was fierce.
We shall soon hear him say something
that will cause us either joy or anger:
either Erec is sending him to you here
as your prisoner, to be at your mercy,
1165 or else he is coming out of audacity,
to brag among us madly
that he has vanquished Erec or killed him.
I believe he brings no other news."
The queen said: "I believe so."
1170 "That may well be," said one and all.
   Then Yder came through the door,
bearing the news to them:

des loges sont tuit avalé;
a l'ancontre li sont alé.

1175 Ydiers vint au perron a val;
la descendi de son cheval.
Et Gauvains la pucele prist
et jus de son cheval la mist.
Li nains de l'autre part descent.

1180 Chevaliers i ot plus de cent;
quant descendu furent tuit troi,
si les mainnent devant le roi.
La ou Ydiers vit la reïne,
jusque devant ses piez ne fine;

1185 salüee l'a tot premiers,
puis le roi et ses chevaliers, *
et dist: "Dame, an vostre prison *
m'anvoie ci uns gentix hom,
uns chevaliers vaillanz et preuz,

1190 cil cui fist hier santir les neuz
mes nains de la corgiee el vis:
vaincu m'a d'armes et conquis.
Dame, le nain vos amaing ci *   [5d]
et ma pucele a merci

1195 por fere quanque il vos plest."
La reïne plus ne se test;
d'Erec li demande novele:
"Or me dites, sire," fet ele,
"savez vos quant Erec vanra?"

1200 "Dame, demain, et s'amanra
une pucele ansanble o lui;
onques si bele ne conui."
Quant il ot conté son message,
la reïne fu preuz et sage;

1205 cortoisemant li dit: "Amis,
des qu'an ma prison estes mis,
molt iert vostre prisons legiere;
n'ai nul talant que mal vos quiere.
Mes or me di, se Dex t'aïst,

1210 comant as non." Et il li dist:
"Dame, Ydiers ai non, li filz Nut."
La verité l'an reconut.
Lors s'est la reïne levee,
devant le roi s'an est alee

1215 et dist: "Sire, avez antandu?
Or avez vos bien atandu

1185. saluee l'a *BPA* = *F*] et si salua *C*, Salue la *H* (de pr.),
   V (*omits* de, *-1*).
1186. puis le roi et *HBPVA* = *F*] Le roi et toz *C*.
1215. avez antandu *HBPVA* = *F*] or auez uev (*i.e.* veu) *C*.
1216. atandu *HBPVA* = *F*] antandu *C*.

52

they all came down from the galleries
and went to meet him.
1175 Yder came to the mounting block below;
there he dismounted.
And Gawain took the maiden
and helped her down from her horse.
The dwarf dismounted on the other side.
1180 More than a hundred knights were there;
when all three had dismounted,
they took them before the king.
As soon as Yder saw the queen,
he went immediately to her feet;
1185 he greeted her first of all,
then the king and his knights,
and said: "My lady, I am sent here
to be your prisoner by a noble man,
a brave and worthy knight,
1190 he whom my dwarf yesterday
struck on the face with his whip:
he has vanquished and beaten me at arms.
My lady, I bring you the dwarf
and my maiden, to be at your mercy
1195 and to do whatever you wish."
The queen kept silent no longer;
she asked him for news of Erec:
"Now tell me, sir," said she,
"do you know when Erec will return?"
1200 "My lady, tomorrow, and he will bring
a maiden with him;
I have never known such a beautiful one."
When he had transmitted his message,
the queen was prudent and wise;
1205 she courteously said to him: "Friend,
since you have surrendered yourself as my prisoner,
your sentence will be very light;
I have no wish that evil should befall you.
But now tell me, as God may help you,
1210 your name." And he said to her:
"My lady, my name is Yder, son of Nut."
It was recognized that he spoke the truth.
Then the queen rose,
went before the king,
1215 and said: "My lord, have you heard?
Now it is well that you have waited

Erec le vaillant chevalier.
Molt vos donai boen consoil hier,
quant jel vos loai a atandre:
1220 por ce fet il boen consoil prandre."
Li rois a dit: "N'est mie fable;
ceste parole est veritable.
Qui croit consoil n'est mie fos; *
buer creümes hier vostre los.
1225 Mes se de rien nule m'amez,
ce chevalier quite clamez
par tel covant de la prison
que il remaigne an ma meison,
de ma mesniee et de ma cort,
1230 et s'il nel fet, a mal li tort."
Li rois ot sa parole dite, *
et la reïne tantost quite
lo chevalier arëaumant,
mes ce fu par tel covenant
1235 qu'a la cort del tot remassist.
Cil gaires preier ne s'an fist:
la remenance a otroiee;   [5e]
puis fu de cort et de mesniee.
Iqui n'avoit gueres esté,
1240 lors furent garçon apresté
qui le corrurent desarmer.
    Or redevons d'Erec parler,
qui ancore an la place estoit
ou la bataille fete avoit.
1245 Onques, ce cuit, tel joie n'ot
la ou Tristanz le fier Morhot
an l'isle Saint Sanson vainqui,
con l'an feisoit d'Erec iqui.
Molt feisoient de lui grant los
1250 petit et grant et gresle et gros;
tuit prisent sa chevalerie.
N'i a chevalier qui ne die:
"Dex, quel vasal! Soz ciel n'a tel."
Aprés, s'an va a son ostel.
1255 Grant los an font et grant parole,
et li cuens meïsmes l'acole,
qui sor toz grant joie an feisoit,
et dit: "Sire, s'il vos pleisoit,

1217. Erec *HBP = F*] D erec *C (VA omit 1217-8).*
1231. *Decorated initial* L *in C (also HP; none in B; VA omit).*
1242. *No large initial, CHPVA; B has a larger than usual initial* O.
    Cf. previous note.
1246. la ou *BPVA = F*] Quant *C.* | le fier M. *BVA = F*] ocist le m. *C,*
    le morlyot *P (H omits 1245-48).*
1247. Saint *BPVA = FR*] quant *C.*

54

for Erec, the valiant knight.
I gave you very good counsel yesterday
when I advised you to wait for him:
1220 that is why it is well to accept counsel."
The king replied: "This is no fable;
these words are full of truth.
He who believes in counsel is no fool;
we did well yesterday to take your advice.
1225 But if you bear any love for me,
proclaim this knight free
from obligation as your prisoner,
on condition that he remain in my house
as a member of my household and my court,
1230 and if he does not do so, may it be to his detriment."
As soon as the king had spoken,
the queen straightaway freed
the knight in the proper manner,
but this was on the condition
1235 that he would remain completely at the court.
He hardly needed to be begged to do so:
he accepted the condition;
thenceforth he was of the court and of the household.
He had scarcely been there at all
1240 when valets were ready
and ran to remove his armor.
   Now we must speak of Erec again,
who was still on the field
where he had fought the battle.
1245 Never, I believe, was there such joy
where Tristan defeated the savage Morholt
on the isle of Saint Sanson,
as was made over Erec there.
He was greatly praised and honored
1250 by small and great, by thin and fat;
everyone esteemed his knightly prowess.
Not a knight was there who did not say:
"God, what a vassal! He has no equal under the heavens."
Afterwards he went back to his lodgings.
1255 They greatly praised and spoke of him,
and the count himself embraced him,
greatly rejoicing above all others,
and said: "Sir, should it please you,

bien devrïez et par reison
1260 vostre ostel prandre an ma meison,
quant vos estes filz Lac le roi;
se vos prenïez mon conroi,
vos me ferïez grant enor,
car je vos tieng por mon seignor.
1265 Biax sire, la vostre merci,
de remenoir o moi vos pri."
Erec respont: "Ne vos enuit,
ne lesserai mon oste enuit,
qui molt m'a grant enor mostree
1270 quant il sa fille m'a donee.
Et qu'an dites vos, sire, dons?
Don n'est biax et riches cist dons?"
"Oïl, biax sire," fet li cuens;
"cist dons si est et biax et buens.
1275 La pucele est molt bele et sage,
et si est molt de haut parage:
sachiez que sa mere est ma suer.
Certes molt en ai lié le cuer
quant vos ma niece avoir deigniez.
1280 Ancor vos pri que vos veigniez
o moi herbergier enuit mes."   [5f]
Erec respont: "Lessiez m'an pes;
nel feroie an nule meniere."
Cil voit n'i a mestier proiere
1285 et dist: "Sire, a vostre pleisir!
Or nos an poons bien teisir,
mes gié et mi chevalier tuit
serons avoec vos ceste nuit
par solaz et par conpaignie."
1290 Quant Erec l'ot, si l'an mercie.
Lors an vint Erec chiés son oste,
et li cuens avoec lui an coste;
dames et chevaliers i ot.
Li chevaliers molt s'an esjot.
1295 Tot maintenant que Erec vint,
sergent corrurent plus de vint
por lui desarmer a esploit.
Qui an cele meison estoit
molt pooit grant joie veoir.
1300 Erec s'ala premiers seoir,
puis s'asistrent tuit par les rans,
sor liz, sor seles et sor bans.
Lez Erec s'est li cuens assis,
et la bele pucele an mis,
1305 qui tel joie a de son seignor *
c'onques pucele n'ot greignor.

1277, 1278 *HBPVA = F1279-80]* interverted C.

56

           you ought rightfully
1260   to take your lodging in my house,
           since you are the son of King Lac;
           should you accept my hospitality,
           you would do me great honor,
           for I would treat you as my lord.
1265   Good sir, by your leave,
           I beg you to stay with me."
           Erec replied: "May it not trouble you,
           but I shall not abandon my host tonight,
           who showed me such great honor
1270   when he gave me his daughter.
           And what then do you say of this, sir?
           Is this gift not fine and rich?" *
           "Yes, good sir," said the count;
           "this gift is indeed beautiful and good.
1275   The maiden is very beautiful and wise,
           and she is of very high lineage:
           know that her mother is my sister.
           Truly my heart is very glad
           because you have deigned to take my niece.
1280   Again I beg you to come
           with me to lodge this night."
           Erec replied: "Leave me in peace;
           I would not do so in any way."
           The count saw that it was useless to insist,
1285   and said: "Sir, as you wish!
           Now we may drop the matter,
           but I and all my knights
           will be with you this night
           for amusement and for company."
1290   When Erec heard this, he thanked him.
           Then Erec came back to his host's,
           with the count beside him;
           ladies and knights were there.
           The knight greatly rejoiced at this. *
1295   As soon as Erec arrived,
           more than twenty men-at-arms came running
           quickly to remove his armor.
           Whoever was in that house
           could see very great joy.
1300   Erec went to sit down first;
           then they all sat down around him,
           on beds, on stools, and on benches.
           The count sat near Erec,
           with the beautiful maiden between them,
1305   who was so joyful because of her lord
           that never was any maiden more so.

Erec le vavasor apele,
parole li dist boene et bele, *
et si li comança a dire:
1310 "Biax amis, biax ostes, biax sire,
vos m'avez grant enor portee,
mes bien vos iert guerredonee:
demain an manrai avoec moi
vostre fille a la cort le roi.
1315 La la voldrai a fame prandre,
et, s'il vos plest un po atandre,
par tans vos anvoierai querre:
mener vos ferai an ma terre,
qui mon pere est et moie aprés;
1320 loing de ci est, non mie pres.
Iluec vos donrai deus chastiax,
molt boens, molt riches et molt biax:
sires seroiz de Roadan,
qui fu fez des le tans Adan,
1325 et d'un autre chastel selonc
qui ne valt mie moins un jonc:
la gent l'apelent Montrevel;
mes peres n'a meillor chastel.
Einz que troi jor soient passez
1330 vos avrai anvoié assez
or et argent et veir et gris
et dras de soie de chier pris
por vos vestir et vostre fame,
qui est ma chiere dolce dame.
1335 Demain droit a l'aube del jor,
an tel robe et an tel ator,
an manrai vostre fille a cort:
je voel que ma dame l'atort
de la soe robe demainne,
1340 qui est de soie tainte an grainne."
Une pucele estoit leanz,
molt preuz, molt saige, molt vaillanz;
lez la pucele au chainse blanc
estoit assise sor un banc,
1345 et sa cosine estoit germainne
et niece le conte demainne.
Quant la parole a antandue, *

[2a]

1309. et si li A = R (Si li a comancie HBP = F)] et cil li C, Ainsi li V.
1313. an manrai HBPVA = F] an uandra C.
1325. d'un HBPA = FR (et dun et dautre c. s. V)] dui C.
1326. valt mie HBPVA = FR] ualent pas C.
1332. soie de HBPVA = F] soie et de C.
1345. et sa c. estoit HBP = F] Qui ert sa c. C, Q. sa c. estoit VA.
1347-50 HBPVA = F1359-62] omitted C.
1347. parole HPV] pucele BA = F. | a HV] ot BPA = F.

58

Erec called to the vavasor,
saying good and fine words to him,
and he began to speak thus:
1310 "Good friend, good host, good sir,
you have greatly honored me,
and you shall be well rewarded for it:
tomorrow I shall take your daughter with me
to the court of the king.
1315 There I wish to take her for my wife,
and, if you will wait a bit,
I shall send for you presently:
I will have you escorted to my land,
which is my father's and later will be mine;
1320 it is far from here, not at all near.
There I will give you two castles,
very fine, rich, and beautiful:
you will be lord of Roadan,
which was built in the time of Adam,
1325 and of another castle nearby
which is worth not a bit less:
people call it Montrevel;
my father has no better castle.
Before three days have passed
1330 I will have sent you much
gold and silver and vair and miniver *
and expensive silken cloth
to clothe you and your wife,
who is my dear sweet lady.
1335 Tomorrow right at daybreak
I shall take your daughter to court,
dressed and adorned as she is now:
I want my lady the queen to clothe her
in one of her very own dresses,
1340 one of scarlet-dyed silk."
There was a maiden in that place,
very prudent, sensible, and worthy;
she was seated on a bench
near the maiden in the white dress,
1345 and she was her first cousin
and the count's own niece.
When she heard this declaration,

que si tres povremant vestue
en voloit mener sa cosine
1350 Erec a la cort la reïne,
a parole en a mis le conte:
"Sire," fet ele, "molt grant honte
sera a vos, plus qu'a autrui,
se cist sires an mainne o lui
1355 vostre niece si povremant
atornee de vestemant."
Et li cuens respont: "Je vos pri,
ma dolce niece, donez li,
de voz robes que vos avez,
1360 la mellor que vos i savez."
Erec a la parole oïe
et dist: "Sire, n'an parlez mie.
Une chose sachiez vos bien:
ne voldroie por nule rien
1365 qu'ele eüst d'autre robe point
tant que la reïne li doint."
Quant la dameisele l'oï,
lors li respont et dist: "Haï!
Biax sire, quant vos an tel guise,
1370 el blanc chainse et an la chemise,
ma cosine an volez mener,
un autre don li voel doner.
Quant vos ne volez antresait   [2b]
que nule de mes robes ait,
1375 je ai trois palefroiz molt buens—
onques meillors n'ot rois ne cuens:
un sor, un vair et un baucent.
Sanz mantir, la ou en a cent,
n'en a mie un meillor del vair:
1380 li oisel qui volent par l'air
ne vont plus tost del palefroi.
Einz nus hom ne vit son desroi:
uns anfes chevalchier le puet.
Tex est com a pucele estuet,
1385 qu'il n'est onbrages ne restis,
ne mort, ne fiert, ne n'est ragis.
Qui meillor quiert ne set qu'il vialt;
qui le chevalche ne s'an dialt,
einz va plus aeise et söef
1390 que s'il estoit an une nef."
    Lors dist Erec: "Ma dolce amie,
ice don ne refus je mie,
s'ele le prant; einçois me plest:
ne voel mie qu'ele le lest."

1351. *Initial* A *in* C.
1377. vair *P = FR*] bai *CH*, noir *BVA. Cf. 1379, 1398.*

60

that Erec wanted to take her cousin
to the queen's court
1350 dressed so very poorly,
she spoke about it to the count:
"Sir," said she, "it will be a great shame
for you, more than for anyone else,
if this lord takes your niece
1355 along with him so poorly
furnished with clothing."
And the count replied: "I beg you,
my sweet niece, give her,
from among your own dresses,
1360 the one you consider the best."
Erec heard this request,
and said: "Sir, do not speak of that.
Let me tell you one thing:
I would not for any reason wish
1365 her to have any other dress,
until the queen gives her one."
When the damsel heard this,
she answered him and said: "Well then!
Good sir, since you wish to take my cousin
1370 with you in such a way,
in the white dress and the chemise,
I want to give her another gift.
Since you absolutely do not want
her to have any dress of mine,
1375 I have three very fine palfreys— *
no king nor count ever had a better one:
one is sorrel, one dapple-gray, and one has white stockings.
In all truth, among a hundred,
there is none better than the gray:
1380 the birds that fly through the air
go no more quickly than that palfrey.
No one ever saw it bolt or rear:
a child can ride it.
It is just right for a maiden,
1385 for it is neither skittish nor balky,
nor does it bite, nor strike, nor get violent.
Whoever seeks a better one knows not what he wants;
whoever rides it does not suffer,
but rather goes more easily and gently
1390 than if he were on a ship."
    Then Erec said: "My sweet friend,
I do not refuse this gift at all
if she accepts it; rather, it pleases me:
I do not wish her to decline it."

61

1395 Tot maintenant la dameisele
    un suen privé sergent apele,
    si li dist: "Biax amis, alez,
    mon palefroi veir anselez,
    si l'amenez isnelemant."
1400 Et cil fet son comandemant:
    le cheval ansele et anfrainne,
    del bel aparellier se painne,
    puis monte el palefroi crenu.
    Ez vos le palefroi venu.
1405 Quant Erec le palefroi vit,
    ne le loa mie petit,
    car molt le vit et bel et gent;
    puis comanda a un sergent
    qu'an l'estable lez son destrier
1410 alast le palefroi l̈ier.
    A tant se departirent tuit;
    grant joie orent fet cele nuit.
    Li cuens a son ostel s'an vet;
    Erec chiés le vavasor let
1415 et dit qu'il le convoiera
    au matin, quant il s'an ira.
    Cele nuit ont tote dormie.
    Au main quant l'aube est esclarcie,
    Erec s'atorne de l'aler:
1420 ses chevax comande anseler
    et s'amie la bele esvoille;
    cele s'atorne et aparoille.
    Li vavasors lieve et sa fame;
    n'i remaint chevalier ne dame
1425 qui ne s'atort por convoier
    la pucele et le chevalier.
    Tuit sont monté, et li cuens monte.
    Erec chevalche lez le conte
    et delez lui sa bele amie, *
1430 qui l'esprevier n'oblia mie:
    a son esprevier se deporte;
    nule autre richesce n'an porte.
    Grant joie ont fet au convoier.
    Avoec Erec volt anvoier
1435 au dessevrer une partie
    li frans cuens de sa conpaignie,
    por ce qu'annor li feïssient *
    se avoec lui s'an alessient,
    mes il dist que nul n'an manroit,
1440 ne conpaignie ne queroit
    fors que s'amie solemant.
    Puis lor dist: "A Deu vos comant!"

1429. lui *HBPVA = FR*] *omitted C (-1).*

1395	At once the damsel
	summoned one of her own servants
	and said to him: "Good friend, go,
	saddle my dapple-gray palfrey,
	and bring it quickly."
1400	And he carried out her order:
	he saddled and bridled the horse,
	strove to equip it well,
	then mounted the shaggy-maned palfrey.
	There was the palfrey brought before them.
1405	When Erec saw the palfrey,
	he was not sparing in his praise,
	for he saw it was handsome and well-bred;
	then he ordered a servant
	to go and tie up the palfrey
1410	in the stable beside his charger.
	Then they all separated;
	they had greatly rejoiced that night.
	The count went to his lodgings;
	he left Erec at the vavasor's
1415	and said that he would accompany him
	in the morning when he went on his way.
	They slept all that night.
	In the morning, when dawn broke,
	Erec prepared for his departure:
1420	he ordered his horses saddled
	and he awakened his beautiful lady;
	she dressed and prepared herself.
	The vavasor and his wife arose;
	there was not a knight nor lady
1425	who did not prepare to accompany
	the maiden and the knight.
	All were on horseback, and the count mounted up.
	Erec rode next to the count,
	and his beautiful lady beside him.
1430	She in no way forgot the sparrow-hawk:
	she amused herself with her sparrow-hawk;
	she took with her no other riches.
	There was great joy as they went along together.
	At parting the generous count
1435	wanted to send with Erec
	a part of his retinue,
	so that they might honor him
	by going with him,
	but he said that he would take no one with him,
1440	and that he sought no company
	other than his lady.
	Then he said to them: "I commend you to God!"

Convoiez les orent grant piece.
Li cuens beise Erec et sa niece
1445 si les comande a Deu le pi.
Li peres et la mere ausi
les beisent sovant et menu;
de plorer ne se sont tenu:
au departir plore la mere,
1450 plore la pucele et li pere.
Tex est amors, tex est nature,
tex est pitiez de norreture:
plorer les feisoit la pitiez
et la dolçors et l'amistiez
1455 qu'il avoient de lor anfant;
mes bien savoient ne por quant
que lor fille an tel leu aloit
don granz enors lor avandroit.
D'amor et de pitié ploroient,
1460 que de lor fille departoient;
ne ploroient por altre chose.   [2d]
Bien savoient qu'a la parclose
an seroient il enoré.
Au departir ont molt ploré;
1465 plorant a Deu s'antre comandent.
Or s'an vont, que plus n'i atandent.
    Erec de son oste depart,
car mervoilles li estoit tart
que a la cort le roi venist.
1470 De s'avanture s'esjoïst:
molt estoit liez de s'avanture,
qu'amie a bele a desmesure,
saige et cortoise et de bon aire.
De l'esgarder ne puet preu faire;
1475 quant plus l'esgarde et plus li plest.
Ne puet müer qu'il ne la best;
volantiers pres de li se tret.
An li esgarder se refet:
molt remire son chief le blont,
1480 ses ialz rianz et son cler front,
le nes et la face et la boche,
don granz dolçors au cuer li toche.
Tot remire jusqu'a la hanche:
le manton et la gorge blanche,
1485 flans et costez et braz et mains.

1447. les *B = F1909*] la *CH = FR*, le *PVA*.
1451. tex est n. *HBPVA = FR*] test est n. *C*.
1453. s *of* les *added above line* (*R's* leur *is erroneous*). | la p. *B = F*
    (li p. *HP*)] granz p. *C*, lamisties *VA* (li p. *in following line, V*).
1461. ne *BPVA = FR*] n *missing, C: corner torn from folio 2.*
    (*H omits 1461-1464.*)

64

They had accompanied them a long way.
The count kissed Erec and his niece
1445 and commended them to God the merciful.
The father and the mother too
kissed them over and over again;
they did not hold back their tears:
at parting the mother wept,
1450 and the maiden wept, as did the father.
Such is love, such is nature,
such is the tenderness for one's offspring:
they wept because of the tenderness
and the sweetness and the friendship
1455 that they had for their child;
and yet they knew full well
that their daughter was going to such a place
where there would be great honor for them.
They were weeping out of love and tenderness,
1460 for they were parting from their daughter;
they wept for no other reason.
They knew full well that in the end
they would be honored as a result.
At parting they wept greatly;
1465 weeping they commended one another to God.
Then they left, tarrying there no more.
    Erec left his host,
for he was extremely impatient
to return to the court of the king.
1470 He rejoiced at his adventure:
he was delighted with his adventure,
for he had an extremely beautiful lady,
wise and courtly and well-bred.
He could not get enough of seeing her;
1475 the more he looked at her, the more she pleased him.
He could not keep from kissing her;
eagerly he drew near to her.
Looking at her restored and delighted him:
he kept looking at her blond hair,
1480 her laughing eyes and her unclouded brow,
her nose and her face and her mouth,
and from this great sweetness touched his heart.
He admired everything, down to her hips:
her chin and her white throat,
1485 her flanks and sides, her arms and hands.

Mes ne remire mie mains
la dameisele le vasal
de boen oel et de cuer leal *
qu'il feisoit li par contançon.
1490 N'an preïssent pas rëançon
li uns de l'autre regarder.
Molt estoient igal et per
de corteisie et de biauté
et de grant debonereté.
1495 Si estoient d'une meniere,
d'unes mors et d'une matiere,
que nus qui le voir volsist dire
n'an poïst le meillor eslire
ne le plus bel ne le plus sage.
1500 Molt estoient d'igal corage
et molt avenoient ansanble.
Li uns a l'autre son cuer anble;
onques deus si beles ymages
n'asanbla lois ne mariages.
1505 Tant ont ansanble chevalchié   [2e]
qu'a droit midi ont aprochié
le chastel de Caradigan,
ou andeus les atandoit l'an.
Por esgarder s'il les verroient,
1510 as fenestres monté estoient
li meillor baron de la cort.
La reïne Ganievre i cort,
et s'i vint meïsmes li rois,
Kex et Percevax li Galois,
1515 et mes sire Gauvains aprés,
et Corz, li filz au roi Arés;
Lucans i fu, li botelliers;
molt i ot de boens chevaliers.
Erec ont choisi qui venoit
1520 et s'amie qu'il amenoit;
bien l'ont trestuit reconeü
de si loing com il l'ont veü.
La reïne grant joie an mainne;
de joie est tote la corz plainne
1525 ancontre son avenemant,
car tuit l'ainment comunemant.
Lués que il vint devant la sale,
li rois ancontre lui s'avale,
et la reïne d'autre part;
1530 tuit li dïent que Dex le gart.
Lui et sa pucele conjoent;
sa grant biauté prisent et loent.

1488. oel *PV* (huil *B*, oil *A*) = *F*] uoel *C* (*H omits 1485-90*).
1496. s *of* unes *added above line.*

66

But the damsel, for her part, looked at the knight
no less than he looked at her,
with favorable eye and loyal heart,
in eager emulation.
1490 They would not have accepted a ransom
to leave off looking at one another.
They were very well and evenly matched
in courtliness and in beauty
and in great nobility.
1495 They were so similar,
of one character and of one substance,
that no one who wanted to speak truly
could have chosen the better one
nor the more beautiful nor the wiser.
1500 They were very equal in spirit
and very well suited to one another.
Each of them stole the other's heart;
never were two such beautiful figures
brought together by law or by marriage.
1505 They rode together until,
right at noon, they approached
the castle of Cardigan,
where they were both expected.
In order to catch sight of them,
1510 the best barons of the court
had gone up to the windows.
Queen Guinevere ran there,
and the king himself came,
Kay and Perceval the Welshman,
1515 and then my lord Gawain,
and Cor, the son of King Arés;
Lucan, the wine-steward, was there;
and there were many good knights.
They observed Erec as he approached
1520 and his lady, whom he was bringing along;
they all clearly recognized him,
from as far away as they could see him.
The queen was overjoyed at this;
the whole court was full of joy
1525 in preparation for his arrival,
for he was well loved by all.
As soon as he came before the hall,
the king came down to meet him,
as did the queen on the other side;
1530 all invoked God's protection on him.
They welcomed him and his maiden;
they praised and made much of her great beauty.

Et li rois meïsmes l'a prise
et jus del palefroi l'a mise.
1535 Molt fu li rois bien afeitiez;
a cele ore estoit bien heitiez.
La pucele a molt enoree:
par la main l'a a mont menee
an la mestre sale perrine.
1540 Aprés, Erec et la reïne
sont andui monté main a main,
et il li dist: "Je vos amain,
dame, ma pucele et m'amie
de povres garnemanz garnie;
1545 si com ele me fu donee,
ensi la vos ai amenee.
D'un povre vavasor est fille.
Povretez mainz homes aville: *
ses peres est frans et cortois,   [2f]
1550 mes d'avoir a molt petit pois,
et molt gentix dame est sa mere,
qu'ele a un riche conte a frere. *
Ne por biauté ne por linage
ne doi je pas le mariage
1555 de la pucele refuser. *
Povretez li a fet user
ce blanc chainse tant que as cotes
an sont andeus les manches rotes.
Et ne por quant, se moi pleüst,
1560 boenes robes asez eüst,
c'une pucele, sa cosine,
li volt doner robe d'ermine,
de dras de soie, veire ou grise;
mes ne volsisse an nule guise
1565 que d'autre robe fust vestue
tant que vos l'eüssiez veüe.
Ma douce dame, or an pansez,
car mestier a, bien le veez,
d'une bele robe avenant."
1570 Et la reïne maintenant
li respont: "Molt avez bien fait:
droiz est que de mes robes ait,
et je li donrai boene et bele,
tot or androit, fresche et novele."
1575 La reïne araumant l'an mainne
an la soe chanbre demainne
et dist qu'an li aport isnel
le fres blïaut et le mantel

1552. riche HBPV = F] gentil CA.
1554. doi HBPVA = F] quier C.
1555. la pucele refuser HBPVA = F] la dameisele esposer C.

And the king himself took her
and set her down from her palfrey.
1535 The king was very well-bred;
on that occasion he was very joyful.
He greatly honored the maiden:
by the hand he led her up
into the great stone hall.
1540 Then Erec and the queen
went up together hand in hand,
and he said to her: "My lady,
I bring you my maiden and my lady
clad in poor garments;
1545 just as she was given to me,
so have I brought her to you.
She is the daughter of a poor vavasor.
Poverty abases many men:
her father is noble and courtly,
1550 but he has little weight of wealth,
and her mother is a very noble lady,
for she has a rich count as her brother.
Neither beauty nor lineage
would be cause for me to disdain
1555 marriage with this maiden.
Poverty has made her wear
this white dress so much that
both sleeves are worn through at the elbows.
And yet, if I had been willing,
1560 she would have had plenty of fine clothes,
for a maiden, her cousin,
wanted to give her an ermine dress,
with silken fabric, vair or miniver;
but I was totally opposed
1565 to her being dressed in any other clothes
until you had seen her.
My sweet lady, now think of this,
for she has need, as you can see,
of a fine and fitting dress."
1570 And the queen answered him
at once: "You have acted very properly:
it is right that she should have one of mine,
and I shall give her one, good and beautiful,
a brand-new one, immediately."
1575 The queen promptly led her
to her private chamber
and ordered brought to her swiftly
the new court dress and the cloak *

69

de la vert porpre croisilliee
1580 qui por son cors estoit tailliee.
Cil cui ele l'ot comandé
li a le mantel aporté
et le blïaut, qui jusqu'as manches
estoit forrez d'ermines blanches.
1585 As poinz et a la cheveçaille
avoit sanz nule devinaille
plus de deus cenz mars d'or batu, *
et pierres de molt grant vertu,
yndes et verz, persses et bises,
1590 avoit par tot sor l'or assises.
Molt estoit riches li blïauz,
mes por voir ne valoit noauz
li mantiax de rien que je sache.   *[6a]*
Ancor n'i avoit mise estache,
1595 car toz estoit fres et noviax
et li blïauz et li mantiax.
Molt fu li mantiax boens et fins:
au col avoit deus sebelins,
es tassiax ot d'or plus d'une once; *
1600 d'une part ot une jagonce,
et un rubi de l'autre part,
plus cler qu'escharbocle qui art.
La pane fu de blanc hermine:
onques plus bele ne plus fine
1605 ne fu veüe ne trovee;
la porpre fu molt bien ovree
a croisetes totes diverses,
yndes et vermoilles et perses,
blanches et verz, bloes et giaunes. *
1610 Unes estaches de cinc aunes
de fil de soie a or ovrees
a la reïne demandees;
les estaches li sont bailliees,
beles et bien aparelliees.
1615 Ele les fet tot maintenant
el mantel metre isnelemant
et s'an fist tel home antremetre

1579. la vert porpre *BA* (le u. p. *V*) = *F*] lautre robe *C*,
      la uerde p. *P (+1)*; *H omits 1579-80.*
1589. *first* s *of* persses *added above line.*
1599. tassiax (tassiaus *P = F*)] estaches *C* (*H omits 1599-1602*).
      Cf. 6760. l plus d'une *P = F*] une *C*. [*F's variants to the
      remaining MSS are* tasiax *VA*, tausseaus *E*, tentax *B*.]
1603. de *HP = F*] dun *CBVA*.
1609. bloes (bloies *B*, bleues *HPVA*) = *F*] indes *C*.
1611. a or *PVA = F*] dor *CH*, bien *B*.
1613. sont *HB = F*] a *C*, ont *PVA*.

70

of rich green cloth with the crossed pattern
1580 which had been tailored for her personally.
He whom she had ordered
brought her the cloak
and the dress, which was lined
with white ermine, even in the sleeves.
1585 At the wrists and at the neck
there were, without any mystery,
more than two hundred marks of beaten gold,
and stones of great power,
violet and green, deep blue and grey-brown,
1590 were everywhere set upon the gold.
The dress was very rich,
but in truth the cloak was,
to my knowledge, worth not a bit less.
No ribbons had yet been placed upon it, *
1595 for both the dress and the cloak
were still brand-new.
The cloak was very good and fine:
at the collar there were two sables,
and an ounce of gold in the fasteners; *
1600 on one side there was a jacinth, *
and a ruby on the other side,
clearer than a burning garnet. *
The lining was of white ermine:
one more beautiful nor finer
1605 was never seen nor found;
the rich cloth was very finely worked
with different crisscross designs,
violet and red and indigo,
white and green, blue and yellow.
1610 The queen requested
some ribbons, made from five ells *
of silken thread wound round with gold;
the ribbons were brought to her,
beautiful and well prepared.
1615 Without delay she had them
speedily attached to the cloak,
and she had it done by a man

qui boens mestres estoit del metre.
    Quant el mantel n'ot que refere,
1620 la franche dame de bon ere
la pucele au blanc cheinse acole
et si li dist franche parole:
"Ma dameisele, a ce blïaut,
qui plus de cent mars d'argent vaut,
1625 vos comant cest chainse changier:
de tant vos voel or losangier.
Et ce mantel afublez sus;
une autre foiz vos donrai plus."
Cele ne le refuse mie:
1630 la robe prant, si l'an mercie.
An une chanbre recelee
l'an ont deus puceles menee;
lors a son chainse desvestu,
que nel prise mes un festu. *
1635 Puis vest son blïaut, si s'estraint,
d'un orfrois molt riche se ceint,
et son chainse por amor Dé *   [6b]
comande que il soit doné;
et le mantel aprés afuble.
1640 Or n'ot mie la chiere enuble,
car la robe tant li avint
que plus bele asez an devint.
Les deus puceles d'un fil d'or
li ont galoné son crin sor,
1645 mes plus luisanz estoit li crins
que li filz d'or qui molt est fins.
Un cercle d'or ovré a flors
de maintes diverses colors
les puceles el chief li metent.
1650 Mialz qu'eles pueent s'antremetent
de li an tel guise atorner *
qu'an n'i truisse rien qu'amander.
Deus fermaillez d'or neelez,
an un topace anseelez,
1655 li mist au col une pucele.
Or fu tant avenanz et bele *
que ne cuit pas qu'an nule terre,
tant seüst l'an cerchier ne querre,
fust sa paroille recovree,
1660 tant l'ot Nature bien ovree.

1623. a *HBPA = F] omitted CV.*
1634. *B = F]* quant ele an la chanbre fu *C (-1). Other mss. have
readings similar to B's:* Qel ne *H,* Car nel *VA,* Que nel *P;*
prise mais *HV,* pr. pas *PA;* .i. festu *PVA,* .i. uestu *H.*
1651. atorner *HBPVA = F]* amander *C.*
1656. Or *HPVA = F]* Qui *C; B omits 1655-6.*

who was a past master at his craft. *
When there was no more to be done on the cloak,
1620 the generous and noble lady
embraced the maiden with the white dress
and spoke generously to her:
"My damsel, I order you to replace
this house dress with this court dress,
1625 which is worth more than a hundred marks of silver:
I wish now thus to honor you.
And put on this cloak over it;
another time I shall give you more."
The maiden did not refuse it:
1630 she took the clothes and thanked her for them.
Two maidens led her away
to a secluded room;
then she removed her old dress,
for she no longer cared a straw for it.
1635 Then she put on her court dress and tightened it,
girded herself with a rich band of orphrey, *
and ordered that her old dress
be given away, for the love of God;
then she put on the cloak.
1640 Now she looked not the least bit sad,
for this attire suited her so well
that she became even more beautiful.
The two maidens braided her golden hair
with a thread of gold,
1645 but her hair shone more brightly
than the golden thread, fine as it was.
A golden chaplet, wrought with flowers *
of many different colors,
was placed on her head by the maidens.
1650 As best they could, they undertook
to adorn her in such a way
that one might find nothing to improve.
Two clasps of nielloed gold, *
set upon a topaz,
1655 were placed at her neck by one maiden.
Now she was so pleasing and beautiful
that I believe her equal
could not be found in any land,
however much one might seek,
1660 so well had Nature fashioned her.

Puis est hors de la chanbre issue;
a la reïne an est venue.
La reïne molt la conjot:
por ce l'ama et molt li plot
1665 qu'ele estoit bele et bien aprise.
L'une a l'autre par la main prise,
si sont devant le roi venues,
et quant li rois les ot veües,
ancontre se lieve an estant.
1670 De chevaliers i avoit tant,
qant eles an la sale entrerent,
qui ancontre eles se leverent,
que je n'an sai nomer le disme,
le treziesme ne le quinzisme,
1675 mes d'auques des meillors barons
vos sai bien a dire les nons,
de ces de la Table Reonde,
qui furent li meillor del monde.
    Devant toz les boens chevaliers
1680 doit estre Gauvains li premiers,   [6c]
li seconz Erec, li filz Lac,
et li tierz Lancelot del Lac,
Gonemanz de Goort li quarz,
et li quinz fu li Biax Coarz.
1685 Li sistes fu li Lez Hardiz,
li sesmes Melianz des Liz,
li huitiesmes Mauduiz li Sages,
li noemes Dodins li Sauvages;
Gaudeluz soit dismes contez,
1690 car an lui ot maintes bontez.
Les autres vos dirai sanz nonbre,
por ce que li nonbrers m'anconbre:
Yvains li preuz se seoit outre; *
d'autre part Yvains li avoutre,
1695 et Tristanz qui onques ne rist
delez Blioberis s'asist.
    Aprés fu Caradué Briébraz,
uns chevaliers de grant solaz,
et Caverons de Roberdic,
1700 et li filz au roi Quenedic,
et li vaslez de Quintareus,
et Ydiers del Mont Delereus,
Galerïez et Quex d' Estraus,
Amauguins et Galez li Chaus,
1705 Gilflez, li filz Do, et Taulas,
qui onques d'armes ne fu las,
et uns vassax de grant vertu:

1687. First s *of* huitiesmes *added above line.*
1692. nonbrers *B = F*] nonbres *CV*, nombres *P*, contes *H*, conter *A*.

74

Then she came out of the room
and came to the queen.
The queen welcomed her warmly:
she loved her and took pleasure in her
1665 because she was beautiful and well-bred.
They took one another by the hand
and came before the king,
and when the king saw them,
he rose to meet them.
1670 So many knights were there
who rose to meet them
when they entered the hall
that I could not name the tenth part,
nor the thirteenth nor the fifteenth,
1675 but I can tell you the names
of some of the best barons
among those of the Round Table,
who were the best in the world.
    Before all the good knights
1680 Gawain must be the first;
the second Erec, son of Lac;
and the third Lancelot of the Lake;
Gonemant of Goort the fourth;
and the fifth was the Fair Coward. *
1685 The sixth was the Ugly Hero;
the seventh Meliant of Liz;
the eighth Mauduit the Wise;
the ninth Dodin the Wildman;
let Gaudelu be counted tenth,
1690 for in him were many good qualities.
The others I shall tell you without numbers,
because the numbering encumbers.
Ywain the Valiant was seated farther on;
on another side Ywain the Bastard,
1695 and Tristan, who never laughed,
was seated by Blioberis.
Afterwards came Caradué Short-Arm,
a knight of great amusement,
and Caveron of Roberdic,
1700 and the son of King Quenedic,
and the youth of Quintareus, *
and Yder of the Sorrowful Mountain,
Galeriet and Kay of Estral,
Amauguin and Galet the Bald,
1705 Girflet, son of Do, and Taulas,
who was never tired of bearing arms,
and a vassal of great courage,

75

Loholz, li filz le roi Artu;
et Sagremors li Desreez—
1710 cil ne doit pas estre oblïez,
ne Bedoiers li conestables,
qui molt sot d'eschas et de tables,
ne Bravaïns, ne Loz li rois,
ne Galegantins li Galois.
1715 Qant la bele pucele estrange
vit toz les chevaliers an range
qui l'esgardoient a estal,
son chief ancline contre val:
vergoigne an ot, ne fu mervoille;
1720 la face l'an devint vermoille—
mes la honte si li avint
que plus bele asez an devint.
Quant li rois la vit vergoignier,
ne se vost de li esloignier;
1725 par la main l'a dolcemant prise   [6d]
et delez lui a destre assise.
De la senestre part s'asist
la reïne, qui au roi dist:
"Sire, si con je cuit et croi,
1730 bien doit venir a cort de roi
qui par ses armes puet conquerre
si bele dame en autre terre.
Bien feisoit Erec a atandre:
or pöez vos le beisier prandre
1735 de la plus bele de la cort.
Je ne cuit qu'a mal nus l'atort:
ja nus ne dira, qui ne mante,
que ceste ne soit la plus gente
des puceles qui ceanz sont
1740 et de celes de tot le mont."
      Li rois respont: "N'est pas mançonge;
ceste, se l'an nel me chalonge,
donrai ge del blanc cerf l'enor."
Puis dist as chevaliers: "Seignor,
1745 que dites vos? Que vos an sanble?
Ceste est de cors, de vis ansanble,
et de quanqu'estuet a pucele,
et la plus gente et la plus bele
qui soit jusque la, ce me sanble, *
1750 ou li ciax et la terre asanble.
Je di que droiz est antresait

1736. Je *BPVA = FR*] Ja *CH*.
1737. qui ne *HBV = F*] que ie *C*, quil ne *P*, que ne *A*.
1749. qui soit jusque la *BV* (dusqala *H*, dusques la *P*,
      jusques la *A*) = *F*] ne qui soit des la *C*.
1719. mervoille *HBPVA = FR*] uermoille *C*.

Loholt, the son of King Arthur,
and Sagremor the Unruly—
1710 he must not be forgotten,
nor Bedoier the constable, *
who knew much of chess and backgammon,
nor Bravaïn, nor King Lot,
nor Galegantin the Welshman.
1715 When the beautiful stranger
saw all the knights gathered round
looking fixedly at her,
she bowed her head:
she was embarrassed, and it was no wonder;
1720 her face became red—
but modesty suited her so well
that she became even more beautiful.
When the king saw that she was embarrassed,
he did not wish to draw away from her;
1725 he took her gently by the hand
and seated her beside him, at his right.
At his left the queen
took her seat and said to the king:
"My lord, as I think and believe,
1730 anyone should be welcome at court
who can win, by deeds of arms,
such a beautiful lady in another land.
We did well to wait for Erec;
now you can bestow the kiss
1735 upon the most beautiful damsel in the court.
I think no one will take it ill;
no one will ever say, without lying,
that this is not the most beautiful
of the maidens present here
1740 and of those in all the world."
The king replied: "This is no lie;
to this one, if no one challenges me,
shall I give the honor of the white stag."
Then he said to the knights: "My lords,
1745 what say you? How does it seem to you?
This damsel, in both body and face,
and in all that befits a maiden,
is the most gracious and the most beautiful
that may be found, it seems to me,
1750 this side of where heaven and earth meet.
I say that it is absolutely right

77

que ceste l'enor del cerf ait.
Et vos, seignor, qu'an volez dire?
Savez i vos rien contredire?
1755 Se nus i vialt metre desfanse,
s'an die or andrioit ce qu'il panse.
Je sui rois, si ne doi mantir,
ne vilenie consantir,
ne fauseté ne desmesure;
1760 reison doi garder et droiture,
qu'il apartient a leal roi
que il doit maintenir la loi,
verité et foi et justise.
Je ne voldroie an nule guise
1765 fere deslëauté ne tort,
ne plus au foible que au fort;
n'est droiz que nus de moi se plaingne,
et je ne voel pas que remaigne
la costume ne li usages   [6e]
1770 que siaut maintenir mes lignages.
De ce vos devroit il peser,
se ge vos voloie alever
autre costume et autres lois
que ne tint mes peres li rois.
1775 L'usage Pandragon, mon pere,
qui rois estoit et emperere,
voel je garder et maintenir,
que que il m'an doie avenir.
Or me dites toz voz talanz;
1780 de voir dire ne soit nus lanz
se ceste n'est de ma meison
la plus bele, et doit par reison *
le beisier del blanc cerf avoir:
la verité an voel savoir."
1785 Tuit s'escrïent a une voiz:
"Par Deu, sire, ne par sa croiz,
vos pöez bien jugier par droit
que ceste la plus bele soit:
an ceste a asez plus biauté
1790 qu'il n'a el soloil de clarté.
Beisier la pöez quitemant;
tuit l'otroions comunemant."
Qant li rois antant qu'a toz plest,
or ne leira qu'il ne la best:

1752. que *HBPVA = F] omitted C* (del blanc cerf).
1782. la plus bele, et doit *PVA (B omits* et) = *F]* ele doit bien et *C,*
et sele ne doit *H.*
1793. *Initial* Q *in C.*

78

that she should have the honor of the stag.
And you, my lords, what do you wish to say?
Have you any objection to this?
1755 If anyone wishes to oppose this,
let him now say what he thinks.
I am the king, and I must not lie
nor consent to any villainy
or falsity or excess;
1760 I must preserve reason and rightness,
for it behooves a loyal king
to maintain law,
truth, faith, and justice.
I should not wish in any way
1765 to commit disloyalty or wrong,
no more to the weak than to the strong;
it is not right that any should complain of me,
and I do not want the tradition or the custom,
which my line is wont to uphold,
1770 to fall into desuetude.
It should rightly grieve you
if I sought to impose upon you
another tradition and other laws
than those held by my father the king.
1775 I want to preserve and uphold
the tradition of my father Pendragon,
who was king and emperor,
whatever may befall me.
Now give me your opinions;
1780 let no one be slow to say in truth
whether this maiden is not the fairest
of my court, and should by right
have the kiss of the white stag:
I want to know the truth of this."
1785 All cried out with a single voice:
"In God's name, Sire, and by his cross,
you can indeed judge by right
that she is the most beautiful:
in her there is far more beauty
1790 than there is brightness in the sun.
You may freely kiss her;
we all concede it with one voice."
When the king heard that it pleased all,
he would not postpone kissing her:

<pre>
1795   vers li se torne si l'acole. *
       La pucele ne fu pas fole:
       bien volt que li rois la beisast;
       vilainne fust s'il l'an pesast.
       Beisiee l'a come cortois
1800   veant toz ses barons li rois
       et si li dist: "Ma dolce amie,
       m'amor vos doing sanz vilenie;
       sanz malvestié et sanz folage
       vos amerai de boen corage."
1805   Li rois par itele avanture
       randi l'usage et la droiture
       qu'a sa cort avoit li blans cers.
       Ici fenist li premiers vers.
           Quant li beisiers del cerf fu pris
1810   a la costume del païs,
       Erec, come cortois et frans,
       fu de son povre oste an espans:
       de ce que promis li avoit,
       covant mantir ne li voloit.
1815   Molt li tint bien son covenant,
       qu'il li anvea maintenant
       cinc somiers sejornez et gras   [6f]
       chargiez de robes et de dras,
       de boqueranz et d'escarlates,
1820   de mars d'or et d'argent an plates,
       de veir, de gris, de sebelins
       et de porpres et d'osterins.
       Quant chargié furent li somier
       de quanqu'a prodome a mestier,
1825   dis chevaliers et dis sergenz
       de sa mesniee et de ses genz
       avoec les somiers anvea,
       et si lor dist molt et pria
       que son oste li saluassent
1830   et si grant enor li portassent,
       et lui et sa fame ansimant,
       con le suen cors demainnemant;
       et quant presantez lor avroient
       les somiers que il lor menoient,
</pre>

1795-98 *HBPVAE = F1831-34*] omitted C.
1795.   li *BPVAE = F*] lui *H*. | se torne *PVA = F*] se torna *H*, se trait et *B*,
        satorne *E*.
1797.   volt *BP*] uaut *H*, vaut *V*, uelt *AE*; vost *F*. |
        beisast *HBPVE = F*] baist *A* (Ml't bien).
1798.   vilainne *HBVAE = F*] Vergoigne *P*. | s'il l'an p. *HBA = F*]
        si len p. *VE*, lempesast *P*.
1807.   avoit *B*] deuoit *CHPAE = F* (*V* omits 1805-08).
1809.   *Initial* Q *HBPVAE = F*] *No large initial,* C.

1795   he turned toward her and embraced her.
      The maiden was not foolish:
      she wished the king to kiss her;
      she would have been uncourtly had it been unpleasant to her.
      In the sight of all his barons,
1800   the king kissed her like a courtly man,
      and said to her: "My sweet friend,
      I give you my love without villainy;
      without wickedness and without folly
      I shall gladly love you."
1805   Through such an adventure did the king
      reestablish the tradition and the right
      which the white stag had at his court.
      Here ends the first movement. *
        When the kiss of the stag had been bestowed
1810   according to the tradition of the land,
      Erec, like a courtly and generous man,
      was concerned for his poor host:
      he did not want to fail to keep his word
      concerning what he had promised him.
1815   He kept his promise very well,
      for he sent him straightaway
      five packhorses, rested and well-fleshed,
      loaded with clothing and with cloth,
      with buckram and with scarlet, *
1820   with gold marks and silver bullion,
      vair and miniver and sable
      and precious Oriental fabrics. *
      When the horses were loaded
      with everything a gentleman needs,
1825   Erec sent ten knights and ten servants
      from his household and his retinue
      to accompany the horses,
      and repeatedly begged them
      to bear greetings to his host
1830   and show him the same great honor,
      and likewise to his wife,
      as they would to himself;
      and when they had presented them
      with the horses they were leading—

1835 l'or et l'argent et les besanz
et toz les riches garnemanz
qui estoient dedanz les males,
an son rëaume d'Estre Gales
amenassent a grant enor
1840 et la dame, et le seignor. *
Deus chastiax lor avoit promis,
les plus biax et les mialz asis
et ces qui mains dotoient guerre
qui fussent an tote sa terre:
1845 Montrevel l'un apeloit l'an;
l'autres avoit non Roadan.
Quant an son roiaume vandroient,
ces deus chastiax lor liverroient,
et les rantes et les justises,
1850 si com il lor avoit promises.
Cil ont bien la chose atornee *
si com Erec l'ot comandee.
L'or et l'argent et les somiers
et les robes et les deniers,
1855 dom il i ot a grant planté,
tot ont son oste presanté
li messagier en es le jor,
qui n'avoient soing de sejor.
El rëaume Erec les menerent
1860 et molt grant enor lor porterent.
El païs vindrent an trois jorz;
des chastiax lor livrent les torz,
que li rois Lac nel contredist.   [8a]
Grant joie et grant enor lor fist;
1865 por Erec son fil les ama.
Les chastiax quites lor clama
et si lor fist asseürer,
chevaliers et borjois jurer
qu'il les tanroient ausi chiers
1870 come lor seignors droituriers.
Quant ce fu fet et atorné,
li messagier sont retorné
a lor seignor Erec arriere.
Il les reçut a bele chiere;
1875 del vavasor et de sa fame,
et de son pere, et del regne, *
lor a demandees noveles;
il l'an dïent boenes et beles.

1851-52 HBPVA = F1887-88] omitted C.
1852. l'ot BPVA = F] la H.
1859. Erec les HBP = F] les an C, et el r. les V, el r. E. lenmenerent A.
1863. que li r. BPV = F] conques r. C, Ainc li r. HA.
1872. li messagier HPA (Li message BV = F)] tot maintenant C.

1835   the gold, the silver, and the bezants *
and all the rich clothes
that were in the trunks—
then to his kingdom in Estre-Gales
they should escort, with great honor,
1840   both the lady and the lord.
He had promised them two castles,
the most beautiful and the best situated
in all his land
and the ones that least feared war:
1845   one was called Montrevel;
the other was named Roadan.
When they came to his kingdom,
Erec's men would cede these two castles to them,
and the revenues and jurisdictions,
1850   just as he had promised them.
They arranged the matter
just as Erec had ordered.
The gold and the silver and the horses
and the clothes and the deniers, *
1855   of which there was a great abundance,
the messengers at once
presented to his host,
for they did not care to delay.
They led them to Erec's kingdom
1860   and showed them great honor.
They arrived there in three days;
they delivered to them the keeps of the castles,
for King Lac did not oppose it.
He joyously welcomed and greatly honored them;
1865   he loved them because of his son Erec.
He ceded the castles to them
and had both knights and burghers
engage by oath and swear
that they would hold them as dear
1870   as their rightful lords.
When this had all been arranged,
the messengers returned
to their lord Erec.
He received them warmly;
1875   he asked them for news
of the vavasor and his wife,
and of his father and of the kingdom;
they told him good and pleasing news.

Ne tarda gueres ci aprés
1880 que li termes vint, qui fu pres,
que ses noces feire devoit.
Li atandres molt li grevoit;
ne volt plus sofrir ne atandre.
Au roi an vet le congié prandre
1885 que an sa cort, ne li grevast,
ses noces feire li lessast.
Li rois le don li otrea,
et par son rëaume anvea
et rois et dus et contes querre,
1890 ces qui de lui tenoient terre,
que nul si hardi n'i eüst
qu'a la Pantecoste ne fust.
N'i a nul qui remenoir ost,
qui a la cort ne vaigne tost,
1895 des que li rois les ot mandez.
Si vos dirai, or m'antandez,
qui furent li conte et li roi.
Molt i vint a riche conroi
li cuens Branles de Colescestre,
1900 qui cent chevax mena an destre;
aprés i vint Menagormon,
qui sires estoit d'Eglimon,
et cil de la Haute Montaigne
i vint a molt riche conpaigne.
1905 De Traverain i vint li cuens
atot cent conpaignons des suens;
aprés vint li cuens Godegrains,   [8b]
qui n'an amena mie mains.
Avoec cez que m'öez nomer
1910 vint Moloas, uns riches ber,
et li sires de l'Isle Noire:
nus n'i oï onques tonoire,
ne n'i chiet foudre ne tanpeste,
ne boz ne serpanz n'i areste,
1915 ne n'i fet trop chaut ne n'iverne.
Et Greslemuef d'Estre Posterne
i amena conpaignons vint,
et Guingamars ses frere i vint:
de l'isle d'Avalons fu sire.
1920 De cestui avons oï dire
qu'il fu amis Morgant la fee,
et ce fu veritez provee.
Daviz i vint de Tintajuel,
qui onques n'ot ire ne duel.
1925 Asez i ot contes et dus,

1891. que *HBPVA = FR*] Q^i *with a bar above, C (apparently combining the usual abbreviations for both* Que *and* Qui).

84

It was not long after this
1880 that the date came which had been set
for Erec to be married.
The waiting greatly tormented him;
he did not want to suffer or wait any more.
He went to ask the king's leave
1885 for his marriage to be performed
at his court, if it did not displease him.
The king granted him the boon,
and throughout his kingdom sent for
kings and dukes and counts,
1890 those who held land from him,
that none should be so bold
as not to be there at Pentecost.
Not one dared stay behind
and not come quickly to court,
1895 as soon as the king had summoned him.
Now listen to me, and I shall tell you
who were the counts and the kings.
Count Branles of Gloucester
came with a very rich entourage,
1900 leading a hundred horses;
then came Menagormon,
who was lord of Eglimon,
and he of the High Mountain
came with a very rich company.
1905 The count of Traverain came
with a hundred of his companions;
then came count Godegrain,
who brought along no fewer.
With those you have heard me name
1910 came Moloas, a powerful baron,
and the lord of the Black Isle:
no one ever heard thunder there;
neither lightning nor tempest strikes,
nor dwells any toad or serpent,
1915 and the weather is not too hot nor is there any winter.
And Greslemuef of Estre-Posterne
brought with him twenty companions,
and his brother Guingamar came:
he was lord of the isle of Avalon.
1920 Of him we have heard tell
that he was the friend of Morgan le Fay,
and it was the proven truth.
David of Tintagel came,
who never felt anger nor sorrow.
1925 There were many counts and dukes,

mes ancore i ot des rois plus.
Garraz, uns rois de Corques fiers,
i vint a cinc cenz chevaliers
vestuz de paisle et de cendax,
1930   mantiax et chauces et blïax.
Sor un cheval de Capadoce
vint Aguiflez, li rois d'Escoce,
et amena ansanble o soi
andeus ses filz, Cadret et Quoi,
1935   deus chevaliers molt redotez.
Avoec ces que vos ai nomez
vint li rois Bans de Ganieret,
et tuit furent juesne vaslet
cil qui ansanble o lui estoient:
1940   ne barbe ne grenon n'avoient.
Molt amena gent anvoisiee;
deus cenz en ot an sa mesniee,
n'i ot nul d'ax, quiex que il fust,
qui faucon ou terçuel n'eüst,
1945   esmerillon ou esprevier,
ou riche ostor sor ou muier.
Quirions, li rois vialz d'Orcel,
n'i amena nul jovancel,
einz avoit conpaignons deus cenz,
1950   don li mains nez avoit cent anz.
Les chiés orent chenuz et blans,   *[8c]*
que vescu avoient lonc tans,
et les barbes jusqu'as ceinturs; *
ces tint molt chiers li rois Artus.
1955   Li sires des nains vint aprés,
Bilis, li rois d'Antipodés.
Cil don ge vos di si fu nains,
et fu Blïant freres germains.
De toz nains fu Bylis li mendres,
1960   et Blïanz ses freres li grendres,
ou demi pié ou plainne paume,
que nus chevaliers del rëaume.
Par richesce et par seignorie
amena an sa conpaignie
1965   Bylis deus rois qui nain estoient,
qui de lui lor terre tenoient,
Gribalo et Glodoalan;

1944. terçuel *B = F*] oisel *C*, cierceul *V*, terceal *A*
      (*H omits 1943-46; P omits 1935-68*).
1946. ou muier *VA = F*] ou gruier *C*, bien manier *B* (*omits* riche);
      HP omit.
1963. seignorie *HBVA = F*] conpaignie *C* (*P omits 1935-68*).

but there were even more kings.
Garras, a fierce king of Cork,
came with five hundred knights
clad in costly silks, *
1930 cloaks and stockings and fitted tunics. *
On a horse from Cappadocia
came Aguiflez, the king of Scotland,
and he brought along with him
both his sons, Cadret and Quoi,
1935 two greatly dreaded knights.
With those that I have named for you
came King Ban of Ganieret,
and all who were with him
were young valets:
1940 they had neither beards nor mustaches.
He brought many joyful people;
he had two hundred in his household,
and every one of them, whatever he might be,
had a falcon or a tercel, *
1945 a merlin or a sparrow-hawk,
or a goshawk, red or moulted.
Quirions, the old king of Orcel,
brought no young men along,
but rather had two hundred companions,
1950 the youngest of whom was a hundred years old.
Their heads were hoary and white,
for they had lived a long time,
and they had beards down to their waists;
King Arthur held them very dear.
1955 The lord of the dwarves came next,
Bilis, king of the Antipodes. *
He of whom I speak was indeed a dwarf,
and full brother of Blïant.
Bilis was the smallest of all the dwarves,
1960 and Blïant his brother the largest,
by half a foot or a full handbreadth,
of all the knights in the kingdom. *
To display his power and his authority
Bilis brought in his company
1965 two kings who were dwarves,
who held their land from him,
Gribalo and Glodoalan;

mervoilles les esgarda l'an.
Quant a la cort furent venu,
1970 formant i furent chier tenu;
an la cort furent come roi
enoré et servi tuit troi,
car molt estoient gentil home.
Li rois Artus, a la parsome,
1975 quant asanblé vit son barnage,
molt an fu liez an son corage.
Aprés, por la joie angraignier,
comanda cent vaslez baignier,
que toz les vialt chevaliers faire.
1980 N'i a nul qui n'ait robe vaire
de riche paisle d'Alixandre,
chascuns tel com il la volt prandre
a son voloir, a sa devise.
Tuit orent armes d'une guise
1985 et chevax corranz et delivres:
li pires valoit bien cent livres.
    Qant Erec sa fame reçut,
par son droit non nomer l'estut,
qu'altremant n'est fame esposee,
1990 se par son droit non n'est nomee.
Ancor ne savoit l'an son non,
mes ore primes le set l'on:
Enyde ot non an baptestire.
L'arcevesques de Quantorbire,
1995 qui a la cort venuz estoit,   [8d]
les beneï, si com il doit.
Quant la corz fu tote asanblee,
n'ot menestrel an la contree
qui rien seüst de nul deduit
2000 qui a la cort ne fussent tuit.
An la sale molt grant joie ot;
chascuns servi de ce qu'il sot:
cil saut, cil tunbe, cil anchante,
li uns conte, li autres chante,
2005 li uns sifle, li autres note, *
cil sert de harpe, cil de rote;
cil flaüte, cil chalemele,
cil gigue, li autres vïele;

1968. mervoilles *BVA* = *F* (me̱ruelle *H*)] a m. *CE*. |
    les esgarda *BVA* = *F*] lesgardoit *C*, les agarda *H*, les amot *E* (*P omits*).
1996. les *HBP* = *F*] la *C*, le *V*; e̱t les beneicons faisoit *A*.
2004. conte *VA* = *F*] sifle *C*, encontre *B*, contre *P*, tombe *E* (*H omits 2003-16*).
2005-06 *BPVE* = 2043-44 *F* (*A has 2006 only*)] *omitted CH*.
2005. sifle *E* = *F*] sible *BV*, tymbre *P* (*A omits 2005; C has sifle in 2004*). |
    li autres *BPV* (li autre *F*)] lautre *E* (-1).
2006. harpe *BPVA* = *F*] lars *E*. | cil *B* = *F*] et cil *PVA*, cil de la r. *E*.

88

        people looked at them with wonder.
        When they had arrived at court,
1970   they were very cordially welcomed;
        at court all three
        were honored and served like kings,
        for they were very noble men.
        At length King Arthur,
1975   when he saw his baronage assembled,
        was very happy in his heart.
        Then, to increase the joy,
        he ordered a hundred youths to bathe,
        for he wanted to make them all knights.
1980   Each one received a shimmering gown *
        of rich silk from Alexandria,
        each just as he wished to have,
        according to his desire and taste.
        They all had matching armor
1985   and swift and trim horses:
        the worst was well worth a hundred pounds.
        When Erec received his wife,
        she had to be named by her proper name,
        for otherwise a woman is not married,
1990   if she is not called by her proper name.
        People did not yet know her name,
        but now they learned it for the first time:
93   Enide was the name given her at baptism. *
        The archbishop of Canterbury,
1995   who had come to court,
        blessed them, as was fitting and proper.
        When the court was all assembled,
        there was no minstrel in the land
        who knew anything of any entertainment
2000   who was not at the court.
        In the hall there was great joy;
        each contributed what he could:
        one jumped, another tumbled, another performed magic,
        one told stories, another sang,
2005   one whistled, another played,
        this one the harp, that one the rote, *
        this one the flute, that one the reed pipe,
        the fiddle or the hurdy-gurdy;

	puceles querolent et dancent:
2010	trestuit de joie fere tancent.

puceles querolent et dancent:
2010 trestuit de joie fere tancent.
Riens n'est qui joie puisse fere
ne cuer d'ome a leesce trere,
qui as noces ne fust le jor.
Sonent tinbre, sonent tabor,
2015 muses, estives et freteles,
et buisines et chalemeles.
Que diroie de l'autre chose?
N'i ot guichet ne porte close:
les issues et les antrees
2020 furent le jor abandonees;
n'an fu tornez povres ne riches.
Li rois Artus ne fu pas chiches:
bien comanda as penetiers
et as queuz et aus botelliers
2025 qu'il livrassent a grant planté,
a chascun a sa volanté,
et pain et vin et veneison.
Nus ne demanda livreison
de rien nule, que que ce fust,
2030 qu'a sa volanté ne l'eüst.
   Molt fu granz la joie el palés,
mes tot le sorplus vos an les,
s'orroiz la joie et le delit
qui fu an la chanbre et el lit
2035 la nuit, quant asanbler se durent.
Evesque et arcevesque i furent.
A cele premiere asanblee,
la ne fu pas Enyde anblee, *
ne Brangiens an leu de li mise.
2040 La reïne s'est antremise
de l'atorner et del couchier,
car l'un et l'autre avoit molt chier.
Cers chaciez qui de soif alainne
ne desirre tant la fontainne,
2045 n'espreviers ne vient a reclain
si volantiers, quant il a fain,
que plus volantiers n'i venissent,
einçois que il s'antre tenissent.
Cele nuit ont bien restoré *
2050 ce que il ont tant demoré.
Quant vuidiee lor fu la chanbre,

[8e]

2026. a chascun a *HBPVE = F*] chascun selonc *C*, et cascun a *A*.
2031. *Initial* M *BVA = F (Initial* G, Grans, *P*)] *No large initial,* C
    (*H omits 2031-34; E omits 2031-81*).
2037. *Initial* A *in* C.
2049. bien *HVA = F*] tant *C*, ml't *BP*.
2050. ce que il *H = F*] de ce quil *CBPVA*.

90

maidens performed rounds and other dances:
2010 all outdid one another in showing their joy.
Nothing that can contribute to joy
or draw the heart of man to happiness
was absent from the wedding that day.
Tambourines and drums resounded,
2015 musettes, flutes and panpipes,
and trumpets and reed pipes.
What should I say of the rest?
No wicket nor door was closed: *
the entrances and exits
2020 were completely free that day;
neither poor man nor rich was turned away.
King Arthur was not stingy:
he ordered the bakers
and the cooks and the wine-stewards
2025 to serve in great quantity,
to each person as he wished,
bread and wine and game.
No one requested
anything, whatever it might be,
2030 without having as much as he wished.
    Great was the joy in the palace,
but I shall spare you the rest of it,
and you will hear the joy and the pleasure
that were in the bedroom and in the bed
2035 that night, when they were to unite.
Bishops and archbishops were present.
At that first union
Enide was not stolen away,
nor was Brangien put in her place.
2040 The queen took charge of
the preparations and the bedding,
for she held both of them very dear.
The hunted stag who pants from thirst
does not so yearn for the fountain,
2045 nor does the hungry sparrow-hawk
return so willingly, when called,
but yet more willingly they came there,
before they held one another.
That night they fully made up for
2050 what they had so long deferred.
When they were left alone in the room,

lor droit randent a chascun manbre.
Li oel d'esgarder se refont,
cil qui d'amor la voie font
2055 et le message au cuer anvoient,
que molt lor plest quanque il voient.
Aprés le message des ialz
vient la dolçors, qui molt valt mialz,
des beisiers qui amor atraient:
2060 andui cele dolçor essaient,
et lor cuers dedanz en aboivrent,
si qu'a grant poinne se dessoivrent.
De beisier fu li premiers jeus.
De l'amor qui est antr'ax deus
2065 fu la pucele plus hardie:
de rien ne s'est acoardie;
tot sofri, que qu'il li grevast.
Ençois qu'ele se relevast,
ot perdu le non de pucele;
2070 au matin fu dame novele.
Ce jor furent jugleor lié,
car tuit furent a gré paié.
Tot fu randu quanqu'il acrurent,
et molt bel don doné lor furent:
2075 robes de veir et d'erminetes,
de conins et de violetes,
d'escarlate grise ou de soie;
qui vost cheval, qui volt monoie,
chascuns ot don a son voloir
2080 si boen com il le dut avoir.
Ensi les noces et la corz
durerent plus de quinze jorz
a tel joie et a tel hautesce;
par seignorie et par leesce
2085 et por Erec plus enorer,   [8f]
fist li rois Artus demorer
toz les barons une quinzainne.
Quant vint a la tierce semainne,
tuit ansanble comunemant
2090 anpristrent un tornoiemant.
Mes sire Gauvains s'avança,
qui d'une part le fïança

2054. la voie font *HBPA* = *F*] ioie refont *C*, cuer refont *V* (*-1*)
          (*E omits 2031-81*).
2056. que *HP* = *F* (Car *BVA*)] mes *C*.
2061. et lor *HBPVA* = *F*] que les *C*.
2091-92 *HBPVA* = *F2129-30 follow 2094 in C.*
2092. qui d'une *HBPVA* = *F*] de lautre *C*, De lune *E*.

they paid homage to each member.
The eyes, which channel love
and send the message to the heart,
2055 renewed themselves with looking,
for whatever they saw greatly pleased them.
After the message of the eyes
came the sweetness, worth far more,
of the kisses that bring on love:
2060 they both sampled that sweetness
and refreshed their hearts within,
so that with great difficulty they drew apart.
Kissing was their first game.
The love between the two of them
2065 made the maiden more bold:
she was not afraid of anything;
she endured all, whatever the cost.
Before she arose again,
she had lost the name of maiden;
2070 in the morning she was a new lady.
That day the minstrels were happy,
for all were paid according to their liking.
All that was owed them was repaid,
and they were given beautiful gifts:
2075 clothes of vair and of ermine,
of rabbit and rich purple cloth,
fur-trimmed scarlet or silk;
whoever wanted a horse or money,
each had a gift according to his wishes,
2080 as good as he should have.
Thus the wedding celebration and the court
lasted more than two weeks
with such joy and such magnificence;
for nobility and for joy
2085 and the more to honor Erec,
King Arthur had all his barons
stay for two weeks.
When it came to the third week,
all together, in common accord,
2090 agreed to undertake a tournament. *
My lord Gawain came forward
and pledged himself for one side

antre Evroïc et Tenebroc.
Et Melis et Meliadoc
2095 l'ont fïancié d'altre partie.
A tant est la corz departie.
    Un mois aprés la Pantecoste
li tornoiz assanble et ajoste
desoz Tenebroc an la plaigne.
2100 La ot tante vermoille ansaigne
et tante bloe et tante blanche, *
et tante guinple et tante manche,
qui par amors furent donees;
tant i ot lances aportees
2105 d'azur et de sinople taintes,
d'or et d'argent en i ot maintes,
maintes en i ot d'autre afeire,
mainte bandee, et mainte veire.
Iluec vit an le jor lacier
2110 maint hiaume, de fer et d'acier,
tant vert, tant giaune, tant vermoil,
reluire contre le soloil;
tant blazon et tant hauberc blanc,
tante espee a senestre flanc,
2115 tanz boens escuz fres et noviax,
d'azur et de sinople biax,
et tant d'argent a bocles d'or;
tant boen cheval baucent et sor,
fauves et blans et noirs et bais:
2120 tuit s'antre vienent a eslais.
D'armes est toz coverz li chans.
D'anbes parz fremist toz li rans;
an l'estor lieve li escrois;
des lances est molt granz li frois.
2125 Lances brisent et escu troent,
li hauberc faussent et descloent,
seles vuident, chevalier tument,
li cheval süent et escument.
La traient les espees tuit   *[9a]*
2130 sor cez qui chieent a grant bruit;
li un corent por les foiz prendre
et li autre por l'estor randre.

2093. Evroïc *H = F*] erec *C*, euroc *B*, euruyn *P*, euroir *V*, ebroic
    (*followed by* de) *E*, .i. roi *A*. | Tenebroc *CH = F*] danebroc *BP*,
    daneboc *V*, daneloc *A*, daneborc *E*.
2094. Melis *HPV*] melic *CE*, meliz *B = F*, milis *A*.
2095. *HBVAE = F* (Le fianca *P*)] ensi fu fete lanhatie *C*.
2099. Tenebroc *H = F*] teneboc *C*; *other variants as in 2093, ex.* danebohc *A*.
2101, 2102 *HBPVAE = F2139-40*] *interverted C*.
2108. et mainte *BPVAE = F* (*H omits* et)] et tante *C*.
2125. escu *BPA = F*] escuz *C*, escus *HV*.

94

between York and Edinburgh.
And Melis and Meliadoc
2095 pledged themselves for the other side.
Then the court disbanded.
        A month after Pentecost
the tournament gathered and was engaged
in the plain below Edinburgh.
2100 There were many bright-red banners,
and many blue and many white,
and many wimples and many sleeves
given as tokens of love;
many lances were brought there,
2105 painted azure and red,
many gold and silver,
many of other colors,
many striped, and many variegated.
There that day was seen the lacing on
2110 of many a helmet, of iron or of steel,
some green, some yellow, some bright red,
gleaming in the sunlight;
many coats of arms and many white hauberks,
many swords at the left-hand side,
2115 many good shields, fresh and new,
of azure and fine red,
and silver ones with golden bosses;
many fine horses, white-stockinged and sorrel,
fawn-colored and white and black and bay:
2120 all came together at a gallop.
The field was all covered with armor.
On both sides the lines stirred noisily;
in the melee the tumult grew;
great was the shattering of lances.
2125 Lances were broken and shields were pierced,
hauberks deformed and torn apart,
saddles were emptied, knights fell,
horses sweated and foamed.
There all drew their swords
2130 above those who fell with great noise;
some ran to take the oaths *
and others to resume the melee.

Erec sist sor un cheval blanc;
toz seus s'an vint au chief del ranc
2135   por joster, se il trueve a cui.
De l'autre part, encontre lui,
point li Orguelleus de la Lande,
et sist sor un cheval d'Irlande
qui le porte de grant ravine.
2140   Sor l'escu, devant la poitrine,
le fiert Erec de tel vertu
que del destrier l'a abatu;
le chaple let et vet avant.
Et Randuraz li vient devant,
2145   filz la Vielle de Tergalo,
et fu coverz d'un cendal blo;
chevaliers ert de grant proesce.
Li uns contre l'autre s'adresce,
si s'antre donent molt granz cos
2150   sor les escuz qu'il ont as cos.
Erec, tant con hante li dure,
le trebuche a la tere dure.
An son retor a encontré
le roi de la Roge Cité,
2155   qui molt estoit vaillanz et preuz.
Les resnes tindrent par les neuz
et les escuz par les enarmes;
endui orent molt beles armes
et molt boens chevax et isniax.
2160   Sor les escuz fres et noviax
par si grant vertu s'antre fierent
qu'andeus les lances peçoierent.
Onques tex cos ne fu veüz: *
ansanble hurtent des escuz,
2165   et des armes et des chevax.
Cengles ne resnes ne peitrax
ne porent le roi retenir:
a la terre l'estut venir,
ainsi vola jus del destrier;
2170   n'i guerpi sele ne estrier,
et nes les resnes de son frain
an porte avoec lui en sa main.

2140. la *HBPA = FR*] le *CV*.
2163. Onques tex cos *HBVA = F* (O. ne fu t. c. *P*)] einz tel cop *C*. |
        fu veüz *HBPVA = F*] furent uev *[i.e. veu] C*.
2164. des escuz *HPA* (les e. *BV*)] lor escu *C*.
2169-70 *HBPVA = F2207-08] omitted C*.
2169. ainsi *HBP = F*] Isci *V*, et si *A*.
2170. n'i *H = F*] Ne *BVA*; *P*: Si g. la s. et lestrier.
2171. et nes *HBVA = F*] en .ij. *[i.e. endeus] C*, Neis *P*. |
        de son *HBPVA = F*] et le *C*.

96

Erec sat upon a white horse;
all alone he came to the head of the ranks
2135 to joust, if he could find an adversary.
On the other side, coming to meet him,
spurred the Arrogant Knight of the Heath,
seated on an Irish horse
that bore him violently forward.
2140 On his shield, in front of his chest,
Erec struck him with such force
that he knocked him down from his charger;
he left the melee and went forward.
And Randuraz came toward him,
2145 son of the Old Woman of Tergalo;
he was covered in blue silk
and was a knight of great prowess.
Each headed for the other,
and they exchanged great blows
2150 on the shields they bore at their necks.
Erec, with all the force of his lance,
knocked him onto the hard ground.
As he was returning he met
the King of the Red City,
2155 who was very valiant and bold.
They held their reins by the knots
and their shields by the straps;
they both had very fine armor
and very good, swift horses.
2160 They struck one another with such strength
on their fresh new shields
that both their lances flew to pieces.
Never had such a blow been seen:
they struck against each other with their shields,
2165 with their armor and with their horses.
Neither cinch nor reins nor breastplate *
could keep the king from falling:
he was forced to the ground,
and so he flew down from his charger;
2170 he left neither saddle nor stirrup behind,
and even the reins of his bridle
he carried off with him in his hand.

97

Tuit cil qui cele joste virent
a mervoilles s'an esbaïrent,
2175 et dïent que trop chier li coste
qui a si boen chevalier joste.
Erec ne voloit pas entandre
a cheval n'a chevalier prandre,
mes a joster et a bien feire
2180 por ce que sa proesce apeire.
Devant lui fet les rans fremir; *
sa proesce fet resbaudir
cez devers cui il se tenoit.
Chevax et chevaliers prenoit
2185 por cez de la plus desconfire.
De mon seignor Gauvain voel dire,
qui molt le feisoit bien et bel.
An l'estor abati Guincel
et prist Gaudin de la Montaingne.
2190 Chevaliers prant, chevax gaaingne:
bien le fist mes sire Gauvains.
Girflez, li filz Do, et Yvains
et Sagremors li Desreez
ces de la ont tex conreez
2195 que tresqu'es portes les anbatent;
asez an prenent et abatent.
Devant la porte del chastel
ont recomancié le cenbel
cil dedanz contre cez defors.
2200 La fu abatuz Sagremors,
uns chevaliers de molt grant pris;
toz estoit retenuz et pris,
quant Erec cort a la rescosse.
Sor un des lor sa lance estrosse;
2205 si bien le fiert soz la memele
que vuidier li covint la sele.
Puis tret l'espee, si lor passe,
les hiaumes lor anbarre et quasse:
cil s'an fuient, si li font rote,
2210 car toz li plus hardiz le dote.
Tant lor dona et cos et bous *
que Sagremor lor a rescos;
el chastel les remet batant.
Les vespres sonerent a tant.
2215 Si bien le fist Erec le jor
que li miaudres fu de l'estor,
mes molt le fist mialz l'andemain:
tant prist chevaliers de sa main
et tant i fist seles vuidier

2181. Devant *HP* = *F*] Deuers *C*. I les rans *P* (le renc *H*, le ranc *F*] lestor *C*.
2218. tant p. *HPVA* = *F*] ml't p. *C*, Que tant *B*.

All those who saw this combat
were wonderfully astounded,
2175 and said that it cost too dearly
to fight against such a fine knight.
Erec was not intent upon
winning horses or taking prisoners,
but on jousting and on doing well, *
2180 to make his prowess evident.
He made the ranks tremble before him;
his prowess excited and encouraged
those on whose side he fought.
He won horses and captured knights,
2185 the more to rout those on the other side.
I wish to speak of my lord Gawain,
who fought well and admirably.
In the melee he struck down Guincel
and captured Gaudin of the Mountain.
2190 He captured knights, he won horses:
my lord Gawain performed very well.
Girflet, son of Do, and Ywain,
and Sagremor the Unruly
took such good care of their adversaries
2195 that they drove them right up to the gates;
they captured and struck down many.
In front of the castle gate
those within renewed the combat
against those on the outside.
2200 There Sagremor, a very worthy knight,
was struck down;
he was captured and made prisoner,
when Erec ran to his rescue.
On one of his adversaries he broke his lance;
2205 he struck him so hard in the chest
that the man was forced from his saddle.
Then he drew his sword, attacked them,
and dented and broke their helmets:
they fled, making a path for him,
2210 for even the bravest feared him.
He gave them so many hits and blows
that he rescued Sagremor from them;
he quickly drove them back into the castle.
At that point vespers sounded. *
2215 Erec fought so well that day
that he was the best of the melee,
but he fought still better the next day:
he captured so many knights
and emptied so many saddles

2220 que nus ne le porroit cuidier,
se cil non qui veü l'avoient;
d'anbedeus parz trestuit disoient
qu'il avoit le tornoi veincu
par sa lance et par son escu.
2225   Or fu Erec de tel renon
qu'an ne parloit se de lui non;
nus hom n'avoit si boene grace,
qu'il sanbloit Ausalon de face,
et de la lengue Salemon,
2230 et de fierté sanbla lyon, *
et de doner et de despandre
refu il parauz Alixandre.
Au repeirier de ce tornoi,
ala Erec parler au roi:
2235 le congié li ala requerre,
qu'aler s'an voloit en sa terre,
mes molt le mercia ençois
con frans et sages et cortois,
de l'enor que feite li ot,
2240 que molt merveilleus gré li sot.
Aprés li a le congié quis *
qu'aler voloit en son païs
et sa fame an voloit mener.
Ce ne li pot li rois veher,
2245 mes, son vuel, n'en alast il mie.
Congié li done et si li prie
qu'au plus tost qu'il porra retort,
car n'avoit baron en sa cort
plus vaillant, plus hardi, plus preu,
2250 fors Gauvain, son tres chier neveu:
a celui ne se prenoit nus.
Aprés celui prisoit il plus
Erec et plus le tenoit chier
que nes un autre chevalier.
2255 Erec ne volt plus sejorner;
sa fame comande atorner,
des qu'il ot le congié del roi,
et si reçut a son conroi
seissante chevaliers de pris
2260 a chevax, a veir et a gris.
Des que son oirre ot apresté,
n'a gueires puis a cort esté.
La reïne congié demande; [9d]
les chevaliers a Deu comande.
2265 La reïne congié li done.
A tele ore con prime sone

2241. li a le c. quis *BPA* = *F* (li a c. requis *V*)] a c. de lui pris *C* (*H omits 2237-42*).

100

2220 that no one could believe it,
       except for those who had seen it; *
       on both sides everyone said
       that he had won the tournament
       with his lance and with his shield.
2225   Now such was Erec's renown
       that people talked of no one else;
       no man had such exceptional qualities,
       for he had the face of Absalom,
       and resembled Solomon in his speech,
2230 and for ferocity was like a lion,
       and in giving and spending
       he was like Alexander.
       Upon his return from this tournament,
       Erec went to speak to the king:
2235 he went to ask permission to leave,
       for he wanted to return to his own land,
       but beforehand he thanked him much,
       as one who is noble, wise, and courtly,
       for the honor he had done him,
2240 for he was extremely grateful to him.
       Then he asked him for his leave,
       for he wanted to return home
       and take his wife with him.
       The king could not refuse him this,
2245 but by his wish he would have stayed.
       He gave Erec his leave, and begged him
       to return as soon as he could,
       for he had no baron in his court
       more valiant, more bold, more gallant,
2250 apart from Gawain, his very dear nephew:
       no one could compare with him.
       After him the king most esteemed
       Erec, and held him dearer
       than any other knight.
2255 Erec wished to stay no longer;
       he ordered his wife to make ready,
       as soon as he had the king's leave,
       and he received in his entourage
       sixty worthy knights,
2260 with horses, and furs of vair and miniver.
       As soon as he had prepared his baggage,
       he scarcely stayed any longer at court.
       He asked the queen's permission to leave;
       he commended the knights to God.
2265 The queen gave him her leave.
       At the hour when prime was sounding *

departi del palés real.
Veant toz monte an son cheval,
et sa fame est aprés montee,
2270 qu'il amena de sa contree;
puis monta sa mesniee tote:
bien furent set vint an la rote,
entre sergenz et chevaliers.
Tant trespassent puiz et rochiers
2275 et forez et plains et montaingnes, *
catre jornees totes plainnes,
a Carnant vindrent a un jor,
ou li rois Lac ert a sejor
en un chastel de grant delit.
2280 Onques nus mialz seant ne vit:
de forez et de praeries,
de vingnes, de gaaigneries,
de rivieres et de vergiers,
de dames et de chevaliers,
2285 de vaslez molt preuz et heitiez,
de gentix clers bien afeitiez
qui bien despandoient lor rantes,
de puceles beles et gentes *
et de borjois bien posteïs
2290 estoit li chastiax bien asis.
Ainz qu'Erec el chastel venist,
deus messagiers avant tramist
qui l'alerent au roi conter.
Li rois fist maintenant monter,
2295 qu'il ot oïes les noveles,
clers et chevaliers et puceles,
et comande les corz soner
et les rues ancortiner
de tapiz et de dras de soie
2300 por son fil reçoivre a grant joie;
puis est il meïsmes montez.
Quatre vinz clers i ot contez,
gentix homes et enorables,
a mantiax gris orlez de sables;
2305 chevaliers i ot bien cinc cenz
sor chevax bais, sors et baucenz;
dames et borjois tant i ot   [9e]
que nus savoir conter nes pot.
Tant galoperent et corrurent
2310 qu'il s'antre virent et conurent,
li rois son fil et ses filz lui.
A pié descendent anbedui,
si s'antre beisent et salüent;

2283, 2284 *HBPA* = F2321-22] *interverted* C (*omitted* V).
2288. de puceles *HBPV* = F (et p. A)] et de dames C.

102

he left the royal palace.
In the sight of all he mounted his horse,
and his wife, whom he had brought from her land,
2270   mounted after him;
then his entire household mounted:
there were easily seven score in the company,
men-at-arms and knights all together.
They passed so many hills and rocks
2275   and forests and plains and mountains
during four full days
that one day they came to Carnant,
where King Lac was staying
in a very pleasant castle.
2280   No one ever saw one better placed:
with forests and with meadows,
with vineyards and plowed fields,
with rivers and with orchards,
with ladies and with knights,
2285   with gallant and healthy young men,
with noble and accomplished clerks
who spent their revenues well,
with beautiful and noble maidens
and with powerful burghers
2290   was the castle well provided.
Before Erec came to the castle,
he sent two messengers ahead,
who went to tell the king.
As soon as he had heard the news,
2295   the king had clerks and knights and maidens
mount upon their horses,
and he ordered the horns to be blown
and the streets to be adorned
with tapestries and silken sheets,
2300   in order to receive his son with great joy;
then he himself mounted up.
There one could count fourscore clerks,
noble and honorable men,
with fur-lined mantles trimmed with sable;
2305   there were easily five hundred knights,
on bay, sorrel, and white-stockinged horses;
there were so many ladies and burghers
that no one could count them.
They galloped and ran
2310   until they saw and recognized one another,
the king and his son.
Both dismounted,
and kissed and greeted each other;

103

de grant piece ne se remüent
2315 d'iluec ou il s'antr'encontrerent.
Li un les autres salüerent.
Li rois grant joie d'Erec fet.
A la foiee l'antrelet,
si se retorne vers Enide.
2320 D'anbedeus parz est an Melide: *
anbedeus les acole et beise;
ne set li quiex d'ax plus li pleise.
El chastel vienent maintenant.
Ancontre son avenemant
2325 sonent trestuit li saint a glais;
de jons, de mantastre et de glais
sont totes jonchiees les rues,
et par desore portendues
de cortines et de tapiz
2330 de dïapres et de samiz.
La ot molt grant joie menee;
tote la gent est aünee
por veoir lor novel seignor:
einz nus ne vit joie greignor
2335 que feisoient juesne et chenu.
Premiers sont au mostier venu;
la furent par devocion
receü a procession.
Devant l'autel del crocefis
2340 s'est Erec a orisons mis. *
Devant l'autel de Nostre Dame   [9f]
menerent dui baron sa fame. *
    Quant ele i ot s'orison fete,   [10a]
un petit s'est arriere trete;
2345 de sa destre main s'est seigniee
come fame bien anseigniee.
A tant fors del mostier s'an vont;
droit a l'ostel revenu sont:
la comença la joie granz.
2350 Le jor ot Erec mainz presanz
de chevaliers et de borjois:
de l'un un palefroi norrois,
et de l'autre une cope d'or;
cil li presante un ostor sor,
2355 cil un brachet, cil un levrier,
et li autres un esprevier,
li autres un destrier d'Espaigne,

2325. saint *PBVA* = *F*] soing *C*, sain *E* = *F1909* (*H omits 2325-30*).
2339. del *HPVA* = *FR* (dou *B*)] des *C*, de *E*.
2343. Q. ele i ot s'orison f. *BPV* = *F* (s'oreison, *F*; sa o. *E*, +*1*)] Q. enyde
ot soferande f. *C* (+*1*), Q. ele a sorison parfaite *H*, Et q. ele ot
sorison f. *A*.

104

for a long time they did not stir
2315 from the spot where they met.
       Greetings were exchanged on all sides.
       The king made much of Erec.
       At length he left him,
       and turned toward Enide.
2320 On both sides he was enraptured:
       he embraced and kissed both of them;
       he did not know which of them pleased him more.
       They soon came to the castle.
       In honor of his arrival
2325 all the bells rang out joyously;
       all the streets were strewn
       with rushes, wild mint and grasses,
       and were hung above
       with hangings and with tapestries
2330 of leafy-patterned silk and samite. *
       There much joy was shown;
       all the people were assembled
       to see their young lord: *
       no one ever saw greater joy
2335 than was displayed by young and old.
       First they went to the church;
       there they were greeted
       by a pious procession.
       Before the altar of the crucifix
2340 Erec knelt in prayer.
       Two barons led his wife
       before the altar of Our Lady.
          When she had completed her prayers,
       she drew back a bit;
2345 with her right hand she crossed herself
       like a well-bred woman.
       Then they left the church;
       they came straight back to the castle:
       there the great joy began.
2350 Erec received many presents that day
       from knights and from burghers:
       from one a Norwegian palfrey,
       and from another a golden cup;
       one gave him a red goshawk,
2355 one a pointer, one a greyhound,
       and another a sparrow-hawk,
       another a Spanish charger,

                cil un escu, cil une ansaigne,
                cil une espee et cil un hiaume.
2360   Onques nus rois an son rëaume
                ne fu plus lieemant veüz
                n'a greignor joie receüz.
                Tuit de lui servir se penerent;
                molt plus grant joie demenerent
2365   d'Enyde que de lui ne firent,
                por la grant biauté qu'an li virent
                et plus ancor por sa franchise.
                An une chanbre fu assise
                desor une coute de paile
2370   qui venue estoit de Tessaile;
                antor li avoit mainte dame. *
                Mes ausi con la clere jame
                reluist desor le bis chaillot
                et la rose sor le pavot,
2375   aussi ert Enyde plus bele
                que nule dame ne pucele
                qui fust trovee an tot le monde,
                qui le cerchast a la reonde.
                Tant fu gentix et enorable,
2380   de saiges diz et acointable,
                de bon ere et de boen atret,
                onques nus ne sot tant d'aguet
                qu'an li poïst veoir folie
                ne malvestié ne vilenie.
2385   Tant ot d'afaitemant apris
                que de totes bontez ot pris
                que nule dame doie avoir,   [10b]
                et de largesce et de savoir.
                Tuit l'amerent por sa franchise:
2390   qui li pooit feire servise
                plus s'an tenoit chiers et prisoit;
                ne nus de li ne mesdisoit,
                car nus n'an pooit rien mesdire.
                El rëaume ne an l'empire
2395   n'ot dame de si boenes mors.
                    Mes tant l'ama Erec d'amors
                que d'armes mes ne li chaloit,
                ne a tornoiemant n'aloit.
                N'avoit mes soing de tornoier:
2400   a sa fame volt dosnoier,
                si an fist s'amie et sa drue.
                En li a mise s'antendue,

2370. Tessaile *FR*] cessaile *C*, thesaile *B*, tessale *P*, tesaile *V*, tesale *A*
            (*H omits 2367-78*).
2385. ot *BVA = F*] a *C* (*H omits 2385-88*).
2396. *No large initial, C.*

106

this one a shield, that one a banner,
this one a sword and that a helmet.
2360 Never was any king more gladly welcomed
in his kingdom
nor received with greater joy.
All strove to serve him;
they made still more
2365 of Enide than they did of him,
for the great beauty they saw in her,
and even more because of her fine character.
In a chamber she was seated
upon a rich silken cushion
2370 which had come from Thessaly;
there were many ladies round her.
But just as the clear gem
shines above the gray-brown pebble
and the rose above the poppy,
2375 so was Enide more beautiful
than any other lady or maiden
that might be found in all the world,
were one to search it all around.
She was so noble and honorable,
2380 wise and gracious in her speech,
well-bred and of pleasant company,
that no one was ever able to observe
that there was in her any folly,
nor meanness nor baseness.
2385 She had so well learned the social graces
that she excelled in all the qualities
that any lady must have,
and in generosity and in good sense.
All loved her for her character:
2390 whoever could be of service to her
esteemed himself the more for it;
no one spoke ill of her,
for no one could find cause to do so.
In the kingdom or in the empire
2395 there was not another lady of such quality.
    But Erec was so in love with her
that he cared no more for arms,
nor did he go to tournaments.
He no longer cared for tourneying:
2400 he wanted to enjoy his wife's company,
and he made her his lady and his mistress.
He turned all his attention to her,

en acoler et an beisier;
ne se queroit d'el aeisier.
2405 Si conpaignon duel en avoient;
sovant entr'ax se demantoient
de ce que trop l'amoit assez.
Sovant estoit midis passez
einz que de lez li se levast.
2410 Lui estoit bel, cui qu'il pesast.
Molt petit de li s'esloignoit,
mes ainz por ce moins ne donoit
de rien nule a ses chevaliers,
armes ne robes ne deniers.
2415 Nul leu n'avoit tornoiemant
nes anveast, molt richemant
aparelliez et atornez.
Destriers lor donoit sejornez
por tornoier et por joster,
2420 que qu'il li deüssent coster.
Ce disoit trestoz li barnages
que granz diax ert et granz domages,
quant armes porter ne voloit
tex ber com il estre soloit.
2425 Tant fu blasmez de totes genz,
de chevaliers et de sergenz,
qu'Enyde l'oï antredire
que recreant aloit ses sire
d'armes et de chevalerie;
2430 molt avoit changiee sa vie.   [10c]
De ceste chose li pesa,
mes sanblant fere n'an osa,
que ses sire an mal le preïst *
asez tost, s'ele le deïst.
2435 Tant li fu la chose celee
qu'il avint une matinee,
la ou il jurent an un lit
ou orent eü maint delit:
boche a boche antre braz gisoient,
2440 come cil qui molt s'antre amoient.
Cil dormi et cele veilla;
de la parole li manbra
que disoient de son seignor
par la contree li plusor.
2445 Quant il l'an prist a sovenir,
de plorer ne se pot tenir;
tel duel en ot et tel pesance

2404. queroit *HBVA = F*] quierent *C*; Ml't pensoit de lui a. *P*.
2409. li *H = F*] lui *C*; Sovant que de son lit l. *BPVA*.
2433. le *HBPVA = F*] nel *C*.
2438. ou *HBPVA = F*] Quil *C*.

	to embracing and kissing;
	he sought no other delight.
2405	His companions were grieved thereby;
	often they lamented among themselves
	that he loved her far too much.
	Often it was past noon
	before he rose from her side.
2410	This pleased him, whoever might be grieved by it.
	He kept very close to her,
	but still for all that gave no less
	of anything to his knights,
	not of arms nor clothes nor deniers.
2415	Wherever there was a tournament
	he sent them there, most richly
	appareled and equipped.
	He gave them fresh chargers
	to tourney and to joust with,
2420	whatever they might cost him.
	All his lords said
	that it was a great shame and sorrow,
	when such a lord as he once was
	no longer wanted to bear arms.
2425	He was so blamed by everyone,
	by knights and men-at-arms alike,
	that Enide heard them say among themselves
	that her lord was becoming recreant
	about arms and knighthood;
2430	he had profoundly changed his way of life.
	This thing weighed upon her,
	but she dared not show it,
	for her lord would probably have taken it ill,
	had she mentioned it.
2435	The matter was hidden from him
	until it happened one morning,
	while they lay in the bed
	where they had many a delight:
	in each other's arms and mouth to mouth they lay,
2440	like those who are deeply in love.
	He slept and she lay awake;
	she remembered what
	many people throughout the land
	were saying about her lord.
2445	When she began to remember that,
	she could not refrain from weeping;
	she felt such pain and sorrow

qu'il li avint par mescheance
qu'ele dist lors une parole
2450 dom ele se tint puis por fole,
mes ele n'i pansoit nul mal.
Son seignor a mont et a val
comança tant a regarder;
le cors vit bel et le vis cler,
2455 et plora de si grant ravine
que, plorant, desor la peitrine
an chieent les lermes sor lui.
"Lasse," fet ele, "con mar fui! *
De mon païs que ving ça querre?
2460 Bien me doit essorbir la terre,
quant toz li miaudres chevaliers,
li plus hardiz et li plus fiers,
li plus lëax, li plus cortois
qui onques fust ne cuens ne rois,
2465 a del tot an tot relanquie
por moi tote chevalerie.
Dons l'ai ge honi tot por voir;
nel volsisse por nul avoir."
    Lors li dist: "Amis, con mar fus!" *
2470 A tant se tot, si ne dist plus.
Et cil ne dormi pas formant:
la voiz oï tot an dormant;
de la parole s'esveilla
et de ce molt se merveilla
2475 que si formant plorer la vit.   *[10d]*
Puis li a demandé et dit:
"Dites moi, dolce amie chiere,
por coi plorez an tel meniere?
De coi avez ire ne duel?
2480 Certes, je le savrai, mon vuel.
Dites le moi, ma dolce amie;
gardez nel me celez vos mie:
por qu'avez dit que mar i fui?
Por moi fu dit, non por autrui:
2485 bien ai la parole antandue."
Lors fu molt Enyde esperdue;
grant peor ot et grant esmai:
"Sire," fet ele, "je ne sai
neant de quanque vos me dites."
2490 "Dame, por coi vos escondites?
Li celers ne vos i valt rien.
Ploré avez, ce voi ge bien;
por neant ne plorez vos mie.
Et an dormant ai ge oïe

2463, 2464 HBPVA = F2501-02] *interverted* C.
2494. dormant HP = F] plorant CBVA.

110

that by mischance it happened
that she made a remark
2450 for which she later counted herself a fool,
but she meant no evil thereby.
She began to contemplate
her lord from head to foot;
she saw his handsome body and fair face,
2455 and wept so violently
that, as she wept,
her tears fell upon his chest.
"Wretch," said she, "unhappy me!
Why did I come here from my land?
2460 The earth should truly swallow me up,
since the very best of knights,
the boldest and the bravest,
the most loyal, the most courtly
that was ever count or king,
2465 has, because of me,
completely abandoned all chivalry.
Now have I truly shamed him;
I should not have wished it for anything."
        Then she said to him: "My friend, how unfortunate for you!"
2470 Then she fell silent, and said no more.
But he was not deeply asleep:
he heard her voice as he slept;
he awoke upon hearing her words,
and was greatly astonished
2475 to see her weeping so bitterly.
Then he questioned her, saying:
"Tell me, dear sweet lady,
why are you weeping in this way?
What causes you anguish or sorrow?
2480 Truly, I will find out—I insist.
Tell me, my sweet lady;
take care not to conceal it from me:
why did you say I was unfortunate?
It was said about me, not any other:
2485 I clearly heard your words."
Then Enide was quite distraught;
she felt great fear and great dismay:
"My lord," said she, "I know
nothing of what you say."
2490 "My lady, why do you dissemble?
Concealment will not avail you.
You have been weeping, I see it clearly;
you do not weep without reason.
And while I slept I heard

111

2495   la parole que vos deïstes."
"Ha! biax sire, onques ne l'oïstes,
mes je cuit bien que ce fu songes."
"Or me servez vos de mançonges.
Apertemant vos oi mantir,
2500   mes tart vandroiz au repantir
se voir ne me reconuissiez."
"Sire, quant vos si m'angoissiez,
la verité vos an dirai;
ja plus ne le vos celerai,
2505   mes je criem qu'il ne vos enuit.
Par ceste terre dïent tuit,
li blonc et li mor et li ros,
que granz domages est de vos
que voz armes antrelessiez.
2510   Vostre pris est molt abessiez:
tuit soloient dire l'autre an
qu'an tot le mont ne savoit l'an
meillor chevalier ne plus preu;
vostres parauz n'estoit nul leu.
2515   Or se vont tuit de vos gabant,
juesne et chenu, petit et grant;
recreant vos apelent tuit.
Cuidiez vos qu'il ne m'an enuit,
quant j'oi dire de vos despit?   *[10e]*
2520   Molt me poise quant l'an le dit,
et por ce m'an poise ancor plus
qu'il m'an metent le blasme sus:
blasmee an sui, ce poise moi,
et dïent tuit reison por coi,
2525   car si vos ai lacié et pris
que vos an perdez vostre pris,
ne ne querez a el antandre.
Or vos an estuet consoil prandre,
que vos puissiez ce blasme estaindre
2530   et vostre premier los ataindre,
car trop vos ai oï blasmer.
Onques nel vos osai mostrer.
Sovantes foiz, quant m'an sovient,
d'angoisse plorer me covient:
2535   si grant angoisse orainz en oi
que garde prandre ne m'an soi,
tant que je dis que mar i fustes."
"Dame," fet il, "droit an eüstes,
et cil qui m'an blasment ont droit.
2540   Apareilliez vos or androit;

2520. q. l'an le dit *B* (on le d. *V*, on le dist *P*) = *F*] q. an lan d. *C*;
Quidies uos dont quil ne manuit *H*; Ce p. moi que on len dist *A*.
This line is repeated in C.

112

2495 the words you spoke."
"Ah, fair lord, you never heard it;
rather, I do believe it was a dream."
"Now you are telling me lies.
I hear you lying openly to me;
2500 you will repent too late
if you do not recognize that I speak the truth."
"My lord, since you press me so,
I shall tell you the truth;
I shall conceal it from you no longer,
2505 but I fear it will distress you.
Throughout this land all are saying,
the blonds and the brunets and the redheads,
that it is a great shame
that you have laid aside your arms.
2510 Your renown has greatly declined:
everyone used to say, last year,
that in all the world no one knew
a better nor a more valiant knight;
your equal was nowhere to be found. *
2515 Now everyone holds you up to ridicule,
young and old, high and low;
all call you recreant.
Do you believe it does not distress me,
when I hear you spoken of with scorn?
2520 It grieves me much when they speak so,
and it grieves me even more because
they place the blame upon me:
I am blamed for it; this grieves me,
and they all say for this reason:
2525 that I have so bound and captured you
that you are losing your renown,
and wish to concern yourself with nothing else.
Now it is fitting that you consider,
so that you may put an end to this blame
2530 and regain your former glory,
for I have heard you blamed too much.
I never dared reveal this to you.
Oftentimes, when I recall it,
I have to weep with anguish:
2535 just now it caused me such anguish
that I could not restrain myself
from saying you were unfortunate."
"My lady," said he, "you were right to do so, *
and those who blame me are also right.
2540 Prepare yourself forthwith;

113

por chevauchier vos aprestez:
levez de ci, si vos vestez
de vostre robe la plus bele
et feites metre vostre sele
2545 sor vostre meillor palefroi."
Or est Enyde an grant esfroi.
Molt se lieve triste et panssive;
a li seule tance et estrive
de la folie qu'ele dist:
2550 tant grate chievre que mal gist. *
    "Ha!" fet ele, "fole malveise,
or estoie je trop a eise,
qu'il ne me failloit nule chose.
Ha! lasse, por coi fui tant ose,
2555 qui tel forssenaige osai dire?
Dex! don ne m'amoit trop mes sire?
Par foi, lasse, trop m'amoit il.
Or m'estuet aler an essil!
Mes de ce ai ge duel greignor,
2560 que ge ne verrai mon seignor,
qui tant m'amoit de grant meniere
que nule rien n'avoit tant chiere.   [10f]
Li miaudres qui onques fust nez
s'estoit si a moi atornez
2565 que d'autre rien ne li chaloit.
Nule chose ne me failloit:
molt estoie boene eüree,
mes trop m'a orguialz alevee,
quant ge ai dit si grant oltraige.
2570 An mon orguel avrai domaige,
et molt est bien droiz que je l'aie:
ne set qu'est biens qui mal n'essaie." *
Tant s'est la dame demantee
que bien et bel s'est atornee
2575 de la meillor robe qu'ele ot,
mes nule chose ne li plot;
einçois li dut molt enuier.
Puis a fet un suen escuier
par une pucele apeler,
2580 si li comande a anseler
son riche palefroi norrois:
onques meillor n'ot cuens ne rois.
Des qu'ele li ot comandé,
cil n'i a respit demandé:
2585 le palefroi veir ansela.
Et Erec un autre apela, *
si li comande a aporter
ses armes por son cors armer.
Puis s'an monta en unes loiges,
2590 et fist un tapiz de Limoiges

114

make ready to ride:
arise from here, and put on
your most beautiful dress
and have the saddle placed
2545 upon your finest palfrey."
Now Enide was sorely afraid.
She arose, very sad and pensive;
she accused and criticized herself
for her ill-advised words:
2550 the goat scratches till it cannot lie comfortably.
"Ah!" said she, "wicked fool,
I was too well off,
for I wanted for nothing.
Ah, wretch, why was I so bold
2555 as to dare speak such madness?
God! Did my lord not love me too much?
In faith, unlucky me, he did indeed.
Now I must go into exile!
But it grieves me even more
2560 that I shall no more see my lord,
who loved me so greatly
that he held nothing else so dear.
The best man who was ever born
had so devoted himself to me
2565 that he cared for nothing else.
I wanted for nothing:
I was most fortunate,
but pride raised me up too high,
since I said such an outrageous thing.
2570 I shall be punished in my pride,
and it is entirely right that I should be:
one does not recognize good fortune who has not tasted misery."
While the lady continued her lamentations
she attractively dressed herself
2575 in her best dress,
but nothing gave her any pleasure;
rather, it caused her much grief.
Then she had a maiden
call for one of her squires,
2580 and ordered him to saddle
her costly Norwegian palfrey:
neither count nor king ever had better.
As soon as she had given the order,
he obeyed without delay:
2585 he saddled the dapple-gray palfrey.
And Erec called for another squire,
and ordered him to bring
his armor, that he might put it on.
Then he went up to a gallery
2590 and had a Limoges rug

115

devant lui a la terre estandre.
Et cil corrut les armes prandre,
cui il l'ot comandé et dit,
ses aporta sor le tapit.
2595 Erec s'asist de l'autre part
sor une ymage de liepart
qui el tapiz estoit portraite.
Por armer s'atorne et afaite.
Premieremant se fist lacier
2600 unes chauces de blanc acier.
Un hauberc vest aprés tant chier
qu'an n'an puet maille detranchier.
Molt estoit riches li haubers,
que an l'androit ne an l'anvers
2605 n'ot tant de fer com une aguille: *[11a]*
n'onques n'i pot coillir reoïlle,
que toz estoit d'argent feitiz,
de menües mailles tresliz,
si ert ovrez si soutilmant,
2610 dire vos puis seüremant,
que ja nus qui vestu l'eüst
plus las ne plus doillanz n'an fust
ne que s'eüst sor sa chemise
une cote de soie mise.
2615 Li sergent et li chevalier
se prenent tuit a mervellier
por coi il se feisoit armer,
mes nus ne l'ose demander.
Quant del hauberc l'orent armé,
2620 un hiaume a cercle d'or jamé,
qui plus cler reluisoit que glace,
uns vaslez sor le chief li lace.
Puis prant l'espee, si la ceint.
Lors comanda qu'an li amaint
2625 le bai de Gascoigne anselé;
puis a un vaslet apelé:
"Vaslez," fet il, "va tost et cor
an la chanbre delez la tor
ou ma fame est; va, se li di
2630 que trop me fet demorer ci;
trop a mis a li atorner. *
Di li qu'el veigne tost monter,
que ge l'atant." Et cil i va;
apareilliee la trova,
2635 son plor et son duel demenant,
et cil li dist tot maintenant:
"Dame, por coi demorez tant?
Mes sires la hors vos atant,

2608. tresliz *E = FR*] trestiz *C*, trellis *H*, traitiz *BV*, faitis *PA*; *cf. 615.*

116

spread out before him on the floor.
And the squire to whom he had given the order
ran to get the armor
and placed it on the rug.
2595 Erec sat on the other side,
upon the image of a leopard
which was portrayed in the rug.
He prepared to arm himself.
First he had the greaves
2600 of shining steel laced on.
Next he put on such an expensive hauberk
that no link could be cut from it.
The hauberk was extremely costly,
for on the outside and on the inside
2605 there was not so much iron as in a needle:
rust could never gather there,
for it was all of fine-wrought silver
in tiny triple-woven links,
and it was so subtly worked,
2610 I can confidently tell you,
that anyone who ever wore it
would be no more tired or sore
than if he had put on
a silken tunic over his chemise. *
2615 The men-at-arms and the knights
all began to wonder
why he was putting on his armor,
but no one dared to question him.
When they had put on his hauberk,
2620 a valet laced upon his head
a helmet, with a bejeweled golden circlet,
which shone more brightly than a mirror.
Then he girded on his sword.
Next he ordered them to bring him
2625 his Gascon bay, all saddled up;
then he called to a valet:
"Valet," said he, "go, run quickly
to the chamber by the tower,
where my wife is; go, and tell her
2630 she is making me wait too long here;
she has taken too long to get dressed.
Tell her to come quickly and to mount,
that I'm waiting for her." The valet went there;
he found her ready,
2635 weeping and grieving,
and he immediately said to her:
"My lady, why do you tarry so?
My lord awaits you outside

117

de totes ses armes armez;
2640 grant piece a que il fust montez,
se vos fussiez apareilliee."
Molt s'est Enyde merveilliee
que ses sires ot an corage,
mes de ce fist ele que sage,
2645 car plus lieemant se contint
qu'ele pot, quant devant lui vint.
Devant lui vint en mi la cort,
et li rois Lac aprés li cort.
Chevalier corent qui mialz mialz: *
2650 il n'i remaint juenes ne chauz
n'aille savoir et demander
s'il an voldra nul d'ax mener;
chascuns s'an porofre et presante,
mes il lor jure et acreante
2655 qu'il n'an manra ja conpaignon,
se sa fame solemant non;
ensi dit qu'il en ira seus.
Molt an est li rois angoisseus:
"Biax filz," fet il, "que viax tu fere?
2660 Moi doiz tu dire ton afere;
ne me doiz nule rien celer.
Di moi quel part tu viax aler,
que por rien nule que te die
ne viax que an ta conpaignie
2665 escuiers ne chevaliers aille.
Se tu as anprise bataille
seul a seul contre un chevalier,
por ce ne doiz tu pas lessier
que tu n'an mainz une partie,
2670 por solaz et por conpaignie,
de tes chevaliers avoec toi:
ne doit seus aler filz de roi.
Biax filz, fai chargier tes somiers,
et mainne de tes chevaliers
2675 trante ou quarante, ou plus ancor,
si fai porter argent et or,
et quanqu'il convient a prodome."
Erec respont a la parsome,
et li conte tot, et devise
2680 comant il a sa voie anprise:
"Sire," fet il, "ne puet autre estre.
Ja n'an manrai cheval an destre;
n'ai que feire d'or ne d'argent,
ne d'escuier, ne de sergent;
2685 ne conpaignie ne demant
fors de ma fame seulemant.
Mes je vos pri, que qu'il aveigne,
se ge muir et ele reveigne,

[11b]

118

with all his armor on;
2640 he would have mounted long since,
had you been ready."
Enide wondered greatly
what her lord had in mind,
but she behaved wisely,
2645 for she acted as joyously as she could,
when she came before him.
She came before him in the middle of the courtyard,
and King Lac came running after her.
Knights came running as fast as they could:
2650 no one, young or old,
refrained from inquiring and asking
whether he wanted to take any of them along;
everyone offered his services,
but he swore and promised them
2655 that he would have no companion
apart from his wife;
he said that he would go alone. *
The king was full of anguish at this:
"Fair son," said he, "what is your purpose?
2660 You must tell me your plans;
you must conceal nothing from me.
Tell me where you want to go,
since, whatever I may say to you,
you wish no squire or knight
2665 to accompany you.
If you have undertaken to fight
in single combat against some knight,
you must not refuse for all that
to take along with you,
2670 for pleasure and companionship,
some portion of your knights:
a king's son must not travel alone.
Fair son, have your packhorses loaded,
and take along thirty or forty
2675 of your knights, or even more,
and have silver and gold brought along,
and everything befitting a gentleman."
At length Erec replied,
and told him everything and related
2680 how he had undertaken his journey:
"Sire," said he, "it cannot be otherwise.
I shall take along no spare horse;
I have no need of gold or silver,
squires or men-at-arms;
2685 I ask no company
other than my wife's.
But, whatever may happen,
if I die and she returns,

119

que vos l'amoiz et tenez chiere,
2690 por m'amor et por ma proiere,
et la mitié de vostre terre
quite, sanz bataille et sanz guerre,
li otroiez tote sa vie."
Li rois ot que ses filz li prie   [11c]
2695 et dist: "Biax filz, je li otroi.
Mes de ce que aler t'an voi
sanz conpaignie, ai molt grant duel;
ja ne le feïsses, mon vuel."
"Sire, ne puet estre autremant.
2700 Je m'an vois; a Deu vos comant.
Mes de mes conpaignons pansez:
chevax et armes lor donez
et quanqu'a chevaliers estuet."
Del plorer tenir ne se puet
2705 li rois, quant de son fil depart;
les genz replorent d'autre part.
Dames et chevalier ploroient:
por lui molt grant duel demenoient.
N'i a un seul qui duel n'an face;
2710 maint s'an pasmerent an la place.
Plorant le beisent et acolent;
a po que de duel ne s'afolent.
Ne cuit que greignor duel feïssent
se a mort navré le veïssent.
2715 Et il lor dist por reconfort:
"Seignor, por coi plorez si fort?
Je ne sui pris ne mahaigniez;
an cest duel rien ne gahaigniez.
Se je m'an vois, je revanrai
2720 quant Deu pleira et je porrai.
Toz et totes vos comant gié
a Deu, si me donez congié,
que trop me feites demorer,
et ce que je vos voi plorer
2725 me fet grant mal et grant enui."
A Deu les comande, et il lui;
departi sont a molt grant poinne.
    Erec s'an va: sa fame an moinne,
ne set ou, mes en avanture.
2730 "Alez," fet il, "grant aleüre,
et gardez ne soiez tant ose
que, se vos veez nule chose,
ne me dites ne ce ne quoi.
Tenez vos de parler a moi,
2735 se ge ne vos aresne avant.

2728. *No large initial, C; introduced by R. F places initial in previous
line (his 2765), as in HBP. No initial in either line, VEA.*

I pray you may love her and hold her dear,
2690   for love of me and because I ask it,
        and that you grant her half your land,
        freely, without battle and without strife,
        for the rest of her life."
        The king heard what his son was asking
2695   and said: "Fair son, I grant her this.
        But seeing you leave unaccompanied
        causes me great sorrow;
        you would not do so, were it up to me."
        "Sire, it cannot be otherwise.
2700   I am leaving; I commend you to God.
        But think of my companions:
        give them horses and arms
        and everything knights need."
        The king could not keep from weeping
2705   when he parted from his son;
        the other people likewise wept.
        Ladies and knights were weeping:
        they displayed great sorrow for him.
        There was no one who did not sorrow;
2710   many fainted upon the courtyard.
        Weeping they kissed and embraced him;
        their sorrow nearly made them harm themselves.
        I believe they would have shown no greater sorrow
        if they had seen him mortally wounded.
2715   And he said, to comfort them:
        "Lords, why do you weep so bitterly?
        I am neither mangled nor taken prisoner;
        you gain nothing by this sorrow.
        If I go away, I shall return
2720   when it pleases God and when I can.
        One and all I commend you
        to God; give me your leave,
        for you are making me wait too long,
        and seeing you weep
2725   causes me great sorrow and anguish."
        He commended them to God, and they did him;
        then they parted with great sorrow.
            Erec rode off, leading his wife,
        knowing not where, but seeking adventure. *
2730   "Ride rapidly," said he,
        "and take care not to be so bold,
        if you see anything,
        as to say this or that to me.
        Take care not to speak to me,
2735   if I do not speak to you first.

Alez grant aleüre avant *
et chevauchiez tot a seür."
"Sire," fet ele, "a boen eür."   [11d]
Devant s'est mise, si se tot.
2740 Li uns a l'autre ne dit mot,
mes Enyde fu molt dolante;
a li seule molt se demante
söef an bas, que il ne l'oie:
"Hé! lasse," fet ele, "a grant joie
2745 m'avoit Dex mise et essauciee;
or m'a an po d'ore abessiee!
Fortune, qui m'avoit atreite,
a tost a li sa main retreite.
De ce ne me chaussist il, lasse!
2750 s'a mon seignor parler osasse,
mes de ce sui morte et traïe,
que mes sires m'a anhaïe.
Anhaïe m'a, bien le voi,
quant il ne vialt parler a moi;
2755 ne je tant hardie ne sui
que je os regarder vers lui."
    Que qu'ele se demante ensi,
uns chevaliers del bois issi,
qui de roberie vivoit;
2760 deus conpaignons o lui avoit,
et s'estoient armé tuit troi.
Molt coveita le palefroi
qu'Enyde venoit chevalchant.
"Savez, seignor, que vos atant?"
2765 fet il a ses deus conpeignons.
"Se nos ici ne gaaignons,
honi somes et recreant
et a mervoilles mescheant.
Ci vient une dame molt bele;
2770 ne sai s'ele est dame ou pucele,
mes molt est richemant vestue.
Ses palefroiz et sa sanbue
et ses peitrax et ses lorains
valent vint mars d'argent au mains.
2775 Le palefroi voel je avoir,
et vos aiez tot l'autre avoir:
ja plus n'an quier a ma partie.
Li chevaliers n'an manra mie
de la dame, se Dex me saut!
2780 Je li cuit feire tel asaut—
ce vos di bien certeinnemant—   [11e]
qu'il conparra molt chieremant;
por ce est droiz que ge i aille

2737. *Line repeated, with spelling* chevalchiez, *as first line of 11d.*

122

Go speedily before,
and ride in complete confidence."
"My lord," said she, "as you wish."
She went before, and kept silent.
2740 Neither said a word to the other,
but Enide was very sorrowful;
to herself she greatly lamented,
but softly, so that he would not hear. *
"Oh, misery," said she, "God had raised
2745 and elevated me to great joy;
now He has so soon abased me!
Fortune, who had beckoned me,
has speedily withdrawn her hand.
I should not care about this, alas!
2750 if I dared speak to my lord,
but I am undone and betrayed,
for my lord has turned to hating me.
He hates me, I see that clearly,
since he does not wish to speak to me;
2755 and I am not so bold
that I dare to look at him."
     While she was lamenting thus,
a knight who lived by robbery
came out of the forest;
2760 he had two companions with him,
and all three of them wore armor.
He greatly coveted the palfrey
that Enide was riding.
"Do you know, my lords, what awaits you?"
2765 said he to his two companions.
"If we don't make a killing here,
we are shamed and dishonored
and incredibly unlucky.
Here comes a very beautiful lady;
2770 whether married or not I don't know,
but she is very richly dressed.
Her palfrey and her saddle,
and her breastplate and her crupper *
are worth at least twenty marks of silver.
2775 I want to have the palfrey,
and you can have all the other goods:
I seek no more for my share.
The knight will carry off nothing
of the lady's, God save me!
2780 I'm planning such an attack on him—
I tell you this quite confidently—
that it will cost him very dearly;
so it is right that I should go

123

feire la premiere bataille."
2785 Il li otroient, et cil point;
tot droit desoz l'escu se joint
et li dui remestrent an sus.
Adonc estoit costume et us
que dui chevalier a un poindre
2790 ne devoient a un seul joindre,
et, s'il l'eüssent anvaï,
vis fust qu'il l'eüssent traï.
  Enyde vit les robeors;
molt l'an est prise granz peors:
2795 "Dex!" fet ele, "que porrai dire?
Or iert ja morz ou pris mes sire,
car cil sont troi et il est seus.
N'est pas a droit partiz li jeus
d'un chevalier ancontre trois;
2800 cil le ferra ja demenois,
que mes sires ne s'an prant garde.
Dex! serai je donc si coarde
que dire ne li oserai?
Ja si coarde ne serai:
2805 jel li dirai, nel leirai pas."
Vers lui se torne en es le pas
et dist: "Biau sire, ou pansez vos?
Ci vienent poignant aprés vos *
troi chevalier qui molt vos chacent;
2810 peor ai que mal ne vos facent."
"Cui?" fet Erec, "qu'avez vos dit?
Or me prisiez vos trop petit!
Trop avez fet grant hardemant,
qui avez mon comandemant
2815 et ma desfanse trespassee.
Ceste foiz vos iert pardonee,
mes, s'autre foiz vos avenoit,
ja pardoné ne vos seroit."
Lors torne l'escu et la lance;
2820 contre le chevalier se lance:
cil le voit venir, si l'escrie.
Quant Erec l'ot, si le desfie.
Andui poignent, si s'antre vienent;
les lances esloigniees tienent,
2825 mes cil a a Erec failli,   [11f]
et Erec a lui maubailli,
que bien le sot droit anvaïr.
Sor l'escu fiert de tel aïr
que d'un chief en autre le fant,
2830 ne li haubers ne li desfant:

2785. point *HBPVA* = *F*] ioint *C*.
2790. joindre *HBP* (aioindre *V*, jondre *A*) = *F*] poindre *C*.

124

	to make the first attack."
2785	They granted him this, and he spurred his horse;
	he positioned himself beneath his shield,
	and the other two remained behind.
	At that time it was customary
	that two knights in an attack
2790	should not join against one,
	and if the others had attacked him,
	it would have been considered treachery.
	Enide saw the robbers;
	she was seized by very great fear:
2795	"Dear God!" she cried, "what can I say?
	My lord will be killed or taken prisoner,
	for they are three and he is alone.
	The game is not equal
	with one knight against three;
2800	that one is about to strike him,
	for my lord is not on his guard.
	God! shall I then be so cowardly
	that I dare not warn him?
	I shall not be so cowardly:
2805	I shall warn him, without fail."
	She immediately turned toward him
	and said: "Fair lord, where are your thoughts?
	Here come three knights spurring after you,
	hunting you, in hot pursuit;
2810	I fear they will do you harm."
	"What?" said Erec, "what did you say?
	You really have too little esteem for me!
	You have shown too great presumption
	by disobeying my orders
2815	and doing what I forbade.
	You will be forgiven this time,
	but if it happens to you again,
	you will not be forgiven."
	Then he turned his shield and lance;
2820	he rode to meet the other knight,
	who saw him coming and challenged him.
	When Erec heard him, he defied him.
	Both spurred their mounts and came together;
	they held their lances lowered,
2825	but the other missed Erec,
	whereas Erec maltreated him,
	for he was skilled in the attack.
	He struck his shield so violently
	that he split it from top to bottom,
2830	and the hauberk afforded no more protection:

125

en mi le piz le fraint et ront,
et de la lance li repont
pié et demi dedanz le cors.
Au retrere a son cop estors,
2835 et cil cheï; morir l'estut,
car li glaives el cuer li but.
Li uns des autres deus s'eslesse,
son conpaignon arrieres lesse,
vers Erec point, si le menace.
2840 Erec l'escu del col anbrace,
si le requiert come hardiz;
cil met l'escu devant le piz,
si se fierent sor les blazons.
La lance vola an tronçons
2845 au chevalier de l'autre part;
Erec de sa lance le quart
li fist par mi le cors passer.
Cist nel fera hui mes lasser:
pasmé jus del destrier l'anversse,
2850 puis point a l'autre a la traversse.
Quant cil le vit vers lui venir,
si s'an comança a foïr:
peor ot; ne l'osa atandre.
An la forest cort recet prandre,
2855 mes li foïrs rien ne li vaut.
Erec l'anchauce et crie an haut:
"Vasax, vasax, ça vos tornez!
Del desfandre vos atornez,
ou ge vos ferrai an fuiant:
2860 vostre fuie ne valt neant."
Mes cil del retorner n'a cure;
fuiant s'an vet grant aleüre.
Erec lo chace si l'ataint;
a droit le fiert sor l'escu paint
2865 si l'anversse de l'autre part.
De ces trois n'a il mes regart:
l'un en a mort, l'autre navré,
si s'est del tierz si delivré
qu'a pié l'a jus del destrier mis.   [12a]
2870 Toz les trois chevax en a pris,
ses lie par les frains ansanble.
Li uns l'autre de poil dessanble:
li premiers fu blans come leiz,
li seconz noirs, ne fu pas leiz,
2875 et li tierz fu trestoz veiriez.
A son chemin est repeiriez,
la ou Enyde l'atandoit.
Les trois chevax li comandoit

2834. An *corrected to* Au *in ms.*

in the middle of his chest he broke and ruptured it,
and he thrust a foot and a half
of his lance into his body.
As he withdrew he turned it aside,
2835 and the other fell; he could not escape death,
for the lance had drunk from his heart.
One of the other two galloped forward,
left his companion behind,
spurred toward Erec and threatened him.
2840 Erec placed his shield in position,
and boldly attacked the other,
who placed his shield before his chest,
and they struck one another on the blazons. *
The other knight's lance
2845 flew into bits;
Erec made the fourth of his lance
pass through the other's body.
That one will trouble him no more today:
Erec knocked him unconscious from his charger,
2850 then spurred obliquely toward the other.
When that one saw him coming toward him,
he began to flee:
he was afraid; he dared not wait for him.
Into the forest he ran to seek refuge,
2855 but fleeing was to no avail.
Erec pursued him and cried aloud:
"Varlet, varlet, come back this way!
Prepare to defend yourself,
or I shall strike you as you flee:
2860 your flight avails you naught!"
But the other had no wish to turn back;
he went on fleeing at a great pace.
Erec pursued and caught up with him;
he struck him full on his painted shield
2865 and knocked him off on the other side.
Erec need fear these three no more:
one he had killed, another wounded,
and so taken care of the third
that he had brought him down on foot.
2870 He took all three horses,
and tied them together by the reins.
Each had a different coat from the others:
the first was white as milk,
the second black, not bad looking,
2875 and the third was all dappled.
Erec came back to the road,
where Enide was waiting for him.
He ordered her to drive

        devant li mener et chacier,
2880   et molt la prist a menacier
        qu'ele ne soit plus si hardie
        c'un seul mot de la boche die,
        se il ne l'an done congié.
        Ele respont: "Nel ferai gié
2885   ja mes, biax sire, se vos plest."
        Lors s'an vont, et ele se test.
            N'orent pas une liue alee,
        qant devant, en une valee,
        lor vindrent cinc chevalier autre,
2890   chascuns la lance sor le fautre,
        les escuz as cos anbraciez
        et les hiaumes bruniz laciez:
        roberie querant aloient.
        A tant la dame venir voient,
2895   qui les trois chevax amenoit,
        et Erec qui aprés venoit.
        Tot maintenant que il les virent,
        par parole antr'ax departirent
        trestot le hernois autresi
2900   con s'il an fussent ja garni.
        Male chose a en covoitise, *
        mes ne fu pas a lor devise
        que bien i fu mise desfansse.
        Assez remaint de ce qu'an pansse, *
2905   et tex cuide prandre qui faut:
        si firent il a cel assaut.
        Ce dist li uns que il avroit
        la dame ou il toz an morroit,
        et li autres dist que suens iert
2910   li destriers veirs, que plus n'an quiert
        de trestot le gaaing avoir.
        Li tierz dist qu'il avroit le noir.
        "Et je le blanc!" ce dist li quarz.   [12b]
        Li quinz ne fu mie coarz,
2915   qu'il dist qu'il avroit le destrier
        et les armes au chevalier:
        seul a seul les voloit conquerre,
        et si l'iroit premiers requerre,
        se il le congié l'an donoient.
2920   Et cil volantiers li otroient.
        Lors se part d'ax et vient avant;
        cheval ot boen et bien movant.
        Erec le vit et sanblant fist
        qu'ancor garde ne s'an preïst.
2925   Quant Enyde les a veüz,

2908. morrroit C.
2925. a HBPVE = F] ot C; les apercut A.

                    128

the three horses in front of her,
2880 and he began to threaten her,
so that she should not again be so bold
as to let a single word escape her lips,
unless he gave her leave to do so.
She replied: "I shall never do it again,
2885 fair lord, since that is your pleasure."
Then they rode on, and she kept silent.
　　They had not gone one league
when, before them, in a valley,
five other knights came toward them,
2890 each with his lance in its rest,
shield on his arm, held to his neck,
and burnished helmet laced on:
they were going in search of robbery.
At that point they saw the lady coming
2895 leading the three horses,
and Erec who was following her.
Just as soon as they saw them,
they divided among themselves, in words,
every bit of their equipment,
2900 just as if they were already in possession of it.
Covetousness is a bad thing,
and it was not to their liking
that a good defense was made against it.
A bird in the hand is worth two in the bush,
2905 and he who thinks to grasp may miss:
so did they in this attack.
One said that he would have
the lady or die in the attempt,
and another said the dappled charger
2910 would be his, that he sought to have
no more of all the booty.
The third said he would have the black.
"And I the white!" said the fourth.
The fifth was no coward,
2915 for he said he would have the knight's
charger and his armor:
he wanted to win them in single combat,
and so he would go attack him first,
if they would give him leave to do so.
2920 And they readily granted him this.
Then he left them and went forward;
he had a good, smooth-gaited horse.
Erec saw him and pretended
he was not yet on his guard.
2925 When Enide saw them,

129

toz li sans li est esmeüz;
grant peor ot et grant esmai:
"Lasse," fet ele, "que ferai?
2930 Ne sai que die ne que face,
que mes sires molt me menace
et dit qu'il me fera enui,
se je de rien paroil a lui.
Mes se mes sires ert ci morz,
de moi ne seroit nus conforz:
2935 morte seroie et mal baillie.
Dex! mes sire ne le voit mie;
qu'atant je dons, malveise fole?
Trop ai or chiere ma parole,
quant je ne li ai dit pieç'a.
2940 Bien sai que cil qui vienent ça
sont de mal faire ancoragié.
Ha! Dex, comant li dirai gié?
Il m'ocirra. Asez m'ocie!
Ne leirai que je ne li die."
2945 Lors l'apele dolcemant: "Sire!"
"Cui?" fet il, "que volez vos dire?"
"Sire, merci! Dire vos vuel
que desbunchié sont de ce bruel
cinc chevalier, don je m'esmai;
2950 bien pans et aparceü ai
qu'il se voelent a vos conbatre.
Arrieres sont remés li quatre,
et li cinquiesmes a vos muet
tant con chevax porter le puet:
2955 ne gart l'ore que il vos fiere.
Li catre sont remés arriere,
mes ne sont gaires de ci loing: *[12c]*
tuit le secorront au besoing."
Erec respont: "Mar le pansastes,
2960 que ma parole trespassastes,
ce que desfandu vos avoie!
Et ne por quant tres bien savoie
que gueres ne me priseiez.
Cest servise mal anpleiez,
2965 que ge ne vos an sai nul gré;
bien sachiez que ge vos an hé;
dit le vos ai et di ancore.
Ancor le vos pardonrai ore,
mes autre foiz vos an gardez,
2970 ne ja vers moi ne regardez,
que vos ferïez molt que fole,
car je n'aim pas vostre parole."
Lors point Erec contre celui,
si s'antre vienent amedui:
2975 l'uns anvaïst l'autre et requiert.

130

her blood raced in her veins;
she felt great fear and great dismay:
"Alas," said she, "what shall I do?
I know not what to say or do,
2930 since my lord threatens me so
and says that he will punish me
if I speak to him of anything.
But if my lord were killed here,
nothing could comfort me:
2935 I would be dead and done for.
God! My lord does not see him;
what am I waiting for, wicked fool?
Now I value my words too highly,
since I have delayed speaking so long.
2940 I know full well that those who are coming
are bent on doing ill.
Oh, God, how will I tell him?
He'll kill me. All right, let him!
I shall tell him nevertheless."
2945 Then she called softly to him: "My lord!"
"What?" said he, "what do you want?"
"My lord, pity! I want to tell you
that five knights have broken cover
from that thicket, and I am very worried;
2950 I have seen them, and I very much think
that they want to fight with you.
Four of them have remained behind,
and the fifth is coming toward you
as fast as his horse can carry him:
2955 I fear that he may strike you at any moment.
The other four have remained behind,
but they are scarcely far from here:
they will all help him, if need be."
Erec replied: "Woe to you, that you
2960 decided to disobey my orders,
and do what I forbade you to!
And yet I knew very well
that you had little esteem for me.
You make bad use of this kindness,
2965 for I am in no way grateful to you;
be assured that I hate you for it;
I have told you this and I tell you again.
I shall forgive you again this time,
but take care another time,
2970 and do not look in my direction,
for you would behave very foolishly,
since I do not like your words."
Then Erec spurred toward the other knight,
and they both came together:
2975 each of them attacked the other.

Erec si duremant le fiert
que li escuz del col li vole,
et si li brise la chanole.
Li estrié ronpent et cil chiet:
2980 n'a peor que il s'an reliet,
que molt s'est quassez et bleciez.
Uns des autres s'est adreciez,
si s'antre vienent de randon.
Erec li met tot a bandon
2985 desoz le manton an la gorge
le fer tranchant de boene forge;
toz tranche les os et les ners,
que d'autre part an saut li fers.
Li sans vermauz toz chauz an raie
2990 d'anbedeus parz par mi la plaie:
l'ame s'an va; li cuers li faut.
Et li tierz de son agait saut,
qui d'autre part d'un gué estoit;
par mi le gué s'an vint tot droit.
2995 Erec point, si l'a ancontré
ainz qu'il par fust issuz del gué;
si bien le fiert que il abat
et lui et le destrier tot plat.
Li destriers sor le cors li jut
3000 tant qu'an l'eve morir l'estut,
et li chevax tant s'esforça
qu'a quelque poinne se dreça.
Ensi en a les trois conquis.
Li autre dui ont consoil pris
3005 que la place li guerpiront,
ne ja a lui ne chanpiront:
fuiant s'an vont par la riviere.
Erec les anchauce derriere,
si an fiert un derriers l'eschine
3010 que sor l'arçon devant l'ancline.
Trestote sa force i a mise:
sa lance sor le dos li brise,
et cil cheï le col avant.
Erec molt chieremant li vant
3015 sa lance, que sor lui a fraite;
del fuerre a tost l'espee traite.
Cil releva, si fist que fos:
Erec li dona tex trois cos
qu'el sanc li fist l'espee boivre;
3020 l'espaule del bu li dessoivre,
si qu'a la terre jus cheï.
A l'espee l'autre anvaï,
qui molt isnelemant s'an fuit
sanz conpaignie et sanz conduit.

Erec struck him with such force
that he tore the shield from the other's neck
and ruptured his windpipe.
The stirrups broke and he fell:
2980 there was no fear he would get up again,
for he was badly broken and wounded.
One of the others headed his way,
and they came violently together.
Without restraint Erec thrust
2985 the keen-edged iron, finely made,
into his throat beneath his chin;
he sliced through all the bones and nerves,
and the iron burst out the other side.
The bright-red blood flowed hotly forth
2990 from both sides of the wound:
his soul left him; his heart failed.
And the third, who was on the other side of a ford,
sprang from his hiding-place;
he came straight through the ford.
2995 Erec spurred forward, and met him
before he had completely cleared the ford;
he struck him so hard that he knocked
both him and his charger completely flat.
The charger lay upon his body
3000 until he was drowned in the water,
and the horse struggled until,
with difficulty, it stood up again.
Thus had Erec defeated three of them.
The other two decided
3005 that they would leave him the field,
and would never fight with him:
they went off, fleeing, along the river.
Erec went chasing after them,
and so struck one in the back
3010 that he bent him over the front saddlebow.
He had put all his strength into it:
he broke his lance upon his back,
and the other fell forward.
Erec made him pay dearly
3015 for the lance he broke upon him;
he quickly drew his sword from its scabbard.
The other got up, but that was foolish:
Erec gave him three such blows
that he made his sword drink his blood;
3020 he severed the shoulder from the trunk,
so that it fell to the ground.
With his sword he attacked the other one,
who was fleeing very speedily,
alone, with no one to escort him.

133

3025 Quant cil voit que Erec le chace, *
tel peor a ne set que face:
n'ose atandre et ganchir ne puet.
Le cheval guerpir li estuet,
qu'il n'i a mes nule fïance;
3030 l'escu giete jus et la lance,
si se lesse cheoir a terre.
Erec ne le volt plus requerre,
qu'a terre cheoir se leissa,
mes a la lance s'abeissa:
3035 cele n'i a mie leissiee,
por la soe qu'il a brisiee.
La lance an porte, si s'an vet,
et les chevax mie ne let;
toz les cinc prant, si les an mainne.
3040 Del mener est Enyde an painne:
les cinc avoec les trois li baille,
si li comande que tost aille
et de parler a lui se taigne,
que max ou enuiz ne l'an vaigne.
3045 Mes ele mot ne li respont,
einçois se tot; et il s'an vont:
les chevax an mainnent toz huit.   *[12e]*
    Chevauchié ont jusqu'a la nuit,
ne vile ne recet ne virent.
3050 A l'anuitier lor ostel prirent
desoz un arbre an une lande.
Erec a la dame comande
qu'ele dorme, et il veillera;
ele respont que nel fera,
3055 car n'est droiz, ne feire nel viaut:
il dormira, qui plus se diaut.
Erec l'otroie, et bel li fu.
A son chief a mis son escu,
et la dame son mantel prant,
3060 sor lui de chief an chief l'estant.
Cil dormi, et cele veilla;
onques la nuit ne someilla:
chascun cheval tint an sa main
tote nuit jusqu'a l'andemain,
3065 et molt s'est blasmee et maudite
de la parole qu'ele ot dite,
et dist que mal a esploitié, *

3025-26. *HVA = F3063-64] omitted CBP.*
3025. *Initial, HVA.* cil *HA]* il *V;* que Erec le chace *H]* .e. qui len cache *V,* lencauce *A.*
3034. *C has* terre *lined through, followed immediately by* lance.
3048. *No initial, CHPBVA; introduced by R.*
3067. et dist que mal a *HBPVAE = F]* ml't a ce dit mal *C.*

134

3025 When he saw Erec pursuing him,
he was so afraid he knew not what to do:
he dared not tarry and he could not escape.
He had to abandon his horse,
for he had no more hope in it.
3030 He threw down his shield and lance,
and let himself fall to the ground.
Erec did not wish to continue his attack,
since he had let himself fall to the ground,
but he stooped to take the lance:
3035 that he did not leave behind,
since he had broken his own.
He carried off the lance and went away,
and he did not leave the horses behind:
he took all five of them, and led them off.
3040 It was difficult for Enide to manage them:
he gave her the five to go with the three,
and ordered her to ride quickly
and to refrain from speaking to him,
lest evil or trouble come to her.
3045 She spoke not a word in reply,
but rather kept silent; they went on their way,
taking along all eight horses.
    They rode until night,
and saw no town nor dwelling.
3050 At nightfall they took their lodging
in a field, beneath a tree.
Erec ordered his lady
to sleep, and he would keep watch;
she replied that she would not sleep,
3055 that it was not right, nor did she wish it:
he could sleep, since he was suffering more.
Erec granted this, and it pleased him.
At his head he placed his shield,
and the lady took her cloak
3060 and spread it over him from head to foot.
He slept, and she kept watch;
never did she sleep that night:
she held the horses in her hand
all night until the next day,
3065 and she bitterly blamed and cursed herself
for the remark she had made,
and said she had acted badly,

ne n'a mie de la mité
tant mal com ele a desservi.
3070 "Lasse," fet ele, "si mar vi
mon orguel et ma sorcuidance!
Savoir pooie sanz dotance
que tel chevalier ne meillor
ne savoit l'an de mon seignor.
3075 Bien le savoie; or le sai mialz,
car ge l'ai veü a mes ialz
que trois ne cinc armez ne dote.
Honie soit ma leingue tote,
qui l'orguel et l'outrage dist *
3080 dont mes cors a tel honte gist."
Ensi s'est la nuit demantee
tresque le main a l'anjornee.
Erec se lieve par matin,
si se remetent au chemin,
3085 ele devant et il derriers.
Androit midi uns escuiers
lor vint devant an un valet;
o lui venoient dui vaslet
qui portoient gastiaus et vin *
3090 et cinc fromages de gaïn
as prez le conte Galoain
a ces qui fauchoient son fain.
Li escuiers sot de voidie: [12f]
quant il vit Erec et s'amie
3095 qui de vers la forest venoient,
bien aparçut que il avoient
la nuit an la forest geü;
n'avoient mangié ne beü,
c'une jornee tot an tor *
3100 n'avoit chastel, vile ne tor,
ne meison fort ne abaïe,
ospital ne herbergerie.
Puis s'apansa de grant franchise:
ancontre ax a sa voie anprise,
3105 si les salue come frans
et dist: "Sire, je crois et pans

3068. ne n'a *HBPVE = F* (nenna *A*)] que nai *C.*
3069. tant mal *HP = F*] le m. *CV*, de m. *A*, t. de m. *B, E (+1).* |
        com ele a *HPE = F* (quele [= qu'ele] a *B*, que ele a *VA*)] que ie ai *C.*
3077. que *HBPVAE = F*] car *C.*
3079. l'outrage *HBPVAE = F*] la honte *C.*
3084. remetent au *HBPVAE = F*] remet an son *C. Cf. 3481.*
3089. gastiaus *HBPVAE = F*] et pain *C.*
3091-92. *HBPVAE = F3129-30*] omitted *C, interverted H.*
3092. fauchoient son *HV = F*] fenoient le *BPAE.*
3099. c'une *B* (Qu'une *H = F*)] A une *C (+1)*; Dune *PVAE. Initial* A *in C.*

136

and had not by half
as much misfortune as she deserved.
3070 "Alas," said she, "how I rue
my pride and my effrontery!
I could be absolutely sure
that there was not such a knight
as my lord nor a better one.
3075 I knew this full well; now I know it better,
for I have seen with my own eyes
that he fears neither three nor five armed men.
May my tongue be completely disgraced,
which spoke the prideful and outrageous things
3080 for which I now lie in such shame."
Thus she lamented all night
until daybreak the following morning.
Erec arose early
and they went on their way again,
3085 she in front and he behind.
Just at noon a squire
came before them in a vale;
two servants were with him,
carrying cakes and wine
3090 and five rich cheeses *
to the meadows of Count Galoain,
to the people cutting his hay.
The squire was clever and quick-witted:
when he saw Erec and his lady
3095 coming from the direction of the forest,
he clearly saw that they had
lain there that night;
they had neither eaten nor drunk,
since for a day's ride in any direction
3100 there was no castle, town, nor tower,
nor fortified manor nor abbey,
nor hospice nor inn.
Then he had a very generous thought:
he set out to meet them,
3105 and greeted them courteously
and said: "My lord, I think and believe

qu'enuit avez molt traveillié,
et cele dame molt veillié
et geü an ceste forest.
3110 De cest blanc gastel vos revest,
s'il vos plest un po a mangier.
Nel di pas por vos losangier,
ne rien nule ne vos demant.
Li gastiax est de boen fromant;
3115 boen vin ai et fromage gras,
blanche toaille et biax henas:
s'il vos plest a desgeüner,
ne vos covient aillors torner.
An ces onbres, desoz ces charmes,
3120 vos desarmeroiz de voz armes,
si vos reposeroiz un po.
Descendez, car ge le vos lo."
Erec a pié a terre mis,
si li respont: "Biax dolz amis,
3125 je mangerai, vostre merci;
ne quier aler avant de ci."
Li sergenz fu de bel servise:
la dame a jus del cheval mise,
et li vaslet les chevax tindrent,
3130 qui ansanble l'escuier vindrent.
Puis se vont aseoir an l'onbre.
Li escuiers Erec desconbre
de son hiaume, et si li deslace
la vantaille devant la face.
3135 Puis a devant ax estandue
la toaille sor l'erbe drue;   *[13a]*
le gastel et le vin lor baille;
un fromage lor pere et taille.
Cil mangierent qui fain avoient,
3140 et del vin volantiers bevoient;
li escuiers devant ax sert,
qui son servise pas ne pert.
Quant mangié orent et beü,
Erec cortois et larges fu:
3145 "Amis," fet il, "an guerredon
vos faz d'un de mes chevax don:
prenez celui qui mialz vos siet!
Et si vos pri qu'il ne vos griet:
arriers el chastel retornez;
3150 un riche ostel m'i atornez."
Et il respont que il fera
volantiers quanque lui pleira;

3107. qu'enuit *BA* = *F* (canuit *V*)] Que enuit *C* (+*1*); Que uos aues *H*,
     Que vos soies *P*.
3113, 3114 *HBPVA* = *F3151-52*] *interverted C.*

you have had little comfort this night,
and this lady has long kept watch
and lain in this forest.
3110 I present you with this white cake,
if you wish to eat a little.
I do not say it to flatter you,
nor do I ask anything of you.
The cake is made of good wheat;
3115 I have good wine and rich cheese,
white cloth and fine goblets:
if you wish to eat,
you need turn nowhere else.
In the shade here, beneath these hornbeams, *
3120 you may remove your armor,
and you may rest a little.
Dismount, for I advise it."
Erec stepped down to the ground,
and replied: "Fair gentle friend,
3125 I shall eat, thanks to you;
I have no wish to go further."
The squire was skilled in serving:
he helped the lady to dismount,
and the servants who had come with him
3130 held the horses.
Then they went to sit in the shade.
The squire helped Erec remove
his helmet, and unlaced
the ventail before his face.
3135 Then he spread the cloth out
in front of them on the thick grass;
he gave them the cake and the wine;
he prepared and cut a cheese for them.
They who were hungry ate,
3140 and readily drank wine;
the squire served them,
and his service was not wasted.
When they had eaten and drunk,
Erec was courtly and generous:
3145 "Friend," said he, "as a reward
I make you a gift of one of my horses:
take the one that suits you best!
And I pray it may not displease you
to return to the town;
3150 prepare rich lodgings there for me."
The squire replied that he would gladly
do whatever pleased him;

puis vint as chevax, ses deslie,
le noir a pris si l'an mercie,

3155   car cil li sanble miaudres estre.
Sus monte par l'estrié senestre;
andeus les a iluec leissiez:
el chastel vint toz esleissiez,
ostel a pris bien atorné.

3160   ez le vos arriers retorné.
"Or tost, sire," fet il, "montez,
que boen ostel et bel avez."
Erec monte, la dame aprés.
Li chastiax estoit auques pres:

3165   tost furent a l'ostel venu.
A joie furent receü:
li ostes molt bel les reçut,
et tot quanque il lor estut
fist atorner a grant planté,

3170   liez et de boene volanté.
Quant li escuiers fet lor ot
tant d'enor con feire lor pot,
a son cheval vient, si remonte.
Par devant les loiges le conte

3175   menoit a ostel son cheval.
Li cuens et troi autre vasal
s'i erent venu apoier;
quant li cuens vit son escuier,
qui sor le noir destrier seoit,

3180   demanda li cui il estoit,
et cil respont que il est suens.   *[13b]*
Molt s'an est merveilliez li cuens:
"Comant?" fet il, "ou l'as tu pris?"
"Uns chevaliers, cui ge molt pris,

3185   sire," fet il, "le m'a doné.
An cest chastel l'ai amené,
s'est a ostel chiés un borjois.
Li chevaliers est molt cortois;
tant bel home onques mes ne vi:

3190   se juré l'avoie et plevi,
ne vos reconteroie mie
sa biauté tote ne demie."
Li cuens respont: "Je pans et croi
qu'il n'est mie plus biax de moi."

3195   "Par foi, sire," fet li sergenz,
"vos estes assez biax et genz;
n'a chevalier an cest païs,
qui de la terre soit naïs,
que plus biax ne soiez de lui,

3172. enor *H* = *F* (onor *PV*, honor *AE*)] amor *C*; Tout le bien que *B*.
3179. seoit *HBE* = *F*] estoit *CA*, uenoit *PV*.

then he went to the horses and untied them,
took the black one and thanked him for it,
3155 for it seemed to him to be the best.
He mounted by the left stirrup;
he left them both there:
he went full speed to the town,
took well-prepared lodgings for them,
3160 and there he was, back again.
"Now, quickly, my lord," said he, "mount up,
for you have good and attractive lodgings."
Erec mounted, with the lady after him.
The town was fairly near by:
3165 they had soon reached their lodgings.
They were joyfully received:
the host gave them a fine welcome,
and everything they needed
he had prepared for them in great plenty,
3170 joyfully and willingly.
When the squire had shown them
all the honor he could,
he went back to his horse, and remounted.
In front of the count's galleries
3175 he led his horse to the stable.
The count and three other vassals
had come there to take their ease;
when the count saw his squire
seated on the black charger,
3180 he asked him whose it was,
and he replied that it was his.
The count was greatly astonished at this:
"What?" said he, "where did you get it?"
"A knight whom I highly esteem,
3185 sire," said he, "gave it to me.
I brought him into this town,
and he is lodging with a burgher.
The knight is very courtly;
I never saw such a handsome man:
3190 even if I had sworn and pledged,
I could not describe to you
his beauty, neither in full nor halfway."
The count replied: "I think and believe
that he is not more handsome than I."
3195 "Upon my word, sire," said the squire,
"you are very handsome and fine;
there is no knight in this land
born of the earth
who is better looking than you,

3200	mes bien os dire de cestui
	qu'il est plus biax de vos assez,
	se del hauberc ne fust lassez
	et quamoissiez et debatuz.
	An la forest s'est conbatuz
3205	toz seus contre huit chevaliers,
	s'an amainne toz les destriers.
	Et avoec lui mainne une dame
	tant bele c'onques nule fame
	la mitié de sa biauté n'ot."
3210	Quant li cuens cele novele ot,
	talanz li prist que veoir aille
	se ce est veritez ou faille.
	"Onques mes," fet il, "n'oï tel.
	Mainne moi dons a son ostel,
3215	que certeinnemant vuel savoir
	se tu me diz mançonge ou voir."
	Cil respont: "Sire, volantiers.
	Ci est la voie et li santiers,
	et jusque la n'a pas grant voie."
3220	"Et molt m'est tart que je les voie,"
	fet li cuens, et lors vint a val.
	Et cil descent de son cheval,
	si a fet le conte monter;
	devant corrut Erec conter
3225	que li cuens veoir le venoit.
	Erec molt riche ostel tenoit,
	que bien an ert acostumez:
	molt i ot cierges alumez
	et chandoiles espessemant.
3230	A trois conpaignons seulemant
	vint li cuens, qu'il n'amenoit plus.
	Erec contre lui leva sus,
	qui molt estoit bien afeitiez,
	si li dist: "Sire, bien vaigniez!"
3235	Et li cuens resalua lui.
	Acointié se sont anbedui
	sor une coute blanche et mole;
	s'antre acointierent de parole.
	Li cuens li porofre et presante
3240	et prie que il li consante
	que de lui ses gaiges repraigne.
	Mes Erec baillier ne li daigne,
	einz dit qu'asez a a despandre;
	n'a mestier de son avoir prandre.
3245	Molt parolent de plusor chose, *
	mes li cuens onques ne repose
	de regarder de l'autre part.

[13c]

3205. contre *BPE*] ancontre *CHV* = *FR* (*+1*), *A* (*omits* huit).

3200   but I dare say of this one
      that he is far handsomer than you,
      save that he is wearied from his hauberk,
      and battered and bruised.
      In the forest he did battle
3205   all alone, against eight knights,
      and has brought back all their chargers.
      And he brings a lady with him,
      so beautiful that no woman ever
      had the half of her beauty."
3210   When the count heard this news,
      he wished to go and see
      whether this was truth or falsehood.
      "Never," said he, "have I heard the like.
      Take me to his lodgings,
3215   for I wish to know for certain
      whether you are telling me falsehood or truth."
      He replied: "Sire, gladly.
      Here is the way and the path,
      and it is not very far away."
3220   "I am impatient to see them,"
      said the count, and then he got down.
      The squire dismounted,
      and had the count mount in his place;
      he ran ahead to tell Erec
3225   that the count was coming to see him.
      Erec had very rich lodgings,
      for that was what he was accustomed to:
      there were many lighted candles,
      both wax and tallow, in profusion.
3230   With just three companions
      came the count, for he brought no more.
      Erec rose to greet him,
      for he was very well-bred,
      and he said: "My lord, welcome!"
3235   And the count greeted him in turn.
      They joined one another
      on a soft white pad;
      they became acquainted.
      The count offered and proposed
3240   and begged him to consent
      to allow him to pay his expenses.
      But Erec did not deign to do so,
      saying that he had plenty to spend;
      he had no need to take his wealth.
3245   They spoke at length of numerous things,
      but the count never stopped
      looking in the other direction.

De la dame s'est pris esgart:
por la biauté qu'an li estoit
3250 tot son pansé an li avoit.
Tant l'esgarda com il plus pot;
tant la covi et tant li plot
que sa biautez d'amors l'esprist.
De parler a li congié prist
3255 a Erec, molt covertemant:
"Sire," fet il, "je vos demant
congié, mes qu'il ne vos enuit:
par corteisie et par deduit
voel lez cele dame seoir.
3260 Por bien vos ving andeus veoir,
ne vos n'i devez mal noter:
a la dame voel presanter
mon servise sor tote rien.
Tot son pleisir, ce sachiez bien,
3265 feroie por amor de vos." *
Erec ne fu mie jalous,
que il n'i pansa nule boise.
"Sire," fet il, "pas ne me poise;
joer et parler vos i loist.   [13d]
3270 Ne cuidiez pas que il m'an poist;
volantiers congié vos an doing."
La dame seoit de lui loing
tant con deus lances ont de lonc,
et li cuens s'est assis selonc
3275 delez li sor un bas eschame.
Devers lui se torna la dame,
qui molt estoit saige et cortoise.
"Ha!" fet li cuens, "com il me poise
quant vos alez an tel viltance!
3280 Grant duel en ai et grant pesance.
Mes se croire me volïez,
enor et preu i avrïez
et molt granz biens vos an vandroit.
A vostre biauté covandroit
3285 grant enor et grant seignorie.
Je feroie de vos m'amie,
s'il vos pleisoit et boen vos iere;
vos serïez m'amie chiere
et dame de tote ma terre.
3290 Quant je vos daing d'amors requerre,
ne me devez pas escondire.
Bien voi et sai que vostre sire
ne vos ainme ne ne vos prise;

144

He had noticed the lady:
because of the beauty that was in her
3250 all his thoughts were of her.
He gazed at her as much as he could;
he coveted her so and she so pleased him
that her beauty inflamed him with love.
Very guilefully he asked Erec
3255 for permission to speak with her:
"My lord," said he, "I ask your
leave, provided it does not upset you:
out of politeness and for pleasure
I wish to sit by that lady.
3260 In good faith I came to see you both,
and you should not take it amiss:
I wish to offer my services
to the lady, above all else.
Be assured that, whatever pleased her,
3265 I would do it for the love of you."
Erec was not the least bit jealous,
for he saw no deceit in this.
"My lord," said he, "it does not upset me at all;
you are free to enjoy her conversation.
3270 Do not believe that I am upset by this;
I gladly give you leave."
The lady sat as far from him
as the length of two lances,
and the count sat down beside her
3275 upon a low stool.
The lady, who was very sensible
and courteous, turned toward him.
"Ah," said the count, "how it grieves me
that you travel in such a shameful fashion!
3280 Great sadness have I and great grief.
But if you were willing to believe me,
you would gain honor and profit,
and great good would come to you thereby.
Great honor and great nobility
3285 would be appropriate to your beauty.
I would make you my lady,
were it pleasing and agreeable to you;
you would be my beloved,
and lady of all my land.
3290 Since I deign to court you with love,
you must not reject me.
I see well and I know that your lord
neither loves nor esteems you;

145

         a boen seignor vos seroiz prise, *
3295   se vos avoec moi remenez.".
         "Sire, de neant vos penez,"
         fet Enyde; "ce ne puet estre.
         Hé! mialz fusse je or a nestre,
         ou an un feu d'espines arse
3300   si que la cendre an fust esparse,
         que j'eüsse de rien faussé
         vers mon seignor, ne mal pansé
         felenie ne traïson!
         Trop avez fet grant mesprison,
3305   qui tel chose m'avez requise:
         je nel feroie an nule guise."
         Li cuens comance a enflamer:
         "Ne me deigneriez amer,
         dame?" fet il; "trop estes fiere.
3310   Por losange ne por proiere *
         ne fereiez rien que je vuelle?
         Bien est voirs que fame s'orguelle,
         quant l'an plus la prie et losange;   *[13e]*
         mes qui la honist et leidange,
3315   cil la trueve meillor sovant.
         Certes, je vos met an covant
         que, se vos mon talant ne feites,
         ja i avra espees treites.
         Ocirre ferai or androit,
3320   ou soit a tort ou soit a droit,
         vostre seignor devant voz ialz."
         "Sire, faire le pöez mialz,"
         fet Enyde, "que vos ne dites: *
         trop sereiez fel et traïtes,
3325   se vos ceanz l'ocieiez.
         Mes, biax sire, or vos apaiez,
         car je ferai vostre pleisir.
         Por vostre me pöez seisir:
         je sui vostre et estre le vuel.
3330   Ne vos ai rien dit par orguel,
         mes por savoir et esprover
         se je porroie an vos trover
         que vos m'amessiez de boen cuer;
         mes je ne voldroie a nul fuer
3335   qu'aüssiez tel traïson fete.
         Mes sires de vos ne se guete:
         se vos einsi l'ocieiez,
         trop grant mesprison feriez

3294. vos seroiz *B = F* (seres *PV*)] seriez *CA* (*Instead of 3292-94 H has*
         Laies mester fait ele sire Vos perdes totes uos pensee Mius ualroie
         estre deuoree, *followed by our 3299*).
3310. Por ... por *BP*] Par ... par *CHVA*.

                              146

you will have a proper lord
3295 if you remain with me."
"Sire, you are wasting your effort,"
said Enide; "that cannot be.
Ah! better that I were not yet born,
or burned in a fire of thorns
3300 so that the ashes might be scattered,
than that I were in any way false
toward my lord, or wickedly contemplated
disloyalty or treason!
You have made a very great error
3305 by requesting such a thing of me:
I would not do it in any way."
The count began to flare up:
"You would not deign to love me,
my lady?" said he; "you are too proud!
3310 Would neither praise nor supplication
make you do what I wish?
It is indeed true that the more one begs
and praises a woman, the more prideful she becomes;
but he who shames and mistreats her
3315 often finds her the better for it.
Truly, I promise you
that, if you do not do as I wish,
swords will be drawn.
Rightly or wrongly,
3320 I shall have your lord slain forthwith,
right before your very eyes."
"Sire, you can do better,"
said Enide, "than what you say:
you would be too disloyal and treacherous
3325 if you killed him right here.
But, good sir, calm yourself,
for I shall do as you desire.
You can take me as your own:
I am yours and I wish to be.
3330 I did not speak out of pride,
but in order to learn and ascertain
whether I could be sure that
you might love me truly;
but I should not at any price
3335 wish you to commit such an act of treason.
My lord is not on his guard:
if you killed him in such a way,
you would be committing too great an offense,

147

et g'en reseroie blasmee.
3340 Tuit diroient par la contree
que ce seroit fet par mon los.
Jusqu'au matin aiez repos,
que mes sires voldra lever:
adonc le porroiz mialz grever,
3345 sanz blasme avoir et sanz reproche."
Ce panse cuers que ne dit boche.
"Sire," fet ele, "or me creez!
Ne soiez pas si esfreez,
mes demain anvoiez ceanz
3350 voz chevaliers et voz sergenz,
si me feites a force prandre:
mes sires me voldra desfandre,
qui molt est fiers et corageus,
ou soit a certes ou a geus.
3355 Feites le prandre et afoler
ou de la teste decoler.
Trop ai menee ceste vie;   *[13f]*
je n'aim mie la conpaignie
mon seignor, ja n'an quier mantir.
3360 Je vos voldroie ja santir
an un lit, certes, nu a nu.
Des qu'a ce an somes venu,
de m'amor estes aseür."
Li cuens respont: "A boen eür,
3365 dame! Certes buer fustes nee;
a grant enor seroiz gardee."
"Sire," fet ele, "bien le croi,
mes avoir an voel vostre foi,
que vos me tandroiz chieremant;
3370 ne vos an cresrai autremant."
Li cuens respont liez et joianz:
"Tenez: ma foi je vos fïanz,
dame, lëaumant come cuens,
que je ferai trestoz voz buens.
3375 Ja de ce ne vos esmaiez:
ne voldroiz rien que vos n'aiez."
Lors en a cele la foi prise,
mes po l'an est et po la prise:
por son seignor fu delivrer.
3380 Bien sot par parole enivrer
bricon, des qu'ele i met s'antante:
mialz est asez qu'ele li mante,
que ses sires fust depeciez.

3362. Des qu'a ce *BV* = *F* (Dus qua co *A*, Desque a *E*)] Desor ce *C*,
    Pus que ci *P*, A ce (ia uenu) *H*.
3365. *Initial* D *in CP*. | Certes *BPVE* = *F*] fet il *CA*, par foi *H*.
3381. s'antante *HBPA* = *F*] lantante *C*, setente *V*.

148

and I would in turn be blamed for it.
3340 Throughout the land all would say
that it had been done on my advice.
Take your repose until the morning,
when my lord will wish to rise:
then you will be better able to harm him
3345 without incurring blame or reproach."
The heart thinks what the mouth does not say.
"Sire," said she, "believe me!
Be not so disturbed,
but tomorrow send in
3350 your knights and your men-at-arms,
and have me taken by force;
my lord, who is very proud and courageous,
will want to defend me,
whether in earnest or in sport.
3355 Have him taken and wounded
or have his head cut off.
Too long have I led this life;
I have no liking for my lord's company,
and do not seek to lie about it.
3360 Indeed, I should already like to feel you
naked, beside me, in a bed.
Since we have agreed on this,
you are assured of my love."
The count replied: "Splendid,
3365 my lady! Surely you were born under a lucky star;
you will be kept with great honor."
"My lord," said she, "I do believe it,
but I wish to have your pledge
that you will hold me dear;
3370 I shall not believe you otherwise."
The count replied, happy and joyful:
"Here: I pledge you my faith,
my lady, loyally, as a count,
that I will do all you wish.
3375 Have no fear on this account:
you will not want for anything."
Then she accepted his pledge,
but it mattered little to her and little she valued it:
it was done to save her lord.
3380 She knew well how to intoxicate a rogue with words
when she put her mind to it:
it was far better that she lie to him
than for her lord to be cut to pieces.

De lez li s'est li cuens dreciez,
3385 si la comande a Deu cent foiz,
mes molt li valdra po la foiz
que fïanciee li avoit.
Erec de ce rien ne savoit
qu'il deüssent sa mort pleidier,
3390 mes Dex li porra bien aidier,
et je cuit que si fera il.
Or est Erec an grant peril
et si ne cuide avoir regart;
molt est li cuens de male part,
3395 qui sa fame tolir li panse
et lui ocirre sanz desfanse.
Come fel prant a lui congié:
"A Deu," fet il, "vos comant gié."
Erec respont: "Sire, et je vos."
3400 Ensi departent antr'ax dos.
De la nuit fu grant masse alee.   [14a]
An une chanbre recelee
furent dui lit a terre fet.
Erec an l'un couchier se vet;
3405 an l'autre est Enyde couchiee,
molt dolante et molt correciee.
Onques la nuit ne prist somoil:
por son seignor fu an esvoil,
car le conte ot bien coneü,
3410 de tant com ele l'ot veü,
que plains estoit de felenie.
Bien set que, s'il a la baillie
de son seignor, ne puet faillir
que il nel face maubaillir:
3415 seürs puet estre de la mort.
De lui ne set nul reconfort:
tote nuit veillier li estuet,
mes ainz le jor, se ele puet
et ses sires la voelle croirre,
3420 avront si atorné lor oirre
que por neant vanra li cuens, *
que ja n'iert soe, ne il suens.
    Erec dormi molt longuemant,
tote la nuit, seüremant,
3425 tant que li jorz molt aprocha.
Lors vit bien Enyde et soucha
que ele pooit trop atandre.
Vers son seignor ot le cuer tandre
come bone dame et lëax:

3407. Onques *HBPVA = F*] Nonques *C.*
3416. t *of* set *inserted, above the line, with a mark below the preceding* e.
3423. *Initial HP = F*] *no initial CBVA.*

150

The count rose from beside her,
3385 and a hundred times commended her to God,
but the pledge he made to her
will be of little worth to him.
Erec knew nothing of the fact
that they might be plotting his death,
3390 but God may well come to his aid,
and I believe that he will indeed do so.
Now was Erec in great danger,
and yet he did not believe he had to be on guard;
the count was very ignoble
3395 in thinking to take his wife from him
and kill him when he was defenseless.
Treacherously he took leave of him:
"I commend you," said he, "to God."
Erec replied: "My lord, and I you."
3400 Thus the two of them parted.
It was already late at night.
In a secluded room
two beds were prepared on the floor.
Erec went to lie down in one;
3405 Enide lay down in the other,
deeply saddened and troubled.
She never slept at all that night:
she kept watch because of her lord,
for she had seen enough of the count
3410 to realize clearly
that he was full of evil intentions.
She knew full well that, if he had the power
over her lord, he would not fail
to do him great injury:
3415 her lord would be sure to die.
Nothing could allay her fears for him:
she must keep watch all night,
but before daybreak, if she could manage it
and her lord was willing to believe her,
3420 they would make their departure
in such a way that the count would come for naught,
and she would never be his, nor he hers. *
    Erec slept a long time
all through the night, confidently,
3425 until daybreak was near.
Then Enide realized
that she might wait too long.
Her heart was tender toward her lord,
like a good and loyal lady:

3430 ses cuers ne fu dobliers ne fax.
Ele se vest et aparoille,
a son seignor vient, si l'esvoille:
"Ha! sire," fet ele, "merci!
Levez isnelemant de ci,
3435 que traïz estes antreset
sanz acoison et sanz forfet.
Li cuens est traïtres provez:
se ci pöez estre trovez,
ja n'eschaperoiz de la place
3440 que tot desmanbrer ne vos face.
Avoir me vialt; por ce vos het.
Mes se Deu plest, qui toz biens set,
vos n'i seroiz ne morz ne pris.
Des her soir vos eüst ocis,
3445 se creanté ne li eüsse   [14b]
que s'amie et sa fame fusse.
Ja le verroiz ceanz venir:
prandre me vialt et retenir,
et vos ocirre, s'il vos trueve."
3450 Or ot Erec que bien se prueve
vers lui sa fame lëaumant.
"Dame," fet il, "isnelemant
feites noz chevax anseler,
et feites nostre oste lever,
3455 si li dites qu'il veigne ça.
Traïsons comença piece a!"
Ja sont li cheval anselé,
et la dame a l'oste apelé.
Erec s'est araumant vestuz.
3460 Ses ostes est a lui venuz:
"Sire," dist il, "quel haste avez,
qui a tele ore vos levez,
ainz que jorz ne solauz apeire?"
Erec respont qu'il a a feire
3465 molt longue voie et grant jornee;
por ce a sa voie atornee,
que molt an est an grant espans,
et dist: "Sire, de mon despans
n'avez ancores rien conté.
3470 Enor m'avez feite et bonté,
et molt i afiert grant merite.
Por set destriers me clamez quite,
que je ai ceanz amenez.
Ne vos soit po; ces retenez.

3433. *Initial* H *in* C.
3473-74 *HBPVA =* F3509-10] *omitted* C.
3473. je ai ceanz *BPV = F* (io ai caiens *H*)] jai ca dedens *A*.
3474. retenez *BVA = F*] receues *H*; Por mon despens les retenes *P*.

152

3430   her heart was neither deceitful nor false.
       She dressed and made ready,
       came to her lord, and awakened him:
       "Ah, my lord," said she, "forgive me!
       Get up quickly from here,
3435   for you are certainly betrayed
       without reason or misdeed on your part.
       The count is a proven traitor:
       if he can find you here,
       you will never escape
3440   without his having you cut to pieces.
       He wants me; that is why he hates you.
       But if it please God, who knows all,
       you will be neither killed nor taken prisoner.
       Already last evening he would have killed you,
3445   had I not made him believe
       that I would be his lover and his wife.
       You'll soon see him come in here:
       he wants to take and keep me,
       and kill you, if he finds you."
3450   Now Erec could tell that his wife
       was proving her loyalty for him.
       "My lady," said he, "have our horses
       speedily saddled,
       and have our host get up,
3455   and tell him to come here.
       Treason has already begun long since!"
       The horses were soon saddled,
       and the lady called for the host.
       Erec promptly got dressed.
3460   His host came to him:
       "My lord," said he, "what's the hurry,
       getting up at such an hour,
       before the daylight and the sun appear?"
       Erec replied that he had
3465   very far to go and a long day's ride;
       for that reason he had prepared his departure,
       for he was extremely concerned about it,
       and he said: "Sir, you have as yet
       made no reckoning of my expenses.
3470   You have shown me honor and kindness,
       and that deserves a rich reward.
       Let me be quit for seven chargers,
       which I brought in here with me.
       Keep them, and may this not be too little.

3475 De plus ne vos puis mon don croistre,
     nes de la monte d'un chevoistre."
     De ce don fu li borjois liez,
     si l'an anclina jusqu'as piez;
     granz merciz et grasces l'an rant.
3480 Lors monte Erec et congié prant,
     si se remetent a la voie.
     Molt vet chastïant tote voie
     Enyde, se nule rien voit,
     qu'ele si hardie ne soit
3485 que ele l'an mete a reison.
     A tant antrent an la meison
     cent chevalier d'armes garni;
     de ce furent tuit escherni
     qu'il n'i ont pas Erec trové.
3490 Lors a bien li cuens esprové
     que la dame l'a deceü.   *[14c]*
     L'esclos des chevax a veü, *
     si se sont tuit mis an la trace.
     Li cuens Erec formant menace
3495 et dit que, s'il le puet ataindre,
     por nule rien ne puet remaindre
     que maintenant le chief n'an praigne.
     "Mar i avra nul qui s'an faigne,"
     fet il, "de tost esperoner!
3500 Qui me porra le chief doner
     del chevalier que je tant hé,
     molt m'avra bien servi an gré."
     Lors le sivent tuit abrivé,
     de mautalant sont aïré *
3505 vers celui qui onques nes vit
     ne mal ne lor a fet ne dit. *
     Tant chevauchent qu'il le choisirent:
     au chief d'une forest le virent,
     einz qu'il se fust anforestez.

3482. Molt *HBPVA = F*] Et *C*.
3483. rien *HBPVA = FR*] *omitted C* (-1).
3500. me *A = F*] man *C*, mem *H*, men *BV*, men *P*.
3504. sont *HBPA = F*] tuit *C*.
3505. vers *HBPVA = F*] de *C*. | qui onques nes vit *BP = F*] conques mes
     ne uirent *C*, qui o. nel uit *H*, quil o. ne uit *A*.
3506-07 *HBPVA = F3542-43*] *omitted C*.
3506. ne mal *BPV = F*] Nil *H*. | ne dit *BPV = F*] ne ne dit *H*. *A*: ne qui
     onques mal ne li dist.
3507. chevauchent *HP = F*] chacierent *BV*, alerent *A*. |
     choisirent *HBPV = F*] consiuent *A*.
3508. au chief d'une forest *HPVA = F* (de la f. *B*)] Erec cheualche cil *C*;
     large space between Erec *and* cheualche, *C*.

3475 I cannot increase my gift to you,
even by the price of a halter."
The burgher was happy with this gift,
and he bowed down at his feet;
he thanked him abundantly.
3480 Then Erec mounted and took his leave,
and they went on their way again.
Erec repeatedly warned
Enide that, if she saw anything,
she should not be so bold
3485 as to speak to him about it.
At that point into the house came
a hundred knights, fully armed;
they were thoroughly discomfited
because they did not find Erec there.
3490 Then the count fully realized
that the lady had tricked him.
He saw the horses' tracks,
and they all set out on their trail.
The count vigorously threatened Erec
3495 and said that, if he could catch him,
nothing would keep him from
cutting off his head without delay.
"Woe to anyone who holds back,"
said he, "from spurring quickly!
3500 Whoever can give me the head
of the knight whom I hate so much
will have served me extremely well."
Then they all followed him impatiently,
furious and wrathful
3505 toward him who had never seen them
nor done them ill by word or deed.
They rode till they caught sight of him:
they saw him at the edge of a forest
before he had entered it.

3510   Lors n'an est uns seus arestez;
      par contançon s'esleissent tuit.
      Enyde ot la noise et le bruit
      de lor armes, de lor chevax,
      et vit que plains estoit li vax.
3515   Des que cele les vit venir,
      de parler ne se pot tenir:
        "Haï! sire," fet ele, "haï!
      Con vos a cist cuens anvaï,
      qui por vos amainne tel ost!
3520   Sire, car chevalchiez plus tost,
      tant qu'an cele forest fussiens;
      espoir tost eschaperïens:
      cil sont ancore molt arriere.
      Se nos alons an tel meniere *
3525   ne pöez de ci eschaper,
      car n'iestes mie per a per."
      Erec respont: "Po me prisiez,
      quant ma parole despisiez;
      je ne vos sai si bel prïer
3530   que je vos puisse chastïer.
      Mes se Dex ait de moi merci
      et eschaper puisse de ci,
      ceste vos iert molt chier vandue,
      se corages ne me remue."
3535   Il se retorne maintenant
      et vit le seneschal venant
      sor un cheval fort et isnel.   *[14d]*
      Devant aus a fet un cenbel
      le tret de catre arbalestees.
3540   N'ot pas ses armes anpruntees,
      car molt se fu bien acesmez.
      Erec les a bien aesmez,
      et voit que bien en i a cent.
      Celui qui si le va chacent
3545   panse qu'arester li estuet.
      Li uns contre l'autre s'esmuet,
      si se fierent par les escuz
      des deus fers tranchanz esmoluz.
      Erec son fort espié d'acier
3550   li fist dedanz le cors glacier:
      ne li escuz ne li haubers
      ne li valut un cendal pers.

3510. n'an est *BVA = F*] san est *C*, ni est *H*, nest *P*. | uns seus *HVA = F*
(sous *B*)] li uns *C*, nis uns daus *P*. | arestez *HBPVA = F*] desseurez *C*.
3511. s'esleissent *BPVA = F*] le leissent *C*. *H*: Que tuit ni ceualcent vers lui
(*rhyming with* Enide a grant paor de lui *in the following line*).
3517. *C presents an exceptionally large initial* H *here, 5 lines tall; there is
no large initial at this point in HBPVA.*

156

3510 Then not one of them stopped;
all raced forward at top speed.
Enide heard the din and the noise
of their armor, of their horses,
and saw that the valley was full of them.
3515 As soon as she saw them coming,
she could not keep from speaking:
"Oh! my lord," said she, "Alas!
What an attack this count is making,
bringing a whole army with him against you!
3520 My lord, ride more quickly,
until we're in this forest;
perhaps we'll quickly escape:
they are still far behind.
If we keep on at this pace,
3525 you cannot escape from here,
for you are not at all evenly matched."
Erec replied: "You have little esteem for me,
since you despise my instructions;
there is nothing I can say to you
3530 that can correct your behavior.
But if God has mercy on me
and I can escape from here,
this will cost you very dearly,
if I don't change my mind."
3535 Then straightaway he turned around
and saw the seneschal coming
on a strong, fast horse.
In front of the others he galloped forth
the distance of four crossbowshots.
3540 His armor was not borrowed,
for he was very well equipped.
Erec estimated their number,
and saw that there were easily a hundred of them.
He thought that he must stop
3545 the one who was pursuing him.
They went at each other,
and struck one another on their shields
with their two sharpened, cutting blades.
Erec made his strong steel sword
3550 slide into his body;
neither the shield nor the hauberk
was worth a piece of blue silk to him.

A tant ez vos poingnant le conte.
Si con l'estoire le reconte,
3555 chevaliers estoit forz et buens,
mes de ce fist que fos li cuens
qu'il n'ot que l'escu et la lance:
an sa vertu ot tel fïance
qu'armer ne se volt autremant.
3560 De ce fist molt grant hardemant
que devant trestotes ses genz
s'esleissa plus de nuef arpanz.
Quant Erec le vit fors de rote,
a lui ganchist; cil nel redote,
3565 si s'antre vienent fieremant.
Li cuens le fiert premieremant
par tel vertu devant le piz
que les estriés eüst guerpiz,
se bien afichiez ne se fust;
3570 de l'escu fet croissir le fust,
que d'autre part an saut li fers,
mes molt fu riches li haubers,
qui si de mort le garanti
que einz maille n'an deronpi.
3575 Li cuens fu forz: sa lance froisse.
Erec le fiert de tel angoisse,
sor l'escu qui fu tainz an jaune,
que de la lance plus d'une aune
par mi le costé li anbat;
3580 pasmé jus del destrier l'abat.
A tant ganchist si s'an retorne.   [14e]
En la place plus ne sejorne;
par mi la forest a droiture
s'an vet poingnant grant aleüre.
3585 Ez vos Erec anforesté,
et li autre sont aresté
sor cez qui en mi le chanp jurent:
molt s'afichent formant et jurent
que il le chaceront einçois,
3590 a esperon deus jorz ou trois,
que il nel praignent et ocïent.
Et li cuens antant ce qu'il dïent,
qui molt ert el costé bleciez.
Contre mont s'est un po dreciez
3595 et les ialz un petitet oevre;
bien aparçoit que malveise oevre
avoit ancomanciee a faire.
Les chevaliers fet arriers traire:
"Seignor," fet il, "a toz vos di
3600 qu'il n'i ait un seul si hardi,

3563. Erec *HBPVA = F*] cil *C* (de la rote).

158

And now the count came spurring on.
As the story relates,
3555   he was a good knight and strong,
but the count acted foolishly in this,
for he had only a shield and a lance:
he had such confidence in his prowess
that he chose to wear no armor.
3560   He acted very boldly,
galloping forward a great distance *
out in front of all his men.
When Erec saw him out by himself,
he turned toward him; the count did not fear him,
3565   and they came bravely at one another.
The count struck Erec first,
on the chest, with such power
that he would have been unhorsed,
had he not been well set in his stirrups;
3570   it cracked the wood of the shield,
so that the iron stuck out the other side,
but the hauberk was very fine,
and it so protected him from death
that not a link of it gave way.
3575   The count was strong; he broke his lance.
Erec struck him with such violence
on his yellow-painted shield
that he thrust more than an ell of his lance
into the count's side;
3580   he knocked him unconscious from his horse.
Then Erec turned and came back.
He stayed no longer in the field;
he went galloping full speed
into the forest.
3585   Now Erec was in the forest,
and the others stopped
over those who lay upon the field:
very loudly they affirmed and swore
that they would pursue him
3590   with all speed for two or three days
until they caught and killed him.
And the count, who was badly wounded
in the side, heard what they were saying.
He rose up a little
3595   and opened his eyes just a bit;
he realized full well that it was
an evil deed that he had undertaken.
He ordered his knights to hold back:
"My lords," said he, "to all of you I say:
3600   let there be not a single one so bold,

fort ne foible, ne haut ne bas,
qui ost aler avant un pas.
Retornez tuit isnelemant!
Esploitié ai vilainnemant;
3605 de ma vilenie me poise.
Molt est preuz et saige et cortoise
la dame qui deceü m'a.
La biautez de li m'aluma:
por ce que ge la desiroie,
3610 son seignor ocirre voloie
et li par force retenir.
Bien m'an devoit max avenir:
sor moi an est venuz li max,
que fos feisoie et deslëax
3615 et traïtes et forssenez.
Onques ne fu de mere nez
miaudres chevaliers de cestui;
ja mes par moi n'avra enui
la ou jel puisse destorner.
3620 Or vos comant a retorner."
Cil s'an vont tuit desconforté.
Le seneschal an ont porté
mort an l'anvers de son escu.
Li cuens a puis asez vescu,
3625 qu'il ne fu pas a mort navrez.   [14f]
Ensi est Erec delivrez.
     Erec s'an vet toz esleissiez
une voie antre deus pleissiez. *
Au desbuschier d'un pleisseïz
3630 troverent un pont torneïz,
par devant une haute tor
qui close estoit de mur an tor
et de fossé lé et parfont.
Isnelemant passent le pont,
3635 mes molt orent alé petit
quant de la tor a mont les vit
cil qui de la tor estoit sire.
De celui savrai ge bien dire
qu'il estoit molt de cors petiz,
3640 mes de grant cuer estoit hardiz.
Quant il vit Erec trespassant,
jus de la tor a val descent
et fist sor un grant destrier sor

3623. mort an l'anvers de *BVA* = *F* (Tot enuerse sor *H*, Mort envers
     desor *P*)] le conte ont mis an *C*.
3624. Li cuens *HBPVA* = *F*] mes il *C*.
3625. a mort *HBPVA* = *F*] soef *C*.
3636. les *HBPVA* = *F*] le *C*.

160

strong or weak, high or low,
as to dare go one step further.
Return speedily, all of you!
I have acted basely;
3605 I deeply regret my villainy.
The lady who has foiled me
is very brave, sensible, and courtly.
Her beauty inflamed me:
because I desired her,
3610 I wanted to kill her lord
and hold her by force.
Evil was certain to come to me thereby:
evil has befallen me,
for I behaved rashly and disloyally,
3615 treacherously and madly.
Never was there born of woman
a better knight than this one;
never will he suffer ill on my account,
if I can prevent it.
3620 Now I command you to turn back."
They went away, sad and discouraged.
They carried off the seneschal,
dead, upon his upturned shield.
The count lived long afterwards,
3625 for he was not mortally wounded.
Thus was Erec delivered.
    Erec galloped off
along a path between two hedges.
Emerging from an enclosed portion of the wood
3630 they found a drawbridge
in front of a high tower
that was enclosed within a wall
and a wide and deep moat.
They quickly crossed over the bridge,
3635 but they had gone a very little way
when from the tower above
the lord of the tower saw them.
Of him I can truly say
that he was very small in stature,
3640 but bold and very courageous.
When he saw Erec coming along,
he came down from the tower
and had a saddle with golden lions

161

metre une sele a lyons d'or;
3645 puis comande qu'an li aport
escu et lance roide et fort,
espee brunie et tranchant,
et hiaume cler et reluisant,
hauberc blanc et chauces treslices,
3650 qu'il ot veü devant ses lices
un chevalier armé passer
a cui se vialt d'armes lasser,
ou il a lui se lassera
tant que toz recreanz sera.
3655 Cil ont son comandemant fet:
ez vos ja le cheval hors tret;
la sele mise et anfrené
l'a uns escuiers amené;
uns autres les armes aporte.
3660 Li chevaliers par mi la porte
s'an est issuz plus tost qu'il pot,
toz seus, que conpaignon n'i ot.
Erec vet par mi un pandant.
Ez vos le chevalier fandant
3665 par mi le tertre contre val,
et sist sor un molt fier cheval
qui si grant esfroi demenoit
que il desoz ses piez fraignoit
les chailloz plus delivremant   [15a]
3670 que mole ne quasse fromant,
et s'an voloient de toz sanz
estanceles cleres ardanz,
car des catre piez est a vis
que tuit fussent de feu espris.
3675 Enyde ot la noise et l'esfroi;
a po que de son palefroi
ne cheï jus pasmee et vainne:
an tot le cors de li n'ot vainne
don ne li remuast li sans,
3680 si li devint pales et blans
li vis con se ele fust morte.
Molt se despoire et desconforte,
car son seignor dire ne l'ose,
qu'il la menace molt et chose
3685 et comande qu'ele se teise.
De deus parz est molt a male eise,
qu'ele ne set lequel seisir,
ou le parler ou le teisir.
A li meïsmes s'an consoille:

3644. une sele *HBPVA* = *F*] la sele *C* (*P*: Une s. m. a fin or).
3658. *Final* s *of* escuiers *inserted above line.*
3671. s'an voloient *P* = *F* (en *H*, si *BVA*)] si li uolent *C*.

162

placed on a big sorrel charger;
3645 then he ordered brought to him
his shield and lance, sturdy and strong,
his sharp and burnished sword,
his bright shining helmet,
white hauberk and thrice-woven greaves,
3650 for before his enceintes he had seen *
an armed knight pass by,
with whom he wished to exhaust himself in combat,
or the other would wear himself out
and declare himself defeated.
3655 They carried out his orders:
there was the horse being led out;
a squire brought it,
saddled and bridled;
another brought his arms.
3660 Through the gate the knight
went out as fast as he could,
all alone, for he had no companion.
Erec was crossing a slope.
Now here was the knight charging
3665 across the hill and down the slope,
seated on a very bold horse
that was making such a racket
that beneath its feet it was shattering
the pebbles more freely
3670 than a mill grinds up wheat,
and in all directions there flew
bright burning sparks,
for it seemed its four feet
were all on fire.
3675 Enide heard the din and the racket;
she almost fell, fainting and weak,
from her palfrey:
in all her body there was no vein
in which the blood did not turn,
3680 and her face became pale and white
as if she were dead.
She greatly despaired and grieved,
for she dared not tell her lord,
lest he threaten and blame her
3685 and order her to be silent.
On both sides she was very badly off,
so that she knew not which course to choose:
speaking or keeping silent.
She deliberated within herself;

3690 sovant del dire s'aparoille
si que la leingue se remuet,
mes la voiz pas issir n'an puet,
car de peor estraint les danz,
s'anclost la parole dedanz.
3695 Ensi se justise et destraint:
la boche clot, les danz estraint,
que la parole hors n'an aille;
a li a prise grant bataille,
et dit: "Seüre sui et certe
3700 que trop recevrai leide perte,
se je ici mon seignor pert.
Dirai li donc tot en apert?
Nenil. Por quoi? Je n'oseroie,
que mon seignor correceroie,
3705 et se mes sires se corroce,
il me leira an ceste broce
seule et cheitive et esgaree;
lors serai plus mal eüree.
Mal eüree? Moi que chaut?
3710 Diax ne pesance ne me faut
ja mes, tant con je aie a vivre,
se mes sires tot a delivre
an tel guise de ci n'estort   [15b]
qu'il ne soit mahaigniez a mort.
3715 Mes se je tost ne li acoint,
cist chevaliers qui ci apoint
l'avra einz mort que il se gart,
que molt sanble de male part.
Lasse, trop ai or atandu!
3720 Si le m'a il molt desfandu,
mes ja nel leirai por desfansse:
je voi bien que mes sires pansse
tant que lui meïsmes oblie;
donc est bien droiz que je li die."
3725 Ele li dit; il la menace,
mes n'a talant que mal li face,
qu'il aparçoit et conuist bien
qu'ele l'ainme sor tote rien,
et il li, tant que plus ne puet.
3730 Contre le chevalier s'esmuet
qui de bataille le semont.
Asanblé sont au chief del pont:
la s'antre vienent et desfïent;
as fers des lances s'antre anvïent
3735 anbedui de totes lor forces.
Ne lor valurent deus escorces
li escu qui as cos lor pandent:

3695. Ensi *BPA* (Issi *H*, Ansi *V*; Einsi *F*)] et si *C*.

3690 often she prepared to speak
so that her tongue moved,
but her voice could not get out,
for out of fear she clenched her teeth,
and withheld the words inside.
3695 Thus she governed and fettered herself:
she closed her mouth, clenched her teeth,
so that the words would not get out;
she battled with herself,
and said: "Sure am I and certain
3700 I will receive too great a loss,
if I lose my lord here.
Shall I then speak openly to him?
Certainly not. Why? I wouldn't dare,
for I would anger my lord,
3705 and if my lord grows angry,
he will leave me in this brush,
alone and wretched and abandoned;
then I shall be even worse off.
Worse off? What does that matter to me?
3710 I shall nevermore lack for grief or sorrow
as long as I live
if my lord does not escape freely
from here in such a way
that he is not mortally mangled.
3715 But if I don't warn him soon,
this knight who is spurring this way
will have killed him before he gets his guard up,
for he seems full of evil intentions.
Wretch, now I have waited too long!
3720 He has indeed forbidden me to speak,
but I shall not let that deter me:
I can see that my lord is deep in thought,
so much so that he forgets himself;
therefore it is quite right that I should tell him."
3725 She spoke to him; he threatened her,
but had no wish to harm her,
for he perceived and knew full well
that she loved him above all else,
and he loved her, with all his might.
3730 Erec rushed at the other knight
who was summoning him to battle.
They met at the head of the bridge:
there they came together and challenged one another;
with their iron-tipped lances
3735 they both attacked with all their strength.
The shields hung at their necks
were not worth two bits of bark:

165

li cuir ronpent et les es fandent
et des haubers ronpent les mailles,
3740 si qu'anbedui jusqu'as antrailles
sont anglaivé et anferré
et li destrier sont aterré.
Ne furent pas navré a mort,
car molt erent li baron fort. *
3745 Les lances ont el chanp gitees;
des fuerres traient les espees,
si s'antre fierent par grant ire.
Li uns l'autre sache et detire,
que de rien ne s'antr'espargnoient.
3750 Granz cos sor les hiaumes donoient
qu'estanceles ardanz an issent
quant les espees ressortissent.
Li escu fandent et esclicent;
lor haubers faussent et deslicent.
3755 An mainz leus lor sont anbatues
les espees jusqu'as charz nues,
que molt s'afebloient et lassent;
et se les espees durassent
longuemant l'une et l'autre antiere,   [15c]
3760 ne se treississent pas arriere,
ne la bataille ne fenist,
tant que l'un morir covenist.
Enyde, qui les esgardoit,
a po de duel ne forssenoit.
3765 Qui li veïst son grant duel fere,
ses poinz tordre, ses chevox trere,
et les lermes des ialz cheoir,
leal dame poïst veoir,
et trop fust fel qui la veïst,
3770 se granz pitiez ne l'an preïst. *
Li uns a l'autre granz cos done;
des tierce jusque pres de none
dura la bataille tant fiere
que nus hom an nule meniere
3775 certainnemant n'aparceüst
li quex le meillor en eüst.
Erec s'esforce et esvertue:
s'espee li a anbatue
el hiaume jusqu'el chapeler,
3780 si que tot le fet chanceler,
mes bien se tint qu'il ne cheï.

3744. li baron *HA = F*] li blazon *C*, ambedui *BPV*.
3752. *HBPVA = F3796*] *omitted C.* quant *HBPV = F*] Et *A.* |
    ressortissent *HBVA = F*] retentissent *P.*
3754. *H(B)PVA = F3798*] *omitted C.* lor *H = F*] Li *PA*, Les *V.* |
    haubers *HVA = F*] hauberc *P.* | *B*: Et de desor les h. glicent.

166

the leather broke and the wood split
and the mail of their hauberks broke,
3740 so that both of them were run through
right into their entrails,
and their chargers were thrown to the ground.
They were not mortally wounded,
for the barons were very strong.
3745 They threw their lances onto the field;
from their scabbards they drew their swords,
and struck each other with great fury.
They heaved and pulled at one another,
sparing each other nothing.
3750 They struck great blows on their helmets
so that sparks flew from them
when their swords rebounded.
Their shields split and flew apart;
their hauberks were battered and broken.
3755 In many places the swords penetrated
all the way to their naked flesh,
so that they grew very weak and tired;
and if their swords had both
remained whole for a long time,
3760 they would not have drawn back,
and the battle would not have ended,
until one of them was killed.
Enide, who was watching them,
nearly went mad from distress.
3765 Anyone who saw her in such a sorrowful state,
wringing her hands, tearing her hair,
and the tears falling from her eyes,
would have seen a loyal lady,
and anyone who saw her would have been most cruel,
3770 if great pity had not seized him.
Each dealt the other great blows;
from mid-morning till mid-afternoon *
the battle raged so fiercely
that no man, by any means,
3775 could have told with certainty
which of them had the better of it.
Erec strove to do his utmost:
his sword penetrated the other's helmet
all the way to the coif of mail, *
3780 so that he quite caused him to reel,
but he managed to keep from falling.

167

Et cil ra Erec anvaï,
si l'a si duremant feru
sor la pane de son escu
3785 qu'au retraire est li branz brisiez,
qui molt ert boens et bien prisiez.
Quant cil vit brisiee s'espee,
par mautalant a jus gitee
la part qui li remest el poing
3790 tant com il onques pot plus loing.
Peor ot; arriers l'estut treire,
que ne puet pas grant esforz feire
an bataille ne an assaut
chevaliers cui s'espee faut.
3795 Erec l'anchauce, et cil li prie
por Deu qu'il ne l'ocie mie.
"Merci," fet il, "frans chevaliers!
Ne soiez vers moi fel ne fiers: *
des que m'espee m'est faillie,
3800 la force avez et la baillie
de moi ocirre ou de vif prandre,
que n'ai don me puisse desfandre."
Erec respont: "Quant tu me prïes,   [15d]
oltreemant vuel que tu dïes
3805 que tu es oltrez et conquis;
puis ne seras par moi requis
se tu te mez an ma menaie."
Et cil del dire se delaie.
Quant Erec le vit delaier,
3810 por lui fere plus esmaier
li ra une anvaïe fete:
sore li cort l'espee trete,
et cil dit, qui fu esmaiez:
"Merci, sire! Conquis m'aiez,
3815 des qu'altremant estre ne puet."
Erec respont: "Plus i estuet,
qu'a tant n'an iroiz vos pas quites:
vostre estre et vostre non me dites,
et je vos redirai le mien."
3820 "Sire," fet il, "molt dites bien.
Je sui de ceste terre rois:
mi home lige sont Irois;
n'i a nul ne soit mes rantiz.
Et j'ai non Guivrez li Petiz;
3825 assez sui riches et puissanz,
qu'an ceste terre, de toz sanz,

3798. soiez *B* (soiiez *F*)] soies *C* (*HPV*); *A is substantially different in this passage*.
3812. l'espee *HBPA* = *F*] espee *CV* (Sus li corut espee tr.)
3816. Erec *HBPVA* = *F*] Et cil *C*.

168

Then he attacked Erec in turn,
and struck him with such force
on the rim of his shield
3785 that his good and precious blade
was broken when he brought it back.
When he saw his sword was broken,
in fury he flung down
the part that remained in his hand,
3790 as far away as he could.
He was afraid; he was obliged to draw back,
for a knight who lacks a sword
cannot make a great effort
in battle or attack.
3795 Erec pursued him, and the other begged him,
for God's sake, not to kill him.
"Have mercy," cried he, "noble knight!
Be not cruel and savage toward me:
since my sword has failed me,
3800 you have the force and the right
to kill me or to take me alive,
since I have nothing with which to defend myself."
Erec replied: "Since you beseech me,
I want you to say without reserve
3805 that you are beaten and defeated;
I shall attack you no more
if you place yourself in my power."
But the other delayed in speaking.
When Erec saw him delay,
3810 to frighten him the more
he made another attack:
he ran upon him, with his sword drawn,
and the other, terrified, cried out:
"Pity, my lord! Consider me defeated,
3815 since it cannot be otherwise."
Erec replied: "I demand more,
for you won't get off with so little:
tell me your name and your situation,
and I shall tell you mine."
3820 "My lord," said he, "what you say is right.
I am the king of this land:
my liegemen are Irish;
every one of them pays me tribute.
And my name is Guivret the Short;
3825 I am very rich and powerful,
for in this land, in all directions,

n'a baron, qui a moi marchisse,
qui de mon comandemant isse
et mon pleisir ne face tot.
3830 Je n'ai veisin qui ne me dot,
tant se face orguellex ne cointes.
Molt voldroie estre vostre acointes
et vostre amis d'or en avant."
Erec respont: "Je me revant
3835 que je sui assez gentix hom:
Erec, filz le roi Lac, ai non.
Rois est mes peres d'Estre Gales.
Riches citez et beles sales
et forz chastiax a molt mes peres;
3840 plus n'en a rois ne empereres,
fors li rois Artus seulemant:
celui an ost je voiremant,
car a lui nus ne s'aparoille."
Quant Guivrez l'ot, molt s'an mervoille,
3845 et dist: "Sire, grant mervoille oi;
onques de rien tel joie n'oi
con j'ai de vostre conuissance;   *[15e]*
avoir pöez tele fïance *
en ma terre et an mon avoir
3850 que ja tant n'i voldroiz manoir
que molt ne vos face enorer.
Ja tant n'i voldroiz demorer
que desor moi ne soiez sire.
Andui avons mestier de mire,
3855 et j'ai ci pres un mien recet;
n'i a pas sis liues ne set.
La vos voel avoec moi mener,
s'i ferons noz plaies sener."
Erec respont: "Boen gré vos sai
3860 de ce qu'oï dire vos ai;
n'i irai pas, vostre merci,
mes itant solemant vos pri
que, se nus besoinz m'avenoit
et la novele a vos venoit
3865 que j'eüsse mestier d'aïe,
adonc ne m'oblïessiez mie."
"Sire," fet il, "je vos plevis
que, ja tant con je soie vis,
n'avroiz de mon secors mestier
3870 que tantost ne vos vaigne aidier
a quanque je porrai mander."
"Ja plus ne vos quier demander,"
fet Erec; "molt m'avez promis.
Mes sire estes et mes amis,
3875 se l'uevre est tex con la parole."
Li uns l'autre beise et acole.

170

there is not a baron whose lands border on mine
who eludes my command
or who does not do exactly as I wish.
3830 All my neighbors fear me,
however arrogant or valiant they may be.
I should very much like to be your confidant
and your friend, from this time forward."
Erec replied: "I in turn boast
3835 that I am quite a noble man:
Erec, son of King Lac, is my name.
My father is king of Estre-Gales.
My father has many rich cities,
beautiful halls, and strong castles;
3840 no king or emperor has more,
except for King Arthur alone:
truly I set him apart,
for no one is his equal."
When Guivret heard this, he was astonished,
3845 and said: "My lord, this is wondrous news;
I never had such joy from anything
as I do from making your acquaintance;
you may so count on
my land and my possessions
3850 that, however long you may wish to stay there,
I shall do you the greatest honor.
However long you may wish to stay there,
you will be my overlord.
We both have need of a doctor,
3855 and one of my castles is near here;
it's not six leagues away or seven.
I wish to take you there with me,
and we shall have our wounds tended."
Erec replied: "I am grateful to you
3860 for what you have said;
I shall not go with you, by your leave,
but I ask just this of you:
that, if any need should befall me
and the news reached you
3865 that I needed help,
then you should not forget me."
"My lord," said he, "I promise you
that, as long as I live,
whenever you need my help,
3870 I will quickly come to aid you
with all the resources at my command."
"I wish to ask no more of you,"
said Erec; "you have promised me much.
You are my lord and my friend,
3875 if the deed is like the words."
Each of them kissed and embraced the other.

171

Onques de si dure bataille
ne fu si dolce dessevraille,
que par amor et par franchise
3880   chascuns, des panz de sa chemise,
trancha bandes longues et lees,
s'ont lor plaies antre bandees.
    Quant il se sont antre bandé,
a Deu s'antre sont comandé.
3885   Departi sont an tel meniere:
seus s'an revet Guivrez arriere;
Erec a son chemin retret,
qui grant mestier eüst d'antret
por ses plaies medeciner.
3890   Einz ne fina de cheminer
tant que il vint an une plaigne   *[15f]*
lez une haute forest plaigne
de cers, de biches et de dains,
et de chevriax et de farains
3895   et de tote autre salvagine.
Li rois Artus et la reïne
et de ses barons li meillor
i estoient venu le jor:
an la forest voloit li rois
3900   demorer catre jorz ou trois
por lui deduire et deporter,
si ot comandé aporter
tantes et pavellons et trez.
El tref le roi estoit antrez
3905   mes sire Gauvains toz lassez,
qui chevalchié avoit assez.
Devant son tref estoit uns charmes;
la ot un escu de ses armes *
pandu, et sa lance de fresne
3910   a une branche par la resne,
s'ot le gringalet aresné,
la sele mise et anfrené.
Tant estut iluec li chevax
que Keus i vint, li seneschax:
3915   cele part vint grant aleüre.
Ausi con par anvoiseüre
prist le cheval et monta sus:
onques ne li contredist nus;
la lance et l'escu prist aprés
3920   qui soz l'arbre erent iluec pres.
Galopant sor le gringalet

3891. que il vint *HBA* = *F* (qu̲il uint enmi *P*, qu̲il vint *V*, *-1*)] qu̲il uindrent *C*.
3911. s'ot *H* (Ot *BPV* = *F*)] et *C*; Ot gringalet *A* (*-1*).
3920. erent *HBPV* (ierent *F*)] estoit *C*. ǀ iluec *F* (iloc *H*, illoec *P*)] iqui *C*,
enqui *BV*; *A*: qu̲i drecoient illuqu̲es pr̲es.

172

Never from such a fierce battle
was there such a sweet parting,
for, moved by love and generosity,
3880 each of them cut long, broad bands
from the tail of his shirt,
and they bound up each other's wounds.
    When they had bandaged each other,
they commended one another to God.
3885 They separated in this way:
Guivret came back alone;
Erec, who was badly in need of dressing
to care for his wounds,
resumed his journey.
3890 He never ceased riding
until he came to a meadow
beside a tall forest full
of stags, does, and fallow deer,
roe deer and game animals
3895 and every other wild beast.
King Arthur and the queen
and the best of his barons
had come there that day;
the king wanted to stay
3900 three or four days in the forest,
to amuse and disport himself,
and he had ordered tents
and pavilions to be brought. *
Into the king's tent had come
3905 my lord Gawain, very tired
from a long ride.
In front of his tent was a hornbeam;
there he had hung a shield with his
coat of arms, and his ash-wood lance,
3910 suspended from a branch by the shoulder-strap,
and he had tied his horse, *
saddled and bridled, by the reins.
The horse had been there some while
when Kay, the seneschal, came there:
3915 he came that way very rapidly.
As if to play a trick,
he took the horse and mounted it:
no one opposed him;
then he took the lance and the shield
3920 that were there nearby beneath the tree.
Galloping on Gawain's horse,

s'an aloit Keus tot un valet,
tant que par avanture avint
qu'Erec a l'ancontre li vint.
3925 Erec conut le seneschal
et les armes et le cheval,
mes Keus pas lui ne reconut,
car a ses armes ne parut
nule veraie conuissance:
3930 tant cos d'espee et tant de lance
avoit sor son escu eüz
que toz li tainz an ert cheüz.
Et la dame par grant veidie,
por ce qu'ele ne voloit mie
3935 qu'il la coneüst ne veïst,   *[16a]*
ausi con s'ele le feïst
por le chaut ou por la poldriere,
mist sa guinple devant sa chiere.
Keus vint avant plus que le pas
3940 et prist Erec en es le pas
par les resnes sanz salüer;
einz qu'il le lessast remüer,
li demanda par grant orguel:
"Chevaliers," fet il, "savoir vuel
3945 qui vos estes et d'ou venez."
"Fos estes quant vos me tenez,"
fet Erec; "nel savroiz enuit."
Et cil respont: "Ne vos enuit,
que por vostre bien le demant.
3950 Je voi et sai certainnemant
que bleciez estes et navrez.
Anquenuit mon ostel prenez:
se vos volez o moi venir,
je vos ferai molt chier tenir
3955 et enorer et aeisier,
car de repos avez mestier.
Li rois Artus et la reïne
sont ci pres en une gaudine,
de trez et de tantes logié.
3960 En boene foi le vos lo gié,
que vos veigniez avoeques moi
veoir la reïne et le roi,
qui de vos grant joie feront
et grant enor vos porteront."

3930. d'espee *HBPVA = F*] despees *C.* | *Second* tant *F* (tans *H*)] trous *A*,
omitted CBPV (Que tans *P*, Car tant *V*).
3943. grant *HBPVA = F*] son *C.*
3958. sont *HBPVA = F*] est *C.*
3966. mes *HPA = F*] *omitted CBV.* | n'iroie *P* (Je niroie *V*)] ni iroie *CB*,
je ni i. *HA = F* (por rien).

174

Kay went off along a vale,
until by chance it happened
that Erec came to meet him.
3925 Erec recognized the seneschal,
and the arms and the horse,
but Kay did not recognize him,
for on his armor appeared
no identifiable markings;
3930 he had taken so many blows on it
from sword and lance
that all the paint had fallen off.
And the lady, very cleverly,
because she did not want
3935 Kay to see or recognize her,
put her wimple over her face,
just as she would have done
to protect herself from heat or dust.
Kay came rapidly forward
3940 and immediately, without greeting him,
seized Erec's reins;
before allowing him to move,
he questioned him most haughtily:
"Knight," said he, "I want to know
3945 who you are and where you're from."
"You are mad to hold me thus,"
said Erec; "you'll not learn it today."
And Kay replied: "May it not trouble you,
for it is for your good that I inquire.
3950 I can clearly see
that you are wounded and injured.
Take my lodgings this night:
if you will come with me,
I shall see that you are richly treated,
3955 honored, and cared for,
for you have need of rest.
King Arthur and the queen
are nearby in a small wood,
encamped in tents and pavilions.
3960 In good faith I advise you
to come with me
to see the queen and the king,
who will welcome you warmly
and show you great honor."

3965 Erec respont: "Vos dites bien,
mes n'iroie por nule rien.
Ne savez mie mon besoing;
ancor m'estuet aler plus loing.
Lessiez m'aler, car trop demor;
3970 assez i a encor del jor."
Keus respont: "Grant folie dites,
qui del venir vos escondites;
espoir vos an repantiroiz,
car je cuit que vos i vanroiz
3975 andui, et vos et vostre fame, *
si con li prestres va au sane, *
ou volantiers ou a enviz.
Anquenuit seroiz mal serviz
(se mes consauz en est creüz), *
3980 se bien n'i estes coneüz.
Venez an tost, car je vos praing."   [16b]
De ce ot Erec grant desdaing:
"Vasax," fet il, "folie feites,
qui par force aprés vos me treites.
3985 Sanz desfïance m'avez pris.
Je di que vos avez mespris,
car toz seürs estre cuidoie;
de rien vers vos ne me gardoie."
Lors met a l'espee la main
3990 et dit: "Vasax, lessiez mon frain!
Traiez vos la! Je vos tieng molt *
por orgueilleus et por estout.
Se aprés vos plus me sachiez,
je vos ferrai, bien le sachiez.
3995 Leissiez m'aler!" Et cil le leisse;
el chanp plus d'un arpant s'esleisse,
puis retorne, si le desfie
com hom plains de grant felenie.
Li uns contre l'autre ganchist,
4000 mes Erec de tant se franchist,
por ce que cil desarmez iere,
de sa lance torna desriere
le fer, et l'arestuel devant.
Tel cop li done ne por quant,
4005 an son escu tot el plus emple,
que hurter li fist a la temple
et que le braz au piz li serre:
tot estandu le porte a terre.
Puis vient au destrier, si le prant;
4010 Enyde par le frain le rant.

3979-80 *HPBVA = F*] *omitted C.*
3980. *HB = F*] Se ml't nestes bien c. *PV,* Se uos ni etes bien c. *A.*
4001. cil *BVA = F*] il *CP,* kex *H. Cf. 3995, 4011.*

176

3965   Erec replied: "You speak well,
        but I would not go there for anything.
        You do not know my need;
        I still must go further.
        Let me go, for I tarry too long;
3970   there is still plenty of daylight left."
        Kay replied: "You speak very unwisely,
        you who refuse to come along;
        perhaps you will regret it,
        for I think you will both come,
3975   you and your wife,
        just as the priest goes to the synod,
        either willingly or unwillingly.
        This night you will be badly served
        (if my counsel is heeded),
3980   if you are not well known there.
        Come along quickly, for I'm taking you."
        For this Erec had great disdain:
        "Vassal," said he, "you are quite mad
        to drag me after you by force.
3985   You have taken me without challenge.
        I say that you have acted wrongly,
        for I believed myself secure from danger;
        I was not on my guard against you."
        Then he put his hand to his sword
3990   and said: "Vassal, let go of my bridle!
        Draw back! I consider you excessively
        haughty and daring.
        If you pull me after you any more,
        be assured that I will strike you.
3995   Let me go!" And Kay did so;
        he galloped away across the field, *
        then turned around and challenged Erec
        like a man full of great wrath.
        Each of them dodged the other's blow,
4000   but Erec behaved nobly
        because the other wore no armor, *
        and turned the head of his lance behind,
        and held the butt in front.
        Nonetheless Erec gave him such a blow
4005   on his shield at the widest part
        that it struck him on the temple
        and pinned his arm against his chest;
        Erec stretched him out full length on the ground.
        Then he came to the charger and took it;
4010   by the reins he gave it to Énide.

Mener l'en vost, mes cil li prie,
qui molt sot de losangerie,
que par franchise li randist;
molt bel le losange et blandist:
4015 "Vasax," fet il, "se Dex me gart,
an ce destrier je n'i ai part;
einz est au chevalier del monde
an cui graindre proesce abonde,
mon seignor Gauvain le hardi.
4020 Tant de la soe part vos di
que son destrier li anvoiez,
por ce que enor i aiez;
molt feroiz que frans et que sages,
et ge serai vostre mesages."
4025 Erec respont: "Vasax, prenez   *[16c]*
le cheval, si l'en remenez:
des qu'il est mon seignor Gauvain,
n'est mie droiz que je l'en main."
Keus prant le cheval, si remonte;
4030 au tref le roi vient, si li conte
le voir, que rien ne l'an cela.
Et li rois Gauvain apela:
"Biax niés Gauvain," ce dit li rois,
"s'onques fustes frans ne cortois,
4035 alez aprés isnelemant;
demandez amïablemant
de son estre et de son afeire.
Et se vos le pöez atreire
tant que avoec vos l'ameigniez,
4040 gardez ja ne vos an feigniez."
Gauvains monte an son gringalet;
aprés le sivent dui vaslet:
ja ont Erec aconseü,
mes ne l'ont mie coneü.
4045 Gauvains le salue et il lui;
salüé se sont amedui.
Puis li dist mes sire Gauvains,
qui de grant franchise estoit plains:
"Sire," fet il, "a vos m'anvoie
4050 li rois Artus an ceste voie.
La reïne et li rois vos mandent
saluz, et prïent et comandent
qu'avoec ax vos vaingniez deduire.
Eidier vos vuelent, non pas nuire,
4055 et il ne sont pas loing de ci."
Erec respont: "Molt an merci
le roi et la reïne ansanble,
et vos qui estes, ce me sanble,

4053. vaingniez *BV* (vegniez *F1909*)] uenez *C*, venes *HPA = F*.

178

He wanted to take it with him, but the other,
who was very skilled in flattery, begged him
to return it, out of generosity;
artfully he flattered and blandished him:
4015 "Vassal," said he, "God protect me,
I have no right to this charger;
rather it belongs to that knight in all the world
in whom the greatest prowess abounds,
my lord Gawain the brave.
4020 So on his behalf I ask you
to send him his charger,
so that you may gain honor thereby;
you will be acting both nobly and wisely,
and I shall be your messenger."
4025 Erec replied: "Vassal, take
the horse and return him;
since he belongs to my lord Gawain,
it is not right that I should take him."
Kay took the horse and got back on;
4030 he came to the king's tent and told him
the truth, keeping nothing hidden.
And the king called Gawain:
"Fair nephew Gawain," said the king,
"if ever you were noble or courteous,
4035 go speedily after him;
ask him, in a friendly way,
about himself and his business.
And if you can persuade him
so that you can bring him back with you,
4040 be sure you do not fail to do so."
Gawain mounted upon his horse; *
two valets followed him;
they soon caught up with Erec,
but they did not recognize him at all.
4045 Gawain greeted Erec and Erec him;
each of them greeted the other.
Then my lord Gawain,
who was full of great nobility, said:
"My lord," said he, "King Arthur
4050 sends me to you upon this path.
The queen and the king send you
greetings, and beg and request
that you come and take pleasure with them.
They wish to help you, not to harm you,
4055 and they are not far from here."
Erec replied: "I sincerely thank
the king and the queen together,
and you, who are, it seems to me,

de bon eire et bien afeitiez.
4060 Je ne sui mie bien heitiez,
einz sui navrez dedanz le cors,
et ne por quant ja n'istrai hors
de mon chemin por ostel prendre.
Ne vos i covient plus atendre;
4065 vostre merci, ralez vos an."
　　　Gauvains estoit de molt grant san.
Arrieres se tret et consoille
a un des vaslez an l'oroille
que tost aille dire le roi   [16d]
4070 que il preigne prochain conroi
de ses trez destendre et abatre
et veigne trois liues ou catre
devant ax en mi le chemin
tandre les aucubes de lin.
4075 "Iluec l'estuet enuit logier,
s'il vialt conoistre et herbergier
le meillor chevalier por voir
c'onques veïst, au mien espoir,
qu'il ne vialt por un ne por el
4080 guerpir sa veie por ostel."
Cil s'an vet; son message a dit.
Destandre fet sanz nul respit
li rois ses trez: destandu sont.
Les somiers chargent, si s'an vont.
4085 Sor l'aubagu monta li rois;
sor un blanc palefroi norrois
remonta la reïne aprés.
Mes sire Gauvains tot adés
ne finoit d'Erec delaier,
4090 et cil li dist: "Plus alai hier
asez que je ne ferai hui.
Sire, vos me feites enui;
lessiez m'aler. De ma jornee
m'avez grant masse destorbee."
4095 Et mes sire Gauvains li dit:
"Encor voel aler un petit
avoeques vos, ne vos enuit,
car grant piece a jusqu'a la nuit."
Tant ont a parler entandu
4100 que tuit li tref furent tandu
devant aus, et Erec les voit:
herbergiez est, bien l'aparçoit.
"Haï!" fet il, "Gauvain, haï!
Vostres granz sans m'a esbahi;
4105 par grant san m'avez retenu.

4065-66. *Space left in C for a 2-line initial letter, not executed. Initial* u *or* v
missing, 4065; normal-sized .G. *begins 4066.*

of noble birth and well-bred.
4060 I am not hale or sound,
but rather my body is wounded,
and nevertheless I will not stray
from my road to take lodgings.
You need wait no longer;
4065 I will thank you to go back."
Gawain was very clever.
He drew back and whispered
to one of the valets
to go quickly and tell the king
4070 that he should take immediate measures
to have his tents taken down,
and he should come three or four leagues
in front of them, right on the road,
to have his linen tents set up.
4075 "That is where he must spend this night,
if he wants to know and give lodging to
the best knight, in truth,
that he ever saw, as I believe,
for he does not want, for any reason,
4080 to abandon his path to seek lodging."
The valet left; he delivered his message.
The king had his tents taken down
without any delay; they were taken down.
They loaded the packhorses and they left.
4085 The king mounted his horse; *
the queen in turn mounted
upon a white Norwegian palfrey.
My lord Gawain, meanwhile,
kept on delaying Erec,
4090 and the latter said to him: "I went much farther yesterday
than I shall go today.
Sir, you are annoying me;
let me go. You have greatly
disrupted my day's travel."
4095 And my lord Gawain said to him:
"I wish to go a bit farther
with you, if you don't mind,
for there is still much time before nightfall."
They spent so much time talking
4100 that all the tents were set up
ahead of them, and Erec saw them;
he was to be lodged, as he clearly saw.
"Oho!" said he, "Gawain, oho!
Your great cleverness has caught me;
4105 you have very cleverly detained me.

181

Des que ore est si avenu,
mon non vos dirai or endroit:
li celers rien ne m'i vaudroit.
Je sui Erec, qui fui jadis
4110   vostre conpainz et vostre amis."
Gauvains l'ot; acoler le va:
son hiaume a mont li sozleva
et la ventaille li deslace;   *[16e]*
de joie l'acole et anbrace,
4115   et Erec lui de l'autre part.
A tant Gauvains de lui se part
et dist: "Sire, ceste novele
sera ja mon seignor molt bele.
Liez en iert ma dame et mes sire
4120   et je lor irai avant dire,
mes einçois m'estuet anbracier
et conjoïr et solacier
ma dame Enyde, vostre fame;
de li veoir a molt ma dame
4125   la reïne grant desirrier:
encor parler l'en oï hier."
Gauvains tantost lez li se tret,
si li demande qu'ele fet,
se ele est bien sainne et heitiee;
4130   cele respont com afeitiee:
"Sire, mal ne dolor n'eüsse,
se an grant dotance ne fusse
de mon seignor, mes ce m'esmaie
qu'il n'a gueires manbre sanz plaie."
4135   Gauvains respont: "Moi poise molt. *
Il apert molt bien a son vout,
qu'il a pale et descoloré,
et g'en eüsse asez ploré,
quant ge le vi si pale et taint,
4140   mes la joie le duel estaint,
car de lui tex joie me vint
que de nul duel ne me sovint.
Or venez petite anbleüre;
g'irai avant grant aleüre
4145   dire la reïne et le roi
que vos venez ci aprés moi.
Bien sai qu'amedui en avront
grant joie, quant il le savront."
Lors s'an part; au tref le roi vient.
4150   "Sire," fet il, "or vos covient *
joie feire, vos et ma dame,
que ci vient Erec et sa fame."
Li rois de joie saut an piez:

4129. heitiee *F*] heitie *C*, haitie *HBPA*, hetie *V*.

182

Since that's the way things are,
I shall tell you my name at once:
hiding it would do me no good.
I am Erec, who used to be
4110 your companion and your friend."
Gawain heard this and went to embrace him;
he lifted up his helmet
and untied his ventail;
for joy he embraced him again and again,
4115 and Erec for his part did likewise.
Then Gawain parted from him
and said: "Sir, this news
will be very pleasing to my lord the king.
My lady and my lord will be delighted,
4120 and I shall go ahead to tell them,
but first I must embrace
and welcome and comfort
my lady Enide, your wife;
my lady the queen is
4125 very eager to see her;
I heard her speak of it only yesterday."
Then Gawain drew near her
and asked her how she was,
whether she was quite healthy and well;
4130 she replied like a well-bred lady:
"My lord, I should have neither pain nor sorrow
were I not extremely concerned
for my lord, but it frightens me
that he has scarcely a limb without a wound."
4135 Gawain replied: "This pains me deeply.
It shows very clearly in his face,
which is pale and colorless,
and I would surely have wept at this,
when I saw him so pale and wan,
4140 but joy extinguishes sorrow,
for he brought me such joy
that I forgot my sorrow.
Now come along at a slow pace;
I shall go swiftly ahead
4145 to tell the queen and the king
that you are coming behind me.
I know well that both of them will be
overjoyed when they learn this."
Then he left; he came to the king's tent.
4150 "Sire," said he, "now you should be
joyful, you and my lady,
for here come Erec and his wife."
The king sprang to his feet for joy:

"Certes," fet il, "molt an sui liez;
4155   ne poïsse novele oïr
qui tant me feïst resjoïr." *
Tantost li rois ist de son tré.   [16f]
Molt ont Erec pres ancontré.
Quant Erec voit le roi venant,
4160   a terre descent maintenant,
et Enyde rest descendue.
Li rois les acole et salue,
et la reïne dolcemant
les beise et acole ausimant:
4165   n'i a nul qui joie n'en face.
Iluec meïsmes an la place
li ont ses armes desvestues,
et quant ses plaies ont veües,
si retorne lor joie en ire.
4170   Li rois molt parfont an sospire, *
puis fet aporter un antret
que Morgue sa suer avoit fet.
Li antrez ert de tel vertu,
que Morgue avoit doné Artu,
4175   que la plaie qui an est ointe,
ou soit sor nerf ou soit sor jointe,
ne faussist qu'an une semainne
ne fust tote senee et sainne,
mes que le jor une foiee
4180   fust de l'antret apareilliee.
L'antret ont le roi aporté,
qui molt a Erec conforté.
Quant ses plaies orent lavees, *
l'antret mis sus et rebandees,
4185   li rois lui et Enyde an mainne
en la soe chanbre demainne,
et dist que por la soe amor
vialt an la forest a sejor
demorer quinze jorz toz plains,
4190   tant que toz soit gariz et sains.
Erec de ce le roi mercie,
et li dist: "Sire, je n'ai mie

4170. *HPV* = *F* (ml't forment *B*)] <u>et</u> le roi <u>et</u> tot son empire *C*; *A has no line
corresponding to 4170.*
4174. Morgue *BVA* = *F* (morge *P*)] morganz *C*; *H omits 4173-74.* |
avoit *PVA* = *F*] ot *C, B* (-1 [*unless B's* do<u>n</u>ey *with dot over* y *is meant to be
trisyllabic*]).
4181. le roi *BPVA* = *FR* (au roi *H*)] .e. [= Erec] *C.*
4182. Erec *HBPVA* = *FR*] le roi *C.*
4183. lavees *HBPVA* = *FR*] bandees *C.*
4184. rebandees *HBVA* = *FR*] relauees *C*, bendees *P* (-1).
4189. demorer *HBPVA* = *F*] seiorner *C.*

"Truly," said he, "I am very glad;
4155 I could hear no other news
that would give me so much joy."
Then the king left his tent.
They met Erec quite close at hand.
When Erec saw the king coming,
4160 he immediately dismounted,
and Enide got down in turn.
The king embraced and greeted them,
and the queen likewise
sweetly kissed and embraced them;
4165 everyone welcomed them joyfully.
Right there on the spot
they removed Erec's armor,
and when they saw his wounds
their joy turned to anger.
4170 The king sighed deeply,
then had an ointment brought
which his sister Morgan had made.
The ointment, which Morgan had given Arthur,
was so wonderfully effective
4175 that the wound to which it was applied,
whether on a nerve or on a joint,
could not fail within a week
to be completely cured and healed,
provided it was treated
4180 with the ointment once a day.
They brought the ointment to the king;
it greatly comforted Erec.
When they had washed his wounds,
put on the ointment and rebandaged them,
4185 the king led him and Enide
into his own chamber,
and said that, out of love for Erec,
he wanted to stay
two full weeks in the forest,
4190 until he was completely healed and well.
Erec thanked the king for this,
and said to him: "Sire, I have no

      plaie de coi je tant me duelle
      que ma voie lessier an vuelle.
4195 Retenir ne me porroit nus:
      demain—ja ne tarderai plus—
      m'an voldrai par matin aler,
      lors que le jor verrai lever."
      Li rois en a crollé le chief,
4200 et dist: "Ci a molt grant meschief,
      quant vos remenoir ne volez.   *[17a]*
      Je sai bien que molt vos dolez;
      remenez, si feroiz que sages,
      car il sera trop granz domages,
4205 se vos an ces forez morez.
      Biax dolz amis, car remenez
      tant que vos soiez respassez."
      Erec respont: "Or est assez.
      Je ai si ceste chose anprise,
4210 ne remanroie en nule guise."
      Li rois ot qu'an nule meniere
      ne remanroit por sa proiere,
      si leisse la parole ester, *
      et comande tost aprester
4215 le souper et les tables metre;
      li vaslet s'an vont antremetre.
        Ce fu un samedi a nuit
      qu'il mangierent poissons et fruit,
      luz et perches, saumons et truites,
4220 et puis poires crues et cuites.
      Aprés souper ne tardent gaire;
      comandent les napes a traire.
      Li rois avoit Erec molt chier;
      an un lit le fist seul couchier:
4225 ne vost qu'avoec lui se couchast
      nus qui ses plaies atochast.
      Cele nuit fu bien ostelez.
      An une chanbre par delez,
      Enyde avoeques la reïne,
4230 sor un grant covertor d'ermine,
      s'an dormirent a grant repos,
      tant que li matins est esclos.
      L'andemain, lués que il ajorne,
      Erec se lieve et si s'atorne:
4235 ses chevax comande anseler
      et fet ses armes aporter;

4196. tarderai *H = F* (targerai *P*)] tardera *CBV*, demoeraj *A* (*omits* ja).
4199. crollé *HBPVA = F*] leue [= levé] *C*.
4211-12 *HBPVA = F4257-58 (4259-60, F1909)*] *omitted C*.
4213. si leisse *BPVA = F*] Or lessiez *C*, Sin laie *H*.
4214. comande tost *HPBVA = F*] si comandez *C*.

wound from which I am suffering so much
that I want to interrupt my journey.
4195 No one could detain me;
tomorrow—I shall tarry no more—
I shall want to leave in the morning,
when I see the day dawning."
At this the king shook his head
4200 and said: "There is something very wrong here,
if you do not wish to stay.
I know full well that you are in great pain;
stay, you will act sensibly,
for it will be a great loss
4205 if you die in this forest.
Fair gentle friend, do stay
until you have recovered."
Erec replied: "That is enough.
I have undertaken this matter,
4210 and would not stay in any manner."
The king heard that there was no way
to convince him to stay,
so he dropped the matter
and ordered the evening meal quickly prepared
4215 and the tables set;
the valets went to work at it.
   It was a Saturday evening
when they ate fish and fruit,
pike and perch, salmon and trout,
4220 and then raw and cooked pears.
They tarried little after the meal;
they ordered the tablecloths removed.
The king held Erec very dear;
he had him sleep alone in a bed:
4225 he did not want anyone to lie with him
who might touch his wounds.
Erec was well lodged that night.
In a nearby chamber
Enide and the queen,
4230 on a great ermine coverlet,
slept in deep repose
until the morning dawned.
The next day, as soon as it was light,
Erec arose and made ready;
4235 he ordered his horses saddled
and had his arms brought to him;

vaslet corent si li aportent.
Ancor de remenoir l'enortent
li rois et tuit li chevalier,
4240 mes proiere n'i a mestier,
que por rien ne vost demorer.
Lors les veïssiez toz plorer
et demener un duel si fort
con s'il le veïssent ja mort.
4245 Erec s'arme; Enyde se lieve.
Au departir a toz molt grieve,
que ja mes reveoir nes cuident.   [17b]
Tuit aprés aus lor tantes vuident;
por lor chevax font anvoier
4250 por ax conduire et convoier.
Erec lor dit: "Ne vos poist pas:
ja avoec moi n'iroiz un pas;
les voz granz merciz, remenez."
Ses chevax li fu amenez,
4255 et il monte sanz demorance;
son escu a pris et sa lance,
si les comande toz a Dé, *
et il i ront lui comandé.
Enyde monte, si s'an vont.
4260 An une forest antré sont;
jusque vers prime ne finerent.
Par la forest tant cheminerent
qu'il oïrent crïer molt loing
une pucele a grant besoing.
4265 Erec a entandu le cri:
bien aparçut, quant il l'oï,
que la voiz de dolor estoit
et de secors mestier avoit.
Tot maintenant Enyde apele:
4270 "Dame," fet il, "une pucele
va par ce bois formant crïant;
ele a, par le mien escïant,
mestier d'aïe et de secors.
Cele part voel aler le cors,
4275 si savrai quel besoing ele a.
Descendez ci, et g'irai la,
si m'atandez andemantiers."
"Sire," fet ele, "volantiers."
Seule la leisse, et seus s'an va,
4280 tant que la pucele trova
qui par le bois aloit crïant
por son ami que dui jaiant
avoient pris, si l'an menoient;

4268. *Final* s *of* secors *added above line.*
4277. si *HBPV = F*] ci *C*.

188

valets ran and brought them.
The king and all his knights
again exhorted him to stay,
4240 but prayers were of no avail,
for he would not stay for anything.
Then you could have seen them all weep
and display such sorrow
as if they beheld him already dead.
4245 Erec put on his armor; Enide arose.
Their departure distressed them all,
for they thought never to see them again.
Everyone, after them, poured out of their tents;
they sent for their horses
4250 in order to accompany and escort them.
Erec said to them: "Be not aggrieved:
you will not go one step with me;
I implore you, stay."
His horse was brought to him,
4255 and he mounted without delay;
he took his shield and his lance,
and commended them all to God,
and they in turn commended him.
Enide mounted, and off they went.
4260 They entered a forest;
they did not stop until about prime.
They rode through the forest
until they heard the distant cry
of a damsel in distress.
4265 Erec heard the cry;
he clearly recognized, when he heard it,
that it was the voice of sorrow
and that it needed help.
Immediately he called to Enide:
4270 "My lady," said he, "some maiden
goes through this wood, crying loudly;
she is, I am sure,
in need of aid and of help.
I want to hurry in her direction,
4275 and find out what her need is.
Dismount here, while I go there,
and wait for me meanwhile."
"My lord," said she, "willingly."
He left her alone, and alone went off,
4280 until he found the maiden
who was crying in the wood
for her lover, whom two giants
had taken prisoner, and were leading away;

vilainnemant le demenoient.

4285   La pucele aloit detirant *
     ses crins, et ses dras desirant
     et sa tandre face vermoille.
     Erec la voit, si s'an mervoille,
     et prie li qu'ele li die

4290   por coi si formant plore et crie.
     La pucele plore et soupire;   *[17c]*
     an sopirant li respont: "Sire,
     n'est mervoille se je faz duel,
     car morte seroie, mon vuel.

4295   Je n'aim ma vie ne ne pris,
     car mon ami an mainnent pris
     dui jaiant felon et crüel
     qui sont si anemi mortel.
     Dex! que ferai, lasse, cheitive,

4300   del meillor chevalier qui vive,
     del plus franc et del plus gentil?
     Or est de mort an grant peril: *
     ancui le feront a grant tort
     morir de molt vilainne mort.

4305   Frans chevaliers, por Deu te pri
     que tu me secores mon ami,
     se tu onques le puez secorre;
     ne t'estovra gueres loing corre:
     ancor sont il de ci molt pres."

4310   "Dameisele, g'irai aprés,"
     fet Erec, "quant vos m'an proiez,
     et tote seüre soiez
     que tot mon pooir an ferai:
     ou avoec lui pris esterai,

4315   ou jel vos randrai tot delivre.
     Se li jaiant le leissent vivre
     tant que je les puisse trover,
     bien me cuit a ax esprover."
     "Frans chevaliers," fet la pucele,

4320   "toz jorz serai mes vostre ancele
     se vos mon ami me randez.
     A Deu soiez vos comandez.

4285. aloit *HBV = F*] saloit *C*, les va *P*. | detirant *HV = F*] tirant *C*, siuant *P*,
      dessirant *B* (desci- *F1909*).
4286. ses crins et ses dras *V*] et ses dras trestoz *C*, Ses mains et ses
      crins *H = F*, Ses dras ... crins *BP = F1896, 1909*. | desirant *CHV = F*]
      detirant *B = F1909*, desrompant *P*.
4302. de mort *HB = F*] erec *C*; *P*: Qui onques fust ne cuens ne rois (*rhyming
      with* cortois *in the preceding line, as does V*); *V*: Qui est de mort en grant
      effrois.
4315. tot *HBPV = F*] a *C*.
4320. serai mes *H = F* (mais serai *BPV*)] seroie *C*.

190

they were vilely mistreating him.
4285 The maiden was tearing
her hair and rending her clothes
and her tender rosy face.
Erec saw her and marveled,
and begged her to tell him
4290 why she was weeping and crying so bitterly.
The maiden wept and sighed,
and sighing she replied: "My lord,
it is no wonder if I show grief,
for I wish that I were dead.
4295 I neither love nor value my life,
for my beloved is taken prisoner
by two evil and cruel giants,
who are his mortal enemies.
God! What shall I do, poor wretch,
4300 for the best knight alive,
the noblest and the most generous?
Now he is in great mortal danger;
today, very wrongfully,
they will make him suffer an ignoble death.
4305 Noble knight, I pray you for God's sake,
assist my beloved,
if ever you can assist him;
you will not need to go far;
they are still very near here."
4310 "Damsel, I will go after them,"
said Erec, "since you beg me to,
and you may be quite sure
that I will do everything in my power:
either I will be taken prisoner with him,
4315 or I will return him to you completely free.
If the giants let him live
until I can find them,
I will certainly give them a fight."
"Noble knight," said the maiden,
4320 "I will always be your servant
if you return my beloved to me.
Be commended to God.

Hastez vos, la vostre merci!"
"Quel part s'an vont?"—"Sire, par ci;
4325 vez ci la voie et les escloz."
Lors s'est Erec mis es galoz,
se li dist que iluec l'atande.
La pucele a Deu le comande
et prie Deu molt dolcemant
4330 que il par son comandemant
li doint force de desconfire
ces qui vers son ami ont ire.
    Erec s'an vet tote la trace;
a esperon les jaianz chace.
4335 Tant les a chaciez et seüz   *[17d]*
que il les a aparceüz
einz que del bois par fussent hors.
Le chevalier vit an pur cors,
deschauz et nu sor un roncin,
4340 con s'il fust pris a larrecin,
les mains lïees et les piez.
Li jaiant n'avoient espiez,
escuz, n'espees esmolues, *
ne lances; einz orent maçues;
4345 escorgiees andui tenoient.
Tant feru et batu l'avoient
que ja li avoient del dos
la char ronpue jusqu'as os;
par les costés et par les flans
4350 li coroit contre val li sans,
si que li roncins estoit toz
an sanc jusqu'au vantre desoz.
Et Erec vint aprés toz seus,
molt dolanz et molt angoisseus
4355 del chevalier, quant il le vit
demener a si grant despit.
Antre deus bois, an une lande,
les a atainz, si lor demande:
"Seignor," fet il, "por quel forfet
4360 feites a cest home tel let,
qui come larron l'an menez?
Trop laidemant le demenez:
ausi le menez par sanblant
con se il fust repris anblant.
4365 Grant viltance est de chevalier
nu despoillier, et puis lïer
et batre si vilainnemant.
Randez le moi: jel vos demant
par franchise et par corteisie;
4370 par force nel demant je mie."

4324. s'an *HBPV = F*] an *C*.

192

Hurry, I implore you!"
"Which way are they headed?"—"My lord, this way;
4325 see here the path and their tracks."
Then Erec set off at a gallop,
telling her to wait for him there.
The maiden commended him to God
and prayed God very softly
4330 that by His will
He might give him the strength to defeat
those who felt ire toward her lover.
    Erec went off along the trail;
he spurred in pursuit of the giants.
4335 So well did he pursue and follow them
that he caught sight of them
before they were completely out of the wood.
He saw the unclad knight,
barefoot and naked upon a draft horse,
4340 bound hand and foot,
as if he had been caught committing larceny.
The giants had neither spears,
shields, sharpened swords,
nor lances; instead they had clubs;
4345 they both held whips.
They had struck and beaten him so much
that on his back they had already
flayed the skin right to the bone;
the blood was running down
4350 along his sides and his flanks,
so that the horse was all covered
in blood, right down to its belly.
And Erec came along all alone,
greatly pained and anxious
4355 for the knight, when he saw him
being treated with such scorn.
Between two woods, in a field,
he caught up with them, and asked them:
"My lords," said he, "for what crime
4360 are you committing such an outrage upon this man,
leading him like a thief?
You are treating him too horribly;
you are leading him as though
he had been caught stealing.
4365 It is most shameful
to strip a knight naked, and then to bind
and beat him so vilely.
Turn him over to me: I ask you this
in generosity and courtesy;
4370 I ask it not by force."

"Vasax," font il, "a vos que tient?
De molt grant folie vos vient
quant vos rien nos an demandez.
S'il vos poise, si l'amandez!"
4375 Erec respont: "Por voir m'an poise.
Ne l'an manroiz hui mes sanz noise;
qant vos bandon m'an avez fait,
qui le porra avoir, si l'ait.
Traiez vos la; je vos desfi!   [17e]
4380 Ne l'an manroiz avant de ci
qu'ainçois n'i ait departiz cos."
"Vasax," font il, "vos estes fos
quant a nos vos volez conbatre.
Se vos estïez or tel quatre,
4385 n'avreïez vos force vers nos
ne c'uns aigniax antre deus los."
"Ne sai qu'an iert," Erec respont.
"Se li ciax chiet et terre font, *
dons sera prise mainte aloe;
4390 tex vaut petit qui molt se loe.
Gardez vos, car je vos requier!"
Li jaiant furent fort et fier,
et tindrent an lor mains serrees
les maçues granz et quarrees.
4395 Erec lor vint lance sor fautre:
ne redote ne l'un ne l'autre
por menace ne por orguel;
einz fiert le premerain an l'uel
si par mi outre le cervel
4400 que d'autre part le haterel
li sans et la cervele an saut,
et cil chiet morz—li cuers li faut.
Quant li autres vit celui mort,
si l'an pesa; n'ot mie tort.
4405 Par mautalant vangier le va:
la maçue a deus mains leva
et cuide ferir a droiture
par mi le chief sanz coverture,
mes Erec le cop aparçut
4410 et sor son escu le reçut.
Tel cop ne por quant li dona
li jaianz que tot l'estona
et par po que jus del destrier
nel fist a terre trebuchier.
4415 Erec de son escu se cuevre,
et li jaianz son cop recuevre
et cuide ferir de rechief
a delivre par mi le chief,
mes Erec tint l'espee trete;
4420 une anvaïe li a fete

194

"Vassal," said they, "what business is it of yours?
It's utter madness on your part
to ask us anything about this.
If you don't like it, do something about it!"
4375 Erec replied: "In truth I do not like it.
You'll take him no further today without a quarrel;
since you have left the matter to me,
let whoever can have him, have him.
Come forward; I challenge you!
4380 You won't take him from here
until we've exchanged blows."
"Vassal," said they, "you're mad,
wanting to fight with us.
Even if there were four of you,
4385 you'd have no more force against us
than a lamb between two wolves."
"I don't know how it will be," Erec replied.
"If the sky falls and the earth collapses,
then many a lark will be taken;
4390 he who boasts a lot is worth little.
Be on your guard, for I'm attacking you!"
The giants were strong and fierce,
and gripped in their hands
the big, square clubs.
4395 Erec came at them, his lance in its rest:
he feared neither one nor the other,
whatever their threats and their pride;
rather he struck the first in the eye,
right through the brain, so that,
4400 at the back of the head,
the blood and brains spurted out
and the giant fell dead—his heart gave out.
When the other saw this one dead,
it grieved him, and with good reason.
4405 Furiously he went to avenge him:
he raised his club with both hands
and thought to strike Erec directly
upon his unprotected head,
but Erec saw the blow coming
4410 and took it on his shield.
Nevertheless the giant gave him
such a blow that he quite stunned him
and nearly made him fall down
from his charger to the ground.
4415 Erec covered himself with his shield,
and the giant prepared another blow
and thought again to strike him
freely on the head,
but Erec held his sword drawn;
4420 he made an attack

195

don li jaianz fu mal serviz:
si le fiert par mi la cerviz
que desi es arçons le fant; [17f]
la böele a terre an espant,
4425   et li cors chiet toz estanduz,
qui fu an deus mitiez fanduz.
Li chevaliers de joie plore,
et reclainme Deu et aore,
qui secors anvoié li a.
4430   A tant Erec le deslïa,
sel fist vestir et atorner
et sor un des chevax monter;
l'autre li fist mener an destre.
Si li demande de son estre,
4435   et cil li dist: "Frans chevaliers,
tu es mes sire droituriers;
mon seignor vuel feire de toi,
et par reison faire le doi,
que tu m'as sauvee la vie:
4440   l'ame me fust del cors partie
a grief tormant et a martire.
Quiex avanture, biax dolz sire,
por Deu t'a ci a moi tramis,
que des mains a mes anemis
4445   m'as osté par ton vaselage?
Sire, je te voel fere homage:
toz jorz mes avoec toi irai;
con mon seignor te servirai."
Erec le vit antalanté
4450   de lui servir a volanté,
se il poïst an nule guise,
et dist: "Amis, vostre servise
ne vuel je pas de vos avoir,
mes ce devez vos bien savoir
4455   que je ving ça an vostre aïe
por la proiere a vostre amie
qu'an ce bois trovai molt dolante;
por vos se conplaint et demande
et molt en a son cuer dolant.
4460   De vos li vuel fere presant:
s'a li rasanblé vos avoie,
puis tandroie toz seus ma voie,
qu'avoec moi n'an iroiz vos mie;
n'ai soing de vostre conpaignie,
4465   mes vostre non savoir desir." *
"Sire," fet il, "vostre pleisir.

4447. toi *HBV = F*] uos *CP.*
4448. te *HBV = F*] uos *CP.*
4461. li *HBPV = F*] lui *C.*

196

that served the giant ill;
he struck him so atop the head
that he split him right down to the saddlebows;
he spilled the guts upon the ground,
4425 and the body fell, stretched out full length,
split into two halves.
The knight wept for joy,
invoked and prayed to God,
who had sent him help.
4430 Then Erec untied him,
and had him dress and make ready
and mount upon one of the horses;
he had him lead the other by hand.
And Erec asked him about himself,
4435 and he replied: "Noble knight,
you are my rightful lord;
I wish to make of you my liege,
and I rightly must do so,
for you have saved my life;
4440 my soul would have been torn from my body *
by painful torment and by torture.
What good fortune, fair gentle lord,
for the love of God, sent you to me here,
so that by your prowess
4445 you freed me from the hands of my enemies?
My lord, I wish to pay you homage:
I shall go with you evermore;
I shall serve you as my liege lord."
Erec saw that he was eager
4450 to serve him as he might wish,
if he could do so in any way,
and said: "Friend, I do not
want service from you,
but you must know
4455 that I came here in your aid
at the behest of your lady,
whom I found most sorrowful in this wood;
because of you she laments and grieves
and her heart is very sorrowful.
4460 I wish to make a present of you to her;
if I reunited you with her,
then I would continue on my way alone,
for you will not be going with me;
I have no desire for your company,
4465 but I wish to know your name."
"My lord," said he, "as you wish.

Quant vos mon non savoir volez,
ne vos doit pas estre celez.
Cadoc de Cabruel ai non;
4470 sachiez qu'ensi m'apele l'on.
Mes quant de vos partir m'estuet,
savoir voldroie, s'estre puet,
qui vos estes et de quel terre,
ou vos porrai trover ne querre
4475 ja mes, quant de ci partirai."
"Ja ce, amis, ne vos dirai,"
fet Erec; "ja plus n'an parlez!
Mes se vos savoir le volez
et moi de rien nule enorer,
4480 dons alez tost sanz demorer
a mon seignor le roi Artu,
qui chace a molt tres grant vertu
an ceste forest de deça,
et, mien escïant, jusque la
4485 n'a mie cinc liues petites.
Alez i tost, et se li dites
qu'a lui vos anvoie et presante
cil qu'il her soir dedanz sa tante *
reçut a joie et herberja,
4490 et gardez ne li celez ja
de quel poinne je ai mis hors
et vostre amie et vostre cors.
Je sui a la cort molt amez:
se de par moi vos reclamez,
4495 servise et enor me feroiz.
La, qui je sui demanderoiz:
nel pöez savoir autremant."
"Sire, vostre comandemant,"
fet Cadoc, "voel je faire tot.
4500 Ja mar an seroiz an redot
que je molt volantiers n'i aille;
la verité de la bataille,
si con l'avez faite por moi,
conterai ge tres bien au roi."
4505 Ensi parlant la voie tindrent

4469-78 *HBPV* = *F4515-24 (4517-26, F1909)*] *omitted C.*
4469. Cabruel (*C 4528*)] tabriole *H*, tabriol *B* = *F*, cardueil *P* (ai a non),
    cabriol *V*.
4470. sachiez qu'ensi *PV* (s. einsi *B* = *F*)] biax sire issi *H*. |
    l'on *B* = *F*] on *HPV*.
4472. voldroie (voudroie *B* = *F*)] ualroie *H*, vorrai se *P*.
4477. ja *BPV* = *F*] ne *H*.
4479. et moi de rien nule *BP* = *F* (et m. de r. bien *H*, et de m. r. n. *V*)] se me
    uolez rien *C*.
4488. l *of* qu'il *inserted, with a short line below.*

Since you wish to know my name,
I must not keep it from you.
My name is Cadoc de Cabruel;
4470 know please that people call me thus.
But if I must depart from you,
I should like to know, if I may,
who you are and from what land,
where I may seek and find you
4475 henceforth, when I have left here."
"That, friend, I shall never tell you,"
said Erec; "say no more about it!
But if you wish to learn it
and honor me in any way,
4480 then go quickly without delay
to my lord King Arthur,
who is hunting in full force
in this forest here,
and, to my knowledge, from here to there
4485 is not even five short leagues.
Go there quickly, and tell him
you are sent to him and presented
by one whom, last night, within his tent,
he joyfully received and lodged,
4490 and be careful not to conceal from him
what trouble I freed you from,
your lady and yourself.
I am much loved at court;
if you mention me,
4495 you will honor and serve me.
There, you will ask who I am;
you cannot find out otherwise."
"My lord," said Cadoc, "I wish to do
everything you order.
4500 You need never fear
that I will not go there most gladly;
I shall carefully tell the king
the truth of the combat,
just as you fought it for me."
4505 Speaking thus they continued their way

199

tant que a la pucele vindrent,
la ou Erec lessiee l'ot.
La pucele molt s'an esjot,
quant son ami revenir voit,
4510 que ja mes veoir ne cuidoit.
Erec par la main li presante
et dist: "Ne soiez pas dolante,
dameisele; veez vos ci
tot lié et joiant vostre ami."
4515 Cele respont par grant savoir:
"Sire, bien nos devez avoir
andeus conquis, et moi et lui;
vostre devons estre anbedui,
por vos servir et enorer.
4520 Mes qui porroit guerredoner   *[18b]*
ceste desserte nes demie?"
Erec respont: "Ma douce amie,
nul guerredon ne vos demant;
amedeus a Deu vos comant,
4525 que trop cuit avoir demoré."
Lors a son cheval trestorné,
si s'an va plus tost que il puet.
Cadoc de Cabruel s'esmuet
d'autre part, il et sa pucele,
4530 s'a recontee la novele
le roi Artus et la reïne.
Erec tote voie ne fine
de chevalchier a grant esploit
la ou Enyde l'atandoit,
4535 qui puis ot eü grant deshet,
qu'ele cuidoit tot antreset
qu'il l'eüst lessiee del tot.
Et il restoit an grant redot
qu'aucuns ne l'an eüst menee,
4540 qui l'eüst a sa loi tornee,
si se hastoit molt del retor.
Mes la chalors qu'il ot le jor
et les armes tant li greverent
que ses plaies li escreverent
4545 et totes ses bandes tranchierent;
onques ses plaies n'estanchierent
tant que il vint au leu tot droit
la ou Enyde l'atandoit.
  Cele le vit, grant joie en ot,
4550 mes ele n'aparçut ne sot
la dolor dom il se plaignoit,
car toz ses cors an sanc baignoit
et li cuers faillant li aloit.
  A un tertre qu'il avaloit,
4555 cheï toz a un fes a val

200

until they came to the maiden,
where Erec had left her.
The maiden greatly rejoiced
when she saw her lover returning,
4510 for she had thought never to see him again.
By the hand Erec presented him to her,
and said: "Do not be sorrowful,
damsel; see here
your lover, happy and joyful."
4515 She replied, full of good sense:
"My lord, we must consider that you
have won us both, myself and him;
we must both be yours,
to serve and honor you.
4520 But who could requite
this service even halfway?"
Erec replied: "My fair friend,
I ask no recompense of you;
I commend you both to God,
4525 for I fear I have tarried too long."
Then he turned his horse about
and rode off as fast as he could.
Cadoc de Cabruel set off
in the other direction, he and his maiden,
4530 and recounted the news
to King Arthur and the queen.
Erec meanwhile kept on
riding at a great pace,
back to where Enide was waiting for him;
4535 she had, meanwhile, felt great sorrow,
for she believed without a doubt
that he had quite abandoned her.
And he in turn was sore afraid
that someone might have led her off,
4540 who would have made her do his will,
and so he hastened to return.
But the heat of the day
and his armor made him suffer
so that his wounds reopened
4545 and all his dressings came apart;
his wounds never stopped bleeding
until he came straight to the place
where Enide was waiting for him.
    She saw him; this gave her great joy,
4550 but she was not aware
of the pain from which he suffered,
for his whole body was bathed in blood
and his heart was failing him.
As he was coming down a knoll,
4555 he fell down all at once

jusque sor le col del cheval;
si com il relever cuida,
la sele et les arçons vuida,
et chiet pasmez con s'il fust morz.
4560 Lors comança li diax si forz,
qant Enyde cheü le vit:
molt li poise quant ele vit,
et cort vers lui si come cele
qui sa dolor mie ne cele.
4565 An haut s'escrie et tort ses poinz;   [18c]
de robe ne li remest poinz
devant le piz a dessirier;
ses chevox prist a arachier
et sa tandre face desire.
4570 "Ha! Dex," fet ele, "biax dolz sire,
por coi me leisses tu tant vivre?
Morz, car m'oci, si t'an delivre!"
A cest mot sor le cors se pasme;
au revenir formant se blasme:
4575 "Ha!" fet ele, "dolante Enyde,
de mon seignor sui omecide!
Par ma folie l'ai ocis:
ancor fust or mes sires vis,
se ge, come outrageuse et fole,
4580 n'eüsse dite la parole
por coi mes sires ça s'esmut.
Ainz boens teisirs home ne nut, *
mes parlers nuist mainte foiee:
ceste chose ai bien essaiee
4585 et esprovee an mainte guise."
Devant son seignor s'est assise,
et met sor ses genouz son chief;
son duel comance de rechief:
"Haï! sire, con mar i fus!
4590 A toi ne s'apareilloit nus,
qu'an toi s'estoit Biautez miree,
Proesce s'i ert esprovee,
Savoirs t'avoit son cuer doné,
Largesce t'avoit coroné,
4595 cele sanz cui nus n'a grant pris.
Mes qu'ai ge dit? Trop ai mespris,
qui la parole ai manteüe
don mes sire a mort receüe,
la mortel parole antoschiee
4600 qui me doit estre reprochiee,
et je requenuis et otroi
que nus n'i a corpes fors moi;

4563. lui *BPV = F*] li *C* (*H is illegible to me; apparently F read* lui *here*).
4583. parlers *BV = FR* (parler *H*)] parlests *C*; Par parler vient mainte folie *P*.

202

upon the neck of his horse;
as he tried to get up again,
he toppled from the saddle
and fell unconscious as though dead.
4560 Then began great sorrowing,
when Enide saw him fallen:
it pained her greatly that she lived,
and she ran toward him like one
who makes no attempt to hide her grief.
4565 She cried aloud and wrung her hands;
upon her breast no portion
of her clothes remained unrent;
she began to tear her hair
and to rend her tender face.
4570 "Oh, God!" said she, "fair sweet lord,
why do you let me live so long?
Death, come kill me, get on with it!"
With these words she fainted upon the body;
when she revived she blamed herself severely:
4575 "Ah!" said she, "sorrowful Enide,
I am the murderess of my lord!
I have killed him by my folly;
my lord would still be alive,
if I, like one both rash and mad,
4580 had not spoken the words
that caused my lord to come here.
A good silence never harmed anyone,
but speaking oftentimes causes harm:
I have truly found this out
4585 by experience, in many a way."
She sat down before her lord
and put his head upon her knees;
her sorrow she began anew:
"Oh, my lord, what misfortune for you!
4590 No other was your equal,
for Beauty was mirrored in you,
Prowess manifested itself in you,
Wisdom had given its heart to you,
Generosity had crowned you,
4595 she without whom no one has great renown.
But what have I said? I have too gravely erred,
mentioning the very words
that have caused my lord's death,
the fatal, poisonous words
4600 with which I must be reproached,
and I acknowledge and concede
that no one is guilty in this but me;

je seule an doi estre blasmee."
Lors rechiet a terre pasmee,
4605 et quant ele releva sus,
si se rescrie plus et plus:
"Dex! que ferai? Por coi vif tant?
La Morz que demore, qu'atant, [18d]
qui ne me prant sanz nul respit?
4610 Trop m'a la Morz an grant despit,
quant ele ocirre ne me daigne;
moi meïsmes estuet que praigne
la vangence de mon forfait:
ensi morrai, mau gré en ait
4615 la Morz qui ne me vialt haidier.
Ne puis morir por souhaidier,
ne rien ne m'i vaudroit conplainte:
l'espee que mes sire a ceinte
doit par reison sa mort vangier.
4620 Ja n'an serai mes an dongier,
n'an proiere ne an souhait."
L'espee hors del fuerre atrait,
si la comance a esgarder;
Dex la fet un petit tarder,
4625 qui plains est de misericorde.
Andemantiers qu'ele recorde
son duel et sa mesavanture,
a tant ez vos grant aleüre
un conte o grant chevalerie,
4630 qui molt de loing avoit oïe
la dame a haute voiz crïer.
Dex ne la vost pas oblïer,
que maintenant se fust ocise,
se cil ne l'eüssent sorprise,
4635 qui li ont l'espee tolue
et arriers el fuerre anbatue.
Puis descendi li cuens a terre,
si li comança a enquerre
del chevalier, qu'ele li die
4640 s'ele estoit sa fame ou s'amie.
"L'un et l'autre," fet ele, "sire; *
tel duel ai ne vos sai que dire,
mes moi poise quant ne sui morte."
Et li cuens molt la reconforte:
4645 "Dame," fet il, "por Deu vos pri,
de vos meïsme aiez merci!
Bien est reisons que duel aiez,
mes por neant vos esmaiez,
qu'ancor porroiz asez valoir.
4650 Ne vos metez an nonchaloir;

4647. duel aiez *BP* = *F* (dol *H*)] u<u>os</u> laiez *C*.

204

I alone must be blamed for it."
Then fainting she fell back upon the ground,
4605 and when she raised up again
she cried out more and more:
"God! What shall I do? Why do I live so long?
Why does Death tarry, what is it waiting for,
that it does not take me without delay?
4610 Death holds me in too great contempt,
since it does not deign to kill me;
I myself must take
the vengeance for my terrible crime:
so I shall die, despite Death,
4615 who does not wish to help me.
I cannot die by wishing,
nor would laments be of any use to me;
the sword that my lord girded on
must by right avenge his death.
4620 No more shall I be in Death's power,
nor plead or wish for it."
She drew the sword from the scabbard
and began to look at it;
God, who is full of mercy,
4625 caused her to delay a little.
While she was recalling
her sorrow and her misfortune,
there came with great speed
a count with a great troop of knights,
4630 who from afar had heard
the lady crying aloud.
God did not wish to abandon her,
for she would have killed herself at once,
had they not surprised her,
4635 taken the sword from her
and shoved it back into the scabbard.
Then the count dismounted
and began to question her
about the knight, that she might tell him
4640 whether she was his wife or his lover.
"The one and the other, my lord," said she;
"my grief is such, I know not what to tell you,
but it pains me deeply that I am not dead."
And the count did much to comfort her:
4645 "My lady," said he, "for God's sake I beg you,
have mercy on yourself!
It is only right that you should feel grief,
but you distress yourself for naught,
for you can still achieve high station.
4650 Do not despair;

confortez vos, ce sera sans:
Dex vos fera liee par tans.
Vostre biautez, qui tant est fine, [18e]
bone avanture vos destine,
4655 que je vos recevrai a fame;
de vos ferai contesse et dame:
ce vos doit molt reconforter.
Et g'en ferai le cors porter,
s'iert mis an terre a grant enor.
4660 Lessiez ester vostre dolor,
que folemant vos deduiez."
Cele respont: "Sire, fuiez!
Por Deu merci, lessiez m'ester!
Ne pöez ci rien conquester;
4665 rien qu'an poïst dire ne faire
ne me porroit a joie atraire."
A tant se trest li cuens arriere
et dist: "Feisons tost une biere
sor coi le cors an porterons,
4670 et avoec la dame an manrons
tot droit au chastel de Limors.
La sera anfoïz li cors;
puis voldrai la dame esposer,
mes que bien li doie peser,
4675 que onques tant bele ne vi
ne dame mes tant ne covi.
Molt sui liez quant trovee l'ai!
Or feisons tost et sanz delai
une biere chevaleresce;
4680 ne vos soit poinne ne peresce!" *
Li auquant traient les espees;
tost orent deus perches colpees
et bastons lïez a travers.
Erec ont mis sus tot anvers,
4685 s'i ont deus chevax atelez.
Enyde chevauchoit delez,
qui de son duel fere ne fine.
Sovant se pasme et chiet sovine;
li chevalier qui la menoient
4690 antre lor braz la retenoient,
si la relievent et confortent.
Jusqu'a Limors le cors an portent
et mainnent el palés le conte.
Toz li pueples aprés aus monte:
4695 dames, chevalier et borjois.
En mi la sale, sor un dois,
ont le cors mis et estandu, [18f]
lez lui sa lance et son escu.

4691. relievent *HBPV = F*] retienent *C*.

206

console yourself, that will be sensible;
God will soon make you happy again.
Your beauty, which is so fine,
destines you for good fortune,
4655 for I shall take you as my wife;
I shall make you my countess and my lady;
this must give you much comfort.
And I shall have the body borne away,
and it will be interred with great honor.
4660 Now leave off your grieving,
for you are behaving senselessly."
She replied: "Sir, begone!
For God's sake, let me be!
You can gain nothing here;
4665 nothing one might say or do
could bring me back to joy."
Then the count drew back
and said: "Let us make a stretcher
on which we will bear away the body,
4670 and we'll take along the lady,
straight to the castle of Limors.
There the body will be buried;
then I shall want to marry the lady,
even though it may grieve her,
4675 for I never saw one so beautiful
nor desired any lady so much.
I'm very glad I found her!
Now quickly and without delay let's make
a horse-borne litter;
4680 let there be no trouble nor laziness!"
Some of them drew their swords;
soon they had cut two poles
and tied sticks across them.
They laid Erec upon this on his back,
4685 and attached two horses to it.
Enide rode beside;
she did not cease her grieving.
Often she fainted and fell backwards;
the knights who were escorting her
4690 supported her in their arms,
and lifted her up and consoled her.
They bore the body away to Limors
and took it into the count's palace.
All the people followed after them:
4695 ladies, knights, and burghers.
In the middle of the great hall, on a table,
they placed the body and laid it out,
his shield and lance beside him.

La sale anpli; granz est la presse:
4700 chascuns de demander s'angresse
quiex diax ce est et quiex mervoille.
Andemantiers li cuens consoille
a ses barons priveemant:
"Seignor," fet il, "isnelemant
4705 voel ceste dame recevoir.
Nos poons bien aparcevoir,
a ce qu'ele est et bele et sage,
qu'ele est de molt gentil lignage;
sa biautez mostre et sa franchise
4710 qu'an li seroit bien l'enors mise
ou d'un rëaume, ou d'un empire.
Je ne serai ja de li pire;
einçois an cuit molt amander.
Fetes mon chapelain mander,
4715 et vos, alez la dame querre:
la mitié de tote ma terre
li voldrai doner an doaire,
s'ele vialt ma volanté faire."
Lors ont le chapelain mandé,
4720 si con li cuens l'ot comandé,
et la dame ront amenee
si li ont a force donee,
car ele molt le refusa,
mes totevoies l'esposa
4725 li cuens, qu'ainsi fere li plot.
Et quant il esposee l'ot,
tot maintenant li conestables
fist el palés metre les tables
et fist le mangier aprester,
4730 car tans estoit ja de soper.
    Aprés vespres, un jor de mai,
estoit Enyde an grant esmai:
onques ses diax ne recessoit,
et li cuens auques l'angressoit,
4735 par proiere et par menacier,
de pes fere et d'esleescier.
Et si l'ont sor un faudestuel
feite aseoir, outre son vuel;
vousist ou non, l'i ont asise
4740 et devant li la table mise.
D'autre part est li cuens asis,   [19a]
qui par un po n'anrage vis,
quant reconforter ne la puet:
"Dame," fet il, "il vos estuet
4745 cest duel lessier et oblïer.

4720. l'ot *HBV = F*] ot *CP*.
4744. *C omits one* il (*-1*).

208

The hall filled up; great was the press:
4700 everyone was pushing to inquire
what grief this was and what a source of wonder.
Meanwhile the count conferred
privately with his barons:
"Lords," said he, "I wish
4705 speedily to receive this lady.
We can easily see,
from both her beauty and her manner,
that she is of very noble lineage;
her beauty and her nobility show
4710 that the honor of a kingdom
or of an empire would be well placed in her.
I shall never be lessened through her;
rather I think to better myself.
Have my chaplain summoned,
4715 and you, go and get the lady:
half of all my land
I wish to give her as a dowry
if she consents to do my will."
Then they summoned the chaplain,
4720 just as the count had ordered,
and in turn they brought the lady
and gave her to him by force,
for she vigorously refused him,
but nonetheless the count
4725 married her, since such was his desire.
And when he had married her,
the constable immediately
had the tables set in the palace
and had the food prepared,
4730 for it was already time for the evening meal.
    After vespers, that day in May,
Enide was greatly dismayed:
never did her grief cease,
and the count pressed her somewhat,
4735 with prayers and with threats,
to make her peace and cheer up.
And upon a faldstool *
they made her sit, against her will;
whether she wished it or no, they seated her there
4740 and set up the table in front of her.
Across from her sat the count,
who was close to going mad
because he could not console her:
"My lady," said he, "you must
4745 leave off and forget this grieving.

209

Molt vos pöez an moi fïer
d'enor et de richesce avoir.
Certainnemant pöez savoir
que por duel nul morz ne revit,
4750   n'onques nus avenir nel vit.
Sovaigne vos de quel poverte
vos est granz richesce aoverte:
povre estïez, or estes riche;
n'est pas Fortune vers vos chiche,
4755   qui tel enor vos a donee
c'or seroiz contesse clamee.
Voirs est que morz est vostre sire;
se vos en avez duel et ire,
cuidiez vos que je m'an mervoil?
4760   Nenil. Mes ge vos doing consoil,
le meillor que doner vos sai:
quant je espousee vos ai,
molt vos devez esleescier.
Gardez vos de moi correcier;
4765   mangiez, quant je vos an semoing!"
"Sire," fet ele, "n'en ai soing.
Certes ja tant con je vivrai, *
ne mangerai ne ne bevrai,
se ge ne voi mangier einçois
4770   mon seignor, qui gist sor ce dois."
"Dame, ce ne puet avenir.
Por fole vos fetes tenir,
quant vos si grant folie dites;
vos en avroiz males merites,
4775   s'ui mes vos an fetes semondre."
Cele ne li vialt mot respondre,
car rien ne prisoit sa menace.
Et li cuens la fiert an la face;
ele s'escrie, et li baron
4780   an blasment le conte an viron:
"Ostez, sire!" font il au conte.
"Molt devreiez avoir grant honte,
qui ceste dame avez ferue
por ce que ele ne manjue.
4785   Trop grant vilenie avez feite: [19b]
se ceste dame se desheite
por son seignor qu'ele voit mort,
nus ne doit dire qu'ele ait tort."
"Teisiez vos an tuit!" fet li cuens.
4790   "La dame est moie et je sui suens,
si ferai de li mon pleisir."

4752. C repeats granz (+1).
4767. Certes ja tant BV = F (C. iamais t. H [omits je])) Sire ia t. C,
       Jamais t. P (viuerai).

210

You can have complete confidence in me
to bring you wealth and honor.
You may know for certain
that grief does not make a dead man live anew,
4750 nor did anyone ever see it happen.
Remember from what poverty
great wealth is opened up to you:
you were poor, and now you're rich;
Fortune is not stingy with you,
4755 since she has given you such honor
that now you will be called 'Countess.'
It is true that your lord is dead;
if you feel grief and sorrow at this,
do you think I am astonished?
4760 Not at all. But I give you this advice,
the best that I can give you:
since I have married you,
you should greatly rejoice.
Beware not to anger me;
4765 eat, since I invite you to!"
"Sir," said she, "I do not care to.
Truly, as long as I shall live,
I shall neither eat nor drink
if I do not first see my lord eat,
4770 who is lying on that table."
"My lady, that cannot be.
You will be considered mad
when you speak so foolishly;
you will be ill rewarded
4775 if you need to be warned again today."
She said not a word in reply,
for she put no value on his threat.
And the count struck her on the face;
she cried out, and the barons
4780 around the count rebuked him:
"Hold, sire!" they said to the count.
"You should be deeply ashamed
of striking this lady
because she does not eat.
4785 You have committed a very great villainy:
if this lady laments
for her lord whom she sees dead,
none should say she is wrong."
"Be silent, all of you!" said the count.
4790 "The lady is mine and I am hers,
and I shall do with her as I will."

Lors ne se pot cele teisir,
einz jure que ja soe n'iert,
et li cuens hauce, si refiert,
4795 et cele s'escria an haut:
"Ahi!" fet ele, "ne me chaut
que tu me dïes ne ne faces:
ne criem tes cos ne tes menaces.
Asez me bat, asez me fier:
4800 ja tant ne te troverai fier
que por toi face plus ne mains,
se tu or androit a tes mains
me devoies les ialz sachier
ou tote vive detranchier!"
4805 Antre ces diz et ces tançons
revint Erec de pasmeisons,
ausi con li hom qui s'esvoille. *
S'il s'esbahi, ne fu mervoille,
des genz qu'il vit an viron lui,
4810 mes grant duel a et grant enui
quant la voiz sa fame antandi.
Del dois a terre descendi
et trait l'espee isnelemant:
ire li done hardemant,
4815 et l'amors qu'an sa fame avoit.
Cele part cort ou il la voit
et fiert par mi le chief le conte
si qu'il l'escervele et esfronte
sanz desfïance et sanz parole:
4820 li sans et la cervele an vole.
Li chevalier saillent des tables:
tuit cuident que ce soit deables
qui leanz soit antr'ax venuz.
N'i remaint juenes ne chenuz,
4825 car molt furent esmaié tuit.
Li uns devant l'autre s'an fuit
quanqu'il pueent a grant eslais; *
tost orent voidié le palés,
et dïent tuit, et foible et fort:
4830 "Fuiez! Fuiez! Veez le mort!"
Molt est granz la presse a l'issue:
chascuns de tost foïr s'argüe;
li uns l'autre anpoint et debote.
Cil qui derriers ert an la rote
4835 volsist estre el premerain front;
ensi trestuit fuiant s'an vont,
que li uns n'ose l'autre atandre.
Erec corrut son escu prandre;
par la guige a son col le pant,

[19c]

4807. con li *HP* = *F*] come *C* (*-1*).

212

Then she could keep silent no more,
but swore that she would never be his,
and the count raised his hand and struck again,
4795 and she cried out loudly:
"Ha!" said she, "I don't care
what you say or do to me:
I fear neither your blows nor your threats.
Beat me, strike me, go ahead:
4800 I'll never find you so fearsome
that I'll do any more or less for you,
even if right now with your own hands
you were to tear out my eyes
or skin me alive!"
4805 In the midst of this talking and quarreling
Erec regained consciousness,
like a man who awakes from sleep.
If he was astonished at the people
he saw around him, it was no wonder,
4810 but he felt deep grief and anguish
when he heard his wife's voice.
He got down from the table
and quickly drew his sword:
wrath made him bold,
4815 and the love he bore for his wife. *
He ran to where he saw her
and struck the count atop the head,
so that he sliced through his brains and his brow,
without challenge and without a word:
4820 the blood and the brains flew out.
The knights jumped up from the tables;
everyone believed it was a devil
that had come among them there.
Neither young nor old remained,
4825 for all were deeply frightened.
One before the other they fled
as fast as they could go, full speed;
they had soon emptied the palace,
and everyone said, both weak and strong:
4830 "Away! Away! The dead man!"
The press at the door was great indeed:
each one rushed to flee;
they struck and shoved each other aside.
He who was at the back of the crowd
4835 wanted to be in the first row;
thus they all ran off,
for one dared not await the other.
Erec ran to take his shield;
he slung it round his neck by the guige,

213

4840 et Enyde la lance prant
si s'an vienent par mi la cort.
N'i a si hardi qui lor tort,
car ne cuidoient pas qu'il fust
nus hom, qui chacier les deüst,
4845 mes deables ou enemis,
qui dedanz le cors se fust mis.
Tuit s'an fuient; Erec les chace,
et trova hors en mi la place
un garçon, qui voloit mener
4850 son cheval a l'aigue abevrer,
atorné de frain et de sele.
Ceste avanture li fu bele:
Erec vers le cheval s'esleisse,
et cil tot maintenant le leisse,
4855 car peor ot grant li garçons.
Erec monte antre les arçons,
puis se prant Enide a l'estrier
et saut sor le col del destrier,
si con li comanda et dist
4860 Erec, qui sus monter la fist.
Li chevax andeus les an porte;
il truevent overte la porte,
si s'an vont, que nus nes areste.
El chastel avoit grant moleste
4865 del conte qui estoit ocis,
mes n'i ot nul, tant fust de pris,
qui voist aprés por le vangier.
Ocis fu li cuens au mangier,
et Erec, qui sa fame an porte,
4870 l'acole et beise et reconforte;
antre ses braz contre son cuer
l'estraint, et dit: "Ma dolce suer,
bien vos ai de tot essaiee.　　　　　　　　　　*[19d]*
Or ne soiez plus esmaiee,
4875 c'or vos aim plus qu'ainz mes ne fis,
et je resui certains et fis
que vos m'amez parfitemant.
Or voel estre d'or en avant,
ausi con j'estoie devant,
4880 tot a vostre comandemant;
et se vos rien m'avez mesdit,
je le vos pardoing tot et quit
del forfet et de la parole."
Adons la rebeise et acole.
4885 Or n'est pas Enyde a maleise,

4848. trova *H* (troue *V*, trueve *F*; trueuent *B*, troe- *P*)] tenoit *C*.
4849. un garçon *HBPV* = *F*] Uns garcons *C*.

214

4840 and Enide took the lance *
     and they came through the middle of the courtyard.
     There was none so bold as to turn to them,
     for they did not believe that there was
     any man who was pursuing them,
4845 but a devil or a demon
     that had gotten into the body.
     Everyone fled; Erec pursued them,
     and outside, in the middle of the square, he found
     a boy, who was about to lead
4850 his horse to drink at the water,
     saddle and bridle all in place.
     This was a fine chance for Erec:
     he rushed toward the horse,
     and the boy let go of it without delay,
4855 for he was extremely frightened.
     Erec got into the saddle;
     then Enide put her foot to the stirrup
     and jumped up to the neck of the charger,
     just as Erec, who had her get on,
4860 instructed her to do.
     The horse bore them both away;
     they found the gate open
     and away they went, for no one stopped them.
     In the castle there was great vexation
4865 because of the count who had been killed,
     but there was no one, of whatever renown,
     who would follow to avenge him. *
     The count was slain at table,
     and Erec, bearing his wife away,
4870 embraced and kissed and comforted her;
     in his arms, against his heart,
     he held her tightly and said: "My sweet sister,
     I have tested you well in every way.
     Now be no more dismayed,
4875 for now I love you more than ever I did,
     and I am once more certain and convinced
     that you love me completely.
     Now I want to be henceforth
     just as I was before,
4880 entirely at your command;
     and if your words offended me,
     I fully pardon and forgive you
     for both the deed and the word."
     Then he kissed and embraced her anew.
4885 Now Enide suffered no more

quant ses sires l'acole et beise
et de s'amor la raseüre.
Par nuit s'an vont grant aleüre,
et ce lor fet grant soatume
4890 que la lune cler lor alume.
    Tost est alee la novele,
que riens nule n'est si isnele.
Ceste novele ert ja alee
a Guivret, et li fu contee
4895 c'uns chevaliers d'armes navrez
ert morz an la forest trovez,
o lui une dame tant bele,
si oel sanbloient estancele, *
et feisoit un duel mervelleus.
4900 Trovez les avoit anbedeus
li cuens Oringles de Limors,
s'an avoit fet porter le cors
et la dame espouser voloit,
mes ele le contredisoit.
4905 Quant Guivrez la novele oï,
de rien nule ne s'esjoï,
qu'araumant d'Erec li sovint;
an cuer et an panser li vint
que il iroit la dame querre,
4910 et feroit le cors metre an terre
a grant enor, se ce est il.
Sergenz et chevaliers ot mil
asanblez por le chastel prandre:
se li cuens ne li volsist randre
4915 volantiers le cors et la dame,
tot meïst an feu et an flame.
A la lune, qui cler luisoit,   [19e]
ses genz vers Lymors conduisoit,
hiaumes laciez, haubers vestuz,
4920 et les escuz as cos panduz,
et si venoient armé tuit.
Et fu ja pres de mie nuit
quant Erec les a parceüz:
or cuide il estre deceüz
4925 ou morz ou pris sanz retenal. *
Descendre a fet de son cheval
Enyde delez une haie;
n'est pas mervoille s'il s'esmaie:
"Remenez ci, dame," fet il,
4930 "un petit delez ce santil,

4886. et beise *BPV = FR*] la beise *C (+1); H omits this line.*
4890. *HBPV = F* (lia *for* lor *in A*)] Que la nuit luisoit cler la lune *C*.
4891. *Initial BVA = FR*] *no large initial CHP.*
4901. Oringles *HBV = F* (origles *P*, orincles *A*)] orguilleus *C. Cf. 5024.*

216

as her lord embraced and kissed her
and reassured her of his love.
Through the night they rode swiftly on,
and it gave them much sweetness
4890 that the moon shone brightly upon them.
　　The news went quickly,
for nothing else is so swift.
This news had already reached
Guivret, for it was recounted to him
4895 that a knight, wounded in combat,
had been found dead in the forest,
and with him a lady so beautiful
that her eyes were like sparks,
and she was showing wondrous grief.
4900 The count Oringle de Limors
had found them both,
and had had the body borne away,
and he desired to marry the lady,
but she refused him.
4905 When Guivret heard the news,
he rejoiced not at all,
for he promptly recalled Erec;
it came to him in heart and mind
that he would go and seek the lady,
4910 and have the body interred
with great honor, if it was he.
A thousand men-at-arms and knights
he had assembled to take the castle;
if the count would not willingly
4915 yield the body and the lady,
he would set everything ablaze.
By the clear light of the moon
he led his people toward Limors;
with helmets laced, in hauberks clad,
4920 and with shields slung about their necks,
thus armored they all came.
It was already near to midnight
when Erec caught sight of them:
then he believed himself betrayed,
4925 or dead or captured without possible rescue.
He had Enide dismount
beside a hedge;
it is no wonder if he was alarmed:
"Stay here, my lady," said he,
4930 "a little while beside this path,

tant que ces genz trespassé soient:
je n'ai cure que il nos voient,
car je ne sai quex genz ce sont
ne quel chose querant il vont.
4935 Espoir nos n'avons d'ax regart,
mes je ne voi de nule part
nul leu ou nos puissiens reduire
s'il nos voloient de rien nuire.
Ne sai se max m'an avandra;
4940 ja por peor ne remandra
que a l'ancontre ne lor aille,
et s'il i a nul qui m'asaille,
de joster ne li faudrai pas.
Si sui je molt duillanz et las;
4945 n'est mervoille se je me duel.
Droit a l'ancontre aler lor vuel,
et vos soiez ci tote coie;
gardez que nus d'ax ne vos voie,
tant qu'il vos aient esloigniee."
4950 A tant ez vos lance beissiee
Guivret, qui l'ot de loing veü;
ne se sont pas reconeü,
qu'an l'onbre d'une nue brune
s'estoit esconsee la lune.
4955 Erec fu foibles et quassez,
et cil fu auques respassez
de ses plaies et de ses cos.
Or fera Erec trop que fos,
se tost conuistre ne se fet.
4960 An sus de la haie se tret,
et Guivrez vers lui esperone;   *[19f]*
de rien nule ne l'areisone,
ne Erec ne li sona mot.
Plus cuida fere qu'il ne pot:
4965 qui plus vialt fere qu'il ne puet,
recroirre ou reposer l'estuet.
Li uns ancontre l'autre joste,
mes ne fu pas igaus la joste,
que cil fu foibles et cil forz.
4970 Guivrez le fiert par tel esforz
que par la crope del cheval
l'an porte a terre contre val.
Enyde, qui tapie estoit,
quant son seignor a terre voit,
4975 morte cuide estre et mal baillie:
hors de la haie estoit saillie,
et cort por aidier son seignor.
S'onques ot duel, lors l'ot graignor.

4973. tapie *BPV = F*] a pie *C*, em pies *H*.

until these people have passed by;
I do not care to have them see us,
for I know not what people they are
nor what it is they seek.
4935 Perhaps we need not fear them,
but I do not see in any direction
any place where we might take refuge
if they wanted to harm us in any way.
I know not whether harm will befall me;
4940 but fear will never prevent me
from going to meet them,
and if any one of them attacks me,
I shall not fail to joust with him.
Yet I am in great pain and very weary;
4945 it is no wonder that I am suffering.
I want to go straight to meet them,
and you, keep very still here;
take care that none of them sees you
till they have left you far behind."
4950 Then came Guivret, with lowered lance,
who had seen him from afar;
they did not recognize each other,
for the moon had hid itself
in the shadow of a dark cloud.
4955 Erec was weak and wounded,
but Guivret was somewhat recovered
from his wounds and from his blows.
Now Erec will act very foolishly
if he does not soon make himself known.
4960 He drew away from the hedge,
and Guivret spurred toward him;
he did not speak to him at all,
nor did Erec say a word to him.
He thought he could do more than he could:
4965 he who wants to do more than he is able
must admit defeat or retire.
They jousted one against the other,
but the joust was not even,
for one was weak and one was strong.
4970 Guivret struck him with such force
that over the horse's croup
he bore him to the ground.
Enide, who was hidden,
when she saw her lord upon the ground,
4975 thought herself dead and done for;
she leapt out of the hedge
and ran to help her lord.
If ever she felt grief, now was it greater.

Vers Guivret vient, si le seisist
4980 par la resne, lors si li dist:
"Chevaliers, maudiz soies tu,
c'un home seul et sanz vertu,
dolant et pres navré a mort
as anvaï a si grant tort
4985 que tu ne sez dire por coi!
Se ci n'eüst ore fors toi,
que seus fusses et sanz aïe,
mar fust feite ceste anvaïe,
mes que mes sires fust heitiez!
4990 Or soies frans et afeitiez,
si lesse ester par ta franchise
ceste bataille qu'as anprise,
que ja n'an valdroit mialz tes pris
se tu avoies morz ou pris
4995 un chevalier qui n'a pooir
de relever—ce puez veoir,
car d'armes a tant cos soferz
que toz est de plaies coverz."
Cil respont: "Dame, ne tamez.
5000 Bien voi que lëaumant amez
vostre seignor, si vos an lo;
n'aiez garde, ne bien ne po,
de moi ne de ma conpaignie.
Mes dites moi, nel celez mie,
5005 comant vostre sires a non,   [20a]
que ja n'i avroiz se preu non.
Qui que il soit, si le me dites,
puis s'an ira seürs et quites;
n'estuet doter ne vos ne lui,
5010 qu'a seür estes anbedui."
Quant Enyde aseürer s'ot,
briémant li respont a un mot:
"Erec a non, mantir n'an doi,
car de bon ere et franc vos voi."
5015 Guivrez descent, qui molt fu liez,
et vet Erec cheoir as piez
la ou il gisoit a la terre:
"Sire, je vos aloie querre,"
fet il, "a Lymors droite voie,
5020 car mort trover vos i cuidoie.
Por voir m'estoit dit et conté
qu'a Lymors en avoit porté
un chevalier a armes mort
li cuens Oringles, et a tort
5025 une dame esposer voloit
qu'ansanble o lui trovee avoit,

4988. mar *HBPV* = *F*] car *C*.

220

Towards Guivret she came, seized
4980 his reins, and said to him:
"Knight, cursed be you,
for you have attacked a man
who is alone and powerless,
in pain and wounded near to death,
4985 so wrongfully that you cannot say why! *
If no one but you were here now,
and you were alone and without help,
this attack would be ill made,
provided my lord were in good health.
4990 Now be generous and noble,
and in your generosity abandon
this combat that you have begun,
for your esteem would never improve
for having killed or captured
4995 a knight who had not the strength
to get up—you can see this,
for he has suffered so many blows
that he is all covered with wounds."
He replied: "My lady, fear not.
5000 I clearly see that you loyally love
your lord, and I praise you for it;
you need not be on your guard at all,
towards me or towards my company.
But tell me, do not conceal it,
5005 the name of your lord,
for you can only gain thereby.
Whoever he may be, tell it to me,
then he will go surely and freely on his way;
neither you nor he need fear,
5010 for you are both safe."
When Enide heard herself reassured,
she replied briefly, in a word:
"His name is Erec, I must not lie,
for I see you are well-born and noble."
5015 Guivret dismounted, full of joy,
and threw himself at Erec's feet
where he was lying on the ground:
"My lord, I was on my way to seek you,"
said he, "straight toward Limors,
5020 for I thought to find you dead.
It was recounted to me as the truth
that Count Oringle had taken to Limors
a knight, who had been killed in combat,
and that he wanted wrongfully
5025 to marry a lady
whom he had found with him,

221

mes ele n'avoit de lui soing.
Et je venoie a grant besoing
por li aidier et delivrer:
5030 se il ne me volsist livrer
la dame et vos sanz contredit,
je me prisasse molt petit
s'un pié de terre li lessasse.
Sachiez, se molt ne vos amasse,
5035 que ja ne m'an fusse antremis.
Je sui Guivrez, li vostre amis,
mes se je vos ai fet enui
por ce que je ne vos conui,
pardoner bien le me devez."
5040 A cest mot s'est Erec levez
an son seant, qu'il ne pot plus,
et dit: "Amis, relevez sus!
De cest forfet quites soiez,
quant vos ne me conoissoiez."
5045 Guivrez se lieve, et il li conte
comant il a ocis le conte
la ou il seoit a la table,
et comant devant une estable
avoit recovré son destrier;   [20b]
5050 comant sergent et chevalier
fuiant crioient an la place:
"Fuiez! Fuiez! Li morz nos chace!";
comant il dut estre antrapez
et comant il est eschapez
5055 parmi le tertre contre val; *
comant sor le col del cheval
an avoit sa fame aportee:
s'avanture li a contee.
Et Guivrez li redist aprés:
5060 "Sire, j'ai un chastel ci pres
qui molt siet bien et an biau leu.
Por vostre aise et por vostre preu
vos i voldrai demain mener,
s'i ferons voz plaies sener.
5065 J'ai deus serors gentes et gaies,
qui molt sevent de garir plaies;
celes vos garront bien et tost.
Enuit ferons logier nostre ost
jusqu'au matin par mi ces chans,

5029. *C has a larger than usual space between* li *and* aidier *("grattage" according to Roques, ed.: 214).*
5053. il *HBV = F*] i *C*; Et conment nus ne li vint pres *P*.
5055-58 *H = F5101-04*] *omitted CBP; V omits 5055-56.*
5055. tertre *H*] chastel *F*.
5057. Et en auoit ... *V (+1)*.

but she cared not for him.
And I was coming in great haste
to help and deliver her:
5030   if he refused to yield freely
the lady and yourself to me,
I would have held myself in low esteem
if I had left him a foot of ground.
Be assured that, if I did not greatly love you,
5035   I should never have been concerned with this.
I am Guivret, your friend,
and if I caused you harm
because I did not recognize you,
you must indeed forgive me."
5040   At these words Erec sat up,
for he could do no more,
and said: "Friend, get up!
You are forgiven for this injury,
since you did not recognize me."
5045   Guivret arose, and Erec told him
how he had slain the count
where he was seated at the table,
and how he had recovered his charger
in front of a stable;
5050   how men-at-arms and knights
fled shouting across the square:
"Away! Away! The dead man is after us!";
how he should have been caught
and how he had escaped
5055   across the hill and down the slope;
how he had borne his wife away
upon the horse's neck:
he recounted his adventure.
And afterwards Guivret said to him:
5060   "My lord, I have a castle near here
that is well situated and in a fine place.
For your comfort and for your benefit
I wish to take you there tomorrow,
and we shall have your wounds taken care of.
5065   I have two sisters, charming and gay,
who know much about healing wounds;
they will heal you well and speedily.
We will have our troops spend
the rest of the night amid these fields,

5070 car grant bien vos fera, ce pans,
enuit un petit de repos:
ci nos loigerons par mon los."
Erec respont: "Ce relo gié."
Iluec sont remés et logié.
5075 Ne furent pas de loigier quoi,
mes petit troverent de quoi,
car il n'i avoit pas po gent;
par ces haies se vont loigent.
Guivrez fist son pavellon tandre
5080 et comande une aesche esprandre
por alumer et clarté feire;
des cofres fet les cierges treire
si les alument par la tante.
Or n'est pas Enyde dolante,
5085 car molt bien avenu li est.
Son seignor desarme et desvest,
si li a ses plaies lavees,
ressuiees et rebandees,
car n'i leissa autrui tochier.
5090 Or ne li set que reprochier
Erec, qui bien l'a esprovee:
vers li a grant amor trovee.
Et Guivrez molt le reconjot:
de coutes porpointes qu'il ot
5095 fist un lit feire haut et lonc,
qu'asez i avoit herbe et jonc;
s'ont Erec couchié et covert.
Et puis li ont un cofre overt
s'an fist hors traire trois pastez.
5100 "Amis," fet il, "or an tastez
un petit de ces pastez froiz.
Vin a eve meslé bevroiz:
j'en ai de boen set barrilz plains,
mes li purs ne vos est pas sains,
5105 car bleciez estes et plaiez.
Biax dolz amis, or essaiez
a mangier, que bien vos fera,
et ma dame ausi mangera,
vostre fame, qui molt a hui
5110 por vos esté an grant enui.
Mes bien vos en estes vangiez:
eschapez estes; or mangiez,
et je mangerai, biax amis."
Delez lui s'est Erec assis
5115 et Enyde, cui molt pleisoit
trestot quanque Guivrez feisoit.
Andui de mangier le semonent;
vin et eve boivre li donent,
car li purs li estoit trop rades.

[20c]

224

5070   because a bit of rest, I believe,
will do you much good this night:
here we will take lodging, by my counsel."
Erec replied: "I too advise this."
There they stayed and took lodging.
5075   They were not hesitant about it,
but they found little to their purpose,
for there were not just a few people;
in the hedges there they took their lodging.
Guivret had his pavilion set up
5080   and ordered a wick to be set afire
to make it light and bright;
from the chests he had the tapers drawn
and they lighted them within the tent.
Now Enide was not sorrowful,
5085   for things had turned out well for her.
She disarmed and disrobed her lord,
and washed his wounds for him,
wiped them and rebandaged them,
for she let no one else touch them.
5090   Now Erec, who had come to know her thoroughly, *
could find nothing to reproach her with:
he had come to feel great love for her.
And Guivret in turn took excellent care of him:
with embroidered quilts
5095   he had a bed made, high and long,
for there was plenty of grass and rushes;
they lay Erec down and covered him.
Then they opened a chest for Guivret
and he had three pâtés drawn forth.
5100   "Friend," said he, "now taste
a bit of these cold pâtés.
You will drink wine mixed with water:
I have seven barrels full of good wine,
but pure wine would not be good for you,
5105   for you are injured and wounded.
Fair sweet friend, now try
to eat, for it will do you good,
and my lady, your wife,
will eat as well, for today
5110   she has suffered greatly because of you.
But you have avenged yourself well:
you have escaped; now eat,
and I too shall eat, fair friend."
Erec sat down beside him,
5115   as did Enide, who was greatly pleased
by everything that Guivret did.
Both of them urged Erec to eat;
they gave him wine and water to drink,
for pure wine was too strong for him.

225

5120 Erec manja come malades
et but petit, que il n'osa,
mes a grant eise reposa
et dormi trestote la nuit,
qu'an ne li fist noise ne bruit.
5125 Au matinet sont esvellié
si resont tuit aparellié
de monter et de chevauchier.
Erec ot molt son cheval chier,
que d'autre chevalchier n'ot cure. *
5130 Enyde ont bailliee une mure,
qui perdu ot son palefroi,
mes n'an fu pas an grant esfroi;
onques n'i pansa par sanblant:
bele mule ot et bien anblant
5135 qui a grant eise la porta.
Et ce molt la reconforta
qu'Erec ne s'esmaioit de rien,
einz li disoit qu'il garroit bien.
A Pointurie, un fort chastel,
5140 qui seoit molt bien et molt bel,
vindrent ainçois tierce de jor.
La demorerent a sejor
les serors Guivret anbedeus,
por ce que biax estoit li leus.
5145 An une chanbre delitable,
loing de noise et bien essorable,
en a Guivrez Erec mené;
a lui garir ont molt pené
ses serors, que il an pria.
5150 Erec an eles se fia,
car celes molt l'aseürerent.
Premiers la morte char osterent,
puis mistrent sus antrait et tante;
a lui garir ont grant antante,
5155 et celes, qui molt an savoient,
sovant ses plaies li lavoient
et remetoient l'antrait sus.
Chascun jor catre foiz ou plus
le feisoient mangier et boivre,
5160 sel gardoient d'ail et de poivre.
Mes qui qu'alast ne anz ne hors,
toz jorz estoit devant son cors
Enyde, cui plus an tenoit.
Guivrez sovant leanz venoit
5165 por demander et por savoir
s'il voloit nule rien avoir.
Bien fu gardez et bien serviz,
car ne fu pas faite a enviz
rien nule qui li fust mestiers,

[20d]

226

5120	Erec ate like a sick man
	and drank little, for he dared not,
	but he rested very comfortably
	and slept the whole night through,
	for the others made no sound or noise.
5125	They awoke at daybreak
	and all prepared anew
	to mount and to ride. *
	Erec greatly prized his horse,
	for he cared to ride no other.
5130	To Enide they gave a mule,
	since she had lost her palfrey,
	but she was not greatly troubled by this,
	and apparently never thought of it:
	she had a fine, easy-gaited mule
5135	that carried her very comfortably.
	And it comforted her greatly
	that Erec was not troubled by anything,
	but rather told her he would recover well.
	To Pointurie, a strong castle,
5140	fine and beautifully situated,
	they came before mid-morning.
	There dwelt tranquilly
	the two sisters of Guivret,
	because the place was beautiful.
5145	To a delightful room,
	far from noise and well aired,
	Guivret led Erec;
	his sisters toiled much to heal him,
	for Guivret begged them to do so.
5150	Erec entrusted himself to them,
	for they greatly reassured him.
	First they removed the dead flesh,
	then applied ointment and dressing;
	they showed great diligence in caring for him,
5155	and, being very knowledgeable,
	they frequently washed his wounds
	and reapplied the ointment.
	Each day four times or more
	they made him eat and drink,
5160	and they kept him away from garlic and pepper.
	But whoever went in or out,
	Enide, to whom it mattered most,
	was at his service every day.
	Guivret often entered there
5165	in order to find out
	whether he desired anything.
	He was well kept and well served,
	for anything he needed
	was not done reluctantly,

227

5170 mes lieemant et volantiers.
A lui garir mistrent grant painne
les puceles: ainçois quinzainne
ne santi il mal ne dolor.
Lors, por revenir sa color,
5175 le comancierent a baignier:
an eles n'ot que anseignier,
car bien an sorent covenir. *
Quant il pot aler et venir,
Guivrez ot fet deus robes feire,
5180 l'une d'ermine et l'autre veire,
de deus dras de soie divers.
L'une fu d'un osterin pers
et l'autre d'un bofu roié
qu'an presant li ot anvoié
5185 d'Escoce une soe cousine.   [20e]
Enide ot la robe d'ermine
et l'osterin qui molt chiers fu;
Erec la veire o le bofu,
qui ne revaloit mie mains.
5190 Or fu Erec toz forz et sains; *
or fu gariz et respassez.
Or fu Enyde liee assez;
or ot sa joie et son deduit:
ansanble gisent par la nuit.
5195 Or ot totes ses volantez;
or li revient sa granz biautez,
car molt estoit et pale et tainte,
si l'avoit ses granz diaus atainte.
Or fu acolee et beisiee;
5200 or fu de toz biens aeisiee;
or ot sa joie et son delit.
Ansanble jurent an un lit,
et li uns l'autre acole et beise:
riens nule n'est qui tant lor pleise.
5205 Tant ont eü mal et enui,

5177. bien an sorent *H* = *F*] bien lor an sot *C* (*P omits 5177-78*).
5187. chiers fu *BP* = *FR* (rices fu *H*, bon fu *V*)] fu chiers *C*.
5193-5200 *HBPVE* = *F5239-46*] omitted *C*.
5193. ot *HBVE* = *F*] a *P*. | sa joie *BPVE* = *F*] samie *H*. |
        deduit *HBPE* = *F*] delit *V*.
5194. ansanble gisent *HB* = *F*] a. iurent *VE*, Or sont ensanle *P*. |
        par la nuit *H* = *F*] ior et n. *BP*, mainte n. *E*, en un lit *V*. *Cf. 5202.*
5196. *HBPV* = *F*] Ore li reuint ml't sa b. *E* (*+1*).
5197. car *HBPE* = *F*] Qui *V*. | molt estoit et *HBPV* = *F*] deuant estoit *E*.
5198. ses *HBV* = *F*] li *PE*. | atainte *HPVE* = *F*] estainte *B*.
5199. fu *BPVE* = *F*] est *H*.
5200. fu *BPVE* = *F*] est *H*. | de toz biens *B* = *F*] del tot bien *HV*, du tout b. *P*.
        E: <u>et</u> de tot son boen aese.

5170 but joyfully and willingly.
The maidens took great pains
to heal him: within a fortnight
he felt neither ache nor pain.
Then, to restore his color,
5175 they began to bathe him:
there was nothing they needed to be taught,
for they knew just how to go about it.
When Erec could get up and move about,
Guivret had two gowns made *
5180 of two different silken fabrics,
one lined with ermine and the other with vair.
One was of deep-blue Oriental silk
and the other of striped brocade
which a cousin had sent him
5185 from Scotland as a present.
Enide had the one with ermine
and the very expensive Oriental silk,
Erec the vair with the brocade,
which was not worth a bit less.
5190 Now Erec was all healthy and strong;
now he was cured and well again.
Now Enide was very joyful;
now she had her joy and her pleasure:
they lay together through the night.
5195 Now she had all that she desired;
now her great beauty returned to her,
for she had been very pale and wan,
so touched had she been by her great sorrow.
Now she was embraced and kissed;
5200 now she had everything she wished;
now she had her joy and her delight.
They lay together in one bed,
and each embraced and kissed the other:
nothing else pleased them so much.
5205 They had had so much pain and trouble,

il por li et ele por lui,
c'or ont feite lor penitance.
Li uns ancontre l'autre tance
comant il li puise pleisir:
5210   del sorplus me doi bien teisir.
Or ont lor amor afermee
et lor grant dolor oblïee,
que petit mes lor an sovient.
Des or raler les an covient,
5215   si ont Guivret congié rové,
cui ami orent molt trové,
que de totes les riens qu'il pot
serviz et enorez les ot.
Erec li dist au congié prandre:
5220   "Sire, je ne puis plus atandre
que je ne m'an aille an ma terre.
Feites apareillier et querre
que j'aie tot mon estovoir:
je voldrai par matin movoir
5225   tantost com il iert ajorné.
Tant ai antor vos sejorné
que je me sant fort et delivre.
Dex, se lui plest, me doint tant vivre
que je ancor an leu vos voie
5230   que la puissance resoit moie
de vos servir et enorer!
Je ne cuit nul leu demorer,
se ne sui pris ou retenuz,
tant qu'a la cort soie venuz
5235   le roi Artus, que veoir vuel
a Quarrois ou a Quaraduel."
Guivrez respont en es le pas: *[20f]*
"Sire, seus n'an iroiz vos pas,
car je m'an irai avoec vos,
5240   et s'an manrons ansanble o nos
conpaignons, s'a pleisir vos vient."
Erec a ce consoil se tient
et dit que tot a sa devise
vialt que la voie soit anprise.
5245   La nuit fet la voie aprester,
car plus n'i vostrent arester;
tuit s'atornent et aparoillent.
Au matinet, quant il s'esvoillent,
sont es chevax mises les seles.
5250   Erec an la chanbre as puceles
va congié prandre einz qu'il s'an tort,

5211. amor afermee *5212 C* (rafermee *H = F*, refermee *B*, afremee *P*)]
       dolor obliee *C*.
5212. dolor obliee *HBP = F (5211 C)*] amor afermee *C*. (*H repeats* or ont lor).

230

he for her and she for him, } ?
that now they had done their penance. } .
They vied with each other
in finding ways of pleasing:
5210 about the rest I must keep silent.
Now they had confirmed their love
and forgotten their great sorrow,
which they little remembered henceforth.
Now they had to go away again,
5215 and they asked leave of Guivret,
whom they had found to be a great friend,
for in every way that he could
he had served and honored them.
When taking leave Erec said to him:
5220 "My lord, I can wait no longer
before returning to my own land.
Have preparations made
so that I may have all I need:
I shall want to set out tomorrow
5225 as soon as it is light.
I have stayed with you so long
that I feel strong and well.
May it please God to let me live so long
that I may meet you again somewhere
5230 and the power may in turn be mine
to serve and honor you!
I do not intend to tarry anywhere,
unless I am captured and held,
until I've come to the court
5235 of King Arthur, whom I wish to see
either at Quarrois or at Quaraduel." *
Guivret immediately replied:
"My lord, you will not leave alone,
for I will go with you,
5240 and we'll take companions along with us,
if that is pleasing to you."
Erec accepted this advice
and said that he wanted the journey undertaken
in whatever way might please Guivret.
5245 That night he had their departure prepared,
for they wished to stay there no longer;
they all outfitted and appareled themselves.
At daybreak, when they awoke,
the horses were saddled.
5250 Erec went to the maidens' chamber,
to take his leave before parting,

et Enyde aprés lui recort,
qui molt estoit joianz et liee
que lor voie ert apareilliee.
5255 As puceles ont congié pris:
Erec, qui bien estoit apris,
au congié prandre les mercie
de sa santé et de sa vie,
et molt lor promet son servise.
5260 Puis a l'une par la main prise,
celi qui plus ert de li pres;
Enide a l'autre prise aprés, *
si sont hors de la chanbre issu,
tuit main a main antre tenu,
5265 si vienent el palés a mont.
Guivrez de monter les semont
maintenant sanz nule demore.
Ja ne cuide veoir cele ore
Enyde qu'il soient monté.
5270 Un palefroi de grant bonté,
söef anblant, gent et bien fet,
li a l'an hors au perron tret.
Li palefroiz fu biax et buens;
ne valoit pas moins que li suens
5275 qui estoit remés a Lymors.
Cil estoit veirs et cist est sors,
mes la teste fu d'autre guise:
partie estoit par tel devise
que tote ot blanche l'une joe
5280 et l'autre noire come choe;   [21a]
antre deus avoit une ligne
plus vert que n'est fuelle de vingne, *
qui departoit del blanc le noir.
Del lorain vos sai dire voir,
5285 et del peitral et de la sele,
que l'uevre an fu et boene et bele:
toz li peitrax et li lorains
estoient d'esmeraudes plains.
La sele fu d'autre meniere,
5290 coverte d'une porpre chiere.
Li arçon estoient d'ivoire,
s'i fu antailliee l'estoire
comant Eneas vint de Troye,
comant a Cartaige a grant joie
5295 Dido an son leu le reçut,
comant Eneas la deçut,
comant ele por lui s'ocist,
comant Eneas puis conquist

5262. Enide *HBPV* = *FR*] .e. *C*.
5276. veirs *HBPV* (vers *F*)] noirs *C. Cf. 1377, 1379, 1398, 2585.*

232

and Enide in turn ran after him,
very joyful and glad
that their departure was prepared.
5255 They took leave of the maidens:
Erec, who was well-mannered,
at leave-taking thanked them
for his health and his life,
and promised them his complete service.
5260 Then he took one of them by the hand,
the one who was nearest to him;
then Enide took the other,
and they came forth from the chamber,
all holding hands together,
5265 and went up into the palace.
Guivret urged them to mount up
straightaway, without delay.
Enide thought she would never see
the moment when they would be mounted.
5270 A well-favored palfrey,
easy-gaited, handsome, and well-made,
was brought out for her to the entrance-steps.
The palfrey was fine and gentle;
it was not worth less than her own
5275 which had stayed at Limors.
That one was dapple-gray and this was sorrel,
but the head was of another sort:
it was divided in such a way
that it had one cheek completely white
5280 and the other as black as a crow;
between the two there was a line,
greener than a vine-leaf, *
that separated the black from the white.
Of the crupper I can tell you truly,
5285 and of the breastplate and the saddle,
that the workmanship was fine and beautiful:
the whole breastplate and the crupper
were full of emeralds.
The saddle was made in another way,
5290 covered with expensive cloth.
The saddle-bows were of ivory,
and there was carved the story
of how Aeneas came from Troy,
how in Carthage with great joy
5295 Dido received him in her bed,
how Aeneas betrayed her,
how she killed herself because of him,
how Aeneas later conquered

233

Laurente et tote Lonbardie,
5300 dom il fu rois tote sa vie.
Soutix fu l'uevre et bien tailliee,
tote a fin or apareilliee.
Uns brez taillierres, qui la fist,
au taillier plus de set anz mist,
5305 qu'a nule autre oevre n'antandi;
ce ne sai ge qu'il la vandi,
mes avoir an dut grant desserte.
Molt ot bien Enyde la perte
de son palefroi restoree,
5310 quant de cestui fu enoree.
Li palefroiz li fu bailliez
si richemant apareilliez,
et ele i monte lieemant; *
puis monterent isnelemant
5315 li seignor et li escuier.
Maint riche ostor sor et muier,
maint faucon et maint esprevier
et maint brachet et maint levrier
fist Guivrez avoec ax porter
5320 por aus deduire et deporter.
     Chevalchié ont des le matin
jusqu'al vespre, le droit chemin,
plus de trante liues galesches,
tant qu'il sont devant les bretesches
5325 d'un chastel fort et riche et bel,   [21b]
clos tot an tor de mur novel;
et par desoz a la reonde
coroit une eve molt parfonde,
roide et bruianz come tanpeste.
5330 Erec an l'esgarder s'areste,
por demander et por savoir
se nus li porroit dire voir
qui de ce chastel estoit sire.
"Amis, savroiz le me vos dire,"
5335 fit il a son boen conpaignon,
"comant cist chastiax ci a non
et cui il est? Dites le moi,
s'il est ou a conte ou a roi;
des que ci amené m'avez,
5340 dites le moi, se vos savez."
"Sire," fet il, "molt bien le sai;
la verité vos an dirai:
Brandiganz a non li chastiax,

5316, 5317 *HBPV = F5362-63*] *interverted* C.
5316. *BPV = F*] Et m. o. s. et gruier C, Oisiax ostoirs sors et m. H.
5321-24 *indentation left for initial* C, *but no initial executed.*
5328. molt *HBPV = F*] si C.

234

Laurentum and all of Lombardy,
5300 where he was king for the rest of his life.
Delicate was the workmanship and well carved,
all embellished with fine gold.
A Breton sculptor, who had made it,
spent more than seven years at the carving,
5305 for he worked on nothing else;
I know not what he sold it for, *
but he must have been richly rewarded.
Enide was very well repaid
for the loss of her palfrey
5310 when she was honored with this one.
The palfrey was given to her
thus richly fitted out,
and she mounted it joyfully;
then the lords and the squires
5315 speedily mounted too.
Many a fine goshawk, both red and moulted, *
many a falcon and many a sparrow-hawk
and many a pointer and many a greyhound
were brought with them at Guivret's behest
5320 for their pleasure and entertainment.
     They rode straight along
from morning until vespers,
more than thirty Welsh leagues,
until they came before the brattices *
5325 of a fortified town, strong and fine,
closed all about by a new wall;
and below it all around
ran a very deep stream,
swift and noisy as a storm.
5330 Erec stopped to look at it,
and to inquire
whether anyone could tell him rightly
who was the lord of this castle.
"Friend, could you tell me,"
5335 said he to his good companion,
"how this castle here is named
and whose it is? Tell me
whether it belongs to a count or a king;
since you have brought me here,
5340 tell me, if you know."
"My lord," said he, "I know it very well;
I shall tell you the truth about it:
the castle is called Brandigan,

qui tant est boens et tant est biax
5345   que roi n'anpereor ne dote.
Se France et la rëautez tote,
et tuit cil qui sont jusqu'au Liege,
estoient anviron a siege,
nel panroient il an lor vies, *
5350   car plus dure de quinze lies
l'isle ou li chastiax est assis,
et tot croist dedanz le porpris
quanqu'a riche chastel covient:
et fruiz et blez et vins i vient,
5355   ne bois ne riviere n'i faut.
De nule part ne crient asaut,
ne riens nel porroit afamer.
Li rois Evrains le fist fermer,
qui l'a tenu an quiteé
5360   trestoz les jorz de son ahé
et tandra trestote sa vie;
mes fermer ne le fist il mie
por ce qu'il dotast nules genz,
mes li chastiax an est plus genz;
5365   que s'il n'i avoit mur ne tor,
mes que l'eve qui cort an tor,
tant forz et tant seürs seroit
que nul home ne doteroit."
"Dex!" fet Erec, "con grant richesce!   [21c]
5370   Alons veoir la forteresce,
et si feisons nostre ostel prandre
el chastel, car g'i voel descendre."
"Sire," fet cil cui molt grevoit, *
"se enuier ne vos devoit,
5375   nos n'i descendrïemes pas:
el chastel a molt mal trespas."
"Mal?" fet Erec. "Savez le vos?
Que que ce soit, dites le nos,
car molt volantiers le savroie."
5380   "Sire," fet il, "peor avroie
que vos n'i eüssiez domage.
Je sai tant an vostre corage
de hardemant et de bonté,
se je vos avoie conté
5385   ce que g'en sai de l'avanture,
qui molt est perilleuse et dure,
que vos i voudrïez aler.
J'en ai sovant oï parler,
que passé a set anz ou plus
5390   que del chastel ne revint nus
qui l'avanture i alast querre;

5352. et *HBPV = F*] Car *C*.

236

and it is so good and fine
5345 that it fears neither king nor emperor.
If France and all the kingdom,
and all those from here to the region of Liège,
surrounded it to lay siege,
they would not take it in their lifetimes,
5350 for the island where the burg is situated
extends for more than fifteen leagues,
and everything grows within the walls
that is needed for a strong town:
fruit and wheat and wine are produced there,
5355 and there is no lack of wood nor water.
From no side does it fear assault,
and nothing could starve it.
It was enclosed by King Evrain,
who has held it peacefully *
5360 all the days of his life
and will hold it as long as he lives;
he did not have it enclosed
because he feared any people,
but the town is finer as a result;
5365 for if there were no wall nor tower,
but only the water that flows around it,
it would be so strong and secure
that it would fear no man."
"God," said Erec, "what great wealth!
5370 Let's go and see the fortress,
and take our lodgings
in the town, for I wish to stay there."
"My lord," said he whom this deeply distressed,
"if you don't mind,
5375 let us not stay there;
there is a very evil ritual in the town."
"Evil?" said Erec. "Do you know what it is?
Whatever it is, tell us,
for I should like to know about it."
5380 "My lord," said he, "I would be afraid
that you would suffer harm from it.
I know that in your heart there is
so much courage and goodness
that, if I told you
5385 what I know of the adventure,
which is very dangerous and difficult,
you would want to go there.
I have often heard tell of it,
for seven years or more have passed
5390 since anyone returned from the town
who went there to seek the adventure;

237

s'i sont venu de mainte terre
chevalier fier et corageus.
Sire, nel tenez mie a geus,
5395   que ja par moi ne le savroiz
de si que creanté m'avroiz,
par l'amor que m'avez promise,
que par vos ne sera requise
l'avanture don nus n'estort
5400   qui n'i reçoive honte et mort."
   Or ot Erec ce qui li siet.
Guivret prie qu'il ne li griet,
et dit: "Haï, biax dolz amis,
sofrez que nostre ostex soit pris
5405   el chastel, si ne vos enuit:
tans est d'osteler mes enuit,
et por ce voel qu'il ne vos poist,
que se il nule enors m'i croist,
ce vos devroit estre molt bel.
5410   De l'avanture vos apel
que seulemant le non me dites,
et del sorplus soiez toz quites."
"Sire," fet il, "ne puis teisir   *[21d]*
que ne die vostre pleisir.
5415   Li nons est molt biax a nomer,
mes molt est griés a asomer,
car nus n'an puet eschaper vis.
L'avanture, ce vos plevis,
la Joie de la Cort a non."
5420   "Dex! an joie n'a se bien non,"
fet Erec; "ce vois je querant.
Ne m'alez ci desesperant,
biax amis, ne de ce ne d'el,
mes feisons prandre nostre ostel,
5425   que granz biens an puet avenir.
Riens ne me porroit retenir
que je n'aille querre la Joie."
"Sire," fet il, "Dex vos en oie,
que vos joie i puissiez trover
5430   et sanz anconbrier retorner!
Bien voi qu'aler vos i estuet. *
Des qu'autremant estre ne puet,
alons: nostre ostex i est pris,
car nus chevaliers de haut pris,
5435   ce ai oï dire et conter,
ne puet an ce chastel antrer,
por ce que herbergier i vuelle,
que li rois Evrains nel recuelle.
Tant est gentix et frans li rois

238

and yet from many a land have come
bold and courageous knights.
My lord, do not consider this a game,
5395 for you will never learn of it from me
until you have pledged,
by the love you have promised me,
that you will never seek
the adventure from which none escapes
5400 without receiving shame and death."
    Now Erec heard something to his liking. *
He begged Guivret not to be aggrieved,
and said: "Ah, fair sweet friend,
permit us to take our lodgings
5405 in the town, if you don't mind;
it is time to find lodging for this night,
and I do not wish to distress you,
for if any honor accrues to me there,
that should bring you great pleasure.
5410 I call upon you to tell me
just the name of the adventure,
and I shall require no more of you."
"My lord," said he, "I cannot keep silent
nor avoid saying what you wish to hear.
5415 The name is beautiful to speak,
but it is painful to achieve,
for no one can escape from it alive.
The adventure, I assure you,
is called the Joy of the Court."
5420 "God! In joy there is naught but good,"
said Erec; "that is what I seek.
Don't go discouraging me here,
fair friend, not in this nor in anything else,
but let us take our lodgings,
5425 for much good may come of this.
Nothing could hold me back
from going in search of the Joy."
"My lord," said he, "may God hear you,
that you may find joy there
5430 and return without hindrance!
I clearly see that you must go there.
Since it cannot be otherwise,
let's go: that is where we will take our lodgings,
for no highly reputed knight,
5435 so I have heard tell,
can enter this town
in search of lodging
without being welcomed by King Evrain.
The king is so noble and gracious

5440 qu'il a fet ban a ses borjois,
si chier con chascuns a son cors,
que prodom qui veigne de hors
an lor meisons ostel ne truisse,
por ce que il meïsmes puisse
5445 toz les prodomes enorer
qui leanz voldront demorer."
Einsi vers le chastel s'an vont,
passent les lices et le pont.
Quant les lices orent passees,
5450 les genz, qui furent amassees
par la rue a granz tropeiax, *
voient Erec, qui tant est biax
que par sanblant cuident et croient
que trestuit li autre a lui soient.
5455 A mervoilles l'esgardent tuit;
la vile an fremist tote et bruit,
tant an consoillent et parolent.   *[21e]*
Nes les puceles qui querolent
lor chant an leissent et retardent.
5460 Totes ansanble le regardent
et de sa grant biauté se saignent;
a grant mervoille le deplaignent:
"Ha! Dex!" dit l'une a l'autre, "lasse!
Cist chevaliers qui par ci passe
5465 vient a la Joie de la Cort.
Dolant an iert einz qu'il s'an tort:
onques nus ne vint d'autre terre
la Joie de la Cort requerre
qu'il n'i eüst honte et domage
5470 et n'i leissast la teste an gage."
Aprés, por ce que il l'antande,
dïent an haut: "Dex te desfande,
chevaliers, de mesavanture!
car tu ies biax a desmesure,
5475 et molt fet ta biautez a plaindre,
car demain la verrons estaindre:
a demain est ta morz venue;
demain morras sanz retenue,
se Dex ne te garde et desfant."
5480 Erec ot bien et si antant
qu'an dit de lui par mi la vile:
il le plaignent plus de set mile,
mes riens ne le puet esmaier.

5440. ban *H = FR*] banc *CB*; a tant fait *P*.
5449. Quant *H* (Et q. *B = F*)] Tant que *C*, T. q. totes les *P*. |
orent *H*] ont *CBP = F*.
5450. les genz *HBP = F*] Et les g. *C*. |
qui furent *H = F* (se f. *B*, qui erent *P*)] qui sont *C*.

240

5440   that he has made a proclamation to his burghers
        that, if they value their lives, *
        no nobleman who comes from outside
        may find lodging in their houses,
        so that he himself may
5445   honor all the noblemen
        who want to stay in the town."
        So they went off toward the town,
        and passed the enceintes and the bridge.
        When they had passed the enceintes,
5450   the people, who were gathered
        along the street in great crowds,
        saw Erec, who was so handsome
        that judging from appearances they thought
        that all the others were in his service.
5455   Everyone looked at him with admiration;
        the whole town was astir with rumors,
        so much were people buzzing and talking.
        Even the maidens dancing their rounds
        left off their singing and postponed it.
5460   All of them together looked at him
        and crossed themselves for his great beauty;
        wondrously they pitied him:
        "Oh, God!" said one to the other, "alas!
        This knight who is passing by
5465   is coming to the Joy of the Court.
        He will suffer from it before he leaves:
        no one ever came from another land
        to seek the Joy of the Court
        without meeting with shame and loss
5470   and forfeiting his head there."
        Then, so that he might hear it,
        they said aloud: "God keep you
        from misfortune, knight,
        for you are extraordinarily handsome,
5475   and much is your beauty to be pitied,
        for tomorrow we shall see it extinguished:
        tomorrow your death has come;
        tomorrow you'll die without delay,
        if God does not protect and defend you."
5480   Erec heard clearly and understood
        what they were saying about him in the town:
        more than seven thousand pitied him,
        but nothing could daunt him.

Outre s'an vet sanz delaier,
5485 saluant deboneiremant
toz et totes comunalmant,
et tuit et totes le salüent.
Li plusor d'angoisse tressüent,
qui plus dotent que il ne fait
5490 ou de sa mort ou de son lait.
Seul de veoir sa contenance,
sa grant biauté et sa sanblance
a si les cuers de toz a lui
que tuit redotent son enui,
5495 chevalier, dames et puceles.
Li rois Evrains ot les noveles
que tex genz a sa cort venoient
qui grant conpaignie menoient,
et bien resanbloit au hernois
5500 que lor sires fust cuens ou rois.
Li rois Evrains en mi la rue   [21f]
vint ancontre ax, si les salue:
"Bien vaigne," fet il, "ceste rote,
et li sires et la genz tote!
5505 Bien vaigniez," fet il; "descendez."
Descendu sont; il fu asez
qui lor chevax reçut et prist.
Li rois Evrains pas n'antreprist
quant il vit Enyde venant,
5510 si la salue maintenant
et corrut aidier au descendre.
Par la main, qu'ele ot bele et tandre,
la mainne an son palés a mont,
si con franchise le semont,
5515 si l'enora de quanqu'il pot,
car bien et bel feire le sot,
sanz folie et sanz mal panser.
Ot feite une chanbre ancenser
d'encens, de mirre et d'aloé:
5520 a l'antrer anz ont tuit loé
le biau sanblant au roi Evrain.
An la chanbre antrent main a main,
si con li rois les i mena,
qui d'ax grant joie demena.
5525 Mes por coi vos deviseroie
la pointure des dras de soie
don la chanbre estoit anbelie?
Le tans gasteroie an folie,
et ge nel vuel mie gaster; *
5530 einçois me voel un po haster,

5492. sanblance *FR* (sam- *H*, sen- *B*)] sablance *C*, sanlace *P*. Cf. *6682.*
5529. gaster *HBP* = *F*] haster *C*.

242

Onward he went without tarrying,
5485 greeting one and all
like one well-born, without making distinctions,
and one and all they greeted him.
Many sweated with anguish,
fearing more than he did himself
5490 either his death or his dishonor.
Just the sight of his bearing,
his great beauty, and his appearance
had so won him the hearts of all
that everyone—knights, ladies, and maidens—
5495 feared the misfortune that would befall him.
King Evrain heard the news
that such people were coming to his court
with a great company,
and it appeared from their equipment
5500 that their lord was a count or a king.
King Evrain came to meet them
in the street and greeted them:
"Welcome," said he, "to this company,
and to the lord and all his people!
5505 Welcome," said he; "do dismount."
They dismounted; there were plenty
who held and took their horses.
King Evrain made no error
when he saw Enide coming,
5510 but immediately greeted her
and ran to help her dismount.
By her beautiful and gentle hand
he led her up into his palace,
just as courtesy required,
5515 and he honored her in all he could,
for he knew full well how to do it,
without any base or foolish thought.
He had had a chamber perfumed
with incense, myrrh, and aloe;
5520 upon entering there everyone praised
King Evrain's fine welcome. *
Hand in hand they entered the chamber,
just as the king had led them there,
rejoicing greatly over them.
5525 But why should I relate to you in detail
the embroidery of the silken tapestries
that embellished the chamber?
I would waste my time in folly,
and I do not wish to waste it;
5530 rather I wish to hurry a bit,

que qui tost va par droite voie
celui passe qui se desvoie:
por ce ne m'i voel arester.
Li rois comanda aprester
5535 le souper, quant tans fu et ore.
Ici ne vuel feire demore,
se trover puis voie plus droite.
Quanque cuers et boche covoite
orent plenieremant la nuit:
5540 oisiax et venison et fruit
et vin de diverse meniere—
mes tot passa la bele chiere,
que de toz mes est li plus dolz
la bele chiere et li biax volz.
5545 Molt furent servi lieemant,   [22a]
tant qu'Erec estrosseemant
leissa le mangier et le boivre
et comança a ramantoivre
ce qui au cuer plus li tenoit:
5550 de la Joie li sovenoit,
s'an a la parole esmeüe;
li rois Evrains l'a maintenue.
"Sire," fet il, "or est bien tans
que je die ce que ge pans
5555 et por coi je sui ci venuz.
Trop me sui del dire tenuz;
or nel puis celer en avant.
La Joie de la Cort demant,
car nule rien tant ne covoit.
5560 Donez la moi, que que ce soit,
se vos an estes posteïs."
"Certes," fet li rois, "biax amis,
parler vos oi de grant oiseuse.
Ceste chose est molt dolereuse,
5565 car dolant a fet maint prodome.
Vos meïsmes a la parsome
an seroiz morz et afolez,
se consoil croirre n'an volez.
Mes se vos me volïez croirre,
5570 je vos löeroie a recroirre
de demander chose si grief,
dons ja ne vandrïez a chief.
N'an parlez plus! Teisiez vos an!
Ne vos vanroit pas de grant san
5575 se vos ne creez mon consoil.
De rien nule ne me mervoil
se vos querez enor et pris;

5549. qui *H = F*] que *C*, donc *B*, dont *P*.
5560. *The* z *of* Donez *is added, on the line, with an insertion mark below.*

244

for he who goes quickly by the direct road
passes him who strays from the path:
therefore I do not wish to tarry.
The king ordered the evening meal prepared,
5535   when the time and the hour had come.
Here I do not wish to linger,
if I can find a more direct route.
Whatever heart and palate desire
they had in abundance that night:
5540   fowl and game and fruit
and wine of various sorts—
but the fine welcome was best of all,
for of all dishes the sweetest is
the fine welcome and the lovely face.
5545   They were served very joyfully,
until suddenly Erec
left off eating and drinking
and began to recall
what he had his heart most set on:
5550   he remembered the Joy,
and began to speak of it;
King Evrain continued the conversation.
"Sire," said he, "now it is truly time
that I tell you what I have in mind
5555   and why I have come here.
I have too long refrained from speaking of it;
now I can conceal it no longer.
I request the Joy of the Court,
for I desire nothing else so much.
5560   Give it to me, whatever it may be,
if it is in your power."
"Truly," said the king, "fair friend,
I hear you speak of great folly.
This subject is very painful,
5565   for it has brought pain to many a good man.
You yourself, in the end,
will be wounded and killed by it,
if you will heed no counsel.
But if you were willing to believe me,
5570   I would advise you to give up
asking for such a painful thing,
in which you could never succeed.
Speak no more of it! Keep silent about it!
You would be very unwise
5575   not to follow my advice.
I do not wonder in the least
if you seek honor and renown;

245

mes se je vos veoie pris
ou de vostre cors anpirié,
5580 molt avroie le cuer irié.
Et sachiez bien que j'ai veüz
mainz prodomes et receüz,
qui ceste Joie demanderent:
onques de rien n'i amanderent,
5585 ainz i sont tuit mort et peri.
Einz que demain soit aseri,
pöez ausi de vos atandre,
se la Joie volez anprandre,
que vos l'avroiz, mes bien vos poist.   [22b]
5590 C'est une chose que vos loist *
a repantir et a retraire,
se vos volez vostre preu faire.
Por ce vos di que traïson
vers vos feroie et mesprison,
5595 se tot le voir ne vos disoie."
Erec l'antant et bien otroie
que li rois a droit le consoille,
mes con plus granz est la mervoille
et l'avanture plus grevainne,
5600 plus la covoite et plus s'an painne,
et dist: "Sire, dire vos puis
que preudome et leal vos truis;
nul blasme ne vos i puis metre
de ce don me vuel antremetre,
5605 comant que des or mes m'an chiee.
Ci an soit la broche tranchiee,
que ja de rien que j'aie anprise
ne ferai tel recreantise
que je tot mon pooir n'an face
5610 ainçois que fuie de la place."
"Bien le savoie," fet li rois;
"vos l'avroiz ancontre mon pois,
la Joie que vos requerez,
mes molt an sui desesperez
5615 et molt dot vostre mescheance.
Mes des or estes an fïance
d'avoir quanque vos covoitiez:
se vos a joie an esploitiez,
conquise avroiz si grant enor
5620 qu'onques hom ne conquist graignor;
et Dex, si con je le desir,
vos an doint a joie partir."
De ce tote la nuit parlerent

5590. que H] qⁱ = qui CB, P (qui me).
5596. otroie BP = F] lotroie CH.
5620. qu'onques HBP = F] Onques C.

246

but if I should see you taken prisoner
or physically wounded,
5580 I should be much aggrieved at heart.
And please know well that I have seen
and welcomed many good men
who requested this Joy:
they never improved their lot in any way,
5585 but rather all of them died and perished there.
Before tomorrow draws to evening,
you may expect a similar fate
if you insist upon the Joy,
for you will have it, but at your cost.
5590 It is a thing that you would better
renounce and withdraw from,
if you want to act in your own interest.
That is why I tell you that
I would betray you and do you wrong
5595 if I did not tell you the whole truth."
Erec heard this and readily granted
that the king had counseled him rightly,
but the greater the wonder
and the more dangerous the adventure,
5600 the more he desired and strove toward it,
and he said: "Sire, I can say
that I find you upright, noble, and true;
I can place no blame on you
for what I wish to undertake,
5605 however it may fall out for me.
Let the matter be decided here and now, *
for never in anything I have undertaken
will I commit such an act of recreance
as to do anything less than my utmost
5610 before fleeing from the field of combat."
"I knew it!" said the king;
"you will have it in spite of me,
the Joy you seek,
but I am in despair
5615 and I greatly fear your misfortune.
But as of now you may be sure
of having what you ardently desire;
if you succeed with joy in this,
you will have conquered a greater honor
5620 than any man has ever conquered;
and God grant, as I desire,
that you may come out of this with joy."
They spoke of this all night

	jusque tant que couchier alerent,
5625	que li lit furent atorné.
	Au matin, quant fu ajorné,
	Erec, qui est an son esvoil,
	voit l'aube clere et le soloil,
	si se lieve tost et atorne.
5630	Enyde a molt grant enui torne
	et molt an est triste et iriee;
	molt an est la nuit anpiriee
	de sopeçon et de peor
	que ele avoit de son seignor,
5635	qui se vialt metre an tel peril.
	Mes tote voie s'atorne il,
	que nus ne l'an puet destorner.
	Li rois, por son cors atorner,
	a son lever li anvea
5640	armes que molt bien anplea.
	Erec nes a pas refusees,
	car les soes furent usees
	et anpiriees et mal mises;
	les armes a volantiers prises
5645	si s'an fet armer an la sale.
	Quant armez fu, si s'an avale
	trestoz les degrez contre val,
	et trueve anselé son cheval
	et le roi qui montez estoit.
5650	Chascuns de monter s'aprestoit,
	et a la cort et as ostés:
	an tot le chastel n'a remés
	home ne fame, droit ne tort, *
	grant ne petit, foible ne fort,
5655	qui aler puise, qui n'i voise.
	A l'esmovoir a molt grant noise
	et grant bruit par totes les rues,
	car les granz genz et les menues
	disoient tuit: "Haï! Haï!
5660	chevaliers, Joie t'a traï,
	ceste que tu cuides conquerre,
	mes ta mort et ton duel vas querre."
	Ne n'i a un seul qui ne die:
	"Ceste Joie, Dex la maudie,
5665	que tant preudome i sont ocis!
	Hui an cest jor fera le pis
	que onques mes feïst sanz dote."
	Erec ot bien et si escote
	que les genz disoient li plus,
5670	car tuit disoient: "Mar i fus,
	biax chevaliers genz et adroiz!

5653-54 *HBPV = F5699-5700*] *omitted* C.

until they retired,
5625 when the beds were prepared.
In the morning, when it was light,
Erec, when he awoke,
saw the clear dawn and the sun,
and he rose quickly and made ready.
5630 Enide was sorely troubled
and deeply sad and distressed;
she had suffered much through the night
from the apprehension and the fear
that she felt on behalf of her lord,
5635 who wanted to place himself in such danger.
But nonetheless he was getting ready,
for no one could dissuade him from it.
The king, in order to equip Erec,
on arising sent him
5640 armor, which Erec put to very good use.
Erec did not refuse it,
for his own was worn
and damaged and in bad shape;
he gladly took the armor
5645 and had himself armed in the hall.
When he was armed, he went
down all the steps
and found his horse saddled
and the king already mounted.
5650 Everyone made ready to mount,
both in the court and in the lodgings;
in all the castle there remained
neither man nor woman, well-formed or ill,
tall or short, weak or strong,
5655 who could go along and did not do so.
When they set out there was great noise
and clamor in all the streets,
for the high folk and the low
were all saying: "Oh! Oh!
5660 Joy has betrayed you, knight,
the one you think to conquer,
but you are seeking your death and sorrow."
There was not one who did not say:
"God curse this Joy,
5665 since so many good men have died there!
This day without doubt it will do
the worst that it has ever done."
Erec heard well and listened to
what the people were saying most,
5670 for all were saying: "Woe to you,
fair, noble, and upright knight!

Certes ne seroit mie droiz
que ta vie si tost fenist,
ne que nus enuiz t'avenist,
5675 don bleciez fusses ne leidiz."
Bien ot la parole et les diz,
mes tote voie outre s'an passe:
ne tint mie la teste basse;
ne fist pas sanblant de coart.

[22d]

5680 Qui qu'an parost, molt li est tart
que il voie et sache et conoisse
dom il sont tuit an tel angoisse,
an tel esfroi et an tel poinne.
Li rois hors del chastel le moinne
5685 an un vergier qui estoit pres,
et tote la gent vont aprés
priant que de ceste besoigne
Dex a joie partir l'an doigne.
Mes ne fet pas a trespasser,
5690 por lengue debatre et lasser,
que del vergier ne vos retraie
lonc l'estoire chose veraie.

El vergier n'avoit an viron
mur ne paliz, se de l'air non,
5695 mes de l'air est de totes parz
par nigromance clos li jarz,
si que riens antrer n'i pooit,
se par un seul leu n'i antroit,
ne que s'il fust toz clos de fer.
5700 Et tot esté et tot yver
y avoit flors et fruit maür,
et li fruiz avoit tel eür
que leanz se lessoit mangier,
mes au porter hors fet dongier;
5705 car qui point an volsist porter
ne s'an seüst ja mes raler,
car a l'issue ne venist
tant qu'an son leu le remeïst.
Ne soz ciel n'a oisel volant,
5710 tant pleise a home par son chant, *
por lui deduire et resjoïr,
qu'iluec ne poïst l'an oïr
plusors de chascune nature.
Et terre, tant com ele dure,
5715 ne porte espice ne mecine

5679-81. *The first letters of these lines—* Ne f, Qui, Que *—are missing
because the upper corner of the folio has been torn off.*
5710. tant *P*] Qui *CHB* = *F*. | par son chant *P*] an chantant *C* (*-1*),
qui ni cant *H* = *F*, tant ne quant *B*.
5711. por *HBP* = *F*] A *C*.

Surely it would not be right
that your life should end so soon,
nor that any misfortune befall you,
5675 to wound you or dishonor you."
He clearly heard the words and the talk,
but nonetheless he went on:
he did not bow his head at all;
he had nothing of the look of a coward.
5680 Whoever may speak of it, he was impatient
to see and learn and know
what it was that caused them such anguish,
such fright and such grief.
The king led him out of the town
5685 and into a garden that was nearby,
and all the people went after,
praying that from this urgent need
God might let him leave with joy.
But it is not proper to pass on,
5690 though tongue be worn out and fatigued,
without telling you, concerning the garden,
a true thing according to the story.
    Around the garden there was
neither wall nor palisade, only air,
5695 but the garden was enclosed on all sides
with air, by black magic,
so that nothing could enter
except through one single place,
any more than if it were enclosed with iron.
5700 And all summer and all winter
there were flowers and ripe fruit,
and the fruit had the peculiar property
that it could be eaten therein,
but it could not be carried out;
5705 whoever wanted to take some away
could never discover how to get out again,
for he could not reach the exit
until he put the fruit back in its place.
Nor is there beneath heaven a flying bird,
5710 however much it pleases man with its song,
to gladden and delight him,
that could not be heard therein,
and several of each sort.
And the earth, however far it spreads,
5715 bears no spice or medicinal plant

qui vaille a nule medecine,
que iluec n'i eüst planté,
s'an i avoit a grant planté.
5720 Leanz par une estroite antree
est la torbe des genz antree,
li rois avant et tuit li autre.
Erec aloit, lance sor fautre,
par mi le vergier chevauchant,
qui molt se delitoit el chant
5725 des oisiax qui leanz chantoient,
qui la Joie li presantoient,
la chose a coi il plus baoit.
Mes une grant mervoille voit
qui poïst faire grant peor
5730 au plus hardi conbateor
de trestoz ces que nos savons, *
se fust Tiebauz li Esclavons,
ou Opiniax ou Fernaguz:
car devant ax sor pex aguz
5735 avoit hiaumes luisanz et clers,
et voit de desoz les cerclers
paroir testes desoz chascun;
mes au chief des pex an voit un
ou il n'avoit neant ancor,
5740 fors que tant solemant un cor.
Il ne set que ce senefie,
ne de neant ne s'an esfrie,
einz demanda que ce puet estre
au roi, qui lez lui ert a destre.
5745 Li rois li dit et si li conte:
"Amis, savez vos que ce monte,
ceste chose que ci veez?
Molt an seroiez esfreez,
se vos ameiez vostre cors,
5750 car cil seus piex qui est dehors,
ou vos veez ce cor pandu,
a molt longuemant atandu
un chevalier; ne savons cui,
se il atant vos ou autrui.
5755 Garde ta teste n'i soit mise,
car li pex siet a la devise.
Bien vos en avoie garni,
einçois que vos venissiez ci.

5730. hardi *HBP = F*] riche *C.*
5731, 5732 *HBP = F5777-78*] *interverted C.*
5731. de trestoz *H = F* (De tous *P*, De toz ices *B*)] Ne nus de *C.* |
       nos *HB = F*] or *C*, nos or *P.*
5732. se fust *B = F* (Si f. *H*, Ne f. *P*)] Ce fu *C.*
5733. ou ... ou *HP = F*] Ne ... ne *C.*

252

of use in any remedy
that was not planted therein,
and there were a great plenty of them.
Through a narrow entry-way
5720 the crowd of people entered,
first the king and then all the others.
Erec rode along through the garden,
his lance in its rest,
delighting in the singing
5725 of the birds that sang therein,
presenting to him the Joy,
the thing to which he most aspired.
But he saw a wondrous thing
that could frighten
5730 the boldest warrior
of all those we know,
be it Thibaut the Slavonian,
or Ospinel or Fernagu:
in front of them on sharpened stakes
5735 there were bright and shining helmets,
and beneath each one he saw
a head appear below the circlet;
but at the end of the stakes he saw one
where there was nothing yet,
5740 apart from a horn.
He did not know what this meant,
but he was not at all worried,
and instead asked the king,
who was beside him on his right, what this might be.
5745 The king answered and recounted to him:
"Friend, do you know the meaning
of this thing you see here?
You would greatly fear it
if you valued your well-being,
5750 for this one stake set apart,
where you see that horn hanging,
has for a long time been waiting
for a knight; we know not whom,
whether it waits for you or another.
5755 Take care your head is not placed there,
for the stake stands for that purpose.
I warned you well of this
before you came here.

Ne cuit que ja mes an issiez,
5760   si soiez morz et detranchiez.
Des ore an savez vos itant
que li piex vostre teste atant,
et se ç'avient qu'ele i soit mise,
si con chose li est promise
5765   des qu'il i fu mis et dreciez,
uns autres pex sera fichiez
aprés celui, qui atandra   *[22f]*
tant que ne sai qui revandra.
Del cor ne vos dirai je plus,
5770   fors c'onques soner nel pot nus;
mes cil qui soner le porra,
et son pris et s'enor fera
devant toz ces de ma contree,
s'avra tel enor ancontree
5775   que tuit enorer le vandront
et au meillor d'ax le tandront.
Or n'i a plus de cest afere:
feites voz genz arriere trere,
car la Joie vanra par tans,
5780   qui vos fera dolant, ce pans."
    A tant li rois Evrains le leisse;
et cil vers Enyde se beisse,
qui delez lui grant duel feisoit,
ne por quant ele se teisoit,
5785   car diax que l'an face de boche
ne vaut neant, s'au cuer ne toche.
Et cil, qui bien conuist son cuer,
li a dit: "Bele douce suer,
gentix dame lëax et sage,
5790   bien conuis tot vostre corage:
peor avez grant, bien le voi,
si ne savez ancor por coi.
Mes por neant vos esmaiez
jusqu'a itant que vos voiez
5795   que mes escuz iert depeciez
et ge dedanz le cors bleciez,
et verroiz de mon hauberc blanc
les mailles covrir de mon sanc,
et mon hiaume frait et quassé,
5800   et moi recreant et lassé,
que plus ne me porrai desfandre,
ainz m'estovra merci atandre
et deprier outre mon vuel.
Lors porroiz fere vostre duel,
5805   que trop tost comancié l'avez.
Douce dame, ancor ne savez

5784. ele *BP*] sele *CH*; cele *F*, s'ele *F1896, 1909*.

254

I do not believe you will ever leave here,
5760 unless you are dead and dismembered.
Now you know this much of it,
that the stake awaits your head,
and if it happens to be put there,
as the thing has been promised
5765 since the stake was placed and raised there,
another stake will be planted
after this one, which will wait
until someone else comes along in turn.
Of the horn I shall tell you no more,
5770 except that no one was ever able to sound it;
but anyone who is able to sound it
will establish his renown and his honor
above all those of my land,
and he will have met with such honor
5775 that all will come to honor him
and will consider him the best among them.
Now there is no more of this matter:
have your people withdraw,
for the Joy will come presently,
5780 and will make you suffer, I think."
  Then King Evrain left him,
and Erec leaned toward Enide,
who was feeling great sorrow at his side,
and yet she kept silent,
5785 for sorrow to which one gives voice
is worth naught if it does not touch the heart.
And he, who knew her feelings well,
said to her: "Fair sweet sister,
noble lady, loyal and wise,
5790 I know well what is in your heart:
you are sorely afraid, I see it clearly,
but you do not yet know why.
Still, you distress yourself for naught,
until such time as you see
5795 that my shield is in pieces
and I am wounded in my person,
and you see the links
of my white hauberk covered with my blood,
and my helmet smashed and broken,
5800 and me tired and defeated,
no longer able to defend myself,
but rather obliged to await
and beg for mercy against my wishes.
Then you can carry out your mourning,
5805 for you have begun it too soon.
Sweet lady, you do not yet know

255

que ce sera, ne ge nel sai:
de neant estes an esmai,
car bien sachiez seüremant,
5810 s'an moi n'avoit de hardemant
fors tant con vostre amors m'an baille,
ne crienbroie je an bataille,
cors a cors, nul home vivant.
Si fais folie, qui m'an vant,
5815 mes je nel di por nul orguel,
fors tant que conforter vos vuel.
Confortez vos! Lessiez ester!
Je ne puis plus ci arester,
ne vos n'iroiz plus avoec moi,
5820 car avant mener ne vos doi,
si con li rois l'a comandé."
Lors la beise et comande a Dé,
et ele i recomande lui,
mes molt li torne a grant enui
5825 quant ele nel siust et convoie
tant qu'ele sache et qu'ele voie
quex avanture ce sera
et comant il esploitera.
Mes a remenoir li estuet,
5830 car avant sivre ne le puet:
ele remaint triste et dolante.
Et cil s'an vet tote une sante,
seus, sanz conpaignie de gent,
tant qu'il trova un lit d'argent
5835 covert d'un drap brosdé a or,
desoz l'onbre d'un siquamor,
et sor le lit une pucele,
gente de cors et de vis bele
de totes biautez a devise,
5840 la s'estoit tote seule assise.
De li ne vuel plus deviser,
mes qui bien seüst raviser
et son ator et sa biauté,
dire poïst por verité
5845 c'onques Lavine de Laurente,
qui tant par fu et bele et gente,
n'en ot de sa biauté le quart. *
Erec s'aproche cele part,
qui de plus pres la vialt veoir;
5850 lez li s'ala Erec seoir.
A tant ez vos un chevalier,
soz les arbres, par le vergier,

5836. lo *of* lonbre *illegible in C* (*MS stained or scraped*).
5847. n'en ot de sa *H*] Not de nule *C*, Not mie de *P*.
5852. soz *HB = F*] sor *CP*.

256

what will occur, nor do I know;
you distress yourself for naught,
for know this without any doubt:
5810 if there were no bravery in me
apart from what your love gives me,
I would not fear to do battle,
hand to hand, with any man alive.
I act foolishly, boasting thus,
5815 yet I do not say this out of pride,
but only because I wish to comfort you.
Console yourself! Let it be!
I cannot stop here any longer,
nor can you go on with me,
5820 for I must lead you no further,
as the king has commanded it."
Then he kissed her and commended her to God,
and she in turn commended him,
but it greatly troubled her
5825 not to follow and accompany him
until she might know and see
what sort of adventure it would be
and how he would fare.
But she had to stay behind,
5830 for she could follow him no further:
she stayed there, sad and sorrowful.
And he went on along a path,
alone, without any company,
until he found a silver bed
5835 covered with a sheet embroidered with gold,
in the shade of a sycamore,
and on the bed a maiden,
gracious of body and fair of face,
endowed with every kind of beauty,
5840 was seated all alone.
I do not wish to describe her further,
but anyone who knew how to examine
both her adornments and her beauty
could say in truth
5845 that never did Lavinia of Laurentum,
who was so very beautiful and noble,
have a quarter of her beauty.
Erec drew near in that direction,
wanting to see her more closely;
5850 he went to sit down beside her.
At that moment a knight came along
beneath the trees through the garden,

257

armé d'unes armes vermoilles,
qui estoit granz a merevoilles,
5855 et s'il ne fust granz a enui,
soz ciel n'eüst plus bel de lui,
mes il estoit un pié plus granz,
a tesmoing de totes les genz,
que chevaliers que l'an seüst.
5860 Einz que Erec veü l'eüst,
si s'escrïa: "Vasax! Vasax!
Fos estes, se ge soie sax,
qui vers ma dameisele alez.
Mien escïant, tant ne valez
5865 que vers li doiez aprochier.
Vos conparroiz ancui molt chier
vostre folie, par ma teste.
Estez arriers!" Et il s'areste,
si le regarde, et cil s'estut.
5870 Li uns vers l'autre ne se mut
tant qu'Erec respondu li ot
trestot quanque dire li plot:
"Amis," fet il, "dire puet l'an
folie ausi tost come san.
5875 Menaciez tant con vos pleira,
et je sui cil qui se teira,
qu'an menacier n'a nul savoir.
Savez por coi? Tex cuide avoir *
le geu joé, qui puis le pert,
5880 et por c'est fos tot en apert
qui trop cuide et qui trop menace.
S'est qui fuie, asez est qui chace, *
mes je ne vos dot mie tant
que je m'an fuie; ainçois atant, *
5885 apareilliez de moi desfandre,
s'est qui estor me voelle randre,
que par force feire l'estuisse
n'autremant eschaper n'an puisse."
"Nenil," fet il, "se Dex me saut!
5890 Sachiez bataille ne vos faut,
que je vos requier et desfi."
Ice sachiez vos tot de fi:
einz puis n'i ot resnes tenues;
n'orent mie lances menues,
5895 ainz furent grosses et plenees,
et si estoient bien fenees,
s'an furent plus roides et forz.
Sor les escuz par tel esforz
s'antre fierent des fers tranchanz
5900 que par mi les escuz luisanz
passa de chascun une toise;
mes li uns l'autre an char n'adoise,

258

dressed in vermilion armor,
so tall that it was a wonder to behold,
5855 and had he not been excessively tall,
there would have been under heaven none fairer,
but he was taller by a foot,
according to everyone's testimony,
than any knight ever known.
5860 Before Erec had seen him,
he shouted out: "Vassal! Vassal!
You are mad, upon my soul,
to go toward my damsel.
By my word, you are not so worthy
5865 that you should approach her.
This very day you will pay most dearly
for your folly, by my head.
Stand back!" And he stopped
and looked at him, and Erec stood firm.
5870 Neither moved toward the other
until Erec had replied
and said everything he wished:
"Friend," said he, "one can speak
folly as easily as wisdom.
5875 Threaten all you like,
and I shall just keep silent,
for there is no wisdom in threats.
Do you know why? One may believe
he has won the game, and then may lose it,
5880 and therefore whoever is too confident
and threatens too much is clearly mad.
If there is one to flee, there is another to pursue,
but I do not fear you so much
as to flee; rather, I am waiting, *
5885 ready to defend myself,
if there is anyone who wants to do battle with me
until I am forced to do so
and cannot otherwise escape."
"No," said he, "God save me!
5890 Be assured that you'll get to fight,
for I attack and challenge you."
Now know this for certain:
reins were held in check no more;
they did not have slender lances,
5895 but rather they were thick and well planed,
and they were well seasoned,
which made them stronger and more rigid.
Upon their shields they struck each other
with the heads of their lances, with such force
5900 that through the shining shields
a fathom of each one passed;
but neither touched the other's flesh,

259

ne lance brisiee n'i ot.
Chascuns au plus tost que il pot
5905 a sa lance sachiee a lui,
si s'antre vienent anbedui
et revienent a droite joste.
Li uns ancontre l'autre joste,
si se fierent par tel angoisse
5910 que l'une et l'autre lance froisse
et li cheval desoz aus chieent.
Et cil qui sor les seles sieent
ne se tienent a rien grevé:
isnelemant sont relevé,
5915 car preu estoient et legier.
A pié sont en mi le vergier,
si s'antre vienent demanois
as boens branz d'acier vïenois
et fierent granz cos et nuisanz
5920 sor les escuz clers et luisanz,
si que trestoz les escartelent
et que li oel lor estancelent;
ne ne se pueent mialz pener
d'aus anpirier et d'ax grever
5925 que il se painnent et travaillent.
Andui fieremant s'antr'asaillent
as plaz des branz et as tranchanz.
Tant se sont martelé les danz
et les joes et les nasez
5930 et poinz et braz et plus assez,
temples et hateriax et cos,
que tuit lor an duelent li os.
Molt sont duillant et molt sont las;
ne por quant ne recroient pas,
5935 ainçois s'esforcent mialz et mialz.
La süors lor troble les ialz,
et le sans qui avoec degote,
si que par po ne voient gote,
et bien sovant lor cos perdoient
5940 come cil qui pas ne veoient
les espees sor aus conduire;
ne ne pooit mes gueres nuire
li uns a l'autre; ne por quant   [23d]
ne dotez ja ne tant ne quant
5945 que tote lor force n'an facent.
Por ce que li oel lor esfacent
si que tot perdent le veoir,
leissent jus lor escuz cheoir
si s'antr'aerdent par grant ire.

5930. *The first* s *of* assez *is added above the line.*
5948. leissent jus *HB = F*] et leissent *C* (*P omits 5945-50*).

260

nor was there a broken lance.
Each of them, as quickly as he could,
5905 violently pulled back his lance,
and they came at each other again
and came back to proper jousting.
They jousted one against the other,
and struck each other with such violence
5910 that both lances shattered
and the horses fell beneath them.
They, who remained seated in their saddles,
considered themselves none the worse off;
speedily they got back up,
5915 for they were bold and nimble.
On foot in the orchard,
they came at each other straightaway
with their good blades of steel from Vienne, *
and they struck mighty and damaging blows
5920 on the bright and shining shields,
so that they broke them all apart,
and their eyes glittered;
they could take no greater pains
to wound and injure one another
5925 than they toiled and strove to do.
Each of them fiercely attacked the other
with the flat of his blade and with the edge.
They had so hammered each other's teeth
and cheeks and nasals *
5930 and wrists and arms and plenty more,
temples and napes and necks,
that all their bones ached.
They were in great pain and very tired;
nonetheless they did not give up,
5935 but instead strove more and more.
The sweat blurred their vision,
as did the blood dripping with it,
so that they could barely see at all,
and often their blows went astray
5940 like those of men who could not see
to direct their swords at each other;
they could scarcely do any more harm
to one another; and yet
never fear in any way
5945 that they did not do all they could.
Because their eyes were growing so dim
that they were completely losing their sight,
they let their shields fall
and seized each other with great fury.

5950 Li uns l'autre sache et detire,
     si que sor les genouz s'abatent;
     ensi longuemant se conbatent,
     tant que l'ore de none passe,
     et li granz chevaliers se lasse
5955 si que tote li faut l'alainne.
     Erec a son talant le mainne
     et sache et tire, si que toz
     les laz de son hiaume a deroz
     et si que devers lui l'ancline.
5960 Cil chiet adanz sor la poitrine,
     ne n'a pooir de relever;
     que que il li doie grever,
     li covint dire et otroier:
     "Conquis m'avez, nel puis noier,
5965 mes molt me torne a grant contraire.
     Et ne por quant de tel afaire
     pöez estre et de tel renon
     qu'il ne m'an sera se bel non;
     et molt voldroie par proiere,
5970 s'estre puet an nule meniere,
     que je vostre droit non seüsse,
     por ce que confort an eüsse.
     Se miaudres de moi m'a conquis,
     liez an serai, ce vos plevis;
5975 mes se il m'est si ancontré
     que pires de moi m'ait outré,
     de ce doi ge grant duel avoir."
     "Amis, tu viax mon non savoir,"
     fet Erec, "et jel te dirai; *
5980 ja ainz de ci ne partirai,
     mes ce iert par tel covenant
     que tu me dïes maintenant
     por coi tu ies an cest jardin.
     Savoir an voel tote la fin,
5985 que ton non dïes et la Joie,
     que molt me tarde que je l'oie."
     "La verité del tot an tot,   [23e]
     sire," fet il, "sanz nul redot,
     vos dirai tot quanque vos plest."
5990 Erec son non plus ne li test:
     "Oïs onques parler," fet il,
     "del roi Lac et d'Erec son fil?"
     "Oïl, sire, bien le conui,
     car a la cort le roi Lac fui
5995 mainz jorz, ainz que chevaliers fusse,
     ne ja, son vuel, ne m'an meüsse
     d'ansanble lui por nule rien."
     "Dons me doiz tu conuistre bien,
     se tu fus onques avoec moi

262

5950	They heaved and pulled at one another
	so that they fell upon their knees;
	in this way they fought on at length,
	until the hour of nones was past, *
	and the tall knight grew weary
5955	and completely out of breath.
	Erec could lead him as he wished
	and heaved and pulled him, so that all
	the laces of his helm were ruptured
	and he made him bow before him.
5960	Face down upon his chest he fell,
	and had no strength to rise again;
	however much it grieved him,
	he was forced to say and grant:
	"You have defeated me, I cannot deny it,
5965	but it is much against my liking.
	Nevertheless you may be
	of such condition and such renown
	that it will bring me only pleasure;
	I should very much like to request,
5970	if it can be in any way,
	that I might know your true name,
	so as to have comfort thereby.
	If a better man than I has defeated me,
	I shall be glad, I promise you;
5975	but if it has befallen me
	that a lesser man has outdone me,
	I must be grieved because of that."
	"Friend, you wish to know my name,"
	said Erec, "and I shall tell you;
5980	never shall I leave here beforehand,
	but this will be upon the condition
	that you tell me without delay
	why you are in this garden.
	I want to know the whole story,
5985	to learn your name and about the Joy,
	and I am very impatient to hear it."
	"The truth in its entirety,
	my lord," said he, "without any doubt,
	I'll tell you all you wish to know."
5990	Erec concealed his name no more:
	"Did you ever hear tell," said he,
	"of King Lac and of his son Erec?"
	"Indeed, my lord, I knew him well,
	for I was at King Lac's court
5995	many a day, before becoming a knight,
	and never, had he had his way,
	would I have left for anything."
	"Then you must know me well,
	if ever you were with me

263

6000 a la cort mon pere le roi."
"Par foi, donc m'est bien avenu!
Or öez qui m'a retenu
an cest vergier si longuemant:
trestot vostre comandemant
6005 voel je dire, que qu'il me griet.
Cele pucele, qui la siet,
m'ama des anfance et je li.
A l'un et a l'autre abeli
et l'amors crut et amanda,
6010 tant que ele me demanda
un don, mes el nel noma mie.
Qui veheroit neant s'amie?
N'est pas amis qui antresait
tot le boen s'amie ne fait,
6015 sanz rien leissier et sanz faintise,
s'il onques puet an nule guise.
Creantai li sa volanté,
et quant li oi acreanté,
si vost ancor que li plevisse.
6020 Se plus volsist, plus an feïsse,
mes ele me crut par ma foi.
Fïançai li, si ne soi quoi
tant qu'avint que chevaliers fui:
li rois Evrains, cui niés je sui,
6025 m'adoba veant mainz prodomes
dedanz cest vergier ou nos somes.
Ma dameisele, qui siet la,
tantost de ma foi m'apela
et dist que plevi li avoie
6030 que ja mes de ceanz n'istroie   *[23f]*
tant que chevaliers i venist
qui par armes me conqueïst.
Reisons fu que je remainsisse,
ainz que ma fïance mantisse,
6035 ja ne l'eüsse je plevi.
Des que ge soi le bien an li,
a la rien que ge oi plus chiere
n'an dui feire sanblant ne chiere
que nule rien me despleüst,
6040 car, se ele l'aparceüst,
el retraissist a li son cuer,
et je nel volsisse a nul fuer
por rien qui poïst avenir.
Ensi me cuida retenir
6045 ma dameisele a lonc sejor;

6022. Fïançai *BP = F*] Fiancie *C*, Creantai *H*.
6036. bien an li *BP*] boen et ui *C*; D. q. io le bien en li ui *H = F*.
    (*F gives the reading from BP in his later editions.*)

264

6000   at my father's court."
        "By my faith, then it has truly happened!
        Now hear who has kept me
        so long in this garden:
        as you have ordered, I wish to tell
6005   everything, however much it may grieve me.
        That maiden, who is sitting there, *
        loved me from childhood, and I loved her.
        Both of us were pleased by this
        and our love grew and improved,
6010   until she asked a boon of me,
        but she did not say what it was.
        Who would refuse his lady anything?
        He is no lover who does not
        unhesitatingly do whatever pleases his lady,
        neglecting nothing and unstintingly,
6015   if ever he can in any way.
        I promised I would do her will,
        and when I had promised her this,
        she still wanted me to swear it on oath.
6020   Had she wished for more, I would have done it,
        but she believed me on my word.
        I made her a promise, but knew not what,
        until it happened that I became a knight;
        King Evrain, whose nephew I am,
6025   dubbed me in the sight of many gentlemen,
        within this garden where we are.
        My damsel, who is sitting there,
        immediately invoked my oath
        and said that I had sworn to her
6030   that I would never leave this place
        until some knight came along
        who defeated me in combat.
        It was right for me to remain,
        rather than be untrue to my oath,
6035   or I should never have sworn to it.
        Since I knew the good in her,
        in the thing that I held most dear,
        I must not show in any way
        that anything displeased me,
6040   for, if she had noticed it,
        she would have withdrawn her love,
        and at no price did I wish that,
        no matter what might happen.
        Thus my damsel thought
6045   to keep me for a long stay;

ne cuidoit pas que a nul jor
deüst an cest vergier antrer
vasaus qui me deüst outrer.
Par ce me cuida a delivre,
6050 toz les jorz que j'eüsse a vivre,
avoec li tenir an prison.
Et ge feïsse mesprison
se de rien nule me fainsisse
que trestoz ces ne conqueïsse
6055 vers cui ge eüsse puissance:
vilainne fust tex delivrance.
Bien vos puis dire et acointier
que je n'ai nul ami si chier
vers cui je m'an fainsisse pas;
6060 onques mes d'armes ne fui las,
ne de conbatre recreüz.
Bien avez les hiaumes veüz
de ces que j'ai vaincuz et morz;
mes miens n'an est mie li torz,
6065 qui reison voldroit esgarder:
de ce ne me poi ge garder,
se ge ne volsisse estre fax
et foi mantie et deslëax.
La verité vos en ai dite,
6070 et, sachiez bien, n'est pas petite
l'enors que vos avez conquise.
Molt avez an grant joie mise
la cort mon oncle et mes amis,
c'or serai hors de ceanz mis.
6075 Et por ce que joie an feront   [24a]
tuit cil qui a la cort vanront,
Joie de la Cort l'apeloient
cil qui la joie an atandoient.
Tant longuemant l'ont atandue
6080 que premiers lor sera randue
par vos, qui l'avez desresniee.
Molt avez matee et fesniee
mon pris et ma chevalerie,
et bien est droiz que je vos die
6085 mon non, quant savoir le volez:
Maboagrins sui apelez, *
mes ne sui nes point coneüz
an leu ou j'aie esté veüz,
par remanbrance de cest non,
6090 s'an cest païs solemant non,
car onques tant con vaslez fui
mon non ne dis ne ne conui.

6053. me fainsisse *BP = FR* (men f. *H*)] mespreisse *C*.

266

she did not think that into this garden
might ever come
a vassal who was to outdo me.
Thus she thought to keep me with her,
6050 all the days of my life,
completely in her power, in prison.
And I should have committed a grievous fault
had I held back in any way
from defeating all those
6055 over whom I had power:
such a deliverance would have been ignoble.
I can truly say and inform you
that I have no friend so dear
that I would have held back at all against him; *
6060 never was I weary of bearing arms
or tired of fighting.
You have seen the helmets
of those I have defeated and killed;
but the fault is not at all mine,
6065 for anyone willing to look aright:
I could not help do what I did,
if I did not want to be false
and faithless and disloyal.
I have told you the truth of this,
6070 and, know you well, it is no small
honor which you have won.
You have brought great joy
to the court of my uncle and my friends,
for now I shall be released from here.
6075 And because all those who come to court
will rejoice at this,
those who awaited the joy of it
called it the Joy of the Court.
They have awaited it so long
6080 that it will first be granted them
by you, who have contended for it.
You have quite defeated and becharmed *
my valor and my prowess,
and it is only right that I tell you
6085 my name, since you wish to know it:
I am called Maboagrain,
but I am not at all well known
in any place where I've been seen,
by recollection of that name,
6090 except in this land,
for while I was a youth I never
spoke my name nor revealed it.

Sire, la verité savez *
de quanque vos requis m'avez,
6095   mes a dire vos ai ancor.
Il a an cest vergier un cor,
que bien avez veü, ce croi:
hors de ceanz issir ne doi
tant que le cor aiez soné,
6100   et lors m'avroiz desprisoné
et lors comancera la Joie.
Qui que l'antande et qui que l'oie,
ja essoines ne le tandra,
quant la voiz del cor antandra,
6105   qu'a la cort ne vaigne tantost. *
Levez de ci, sire; alez tost
por le cor isnelemant prandre,
que n'i avez plus que atandre,
s'an feites ce que vos devez."
6110   Maintenant s'est Erec levez,
et cil se lieve ansanble o lui;
au cor an vienent anbedui.
Erec le prant et si le sone;
tote sa force i abandone
6115   si que molt loing an va l'oïe.
Molt s'an est Enyde esjoïe *
quant ele la voiz antandi,
et Guivrez molt s'an esjoï.
Liez est li rois et sa gent liee:
6120   n'i a un seul cui molt ne siee
et molt ne pleise ceste chose;   *[24b]*
nus n'i cesse ne ne repose
de joie feire et de chanter.
Ce jor se pot Erec vanter
6125   c'onques tel joie ne fu feite;
ne porroit pas estre retreite
ne contee par boche d'ome,
mes je vos an dirai la some
briémant sanz trop longue parole.
6130   Par le païs novele vole
qu'ainsi est la chose avenue.
Puis n'i ot nule retenue
que tuit ne venissent a cort;
de toz sanz li pueples i cort,
6135   qu'a pié que a cheval batant,
que li uns l'autre n'i atant.

6093. verité *HP = F*] veritez *C*.
6105. qu'a *HB = F*] Qu<u>e</u> a *CP* (*P omits* la). | tantost *HBP = F*] tost *C*.
6117-18 *HBPV = F6163-64*] *omitted C*.
6117. quant ele la voiz *BPV = F*] Qant la uois del cor *H*.
6118. et Guivrez *HBV = F*] et li rois *P*.

268

My lord, you know the truth
of everything you asked me about,
6095 but I have still more to tell you.
There is in this garden a horn,
which you clearly saw, I believe:
I must not leave this place
until you have sounded the horn,
6100 and then you will have freed me from prison
and then will the Joy begin.
Whoever hears and understands it
will be held back by no obstacle,
when he hears the voice of the horn,
6105 from coming to the court at once.
Arise from here, my lord; go right away,
swiftly to take the horn,
for there is no reason to delay;
so do with it what you must."
6110 At once Erec arose,
and the other arose with him;
they came together to the horn.
Erec took it and sounded it;
he put all his strength into it
6115 so that the sound was heard afar.
At this Enide greatly rejoiced
when she heard the voice of the horn,
and Guivret too greatly rejoiced.
Happy was the king as were his people;
6120 there was not a one whom this thing
did not greatly suit and please;
everyone sang and rejoiced
without cease or rest.
That day Erec could boast
6125 that never had there been such rejoicing;
it could not be described
nor recounted by mouth of man,
but I shall tell you briefly the sum of it,
without speaking at too great length.
6130 The news flew throughout the land
that the thing had happened in this way.
Then there was no preventing
all the people from coming to court;
from all directions they came running,
6135 some on foot, some rapidly on horseback,
for no one waited for anyone else.

Et cil qui el vergier estoient
d'Erec desarmer s'aprestoient,
et chantoient par contançon
6140 tuit de la joie une chançon,
et les dames un lai troverent
que le Lai de Joie apelerent,
mes n'est gueres li lais saüz.
Bien est de joie Erec paüz
6145 et bien serviz a son creante,
mes celi mie n'atalante
qui sor le lit d'argent seoit.
La joie que ele veoit
ne li venoit mie a pleisir—
6150 mes mainte gent covient sofrir
et esgarder ce qui lor poise.
Molt fist Enyde que cortoise:
por ce que pansive la vit
et seule seoir sor le lit,
6155 li prist talanz que ele iroit
a li si li demanderoit
de son afeire et de son estre,
et anquerroit s'il pooit estre
qu'ele del suen li redeïst,
6160 mes que trop ne li desseïst.
Seule i cuida Enyde aler,
que nelui n'i cuida mener,
mes des dames et des puceles,
des mialz vaillanz et des plus beles,
6165 la suioient une partie   [24c]
par amor et par conpaignie,
et por celi feire confort
a cui la joie enuioit fort,
por ce qu'il li estoit a vis
6170 c'or ne seroit mes ses amis
avoec li tant com il soloit,
quant il del vergier issir doit.
A cui que il desabelisse, *
ne puet müer qu'il ne s'an isse,
6175 que venue est l'ore et li termes;
por ce li coroient les lermes
des ialz tot contreval le vis.
Molt plus que je ne vos devis
estoit dolante et correciee,
6180 et ne por quant si s'est dreciee; *
mes de nule ne li est tant
de ces qui la vont confortant
que ele an lest son duel a feire.

6173. A cui que il *H = F*] A c. quil onques *C*, Mais que q. li *B*, Mais que
il bien li *P*. | desabelisse *HB = F*] abelisse *C*, despleust *P*.

270

And those who were in the garden
made ready to remove Erec's armor,
and all tried to outdo one another
6140 in singing a song about the joy,
and the ladies composed a lay
which they called the Lay of Joy,
but the lay is little known.
Erec truly had his fill of joy
6145 and was well served according to his wishes,
but it was far from pleasing her
who sat upon the silver bed.
The joy she saw
did not please her a bit—
6150 but many people must permit
and look at what distresses them.
Enide behaved most courteously:
because she saw the maiden sitting pensively
by herself upon the bed,
6155 she decided she would go
to her and ask her
about her business and her situation,
and would inquire whether she might
tell her in turn about her own,
6160 provided that did not overly displease her.
Enide thought to go there alone
and to take no one else with her,
but some of the ladies and the maidens,
among the worthiest and most beautiful,
6165 followed her, moved by friendship
and the desire to keep her company,
and to bring comfort to her
who was greatly distressed by the Joy,
because it seemed to her
6170 that henceforth her lover would no longer
be with her as he was accustomed,
since he was to leave the garden.
Whoever might be displeased by it,
he could not help leaving it,
6175 since the appointed hour and term had come;
therefore the tears were running
from her eyes all down her face.
She was much more saddened and upset
than what I have described to you,
6180 but nonetheless she arose;
yet of those who were comforting her
none meant so much to her
that she would leave off grieving.

271

Enyde, come de bon eire,
6185 la salue; cele ne pot
de grant piece respondre mot,
car sopir et sanglot li tolent
qui molt l'anpirent et afolent.
Grant piece aprés li a randu
6190 la dameisele son salu,
et quant ele l'ot esgardee
une grant piece et ravisee,
sanbla li qu'ele l'ot veüe
autre foiee et coneüe,
6195 mes n'an fu pas tres bien certainne;
ne d'anquerre ne li fu painne
dom ele estoit, de quel païs,
et don ses sires ert naïs:
d'aus deus demande qui il sont.
6200 Enyde tantost li respont
et la verité li reconte:
"Niece," fet ele, "sui le conte
qui tient Laluth an son demainne,
fille de sa seror germainne;
6205 a Laluth fui nee et norrie."
Ne puet müer que lors ne rie
cele qui tant s'an esjoïst,
einz que plus dire li oïst,
que de son duel mes ne li chaut.   [24d]
6210 De leesce li cuers li saut,
car ne puet sa joie celer;
beisier la vet et acoler
et dist: "Je sui vostre cosine;
sachiez que c'est veritez fine,
6215 et vos estes niece mon pere,
car il et li vostres sont frere.
Mes je cuit que vos ne savez,
ne oï dire ne l'avez,
comant je ving an ceste terre.
6220 Li cuens vostre oncles avoit guerre,
si vindrent a lui an soldees
chevalier de maintes contrees.
Ensi, bele cosine, avint
que avoec un soudoier vint *
6225 li niés le roi de Brandigan;
chiés mon pere fu pres d'un an,
bien a, ce croi, douze anz passez.
Ancor estoie anfes asez,
et il ert biax et avenanz;

6199. *The* s *of* aus *is inserted above the line.*
6211. car *B*] Ne *C*; Sa j. ne p. mes c. *H = F*; Ensi fu demie loee *P (rhyming with* Puis la baisie et acolee *in the following line).*

272

Enide, like a well-born woman,
6185 greeted her; for a long time
the maiden could not reply,
for sighs and sobs prevented her
and hurt and made her most unwell.
Long afterwards the maiden
6190 returned her greeting,
and when she had looked long at Enide
and examined her attentively,
it seemed to her that she had seen her
before and been acquainted with her,
6195 but she was not really certain;
she eagerly inquired of her
where she was from, from what land,
and where her lord was from;
she asked her who both of them were.
6200 Enide at once replied
and recounted the truth to her:
"I am the niece," said she, "of the count
who holds Laluth in his domain,
the daughter of his own sister;
6205 I was born and raised in Laluth."
The maiden could not keep from laughing then,
before she heard her say any more;
she was so overjoyed at this
that she cared no more for her grief.
6210 Her heart leapt for happiness,
for she could not conceal her joy;
she went to kiss and embrace her
and said: "I am your cousin;
know that this is the absolute truth,
6215 and you are my father's niece,
for he and yours are brothers.
But I believe you do not know
and have not heard
how I came to this land.
6220 The count your uncle was at war,
and knights from many lands
came to serve him for pay.
Thus, fair cousin, it happened
that with a mercenary came
6225 the nephew of the King of Brandigan;
he spent nearly a year with my father,
fully twelve years ago, I believe.
I was still just a young child,
and he was handsome and pleasing;

273

6230 la feïmes noz covenanz
antre nos deus, tex con nos sist.
Einz ne vos rien qu'il ne volsist,
tant qu'a amer me comança,
si me plevi et fïança
6235 que toz jorz mes amis seroit
et que il ça m'an amanroit;
moi plot et a lui d'autre part.
Lui demora et moi fu tart
que ça m'an venisse avoec lui;
6240 si nos an venimes andui
que nus ne le sot mes que nos.
A cel jor antre moi et vos
estïens juenes et petites.
Voir vos ai dit; or me redites,
6245 ausi con ge vos ai conté,
de vostre ami la verité,
par quel avanture il vos a."
"Bele cosine, il m'espousa
si que mes peres bien le sot
6250 et ma mere qui joie en ot.
Tuit le sorent et lié an furent
nostre parant, si com il durent.

[24e]

Liez an fu meïsmes li cuens,
car il est chevaliers si buens
6255 qu'an ne porroit meillor trover,
ne n'est or pas a esprover
de bonté ne de vaselage:
ne set l'an tel de son aage,
ne cuit que ses parauz soit nus.
6260 Il m'ainme molt, et je lui plus,
tant qu'amors ne puet estre graindre.
Onques ancor ne me soi faindre
de lui amer, ne je ne doi.
Voir, mes sires est filz de roi,
6265 et si me prist et povre et nue;
par lui m'est tex enors creüe
qu'ainz a nule desconseilliee
ne fu si granz apareilliee.
Et, s'il vos plest, jel vos dirai,
6270 si que de rien n'an mantirai,
comant je ving a tel hautesce;
ja del dire ne m'iert peresce."
Lors li conta et reconut
comant Erec vint a Laluth,
6275 car ele n'ot del celer cure.
Bien li reconta l'avanture
tot mot a mot, sanz antrelais;

6240. nos an venimes *HBP = FR*] nos uenimes *C (-1).*

274

6230   there we exchanged vows
        between the two of us, such as pleased us.
        I never wanted anything that he did not want,
        until at length he began to love me,
        and he swore to me and promised
6235   that he would always be my lover
        and that he would bring me here;
        this pleased me and him as well.
        He was impatient and so was I
        to come away here with him;
6240   we both came here in such a way
        that no one knew of it but us.
        At that time both you and I
        were young and little.
        I've told you the truth; now tell me in turn,
6245   just as I have told you,
        the truth about your lover,
        and by what chance he has you."
        "Fair cousin, he married me
        in such a way that my father knew it well
6250   and it gave my mother joy.
        All our relatives knew of it and
        were happy, as they should have been.
        The count himself was happy about it,
        for my lord is such a fine knight
6255   that one could find no better,
        and he is beyond proving himself
        in goodness and in valor:
        no one else of his age measures up to him,
        and I believe no one is his equal.
6260   He loves me deeply and I love him even more,
        so that love cannot be greater.
        I could never pretend
        to love him, nor should I.
        Truly, my lord is the son of a king,
6265   and yet he took me poor and naked;
        through him my honor has increased so much
        that such was never bestowed upon
        any poor, unprotected creature.
        And, if you wish, I shall tell you,
6270   and it will be nothing but the truth,
        how I attained such a lofty station;
        it will not trouble me at all to do so." *
        Then she recounted and revealed
        how Erec had come to Laluth,
6275   for she had no wish to conceal it.
        She fully told her the whole adventure,
        word for word, omitting nothing;

275

mes a reconter vos an lais,
por ce que d'enui croist son conte
6280 qui deus foiz une chose conte.
Que qu'eles parolent ansanble,
une dame seule s'an anble,
qui as barons le vet conter
por la joie croistre et monter.
6285 De ceste joie s'esjoïrent
tuit ansanble cil qui l'oïrent,
et quant Maboagrains le sot,
sor toz les autres joie en ot.
Ce que s'amie se conforte,
6290 et la dame qui li aporte
la novele hastivemant,
l'a fet molt lié soudenemant.
Liez an fu meïsmes li rois,
qui grant joie feisoit einçois,
6295 mes or la fet asez graignor.
Enyde vient a son seignor
et sa cosine o lui amainne,   [24f]
plus bele que ne fu Elainne
et plus gente et plus avenant.
6300 Contre eles corent maintenant
antre Erec et Maboagrain
et Guivret et le roi Evrain,
et trestuit li autre i acorent,
si les salüent et enorent,
6305 que nus ne s'an faint ne retret.
Maboagrains grant joie fet
d'Enyde, et ele ausi de lui.
Erec et Guivrez anbedui
refont joie de la pucele;
6310 grant joie font et cil et cele,
si s'antre beisent et acolent.
De raler el chastel parolent,
car trop ont el vergier esté;
de l'issir sont tuit apresté,
6315 si s'an issent joie feisant,
et li uns l'autre antre beisant.
Trestuit aprés le roi s'an issent,
mes ainz que el chastel venissent,
furent asanblé li baron
6320 de tot le païs an viron,
et tuit cil qui la Joie sorent
i vindrent, qui venir i porent.
Granz fu l'asanblee et la presse:
chascuns d'Erec veoir s'angresse,
6325 et haut et bas et povre et riche.
Li uns devant l'autre se fiche,
si le salüent et anclinent,

276

but I shall spare you the retelling,
for he who tells a thing twice
6280 boringly expands his tale.
While they were speaking together,
one lady walked away alone,
and went to tell the barons about it,
in order to augment and increase the joy.
6285 Everyone who heard it rejoiced *
together at this joy,
and when Maboagrain learned of it
he rejoiced more than all the others.
The fact that his lady was consoled,
6290 and that the lady hastily
brought him the news,
made him suddenly very happy.
The king himself was happy about it;
he had been very joyful before,
6295 but now his joy was even greater.
Enide came to her lord
and brought her cousin with her,
who was more beautiful than Helen
and more noble and more pleasing.
6300 Together Erec and Maboagrain
and Guivret and King Evrain
all ran immediately to meet them,
and all the others came running,
and greeted them and honored them,
6305 for no one dawdled or held back.
Maboagrain rejoiced over
Enide, as she did over him.
In turn, Erec and Guivret both
rejoiced over the maiden;
6310 everyone greatly rejoiced,
and kissed and embraced one another.
They spoke of returning to the town,
for they had been too long in the garden;
they all made ready to leave there,
6315 and they did so joyfully,
kissing one another.
Following the king they all went forth,
but before they came to the town,
the barons had assembled
6320 from the country all around,
and all those who knew of the Joy,
who could come there, did so.
Great was the gathering and the press:
everyone was striving to see Erec,
6325 high and low, poor and rich.
They planted themselves one in front of another,
and greeted him and bowed,

277

et dïent tuit, c'onques ne finent:
"Dex saut celui par cui ressort
6330 joie et leesce an nostre cort!
Dex saut le plus boen eüré
que Dex a feire ait anduré!"
Ensi jusqu'a la cort l'an mainnent
et de joie faire se painnent,
6335 si con li cuer les an semonent.
Harpes, vïeles i resonent,
gigues, sautier et sinphonies
et trestotes les armonies
qu'an porroit dire ne nomer;
6340 mes je le vos vuel assomer
briémant, sanz trop longue demore.   [25a]
Li rois a son pooir l'enore,
et tuit li autre sanz feintise;
n'i a nul qui de son servise
6345 ne s'aparaut molt volantiers.
Trois jorz dura la Joie antiers
einz qu'Erec s'an poïst torner.
Au quart ne volt plus sejorner
por rien qu'an li seüst proier.
6350 Grant joie ot a lui convoier,
et molt grant presse au congié prandre.
Ne pooit pas les saluz randre
an demi jor par un et un,
s'il volsist respondre a chascun:
6355 les barons salue et acole,
les autres a une parole
comande a Deu toz et salue.
Et Enyde ne rest pas mue
au congié prandre des barons:
6360 toz les salue par lor nons,
et il li tuit comunemant.
Au departir molt dolcemant
beise et acole sa cosine.
Departi sont; la Joie fine.
6365   Cil s'an vont, et cil s'an retornent.
Erec et Guivrez ne sejornent,
mes a joie lor voie tindrent
tant que au chastel tot droit vindrent
ou li rois lor fu anseigniez.
6370 Le jor devant estoit seniez.
Ansanble o lui priveemant
en ses chanbres ot seulemant *
cinc cenz barons de sa meison;
onques mes an nule seison

6372. ot *F1896, 1909*] tant *CPB = F*, not *H*.
6373. tant, *lined out, follows* barons *in C*.

278

and they all said, incessantly:
"God save him through whom
6330   joy and happiness revive in our court!
God save the most fortunate man
ever created by God's labors!"
Thus they brought him to the court
and strove to show their joy,
6335   just as their hearts commanded them.
Harps and hurdy-gurdies resounded,
fiddles, psalteries, symphonia, *
and all the stringed instruments
that one could tell or name;
6340   but I wish to sum it up for you
briefly, without too long a delay.
The king honored Erec all that he could,
as did all the others unstintingly;
there was no one who did not prepare
6345   most willingly to serve him.
Three whole days the Joy lasted
before Erec could go on his way.
On the fourth he wished to stay no more,
however they might beseech him.
6350   There was great joy in escorting him,
and a great press at leave-taking.
In half a day he could not have returned
their salutations one by one,
had he wished to reply to each one:
6355   he saluted and embraced the barons;
the others with a single word
he saluted and commended to God.
For her part Enide was not mute
when taking leave of the barons:
6360   she saluted them all by their names,
and together they all returned her salutation.
At parting very tenderly
she kissed and embraced her cousin.
They departed; the Joy had come to an end.
6365   They went on their way, and the others turned back.
Erec and Guivret did not delay,
but joyfully pursued their way
until they came straight to the castle
where they had been told the king was staying.
6370   He had been bled the previous day.
Together with him, in private
in his chambers, there were only
five hundred barons of his household;
never before in any season

279

6375   ne fu trovez li rois si seus,
si an estoit molt angoisseus
que plus n'avoit gent a sa cort.
À tant uns messages acort,
que il orent fet avancier
6380   por lor venue au roi noncier,
si s'an vint tost devant la rote;
le roi trova et sa gent tote,
si le salue come sages
et dist: "Sire, ge sui messages
6385   Erec et Guivret le Petit."   [25b]
Aprés li a conté et dit
qu'a sa cort veoir le venoient.
Li rois respont: "Bien veignant soient,
come baron vaillant et preu!
6390   Meillors d'aus deus ne sai nul leu;
d'aus iert molt ma corz amandee."
Lors a la reïne mandee
si li a dites les noveles.
Li autre font metre lor seles
6395   por aler contre les barons;
einz ne chaucierent esperons,
tant se hasterent de monter.
Briémant vos voel dire et conter
que ja estoit el borc venue *
6400   la rote de la gent menue,
garçon et queu et botellier,
por les ostex aparellier;
la granz rote venoit aprés,
s'estoient ja venu si pres
6405   qu'an la vile estoient antré.
Maintenant se sont ancontré,
si s'antre salüent et beisent.
As ostex vienent, si s'aeisent,
si se desvestent et atornent;
6410   de lor beles robes s'aornent, *
et quant il furent atorné
a la cort s'an sont retorné.
A cor vienent, li rois les voit,
et la reïne, qui desvoit
6415   d'Erec et d'Enyde veoir.
Li rois les fet lez lui seoir, *
si beise Erec et puis Guivret;
Enyde au col ses deus braz met

6399. borc *HBP = FR*] bois *C.*
6410. s'aornent *F* (saournent *V*)] s̓atornent *CHPB. H has* aornent *in 6409.*
6415. veoir *HBV = F* (veoirs *P*)] acoler *C.*
6416-21 *HBPV = F6462-67] omitted C.*
6418. au ... braz *HBV = F*] les bras au col *P.*

6375   had the king been so alone,
and he was greatly distressed
that he did not have more people at his court.
Just then a messenger ran up,
whom they had sent ahead
6380   to announce their arrival to the king,
and he came quickly ahead of the company;
he found the king and all his people,
and he greeted him properly
and said: "Sire, I am the messenger
6385   of Erec and Guivret the Short."
Then he informed the king
that they were coming to see him at his court.
The king replied: "May they be welcome,
like worthy and valiant barons!
6390   I know no better than those two anywhere;
my court will be much improved by them."
Then he sent for the queen
and told her the news.
The others had their horses saddled
6395   to go to meet the barons;
never did they boot on their spurs,
so eager were they to mount.
Briefly I wish to tell and relate
that the crowd of lesser folk,
6400   valets, cooks, and wine-stewards,
had already come to the burg
to prepare the lodgings;
the major company came after,
and they had already come so near
6405   that they had entered the town.
The two groups immediately met,
and they greeted and kissed one another.
They came to their lodgings, made themselves comfortable,
took off their clothes and put on others;
6410   they adorned themselves with their fine garments,
and when they were all turned out,
they returned to the court.
They arrived at court, the king saw them,
and the queen, who fervently wished
6415   to see Erec and Enide.
The king had them sit beside him,
and kissed Erec and then Guivret;
he embraced Enide with both his arms

si la rebeise et fet grant joie.
6420 La reïne ne rest pas coie
d'Erec et d'Enyde acoler:
de li poïst l'en oiseler,
tant estoit de grant joie plainne.
Chascuns d'ax conjoïr se painne,
6425 et li rois pes feire comande,
puis anquiert Erec et demande
noveles de ses avantures.
Quant apeisiez fu li murmures,
Erec ancomance son conte:
6430 ses avantures li reconte,
que nule n'en i antroblie.
Mes cuidiez vos que je vos die
quex acoisons le fist movoir?
Naie, que bien savez le voir
6435 et de ice et d'autre chose,   [25c]
si con ge la vos ai esclose; *
li reconters me seroit griés,
que li contes n'est mie briés,
qui le voldroit recomancier
6440 et les paroles ragencier
si com il lor conta et dist:
des trois chevaliers qu'il conquist,
et puis des cinc, et puis del conte
qui feire li volt si grant honte,
6445 et puis des jaianz dist aprés.
Trestot en ordre, pres a pres,
ses avantures lor conta
jusque la ou il esfronta
le conte qui sist au mangier,
6450 et con recovra son destrier.
"Erec," dist li rois, "biax amis,
or remanez an cest païs,
en ma cort, si con vos solez."
"Sire, des que vos le volez,
6455 je remandrai molt volentiers
deus anz ou trois trestoz antiers,
mes priez Guivret tot ausi
del remenoir, et gel li pri."
Li rois del remenoir le prie
6460 et cil la remenance otrie.
Ensi remainnent amedui:
li rois les retient avoec lui,
ses tint molt chiers et enora.

6419. rebeise *HV = F*] baise *B (-1), P*. |
fet grant joie *BV = F*] li fait i. *H*, fist ml't gr. i. *P*.
6420. ne rest pas *BPV = F*] ne (?) se taist *H*.

282

and kissed her and made much of her.
6420 The queen, for her part, was not slow
about embracing Erec and Enide:
one could have gone birding with her, *
so full of great joy was she.
Each one strove to make them welcome,
6425 and the king called for silence,
then questioned Erec and asked
for news of his adventures.
When the murmur had died down,
Erec began his tale:
6430 he told the king his adventures,
forgetting not a one of them.
But do you expect me to tell you
the reason that made him set out?
No indeed, for you well know the truth
6435 of this and of other things,
just as I have disclosed it to you:
telling it again would be tedious for me,
for the tale is not short,
whoever might want to begin it anew
6440 and rearrange the words
as he recounted it and told them:
of the three knights that he defeated,
and then the five, and of the count
who wanted to bring him so much shame,
6445 and then he told them of the giants.
All in order, one after the other,
he told them of his adventures
up to the point where he sliced through the brow
of the count who was seated at table,
6450 and how he recovered his charger.
"Erec," said the king, "fair friend,
now stay in this land,
at my court, as is your custom."
"Sire, since you wish it,
6455 I shall most willingly stay
two or three full years,
but ask Guivret likewise
to stay, and I ask him as well."
The king asked him to stay
6460 and Guivret agreed to do so.
Thus both of them stayed:
the king kept them with him
and held them most dear and honored them.

Erec a cort tant demora,
6465 Guivrez et Enyde antr'aus trois,
que morz fu ses peres li rois,
qui vialz ert et de grant aage.
Maintenant murent li message:
li baron qui l'alerent querre,
6470 li plus haut home de sa terre,
tant le quistrent et demanderent
que a Tintajuel le troverent,
uit jorz devant Natevité.
Cil li distrent la verité,
6475 comant il estoit avenu
de son pere, le viel chenu,
qui morz estoit et trespassez.
Erec an pesa plus asez
qu'il ne mostra sanblant as genz,   [25d]
6480 mes diaus de roi n'est mie genz,
n'a roi n'avient qu'il face duel.
La ou il ert, a Tintajuel,
fist chanter vigiles et messes,
promist et randi les promesses
6485 si com il les avoit promises,
as meisons Deu et as eglises.
Molt fist bien ce que fere dut:
povres mesaeisiez eslut
plus de cent et seissante et nuef,
6490 si les revesti tot de nuef;
as povres clers et as provoires
dona, que droiz fu, chapes noires
et chaudes pelices desoz.
Molt fist por Deu grant bien a toz:
6495 a ces qui an orent mestier *
dona deniers plus d'un setier.
Qant departi ot son avoir,
aprés fist un molt grant savoir,
que del roi sa terre reprist;
6500 aprés si li pria et dist
qu'il le coronast a sa cort.
Li rois dist que tost s'an atort,
car coroné seront andui,
il et sa famë avoec lui, *
6505 a la Natevité qui vient,
et dist: "Aler nos an covient *
de ci qu'a Nantes an Bretaigne;
la porteroiz roial ansaigne, *

6464. *No initial in C.*
6495. qui an orent *HBP = F*] quan auoient *C.*
6507. de ci *B = F*] de si *CHP.*
6508. porteroiz *HBP = F* (porteres *HP*)] porteront *C.*

284

Erec remained at court,
6465 with Guivret and Enide, all three together,
until death came to his father the king,
who was old and very advanced in years.
Messengers set forth at once:
the barons who went in search of him,
6470 the highest-placed men in his land,
sought and inquired about him until
they found him at Tintagel,
a week before Christmas.
They told him the truth,
6475 what had happened
to his father, the white-haired old man,
who had died and passed away.
This weighed upon Erec much more
than he showed people outwardly,
6480 but grieving is uncourtly on the part of a king,
and it does not befit a king to show grief.
At Tintagel, where he was,
he had vigils and masses sung,
made promises and honored them
6485 as he had promised,
to the hospices and churches.
He did very well what was fitting and proper:
more than one hundred sixty-nine
poor unfortunates he chose,
6490 and dressed them all anew;
to the poor clerics and priests
he gave, as was right, black copes *
and warm pelisses to go under them.
In God's name he did great good to all:
6495 to those who were in need
he gave more than a pint of deniers. *
When he had shared his wealth,
he performed an act of great wisdom,
for he took back his land from the king;
6500 then he entreated and requested
that he crown him at his own court.
The king told him to make ready without delay,
for they would both be crowned,
he and his wife with him,
6505 at the coming Christmas,
and he said: "We must go
from here to Nantes in Brittany;
there you will wear the royal insignia,

France

285

corone d'or et ceptre el poing:
6510 cest don et ceste enor vos doing."
Erec le roi an mercia
et dist que molt doné li a.
A la Natevité ansanble
li rois toz ses barons asanble;
6515 trestot par un et un les mande
et les dames venir comande.
Toz les manda; nus n'i remaint.
Et Erec an remanda maint:
maint venir en i comanda;
6520 plus en i vint qu'il ne cuida,
por lui servir et enor fere.
Ne vos sai dire ne retrere
qui fu chascuns ne de lor non,   *[25e]*
mes qui qu'i venist ne qui non,
6525 Erec n'oblia pas le pere
ma dame Enyde ne sa mere.
Cil fu mandez premieremant,
et vint a cort molt richemant
con riches ber et chastelains;
6530 n'ot pas rote de chapelains
ne de gent fole n'esbaïe,
mes de bone chevalerie
et de gent molt bien atornee.
Chascun jor font molt grant jornee;
6535 tant chevalchierent chascun jor
qu'a grant joie et a grant enor,
la voille de Natevité,
vindrent a Nantes la cité.
Onques nul leu ne s'aresterent
6540 jusqu'an la haute sale antrerent
ou li rois et ses genz estoient. *
Erec et Enyde les voient:
savoir pöez que joie an orent.
Ancontre vont, plus tost qu'il porent,
6545 si les salüent et acolent;
molt dolcemant les aparolent
et font joie, si com il durent.
Quant antre conjoï se furent,
tuit catre main a main se tindrent,
6550 jusque devant le roi s'an vindrent
si le salüent maintenant
et la reïnë ansemant,

6541. *HBPV = F6587] omitted C.* I ses genz *B* (ses janz *F*)] sa gent *HPV*.
6543. *HBPV = F6589] omitted C.* I que *HBV = F*] grant *P.* I
an orent *HBP = F*] auoient *V*.
6544. plus tost qu'il porent *B = F* (que p. *H*, qui p. *V*)] plus ne deloient *C*;
Au p. t. que il onkes p. *P*.

286

golden crown and scepter in hand:
6510 this gift and this honor I give you."
Erec thanked the king for this,
and said that he had given him much.
At Christmas the king
brought together all his barons;
6515 he summoned them all individually
and ordered the ladies to come.
He summoned them all; no one stayed behind.
And Erec in turn summoned many:
many he ordered to come there;
6520 more of them came than he expected,
to serve him and to honor him.
I cannot tell you or describe
who each one was or give their names,
but whoever came and who did not,
6525 Erec did not forget the father
or the mother of my lady Enide.
He was the first one summoned,
and he came to court very richly,
like a powerful baron and chatelain;
6530 he did not have a troop of chaplains
or of silly or gaping folk,
but of good knights
and people well turned out.
Each day they journeyed far;
6535 they rode so far each day
with great joy and great honor
that on the day before Christmas
they came to the city of Nantes.
Nowhere did they stop
6540 until they entered the great hall
where the king and his people were.
Erec and Enide saw them:
you may be sure this gave them joy.
They went to meet them, as quickly as they could,
6545 and greeted and embraced them;
they spoke to them most tenderly
and welcomed them with proper joy.
When they had greeted one another,
all four, holding hands,
6550 came before the king
and greeted him at once
and the queen likewise,

287

qui delez lui seoit an coste.
Erec tint par la main son oste
6555 et dist: "Sire, veez vos ci
mon boen oste et mon boen ami,
qui me porta si grant enor
qu'an sa meison me fist seignor.
Einz qu'il me coneüst de rien,
6560 me herberja et bel et bien:
quanque il ot m'abandona;
neïs sa fille me dona,
sanz los et sanz consoil d'autrui."
"Et ceste dame ansanble o lui,
6565 amis," fet li rois, "qui est ele?"
Erec nule rien ne li cele:
"Sire," fet il, "de ceste dame
vos di qu'ele est mere ma fame."
"Sa mere est ele?"—"Voire, sire."   *[25f]*
6570 "Certes donc puis je tres bien dire *
que molt doit estre bele et gente
la flors qui ist de si bele ante,
et li fruiz miaudres qu'an i quiaut,
car qui de boen ist, söef iaut. *
6575 Bele est Enyde, et bele doit
estre, par reison et par droit,
que bele dame est molt sa mere;
biau chevalier a en son pere.
De rien nule ne les angine,
6580 car molt retret bien et religne
a anbedeus de mainte chose."
Ci se test li rois et repose,
si lor comande qu'il s'asieent.
Cil son comandemant ne vieent:
6585 assis se sont tot maintenant.
Or a Enyde joie grant,
car son pere et sa mere voit,
que molt lonc tans passé avoit
que ele nes avoit veüz.
6590 Molt l'an est granz joies creüz;
molt l'en fu bel et molt li plot,
s'an fist joie quanqu'ele pot,
mes n'en pot pas tel joie faire
qu'ancor n'an fust la joie maire.
6595 Ne je n'an voel ore plus dire,
car vers la gent li cuers me tire,
qui la estoit tote asanblee
de mainte diverse contree.
Asez i ot contes et rois,
6600 Normanz, Bretons, Escoz, Irois; *

6600. Irois *HBE = F*] einglois *CP* (*missing V*).

288

who was seated at his side.
Erec held his host by the hand
6555 and said: "Sire, you see before you
my good host and my good friend,
who bore me such great honor
that he made me lord in his house.
Before he knew anything of me,
6560 he generously gave me lodging:
he put all he had at my disposal;
he even gave me his daughter,
without advice or counsel from anyone."
"And this lady with him,
6565 friend," said the king, "who is she?"
Erec concealed nothing from him:
"Sire," said he, "of this lady
I tell you that she is the mother of my wife."
"She is her mother?"—"Indeed, sire."
6570 "Certainly then I can truly say
that the flower that comes from such a beautiful stem
must be very beautiful and noble,
and the fruit better that one gathers there,
for what comes from a good source smells sweet.
6575 Enide is beautiful, and beautiful
she must be, by reason and by rights,
for her mother is a very beautiful lady,
her father a handsome knight.
She does not betray them in any way,
6580 for she greatly resembles
and takes after them both in many ways."
Here the king stopped and fell silent,
and ordered them to be seated.
They did not disobey his order:
6585 they sat down at once.
Now Enide was very joyful,
for she saw her father and mother,
because she had not seen them
for a very long time.
6590 Her joy was increased by this;
she was very glad and very pleased,
and she showed her joy as much as she could,
but she could not show it so much
that it was not still greater within her.
6595 But I wish to say no more of this,
for inclination draws me toward the people
who were all assembled there
from many diverse lands.
There were many counts and kings,
6600 Normans, Bretons, Scotsmen, Irish;

289

d'Eingleterre et de Cornoaille
i ot molt riche baronaille,
car des Gales jusqu'an Anjo,
ne el Mainne ne an Peito,
6605   n'ot chevalier de grant afeire *
ne gentil dame de bon eire
don les meillors et les plus gentes
ne fussent a la cort a Nantes,
que li rois les ot toz mandez.
6610   Or öez, se vos comandez,
la grant joie et la grant hautesce,
la seignorie et la richesce,
qui a la cort fu demenee.
Einçois que tierce fust sonee,
6615   ot adobez li rois Artus   [26a]
quatre cenz chevaliers et plus,
toz filz de contes et de rois:
chevax dona a chascun trois
et robes a chascun trois peire,
6620   por ce que sa corz miaudre apeire. *
Molt fu li rois puissanz et larges:
ne dona pas mantiax de sarges,
ne de conins ne de brunetes,
mes de samiz et d'erminetes,
6625   de veir antier et de dïapres,
listez d'orfrois roides et aspres.
Alixandres, qui tant conquist
que desoz lui tot le mont mist,
et tant fu larges et tant riches,
6630   fu anvers lui povres et chiches.
Cesar, l'empereres de Rome,
et tuit li roi que l'en vos nome
an diz et an chançons de geste,
ne dona tant a une feste
6635   come li rois Artus dona
le jor que Erec corona;
ne tant n'osassent pas despandre
antre Cesar et Alixandre
com a la cort ot despandu.
6640   Li mantel furent estandu
a bandon par totes les sales;

6604.   ne el Mainne ne an *HP = F* (m. nen *E* (*-1*), ou m. ne iusquen *B*)]
Nan alemaigne nan *C*.
6611-12 *HPBE = F6657-58] omitted C, missing V*.
6611.   grant hautesce *HE = F*] leesce *B* (*-1*), *P* (grande ioie).
6612.   *HE omit* et. | richesce *HE = F*] hautesce *BP*.
6613.   qui *HBP = F*] que *E*. | a la cort fu *H = F*] fu a la c. *BPE*; Quant la
corz fu tote asanblee *C; missing V*.
6620.   miaudre *HB = F*] mialz *C* (*P omits 6619-20*).

290

from England and from Cornwall
there was a rich gathering of barons,
for from Wales all the way to Anjou,
in Maine or in Poitou,
6605 there was no important knight *
nor noble lady of fine lineage;
the best and the most noble of them
were all at the court at Nantes,
for the king had summoned them all.
6610 Now hear, if you will,
the great joy and the great ceremony,
the nobility and the magnificence
that were displayed at the court.
Before tierce had sounded,
6615 King Arthur had dubbed
four hundred knights and more,
all sons of counts and of kings;
he gave each of them three horses
and to each three pairs of cloaks,
6620 to improve the appearance of his court.
The king was very powerful and generous:
he did not give cloaks made of serge,
nor of rabbit nor of dark-brown wool,
but of samite and of ermine,
6625 of whole vair and mottled silk,
bordered with orphrey, stiff and rough.
Alexander, who conquered so much
that he subdued the whole world,
and was so generous and rich,
6630 compared to him was poor and stingy.
Caesar, the emperor of Rome,
and all the kings you hear about
in narrative and epic poems, *
did not give so much at a celebration
6635 as King Arthur gave
the day he crowned Erec;
nor did Caesar and Alexander between them
dare to expend as much
as was spent at the court.
6640 The cloaks were spread out
freely through all the rooms;

291

tuit furent gitié hors des males,
s'an prist qui vost, sanz contrediz.
En mi la cort, sor un tapiz,
6645 ot trante muis d'esterlins blans,
car lors avoient a cel tans
coreü des le tans Merlin
par tote Bretaigne esterlin.
Iluec pristrent livreison tuit:
6650 chascuns an porta cele nuit
tant com il vost a son ostel.
A tierce, le jor de Nöel,
sont ilueques tuit asanblé.
Tot ot Erec le cuer anblé
6655 la granz joie qui li aproche.
Or ne porroit lengue ne boche
de nul home, tant seüst d'art,
deviser le tierz ne le quart
ne le quint de l'atornemant   *[26b]*
6660 qui fu a son coronemant.
Donc voel ge grant folie anprandre,
qui au descrivre voel antandre;
mes des que feire le m'estuet,
or aveigne qu'avenir puet: *
6665 ne leirai pas que ge n'an die
selonc mon san une partie.
      En la sale ot deus faudestués
d'ivoire, blans et biax et nués,
d'une meniere et d'une taille.
6670 Cil qui les fist, sanz nule faille,
fu molt soutix et angigneus,
car si les fist sanblanz andeus,
d'un haut, d'un lonc et d'un ator,
ja tant n'esgardessiez an tor
6675 por l'un de l'autre dessevrer,
que ja i poïssiez trover
an l'un qui an l'autre ne fust.
N'i avoit nule rien de fust,
se d'or non et d'ivoire fin.
6680 Antaillié furent de grant fin,
car li dui manbre d'une part
orent sanblance de liepart,
li autre dui de corquatrilles.
Uns chevaliers, Bruianz des Illes,
6685 en avoit fet don et seisine
le roi Artus et la reïne.

6664. *HB* = *F* (Si a. *E*)] et cest chose quan feire p. *C* (*P omits 6661-64*;
     missing V).
6670. s *of* les *inserted, above the line.*
6685. don et *HPV* = *FR*] de lun *C*, don a sauine *B*.

all of them were thrown out of the trunks,
and whoever wished could take some, undisputed.
In the middle of the courtyard, on a tapestry,
6645 were thirty hogsheads of white sterlings, *
for at that time
the sterling was in use throughout Brittany
and had been since the time of Merlin.
There all helped themselves:
6650 each one carried off that night
as much as he wished to his lodgings.
At tierce, on Christmas day,
they all assembled there.
The great joy coming to him
6655 quite stole Erec's heart away.
Now neither tongue nor mouth
of any man, however much he knew of art,
could describe the third or the fourth
or the fifth of the display
6660 that was present at his coronation.
So I wish to undertake a foolish venture,
wishing to take on its description;
but since I must do so,
then come what may:
6665 I shall not refrain from telling
a part of it, according to my understanding.
    In the hall were two faldstools
of ivory, white and beautiful and new,
of one style and of one size.
6670 He who made them was, without any doubt,
extremely subtle and ingenious,
for he made the pair of them so alike,
one in height, length, and ornamentation,
that you might look at them from every side,
6675 to distinguish one from the other,
without ever being able to find
anything in one not present in the other.
There was nothing in them made of wood,
but only of gold and fine ivory.
6680 They were very finely carved,
for two of the legs
had the form of leopards,
and the other two of crocodiles.
A knight, Bruiant of the Isles,
6685 had made a gift of them in homage *
to King Arthur and the queen.

Li rois Artus sor l'un s'asist;
sor l'autre Erec aseoir fist,
qui fu vestuz d'un drap de moire.
6690 Lisant trovomes an l'estoire
la description de la robe,
si an trai a garant Macrobe,
qui an l'estoire mist s'antante,
que l'an ne die que je mante. *
6695 Macrobe m'anseigne a descrivre,
si con je l'ai trové el livre,
l'uevre del drap et le portret.
Quatre fees l'avoient fet
par grant san et par grant mestrie.
6700 L'une i portraist Geometrie,
si com ele esgarde et mesure
con li ciax et la terre dure,
si que de rien nule n'i faut,   *[26c]*
et puis le bas, et puis le haut,
6705 et puis le lé, et puis le lonc,
et puis esgarde par selonc
con la mers est lee et parfonde,
et si mesure tot le monde.
Ceste oevre i mist la premerainne.
6710 Et la seconde mist sa painne
en Arimetique portraire,
si se pena de molt bien faire,
si com ele nonbre par sans
les jorz et les ores del tans,
6715 et l'eve de mer gote a gote,
et puis la gravele trestote
et les estoiles tire a tire;
bien an set la verité dire,
et quantes fuelles an bois a:
6720 onques nonbres ne l'an boisa,
ne ja n'an mantira de rien,
car ele i viaut antandre bien.
Tex ert l'uevre d'Arimetique.
Et la tierce oevre ert de Musique,
6725 a cui toz li deduiz s'acorde,

6694. que l'an ne die *HB = F*] Qui lantendie *C.* |
   je mante *B = F* (ien m. *H*)] ie ne m. *C.* (*P omits 6689-96.*)
6700. *HB = FR*] An fu louraigne establie *C; P's text is not parallel.*
6701. ele *HB = FR*] il *C; P has* Li premiere i auoit portrait Par droit compas
   et par mesure *instead of 6699-6701.*
6724. darmetique *in text, marked for correction, with* de musiq[ue] *added in
   margin (only the left-hand portion of the letter* q *is still visible at the edge
   of the leaf).*

294

King Arthur sat on one;
he had Erec sit on the other,
dressed in moiré cloth.
6690 Reading we find in the story
a description of the robe,
and I claim as my guarantor Macrobius, *
who applied himself to history,
lest anyone should say that I am lying.
6695 Macrobius teaches me how to describe,
as I found it in the book, *
the handiwork of the cloth and the portrayal.
Four fairies had created it
with great skill and great mastery.
6700 One of them portrayed Geometry,
how she examines and measures
the extent of the earth and sky,
so that nothing is omitted,
and then the bottom, and then the top,
6705 and then the breadth, and then the length,
and then she examines all along
how broad the sea is and how deep,
and so she measures all the world.
This work was the first one's contribution.
6710 And the second put her effort
into portraying Arithmetic,
and she took pains to do it well,
how she numbers rightly
the days and the hours of time,
6715 and the water of the sea drop by drop,
and then all the grains of sand
and the stars one after the other;
she can well tell the truth of this,
and how many leaves are in a wood:
6720 no number ever deceived her,
and she will never lie about anything,
for she wants to be attentive to it.
Such was the work of Arithmetic.
And the third work was that of Music,
6725 with which all pleasures harmonize,

chanz et deschanz et son de corde, *
d'arpe, de rote et de vïele.
Ceste oevre estoit et boene et bele,
car devant li gisoient tuit
6730 li estrumant et li deduit.
La quarte, qui aprés ovra,
a molt boene oevre recovra,
que la meillor des arz i mist:
d'Astronomie s'antremist,
6735 cele qui fet tante mervoille
et as estoiles se consoille
et a la lune et au soloil.
En autre leu ne prant consoil
de rien qui a feire li soit;
6740 cil la consoillent bien a droit
de quanque cele les requiert, *
et quanque fu et quanque iert
li font certainnemant savoir,
sanz mantir et sanz decevoir.
6745 Ceste oevre fu el drap portreite
don la robe Erec estoit feite,
a fil d'or ovree et tissue.   *[26d]*
La pane qui i fu cosue
fu d'unes contrefetes bestes
6750 qui ont totes blondes les testes
et les cos noirs com une more *
et les dos ont vermauz desore,
les vantres noirs et la coe inde.
Itex bestes neissent en Inde
6755 si ont berbioletes non;
ne manjüent s'espices non, *
quenele et girofle novel.
Que vos diroie del mantel?
Molt fu riches et boens et biax.
6760 Catre pierres ot es tassiax:
d'une part ot deus crisolites *
et de l'autre deus ametistes,

6726. son *H*] sanz *CB*. | de corde *H* = *F*] descorde *C*, dacorde *B*. *P combines*
      6724-26: La tierce musike i assist .I. art ki acordance fist.
6729. li *B* = *F*] lui *CHP*.
6736. se *HBP* = *F*] san *C*.
6738. ne *B* = *F* (ne quiert *H*; Aillors ne prent ele c. *P*)] nan *C*.
6740. consoillent *HBP* = *F*] consoille *C*.
6741. les *H* = *F*] li *C*, lor *B* (*P omits 6741-42*).
6743. li font *HBP* = *F*] Lestuet *C*.
6751. cos *F* (cols *BP*)] cors *CH*; s *of* cors *added above line in C*.
6752. noirs (*lined out*) *follows* ont *in C*.
6756. s'espices *B* (sespisses *H*, s'especes *F*)] se poissons *C*, Si ne m. fors
      poisson *P*.

song and descant and sounds of strings,
of harp, of rote, of hurdy-gurdy.
This work was good and beautiful,
for before her lay all
6730 the instruments and delights.
The fourth one, who worked next,
accomplished a most excellent work,
for she contributed the best of the arts:
she concerned herself with Astronomy,
6735 who makes so many wonders
and seeks counsel from the stars
and from the moon and sun.
Nowhere else does she take counsel
about what she must do;
6740 these advise her very well
about whatever she asks of them,
and whatever was and whatever will be
they make her know with certainty,
without lying and without deception.
6745 This work was portrayed in the cloth
from which Erec's robe was made,
worked and woven with golden thread.
The fur lining that was sewn into it
was from monstrous beasts
6750 that have completely blond heads
and necks as black as a mulberry
and their backs are bright red above,
their bellies black and their tails indigo.
Such beasts are born in India,
6755 and are called berbiolettes;
they eat nothing but spices,
cinnamon, and fresh clove.
What should I tell you of the cloak?
It was very rich and fine and handsome.
6760 There were four stones on the fasteners:
on one side were two chrysolites *
and on the other two amethysts,

qui furent assises en or.
Enyde n'estoit pas encor
6765   venue el palés a cele ore;
quant li rois voit qu'ele demore,
Gauvain i comande a aler
por Enyde el palés mener.
Gauvains i cort, ne fu pas lanz,
6770   o lui li rois Carodüanz
et li larges rois de Gavoie;
Guivrez li Petiz le convoie,
aprés va Ydiers, li filz Nuht.
Des autres barons i corut,
6775   et tot por les dames conduire,
don l'en poïst un ost destruire,
que plus en i ot d'un millier.
Quanque pot, d'Enide atillier
se fu la reïne penee.
6780   El palés l'en ont amenee
d'une part Gauvains li cortois,
de l'autre part li larges rois
de Gavoie, qui molt l'ot chiere
tot por Erec, qui ses niés iere.
6785   Quant eles vindrent el palés,
contre eles cort a grant eslés
li rois Artus, et par franchise
lez Erec a Enyde assise,
car molt li vialt grant enor feire.
6790   Maintenant comanda fors treire
deus corones de son tresor,   *[26e]*
totes massices de fin or.
Quant il l'ot comandé et dit,
les corones sanz nul respit
6795   li furent devant aportees,
d'escharbocles anluminees,
que catre en avoit en chascune.
Nule riens n'est clartez de lune
a la clarté que porroit randre
6800   des escharbocles la plus mandre.
Por la clarté qu'eles gitoient,
tuit cil qui el palés estoient
si tres duremant s'esbaïrent
que de piece gote ne virent;
6805   neïs li rois s'an esbaï,
et ne por quant molt s'esjoï,
qu'il les vit si cleres et beles.
L'une fist prandre a deus puceles
et l'autre a deus barons tenir.

6771. Gavoie *H = FR* (galuoie *B*)] sauoie *CP*.
6783. Gavoie *H = FR* (galuoie *B*)] sauoie *CP*.

which were set in gold.
Enide had not yet
6765 come to the palace at that time;
when the king saw that she delayed,
he ordered Gawain to go
to bring Enide to the palace.
Gawain ran to her without delay,
6770 and with him were King Caroduant
and the generous King of Gavoie;
Guivret the Short accompanied him,
and then came Yder, son of Nut.
So many other barons ran there,
6775 just to escort the ladies,
that one could have destroyed an army,
for there were more than a thousand of them.
The queen had taken great pains
to adorn Enide as well as she could.
6780 They brought her to the palace,
Gawain the courtly on one side,
and on the other the generous king
of Gavoie, who held her very dear
because of Erec, who was his nephew.
6785 When they arrived at the palace,
King Arthur ran swiftly
to meet them, and nobly
seated Enide beside Erec,
for he wanted to do her great honor.
6790 At once he ordered brought forth
from his treasure two crowns,
both of fine solid gold.
When he had spoken and given this order,
the crowns, without any delay,
6795 were brought before him,
glowing with garnets,
for there were four of them in each one.
The light of the moon is nothing
compared to the light the very least
6800 of those garnets could shed.
Because of the light they gave forth,
all those who were in the palace
were so thoroughly dazzled
that for a while they could not see a thing;
6805 even the king was dazzled by it,
and yet he greatly rejoiced,
seeing them so bright and beautiful.
He had two maidens take one of them
and two barons hold the other.

6810 Puis comanda avant venir
les evesques et les prïeus
et les abez religïeus,
por enoindre le novel roi
selonc la crestïene loi.
6815 Maintenant sont avant venu
tuit li prelat, juesne et chenu,
car a la cort avoit assez
clers et evesques et abez.
L'evesques de Nantes meïsmes,
6820 qui molt fu prodom et saintismes,
fist le sacre del roi novel
molt saintemant et bien et bel,
et la corone el chief li mist.
Li rois Artus aporter fist
6825 un ceptre qui molt fu löez.
Del ceptre la façon öez,
qui fu plus clers c'une verrine,
toz d'une esmeraude anterine,
et si avoit plain poing de gros.
6830 La verité dire vos os
qu'an tot le monde n'a meniere
de poisson, ne de beste fiere,
ne d'ome, ne d'oisel volage,
que sa chascuns lonc sa propre ymage *
6835 n'i fust ovrez et antailliez.   *[26f]*
Li ceptres fu au roi bailliez,
qui a mervoilles l'esgarda,
si le mist, que plus ne tarda,
li rois Erec an sa main destre:
6840 or fu rois si com il dut estre.
Puis ont Enyde coronee.
Ja estoit la messe sonee,
si s'an vont a la mestre eglise
oïr la messe et le servise;
6845 a l'eveschié s'an vont orer.
De joie veïssiez plorer
le perë et la mere Enyde,
qui ot a non Tarsenesyde;
por voir ot non ensi sa mere,
6850 et Licoranz ot non ses pere;
molt estoient anbedui lié.
Quant il vindrent a l'eveschié,
ancontre s'an issirent hors,
a reliques et a tresors,
6855 croiz et textes et ancenssier, *
trestuit li moinne del mostier,

6855. croiz et *HB = F* (Crois *P, omits* et)] o croiz o *C*. | textes *B = F*]
teptre *C*, tieutes *H*, candeler *P*. | et a. *HBP = F*] o a. *C*.

300

6810 Then he ordered the bishops
and the priors and the abbots
of the religious orders to come forward
to anoint the new king
according to Christian law.
6815 At once all the prelates,
young and old, came forward,
for at the court there were many
clerics and bishops and abbots.
The bishop of Nantes himself,
6820 who was a very saintly gentleman,
performed the coronation of the new king,
most piously and fittingly,
and put the crown upon his head.
King Arthur ordered a scepter
6825 brought forth which was greatly praised.
Hear how the scepter was made:
it was brighter than stained glass,
made from one solid emerald,
and it was as big as a fist.
6830 I dare to tell you the truth,
that in all the world there is no manner
of fish, nor of wild beast,
nor of man, nor of flying bird,
which was not wrought and carved there,
6835 each according to its proper image.
The scepter was given to the king,
who looked at it with wonder;
then, without delay,
he placed it in Erec's right hand:
6840 now he was king as he should be.
Then they crowned Enide.
The bells had already rung for mass,
so they went to the main church
to hear the mass and the service;
6845 they went to pray at the cathedral.
You would have seen Enide's father
weep for joy, and also her mother,
whose name was Tarsenesyde;
truly that was her mother's name,
6850 and her father's name was Licorant;.
both of them were very happy.
When they arrived at the cathedral,
all the monks of the monastery
issued forth to meet them,
6855 with relics and with treasures,
crosses and gospels and censers,

et o chasses a toz cors sainz,
car an l'eglise en avoit mainz:
a l'encontre orent tot hors tret,
6860 et de chanter n'i ot po fet.
Onques ansanble ne vit nus
tant rois, tant contes, ne tant dus,
ne tant barons a une messe;
si fu granz la presse et espesse
6865 que toz an fu li mostiers plains:
onques n'i pot antrer vilains,
se dames non et chevalier.
Dehors la porte del mostier
en avoit ancores assez;
6870 tant en i avoit amassez
que el mostier antrer ne porent.
Quant tote la messe oïe orent,
si sont el chastel retorné.
Ja fu tot prest et atorné,
6875 tables mises et napes sus.
Cinc cenz tables i ot et plus,
mes ne vos voel pas feire acroire
chose qui ne sanble estre voire:
mançonge sanbleroit trop granz
6880 se je disoie que cinc cenz   [27a]
tables fussent mises a tire
en un palés; ja nel quier dire.
Ainz en i ot cinc sales pleinnes,
si que l'en pooit a granz peinnes
6885 voie antre les tables avoir.
A chascune table, por voir,
avoit ou roi ou duc ou conte,
et cent chevaliers tot par conte *
en chascune table seoient.
6890 Mil chevalier de pein servoient
et mil de vin et mil de mes,
vestuz d'ermins peliçons fres.
Des mes divers don sont servi,
ne por quant se ge nel vos di,
6895 vos savroie bien reison randre,
mes il m'estuet a el antendre *
que a reconter le mangier:
asez an orent sanz dangier;

6878. *HBA = F6924] omitted C (P omits 6877-82); missing V (cf. 6834-93).*
6879. granz *HB = F*] uoire *C*; Mon cuer sanbleroit trop greuans *A.*
6880. *HB = F6926] omitted C (P, V: cf. 6878);* Se ie diee que ces .v..c. *A.*
6897-6912 *HPE = F6943-58] omitted CBVA. V and A have divergent endings; see Textual Notes. F's text follows that of H, except for lines 6907 and 6912.*
6897. *HP*] quaconteroie lor m. *E.*
6898. *HE*] A. orent et *P.*

and reliquaries with holy relics,
for in the church there were many of them;
to meet them they had brought everything out,
6860 and there was not just a little singing.
Never did anyone see together
so many kings, counts, dukes,
and barons at one mass;
so great was the crowd and so thick
6865 that the church was completely full:
no peasant could enter there,
but only ladies and knights.
Outside the door of the church
there were many more of them;
6870 so many had gathered
that they could not enter the church.
When they had heard the whole mass,
they returned to the castle.
All was ready and in order,
6875 tables set and tablecloths laid.
Five hundred tables there were and more,
but I do not wish to make you believe
something that does not seem true:
it would appear too great a lie
6880 if I said that five hundred
tables were set up together
in one great hall; I do not wish to say that. *
Rather, there were five halls full,
so that one could only with great difficulty
6885 find a way between the tables.
At each table, in truth,
there was either a king or a duke or a count,
and a hundred knights, by actual count,
were seated at each table.
6890 A thousand knights served the bread
and a thousand the wine and a thousand the food,
dressed in new ermine pelisses.
Of the various dishes they were served,
if I do not tell you,
6895 I could nevertheless give you an account,
but I must attend to something else
besides telling about the food:
they had plenty, without fail;

a grant joie et a grant planté
6900   servi furent a volanté.
     Quant cele feste fu finee,
li rois departi l'asanblee
des rois et des dus et des contes,
dont asez estoit granz li contes,
6905   des autres genz et des menues
qui a la feste sont venues.
Molt lor ot doné largemant
chevax et armes et argent,
dras et pailes de mainte guise,
6910   por ce qu'il ert de grant franchise
et por Erec qu'il ama tant.
Li contes fine ci a tant.

Explycyt li romans d'Erec et d'Enyde.

6901. *HP*] et quant la f. *E.*
6902. *H*] sasanlee *P*, sablenblee [*sic*] *E.*
6903. *HP*] De rois.de.dus.et de c. *E* (*-1*).
6905. autres *H*] grandes *P*; Et des autres genz m. *E* (*-1*).
6906. sont *HP*] erent *E.*
6907. ot *E = F*] ont *H*, a *P.*
6908. *HP*] Chiuals armes or et a. *E.*
6909. *HP*] Dras de soie de m. g. *E.*
6910. ert *H*] est *P = F1909*, Quar plains estoit de gr. fr. *E.*
6911-12 *not in E, which substitutes*
        Et li iogleor en ont tant
        Ni a cil ne sen aut chantant
        A cest mot finerons le conte
        Dex vos garisse tuit de honte.
6912. *P = F*] Huimais pores oir auant *H.*
Expl. *C*] Eplicit [*sic*] derec et denide *B*, Chi fine derec et denide *P*;
      none in HVAE.

with great joy and great abundance
6900 they were served as they desired.
When that celebration was over,
the king dismissed the gathering
of kings and dukes and counts,
whose number was very large,
6905 and of other people and lesser folk
who had come to the celebration.
He had most generously given them
horses and arms and money,
clothes and costly silks of many kinds
6910 because he was extremely noble
and because of Erec whom he loved so much.
The tale ends here at this point.

Here ends the romance of Erec and Enide.

Textual Notes

The Textual Notes are primarily of two types. Some, indicated by asterisks in the Old French text, explore questions of a textual and interpretive nature. Others, indicated by asterisks in the translation, explain certain words and expressions potentially unfamiliar to the modern reader. These relate specifically to medieval institutions or customs and are frequently essential to a proper understanding of the text.

2-3. Proverb; cf. Morawski 2313: *Tel(le) chose ait on en despit que puis est moult regretee.*

42. Chrétien seems to have been fond of this sort of parallel construction, in which two nouns, adjectives, or verbs with similar or identical meaning are conjoined. This frequently poses problems for the translator; in some cases it has seemed preferable to use a single word in the translation.

61-62. Proverb, Morawski 1593.

98. Exotic locations were undoubtedly prized as sources of fashionable materials, but the choice of this particular name was probably "determined by demands of rhyme"—a fairly common practice. See West: xiii.

104. This is a common stylistic device in OF: a general negation is immediately modified by an exception, usually introduced by *fors,* often coupled with *seulemant (solemant).*

159. OF *anbleüre,* MF *amble,* refers to a gait used by horses and some other quadrupeds, in which both feet on one side leave and return to the ground together. This can be quite a rapid gait, as is clearly suggested here (*aler isnelemant,* 153-54); I have therefore preferred to avoid using 'amble', since that term also means "a leisurely pace" (*AHD*).

231. Proverb, Morawski 754.

307

239. Although Erec had his sword with him (104), he was nevertheless 'unarmed' since he was not wearing armor. Cf. Stone, 17: "ARMED. In the middle ages, and up to the 17th century, 'armed' meant wearing armor and had no reference to carrying arms. A man without armor was said to be 'unarmed,' even though carrying a number of weapons."

265. I.e. the day after tomorrow (today being day 1); cf. 334, 339.

285. OF *barons* is sometimes used to refer to only the highest nobles; at other times its value seems more general. Cf. Foulet, *baron.*

298. This may also be an evil word (*parole*), referring to Arthur's announcement (289-90) or to the collective reaction to it (291-97) —the very reaction predicted by Gawain (49-58).

345. In a narrow sense, OF *chastel* refers to a fortified residence, 'castle', as in 28; used more broadly it refers to the town which frequently grew up around the fortress, which was in turn protected by walls and other fortifications.

352. The sparrow-hawk (also 'sparrowhawk', 'sparrow hawk'; early forms 'sparhawk', 'spar-hawk'; OF *esprevier*) was the smallest of the hunting-birds. The term 'hawk' may be "used indifferently to mean either the long-winged species (falcon) or the short-winged bird commonly known as a 'hawk', and to include either or both sexes" (Wood & Fyfe: 613). When one wishes to distinguish between the sexes, 'falcon' is used for the female of all long-winged hawks, and 'tercel' (also 'tiercel', 354) for the male (but the male sparrow-hawk is called a 'musket'). To moult is to go through the annual process of shedding old feathers and acquiring new plumage. This does not happen during the bird's first year; a red hawk (also called a 'sorehawk' or 'sorrel hawk') is less than a year old and still has its first reddish-brown plumage. A goshawk is a short-winged hawk, about six times as large as the sparrow-hawk (Mavrogordato, 1973: 155-61).

356. For more details, see Kibler (1981): 302, n. 1641-42.

375. "A *vavasor* was the vassal of an important noble, rather than of the king. ... The vavasor generally held an outlying fief and lived in the sort of manor house which formed an important stop along the routes of itinerant knights." (Kibler, 1981: 303, n. 2022.) The use of *mes* ("but") in 376 is explained by the contrast between the man's rank, inherent in his title, and the poverty of his present situation: he was a *vavasor*, but his court was very poor.

381. The OF term *preudom* (382) encompassed a host of masculine virtues: good breeding, upright moral character, generosity, prowess and valor in combat... everything that made a 'good man' in twelfth-century noble society.

382. Hospitality is a basic ingredient in medieval romance. For an in-depth treatment of the subject, with specific reference to *EE* as well as other romances, see Bruckner, *Narrative Invention* (1980).

403. The *chemise* was an undergarment, worn by both sexes. Since it was worn next to the skin, the material was often very soft and fine. It had long sleeves, and was laced on the sides. A woman's *chemise* was long, extending to the feet; the man's was shorter. (Goddard: 91-97.) The Saxons called the same garment a 'smock'; the Normans introduced the name 'chemise' (Cunnington, 1951: 31).

405. "The *chainse* was a dress of washable material. It was laid in pleats, and long." It was "an outer dress, worn as a house dress or at court" (Goddard: 69-75).

417. The rhyming of a word with itself is uncharacteristic of Chrétien: "it seems probable that the original had ... *sot* : *pot*" (Reid, 1976: 18, n. 16). This case is quite distinct from that of the so-called "identical rhyme" ("rime du même au même", Roques: L), where the same spelling involves what are really two different words, whether or not etymologically related, e.g. *prest*, verb : *prest*, adjective (259-60); *cort*, verb : *cort*, noun (311-12)—a technique of which Chrétien was apparently quite fond and which he exploited with considerable virtuosity.

424. This is only the first of several references to the Tristan-Iseult story in Chrétien's works. Not only was he quite familiar with this material (as was his audience), but in line 5 of *Cligés*, his second (surviving) romance, he specifically claims to have written *del roi Marc et d'Ysalt la blonde*—a work which, unfortunately, has not survived.

468. The line could also be punctuated with the comma after *assez* (as Foerster did in his 1909 ed.), in which case it would be translated 'plenty of hay and oats, fresh and wholesome.'

473, 474. I have adopted Foerster's reading for these lines, which has the advantage of making 473 part of the vavasor's instructions, and avoids *C*'s problem of near-repetition (474 and 476) in the narration.

496. I agree with Reid (1976: 5-6) that *pains et vins* "is undoubtedly what Chrétien wrote." Cf. his discussion of the same passage, 1984: 21-22, and note to 417, above.

615. The hauberk (OF *hauberc*) was "a long tunic made of chain mail" (*AHD*; illus.); the greaves (OF *chauces*) protected each leg below the knee.

631-38. For an extensive discussion and analysis of the theme of the "rash boon", in which someone agrees to grant a request before knowing what that request is, see Frappier (1969). The present passage is examined as the first example of the device in Chrétien, pp. 8-11. Cf. Kibler (1981): 298, n. 168-70.

655-57. This statement is surprising, given the relatively short distance Erec has come from Cardigan: he spent less than a full day following the ill-mannered knight from the forest to the present site, and the vavasor's reply, 670-71, confirms the fact that his fame has preceded him. Following the battle, 1033-34, Erec clearly states the relatively short distance back to Cardigan, and he and Enide later arrive there in about half a day's ride, 1505-07.

693. *Coste* (*colte, coute*) may mean variously feather bed, mattress, blanket, cushion or pillow.

710. For a discussion of this observation, see Topsfield (1981: 323, n. 18), who maintains that Chrétien is explicitly declaring that Enide "is entirely human, with no trace in her of the traditional Celtic fairy mistress"; for an opposing view, see Adler (1945): 923.

711-12. Roques listed *fer* : *cerf* among the "rimes approximatives" (p. xxxvii), but he printed *cer* in 712, which is the reading in *C*. Only *cerf* appears elsewhere (16 occurrences), always in the context of *le blanc cerf*; the nominative form is uniformly *cers* (four occurrences).

714. The ventail was a detachable portion of the coat of mail, attached to the mail hood or coif of mail, protecting the lower part of the face.

724. The guige of a shield was "a long strip of leather which went round the neck and formed an additional support for it" (Planché).

726. Cf. Foulet, *arestuel*: 'base of the lance by which one grasped it and where there was probably a notch or some other device to keep the hand in position' (my translation).

733. 'Bay' is reddish-brown or chestnut-colored.

865. Literally, they drew apart [by] more than an *arpant*. This unit of measure was used for both area and length, and occurs frequently in scenes of combat. Neither T.-L. nor Godefroy indicates the precise distance involved; Jenkins (*Roland*, gl.) gives "the distance of 120 feet", but indicates no source in support of this precision.

871. The cantle is "the rear part of a saddle" (*AHD*).

871-72. *derriers* : *estriés* could be added to the list of "approximate rhymes". Cf. Roques: xxxvii.

903-06. While not absolutely indispensable, these lines provide a transition from Yder's discussion of their combat to the mention of their ladies in 908.

940. The coif was a heavy skullcap, worn under a helmet or mail hood.

942. A boss was a circular protuberance or swelling in the center of the exterior surface of a shield.

979-84. The latter part of each of these lines (4-6 syllables) is preserved in a fragment, along with our lines 1012-18, 1046-52, and portions of 1080-86. See Introduction, pages xxvi-xxvii.

1005-06. *sache* : *domage* is another case of "approximate rhyme"; cf. Roques: xxxvii.

1021. *C*'s *oltrage* is likely an anticipation of the following line. Cf. Hunt (1979): 262.

1075-80. One group, *tuit li plusor*, 1078, is contrasted with another, *qui* (= *cil qui*), 1080. *HP* read *Sa pucele et cil qui l'amoient*, as do the remaining manuscripts, according to Foerster, except for *VA*, which have *La*. The manuscript of which a fragment was edited by Thomas (see note to 979-84) seems to have been like *HP[BE]*, but apparently only the first two words of the line, *Sa pucele*, have survived.

1089. The seneschal was "an official in a medieval noble household in charge of domestic arrangements and the administration of servants" (*AHD*).

1121. Despite the OF *chevalier errant*, this is not a 'knight errant'—something that an observer could only guess at, since that term relates not to outward appearance but rather to the state of mind of the individual—but simply a knight on the move. Cf. Roques: 253 and Louis: 188.

1165. I agree with Reid (1976: 13) that *C*'s *se* is illogical and a slip for *cil*. The adopted reading presents a stylistically pleasing opposition: either Erec is sending this knight because he has defeated him, or else the knight is coming to brag that he has defeated Erec. (If *C* were not emended, then it must be seen as presenting an anacoluthon: *s'il* would have to depend on some structure such as *nos savrons*, which is not actually present in the text.)

311

1186. *C*'s text is unsatisfactory: since Erec's instructions to Yder were to go directly to the queen and deliver himself into her hands (1030-37), to which Yder agreed (1063-65) and as he himself announces (1187-88 and 1193-95), it does not seem logical that he would come directly to the queen's feet, only to address first the king and all his knights, as *C* has him do.

1187-88. *prison* : *hom* may be considered another "approximate rhyme" in *C*.

1193-95. Instead of *C*'s text, Foerster gives the following (1909 ed., with his numbering and punctuation):

> 1193 Dame, le nain vos amain ci:
> Venuz est a vostre merci.
> 1195 Moi et ma pucele et mon nain
> An vostre prison vos amain,
> 1197 Por feire tot quanque vos plest."

His 1195-96, from *PVAE*, are omitted by *CHB*. F argues (*Anm*) that these lines, though poorly supported, are indispensable, since all three—Yder, his damsel, and the dwarf—must be mentioned. (Cf. note to 1186, above.) Micha: 88 makes the same point. But *C*'s version is satisfactory, since Yder does in fact mention all three: himself (1187-88), the dwarf (1193), and the damsel (1194).

1223. Proverb; cf. Morawski 777: *Fous est qui ne croit consoill.*

1231. Since the scene has not changed from what immediately precedes, I have displaced the break from here to 1242. A possible explanation for the position of the large initials in *C* is furnished by the theory of oral performance, requiring the subdivision of the narrative into manageable segments. If one session stopped at 1230, then 1231-41 (particularly 1231-38) would serve to remind the audience of the action at the beginning of the following session. Cf. Titchener (1925).

1272. Chrétien seems to be indulging in a bit of word play here, involving the conjunction *dons, don*, and the noun *dons*. It is unfortunately impossible to convey this in translation.

1294. This presumably refers to the vavasor and his reaction to Erec's return to his house; *H* has *vavasors* in this line, as does Foerster. Roques, in his "Index des noms propres et des personnages anonymes", however, included this line neither among the references to Erec nor among those to the vavasor.

1305-06. The various manuscripts do not present parallel readings for this passage. Instead of 1305-06, Foerster gives the following (1909 ed., with his numbering and punctuation):

1307	Qui de l'alete d'un plovier
	Peissoit sor son poing l'esprevier,
	Por cui la bataille ot esté.
1310	Mout avoit le jor conquesté
	Enor et joie et seignorage.
	Mout estoit liee an son corage
	De l'oisel et de son seignor:
	Ne pot avoir joie greignor
1315	Et bien an demostra sanblant.
	Ne fist pas sa joie an anblant;
	Que bien le sorent tuit et virent.
	Par la meison grant joie firent
1319	Tuit por amor de la pucele.

F1313-14 correspond to our 1305-06; *VA*'s versions of these lines are identical to *C*'s. Only *B* has all the lines given by F: 1307-12 are completely omitted by *C*, while *VA* insert them after our 1430; *P* omits 1311-12, *H* omits 1315-16, and *CVA* omit 1315-19.

1308. *CVA* have this line; *HBP* omit it.

1331. Vair (OF *veir* or *vair*) and miniver (OF *gris* or *petit-gris*) were both furs, highly prized for trim on medieval garments. Their exact origin is uncertain, though they probably came from different kinds of squirrel. It is thought that a confusion between *vair* and *verre* is responsible for the story of Cinderella's 'glass' slippers (Louis: 193). *Vair* was also used as a color adjective to mean 'variegated', e.g. in describing a horse, as in 1377, 1379, and 1398.

1347-50. These lines, omitted only by *C*, provide a smoother transition between the introduction of the cousin (1341) and her intervention in the scene (1351-ff.).

1375. A palfrey (OF *palefroi*) was a woman's saddle horse.

1429. *VA* end this line with *samie bele*, and then have *Qui resemble rose novele* instead of 1430, followed in *VA* by F1307-12. (See note to 1305-06, above.)

1437-38. Foerster ultimately adopted (1909: xlvi and 195-96) *C*'s spellings of these two imperfect subjunctives (with the minor difference of *ali-* instead of *ale-*), but added an accent to show the stress on the third syllable: *feïssiént, alissiént*. See his *Anm* for an extended discussion of these verbs. Roques (xxxvii) calls this accentuation "plus bourguignonne que champenoise."

313

1488. *C*'s usual spelling is *oel*: 433, 1123, 2053, 4898, 5922, 5946; *uel* occurs in 4398. Roques printed *voel* here, but the expression *de bon
voel* is unattested in Godefroy, whereas *de bon oil* is supported. Cf.
Reid (1976): 2.

1548. Proverb; cf. Morawski 1716: *Povreté abaisse courtoisie.*

1552. *C*'s *gentil* is likely an inadvertent repetition from the previous line.

1555. I agree with Reid (1976): 9-10 (seconded by Hunt, 1979: 262) that *C*
makes little sense in these lines, and that scribal error is to blame
for Guiot's text being at variance with that of the other manuscripts.

1578. The *bliaut* was the usual court costume of the nobility. "The lady's
bliaut was an elaborate dress, of the costliest materials, with bands of
embroidery at the high neck and at the wrists of the long sleeves,
often lined with fur, cut in two parts as a rule, with a skirt (*gironée*)
very long and full, and longwaisted bodice (*le cors*), adjusted closely
to the figure by means of lacings (*laz*) at the sides" (Goddard: 47-
48). For more details and an abundance of illustrative quotations,
see Goddard, especially 47-55. Numerous lines from the present
passage (our 1578-1658, F1590-1670, R1570-1650) are quoted, 17-
18, as an illustration of the complete costume of the time. For details of the cloak (OF *mantel*), see Goddard: 163-70.

1587. Here as in other places where numbers are involved, the manuscripts
show considerable variation: *demi marc HBP* (*mar B*), *xx.* [*vint*] *mars V*
(*dor tout b.*), *.c.* [*cent*] *mars A*. F1599 = *HP*(*B*); R1579 = *C*.

1594. "The *atache* [*C*'s *estache* is a variant spelling] was the ribbon by which
the *mantel* was fastened" (Goddard: 32); cf. Foulet, *estache*: "cordon
servant à fermer le collet du 'mantel'."

1599. The presence of *estache* here seems inconsistent with what is said in
1594. Moreover, in 1610, the queen specifically requests some
estaches, they are brought to her (1613), and she has them put on the
cloak (1615-18). "The *tassels* were metal ornaments placed on the
front edge of the *mantel*, at the height of the shoulders, like a modern
clasp, except that, instead of being provided with a hook for fasten-
ing, ribbons (*ataches*) were run through them which, when tied, held
the *mantel* in place." (Goddard: 209; she also refers to them as
"plaques" in the article *mantel*, 164). Among the examples she
quotes these lines (F1611-13) and our 6760-63 (F6806-09).

1600. The jacinth (OF *jagonce*) is a reddish-orange variety of zircon, also
called 'hyacinth.'

1602. The garnet (OF *escharbocle*) is a deep red precious stone, highly esteemed for its supposed miraculous properties.

1609. Since *yndes* already occurs in 1608, it seems unlikely that Chrétien wrote *indes* here.

1611. The ell (OF *aune*) was a unit of linear measure, formerly used for measuring cloth.

1618. Chrétien again seems to be indulging in word play, involving the verb (*antre*)*metre* and the noun *mestres*. As before, 1272, the translation cannot convey this.

1634. *C*'s text, besides being one syllable short, seems definitely weaker.

1636. Orphrey (OF *orfrois*) was elaborate embroidery, or material so embroidered or woven with gold thread (Goddard: 178-82).

1637. For the form *Dé*, contrasted with *Deu* in non-rhyming position, see Woledge (1979): 721.

1647. This chaplet is discussed by Goddard under OF *cercle*, 68.

1651. Roques attempted to justify the presence of *amander* in two successive lines (218, note to R1643-44). I agree with Reid (1976: 6-7) that the first of these "is simply a blunder on Guiot's part due to anticipation of *amander* in [R]1644" (7).

1653. Niello is a black metallic alloy, used to fill an incised design on the surface of another metal.

1656. Again I agree with Reid (1976: 12), against Roques: it would be extremely strange for Chrétien to offer such lavish praise of *une pucele* who was merely one of the queen's serving-maids.

1684. For an account of this name, as well as that of the 'Ugly Hero' in 1685, see Adler (1946-47): 218-24.

1693-1714. This second list, which mentions 21 knights over 22 lines in *C*, expands to include 42 knights in 46 lines in *B* (F's text); most manuscripts are intermediate in length; *H* is shortest, with 21 names in 18 lines. Here as elsewhere the forms of the proper names show extensive variation; I have retained *C*'s spelling throughout. The interest presented by the other names is slight; see F's editions for complete details. For purposes of comparison, the corresponding line numbers are as follows:

	Roques	Foerster
1693-94	= 1685-86	= 1707-08
1695-96	= 1687-88	= 1713-14
1697-1704	= 1689-96	= 1719-26
1705-14	= 1697-1706	= 1729-38

1693. West, *Index*, identifies this Yvain with Chrétien's *Chevalier au lion*. Other manuscripts are more specific: *Et Yvains li fiz Uriien* (F1706; F1705-06, with variations, are present in all manuscripts except *C*). F1707 has *Yvains de Loenel fu outre*, but this is supported only by *B*, with distant variants in *VA*.

1701. A *vaslez* (diminutive of *vassal*) was a young man in service to a knight.

1711. The constable (OF *conestable*) was an officer of the court, originally in charge of the horses; in wartime he commanded the cavalry.

1749. Emendation based on Reid (1976): 12-13.

1782. Emendation based on Micha 88 and, particularly, Reid (1976): 3-4. Cf. moreover Guinevere's words, 1734-40: Enide clearly satisfies the conditions (already mentioned by Gawain, 45-48) for the kiss of the white stag. F1818 followed *HE* for his 1890 ed. but *PVA(B)* in his subsequent editions.

1795-98. While not indispensable, these lines furnish an element of commentary by the narrator concerning the maiden's part in—and her attitude toward—this ceremonial custom.

1808. Much has been written concerning the meaning of *vers* in this line; see, for example, Kelly (1970): 189-90, 195-96. Frappier (1957; 1968: 89-90)used "prélude" to refer to this portion of the romance; cf. Cormier (1982): 66-67 and 184-85.

1819. Buckram (OF *boquerant*) is "a coarse cotton fabric heavily sized with glue" (*AHD*); scarlet (OF *escarlate*) was a fabric, wool or silk; originally blue, it was later most often bright red (Louis, gl.).

1822. *Porpre*, like *escarlate*, was a fabric; it could be of various colors. *Osterin* was a kind of silk, of Oriental origin (Louis, gl.).

1835. Bezants were gold coins issued in Byzantium.

1840. F noted this line as hypometric (-1) in *CV*, but there is a dot in *C* after *dame*, indicating a strong pause; the word is thus to be read *da-me*, in two syllables. Cf. 1876.

1851-52. Omission of these lines in *C* can be explained as a case of eye-skip: having copied 1850 beginning *si com*, the scribe went on to just below the next *si com*, in 1852. The passage reads better with the two lines restored.

1854. The denier was a small coin of varying value, current in France and in western Europe generally from the eighth century until the French Revolution. It was sometimes, like the former British penny, 1/240 of a pound (*livre*).

1876. A dot in *C* after *pere* marks a hiatus; the word is thus to be read in two syllables, *pe-re*, and the line is not "(-1)" as per F. Cf. 1840. Roques calls *fame* : *regne* a case of imperfect rhyme, and says "il faut lire *fanme* : *rangne*" (Notes crit., 219-20). F printed *ranne*, which occurs in no manuscript (*renne H, regne CBVA, resgne E, sa dame P*). Wace, *Brut* 10501-02, rhymes *regnes* : *femes* (cited by Nitze (1954: 693); *Eneas* 379-80 rhymes *feme* : *regne*. There are in fact numerous cases in *C* of *e* + nasal consonant rhyming with *a* + nasal consonant: cf. 411-12, 649-50, 809-10, 941-42, 1737-38, 1949-50, 2131-32, 2287-88, etc.

1929. *Paisle* and *cendal* were both types of silk, highly valued for such articles of clothing as the court dress (*bliaut*). They are often described as *riche* (1981) or *chier*, and described as being of exotic origin.

1930. For details concerning the *bliaut* as a man's garment, see Goddard: 55-59.

1944-46. See notes to 352-54 for most of these terms referring to hunting birds. The merlin is also called 'pigeon hawk.'

1953-54. This case of "approximate rhyme" is all the more striking in that it involves two unusual forms: *ceinturs* (masculine) and *Artus*, instead of Chrétien's usual rhyming form, *Artu*. Roques: 220, note to 1939-40, states that this is the unique example of *Artus* as a rhyme-form in Chrétien, but in fact it occurs again in 6615 (R6599). F1992 printed *Arturs*, the spelling of *H* (*P* omits 1935-68 = F1973-2006).

1956. For a discussion of this personnage, see Loomis: 142-44, 479, and Frappier (1970): 15-17.

1962. *C* presents an anacoluthon, passing from superlative (*li grendres*) to comparative (*que nus*), which I have avoided in my translation. See Micha: 85-86 for a discussion of this passage.

1980. The word *robe* had various meanings. When designating a single garment, "it is not necessarily a dress ... but as a rule it is evidently used as in the modern sense." (Goddard: 199). It is clear from this passage that it is something a knight would wear. Cf. 5179 and note.

1993. Much has been written concerning *retardatio*, the technique of postponing the revelation of a character's name until long after that character's first appearance (Enide's was in line 402).

2005-06. This is likely a case of eye-skip in *C*; it is easy to see how scribal errors could occur in a series of this sort.

2006. 'Rote' (also written *rotte*) was another name for the triangular psaltery, a stringed instrument played by plucking the strings with the fingers or a plectrum or pick (*New Grove* 15: 383-87 and 16: 261-65). Cf. Louis: 191-92.

2018. A wicket (OF *guichet*) was a small door or gate, sometimes concealed, sometimes built into or near a larger one.

2038. The other manuscripts name Iseult in this line.

2049. *C*'s *tant* is likely an anticipation of the following line.

2090. For a discussion of the organization and other aspects of the tournament, see Pastoureau (1976): 132-36.

2101-02. The problem of *C*'s order in this couplet (R2085-86) is discussed by Reid (1976): 8 and (1984): 22.

2131. Knights who were taken prisoner had to promise to pay a ransom to those who captured them. See Pastoureau (1976): 134.

2163-64. Although *C*'s version of these lines is unique, there is little reason to prefer F's reading for 2163. The change is motivated by the need for a parallel construction between *des escuz* in 2164 and *des armes et des chevax* in 2165. The change from *escu* to *escuz* then requires the modification of 2163, in order to preserve the rhyme.

2166. A cinch is a strap encircling an animal's body to secure a load or a saddle upon its back.

2179. It should perhaps be noted that, at least within the context of the tournament, *joster* does not yet refer to the tilting match so familiar from filmed versions of medieval tales. That form of single combat did not exist before the 14th century. See Pastoureau 133.

2181. Considering the meanings of *devers* (cf. 2183) and *estor*, it is difficult to make sense of *C*'s apparently unique reading. Foerster assumed a lacuna following this line (his 2219), which would have made it clear that the following lines refer to Gawain, but no such text occurs in any of the surviving manuscripts. I agree with Roques, who suggests (xxxvi) that the contradiction between 2177-78 and 2184 (his 2159-60; 2166) is only apparent, in that Erec's *intention* is not to win horses and capture prisoners, but his victories nevertheless result in his doing so—as he continues to do on the following day, 2218-ff. See Hunt (1979: 261) for further discussion of this passage.

2211-12. This may be another case of "approximate rhyme", but it is perhaps more likely that the variant spellings in the rhyme words *bous* : *rescos* are merely a case of free variation on the part of Guiot, and do not represent a difference in sound. Cf. *esposee*, 4726, and *espousee*, 4762.

2214. The seven canonical hours were matins, prime, tierce, sext, nones, vespers, and complin(e). In *Erec et Enide* we find *prime*, *tierce*, *none*, and *vespre(s)*, corresponding roughly to 6:00 a.m., 9:00 a.m., 3:00 p.m., and 6:00 p.m.; *midi(s)* replaces *sexte*. For a discussion of Chrétien's use of time and time expressions, see Ménard (1967), particularly 384-91.

2221. The pronoun *l'* could also be interpreted as referring to Erec, 'him.'

2230. Foerster printed *lion* in his 1890 edition, but later editions have *Sanson*, a conjecture based on Hartmann von Aue's text and the fact that the other comparisons in this passage all involve personal names. *BPVA* have *lion*; (*H* omits 2227-32). Cf. Frappier (1970): 29, n. 35.

2241. Given the context of 2244-ff., *quis* makes better sense.

2266. Prime was around 6:00 a.m. See note to 2214.

2275-76. *montaingnes* : *plainnes* may be considered another "approximate rhyme" in *C*.

2288. *dames* already appears in 2284.

2320. For *Melide*, derived from *Melita* (= Malta), meaning 'land of bliss', see F's extensive discussion (his 2358) and the further remarks in his 1909 ed. See also G. Paris (1891): 149 and Williams (1954-55): 460, n. 10.

TEXTUAL NOTES

2330. *Dïapre* was a silk fabric, decorated with leafy branches and flowers; cf. 97. Samite was a heavy silk fabric, often interwoven with gold or silver; both of these were used for garments, as well as for purely decorative purposes, as in this line.

2333. Maddox (1978): 56 and Sargent (1977): 395 agree that *novel* means "young" in this line, whereas Luttrell (1980): 277-80 maintains that *novel* means "récemment créé, nouvellement promu à ce statut"— which it surely does in 2070.

2340. Following 2340 *C* presents the first of two digressions, each of which is found in none of the other manuscripts. The first, detailing the offerings made by Erec at the church at Carnant, occupies 24 lines (R2323-46). Frappier (1970): 17-26 convincingly argues that these lines are not Chrétien's, but were likely added later by the scribe Guiot. See also Micha (1939; 1966): 282-83, and Roques, xlix (*d*); cf. Woledge (1979a): 11. The same discussions apply to the passage detailing Enide's offerings (see note to 2342). *C*'s text follows, with abbreviations resolved and punctuation added as in the rest of the present edition; the line numbers are those of Roques' text.

2323 seissante mars i presanta
d'argent, que molt bien anplea,
2325 et une croiz, tote d'or fin,
qui fu ja au roi Costantin.
De la voire croiz i avoit,
ou Damedex por nos s'estoit
crocefïez et tormantez,
2330 qui de prison nos a gitez
ou nos estïens trestuit pris
par le pechié que fist jadis
Adanz par consoil d'aversier.
Molt feisoit la croiz a prisier:
2335 pierres i avoit precïeuses,
qui estoient molt vertueuses.
El mi leu et a chascun cor
avoit une escharbocle d'or;
assises furent par mervoille—
2340 nus ne vit onques sa paroille:
chascune tel clarté gitoit,
de nuiz, con se il jorz estoit
au matin quant li solauz luist;
si grant clarté randoit par nuit
2345 que ardoir n'estuet el mostier
lanpe, cierge, ne chandelier.

320

2342. Following 2342 *C* presents a second digression, this one 28 lines in length (R2349-76); no corresponding passage, concerning Enide's actions and her offering, occurs in any of the other manuscripts. Cf. note to 2340. See also Imbs (1970): 426, "passage interpolé" and 430, "le passage ... est probablement apocryphe". *C*'s text follows, with R's line numbers (abbreviations resolved and punctuation added). In 2354, R corrected *nut* to *nus*.

2349 Jesu et la virge Marie
2350 par boene devocion prie
que an lor vie lor donast
oir qui aprés ax heritast.
Puis a ofert desor l'autel
un paisle vert, nut ne vit tel,
2355 et une grant chasuble ovree.
Tote a fin or estoit brosdee,
et ce fu veritez provee
que l'uevre an fist Morgue la fee
el Val Perilleus, ou estoit.
2360 Grant antante mise i avoit;
d'or fu de soie d'Aumarie.
La fee fet ne l'avoit mie
a oes chasuble por chanter,
mes son ami la volt doner
2365 por feire riche vestemant,
car a mervoille ert avenant.
Ganievre, par engin molt grant,
la fame Artus le roi puissant,
l'ot par l'empereor Gassa;
2370 une chasuble feite en a,
si l'ot maint jor en sa chapele
por ce que boene estoit et bele.
Qant Enide de li torna,
cele chasuble li dona;
2375 qui la verité an diroit,
plus de cent mars d'argent valoit.

2371-82. The punctuation in these lines is based on Sargent (1973: 770).

2433. This emendation is based on Reid (1976): 15.

2458. Foerster's version of this line (2496) is significantly different: *Et dist: "Lasse, con mar m'esmui* (the verb leading directly to the complement *de mon païs* in the following line). Lacy (1980): 42 observes that this monologue of Enide's (R2492-2503, our 2458-69) "is practically the first time she has spoken, and it is literally the first time Chrétien has quoted her words."

2469. Love (1982): 263, n. 4, observes that this is the one and only time that Enide uses *tu* in speaking to Erec; in fact she does so again in 4571 and 4589-94. It is significant that on both occasions she believes he cannot hear her.

2514. This description of Erec by Enide may be seen as an echo of his description of her in 1041-42.

2538-39. For the interpretation of these lines, cf. Zaddy (1973): 10 and Buckbee (1985): 62-63.

2550. Proverb (Morawski 2297), used by Villon in his "Ballade des proverbes", line 1.

2572. Proverb; cf. Morawski 1356: *Ne set que c'e[s]t biens qui n'essaie qu'est maus.*

2586-625. See Frappier (1970): 26-30 for a discussion of this passage.

2614. Pastoureau, 116, states categorically that such a garment never existed, an ordinary hauberk already being sufficiently costly that only a small number of rich knights could afford one.

2631. One would expect *soi atorner*, but *HBPVE* all have *li* (*en li, H; A* omits 2631-32).

2649-50. This may be another case of "approximate rhyme," but the rhyming of *mialz* with *chauz* is likely indicative of the vocalization of the pre-consonantal *l*, in which case no difference in sound would have been intended.

2657. Erec clearly intends to have no other companion than his wife. He will thus be "alone," without the normal retinue befitting his station.

2729. *Aventure* is a highly charged word in this context, implying anything out of the ordinary, in particular the dangerous and demanding situations that allow knights errant to demonstrate their prowess and augment their renown. Compare Arthur's reference to the *forest avantureuse*, scene of the hunt for the white stag (65).

2736. Foerster (1896, 1909) indicated a lacuna following this line. It does not seem necessary to suppose, as he did, that Chrétien must have had Erec specifically include here the condition that Enide was not to look at him (as she says she dares not do, 2755-56, and as he instructs her later, 2970). Since she was riding ahead, she would have had to turn around to speak to him—and in doing so would have revealed she was about to speak. Cf. Roques, xxxvi; Hunt (1979): 261-62.

2743. The pronoun *l'* could be interpreted as referring either to Enide herself or to what she was saying.

2773. The crupper (OF *lorain*) is "a leather strap looped under a horse's tail and attached to a harness or saddle to keep it from slipping forward" (*AHD*).

2808-10. Foerster and Roques also print *vos* in these three lines, but it is impossible to be certain of *C*'s reading, given the customary spelling *uos* and the great similarity between u and n in the manuscript. The difference is of course significant: does Enide's expression of concern involve both of them (*nos*) or only Erec (*vos*)? F (1890) gives the variant *nos* for *BPE* in 2808 (F2846); for *B* in 2809 (F2847); for *CPBVE* in 2810 (F2848). My own examination of the manuscripts yields slightly different findings: *B* has *nos* in all three lines; *P* has *nous* in 2808 but *v⁹* = *vos* in 2809-10. *HVA* have *vos* (u⁹, v⁹, uos, vos) in all three lines. (I was unable to verify this portion of *E*.)

2843. The blazon is the coat of arms with which each shield was decorated; this usage may be seen as an example of synecdoche, in which the decorated portion refers to the entire shield. Cf. *l'escu paint*, 2864.

2901. Proverb; cf. Morawski 434: *Couvoitise fait trop de mal.*

2904. Proverb; cf. Morawski 1320: *Moult r. de ce que fol p..*

3025-26. Though perhaps not indispensable, these lines help to prepare the knight's total submission in the following lines.

3067-69. *C* presents a quite uncharacteristic shift from indirect to direct quotation between 3067 and 3068 (R3099-3100), unique among the manuscripts. The reading chosen by F has the advantage of presenting a smoother transition from narration to quotation.

3079. *C*'s reading is likely due to anticipation of the following line.

3089. Given *gastel* (3110, 3137), *gastiax* (3114), and the absence of further mention of *pain*, this correction seems desirable in the interest of internal consistency.

3090. Roques explains this cheese as "fromages faits, après la fauchaison, du lait plus gras de vaches mieux nourries."

3099. Roques (3129) corrected this to *q'une*, based on *H* (which he calls *R*), but *C* uniformly uses *c'* for the elided form of *que* before *une* (939, 1561, 6827), as well as before *un* (2882, 4982) and *uns* (781, 1048, 4386, 4895).

TEXTUAL NOTES

3119. A hornbeam (OF and MF *charme*) is a kind of tree, also called 'yoke-elm' and 'ironwood', known for its hard, whitish, fine-grained wood.

3245. Roques (3275) rejected *plusor* in favor of *mainte*, the reading of *H* (his *R*). This correction is unnecessary, however, since *plusor* can be used with a singular noun. Cf. T.-L. 7: 2038 [i.e. 1238]: 7-36.

3265-66. This is likely another instance of variant spellings in the rhyme words (*vos* : *jalous*) being merely a case of free variation on the part of Guiot, rather than representing a difference in sound. Cf. 2211-12 and note.

3294. Given the present indicative *remenez* in 3295, the future seems more appropriate than the conditional in 3294.

3310. F printed *Par ... par* in his 1890 ed., but in the *Anmerkungen* he recommended *Por ... por* and adopted that reading in his subsequent editions.

3323-24. Roques listed *dites* : *traïtres* among the "rimes approximatives" (p. xxxvii), but he printed *traïtes* in his 3354, which is the reading in *C*. Both forms occur elsewhere: *traïtres* in 3437 and *traïtes* in 3615.

3421-22. These lines, omitted by *HBPVAE*, rejected by F, occur only in *C*; Micha criticizes them for spoiling the suspense of the episode (1939: 283).

3422. The pronoun *il* could also refer to Erec, and *suens* to the count: 'nor would he (Erec) [be his].' Louis: 91 translates "il [le comte] ne tiendra jamais ni elle, ni lui [Erec]." Micha paraphrases "ni Enide ni Erec ne lui appartiendront" (1939: 283).

3492. For a discussion of this line, see F (1890), *Anm.* 3528; Roques, notes, 3520; Reid (1976): 13-14.

3504. *C*'s *tuit* is likely a careless repetition from the preceding line.

3506-07. In addition to being the only manuscript that omits these lines, *C* presents a very unlikely identical rhyme (*virent* : *virent*) in our 3505 and 3508. Cf. Reid (1976): 5, 7.

3524. As in 2808, the manuscripts are divided: *C* has *nos alons*, whereas *HBVA* = *F* have *vos alez* and *P* has *vos erres*. *C*'s version of Enide's words is nevertheless defensible: she and Erec are in fact proceeding at the same pace, but it is Erec alone who will not escape from the scene, if the count and his men catch up with them.

3561. For the interpretation of *arpant*, see note to 865.

3628. Following this line F adds four lines from *PBVA* (missing *CHE*):

> ... pleissiez,
> F3665   Il et sa fame devant lui.
> A esperon an vont andui.
> Tant ont erré et chevauchié
> F3668   Qu'il vindrent an un pré fauchié.

I agree with Micha (1939): 88, n. 1, and 90, that these lines are "une interpolation [qui] rompt la suite du récit." Hunt (1969: 262) presents a contrary opinion, grouping this with other instances where "an inferior reading in Guiot appears to be the result of repetition of a preceding word or an anticipation of a following one"—but if this were a case of inaccurate copying, one would expect to find a different reading in either 3628 or 3629.

3650. The enceintes (OF *lices*) were the walls encircling a fortified castle.

3744. *C*'s *li blazon* presumably refers to the same objects as *li escu* in 3737. If so, the text seems to present a contradiction, since the shields are first said to afford very little protection, and then are credited with preventing their being mortally wounded. F adds 4 lines from *BPVAE* (missing *CH*) following 3743-44 (his 3784, 3783):

> F3784   Ne furent pas navré a mort,
> F3785   Mes duremant furent blecié.
> Isnelemant sont redrecié,
> S'ont a aus lor lances retreites: (; 1890)
> Ne furent maumises ne freites; (. 1890)
> F3789   Anmi le chanp les ont gitees.

But this seems to present a contradiction with the following line: if the lances were neither damaged (*maumises*) nor shattered (*freites*), why did they throw them onto the field?

3770. Following this line *H* has two lines that appear in no other manuscript:

> Et li chevalier se conbatent
> Des hiaumes les pieres abatent

In his 1890 *Anm.* to 3814, F speculated that these lines might very well be original; he incorporated them into his 1896 and 1909 editions (F3815-16).

3772. Tierce was around 9:00 a.m.; nones around 3:00 p.m. See note to 2214.

3779. The coif of mail (OF *chapeler* or *chapelier*) was a mail hood, worn by knights under the helmet. Stone; cf. Pastoureau, 117.

3798. Since the knight uses *avez* in 3800, the familiar *soies* seems inappropriate. In *HP* the usual spelling of the *vous*-form is *soies*, so there may be no inconsistency here; spelling in *V* varies between *soies* and *soiez*.

3848-51. Although Guiot's text makes perfectly good sense, one may question the similarity of lines 3850 and 3852. Reid (1976): 7 sees a case of anticipation, but admits that "the manuscript tradition is so confused that it is difficult to see exactly what stood in Guiot's model." F's text follows.

> F3892   Avoir poez an moi fiance!
>   Et s'il vos plest a remenoir
>   An ma terre et an mon menoir,
> F3895   Mout vos i ferai enorer.

3893 and 3894 are interverted *BPV*; other variants are relatively minor.

3903. Foulet, under *paveillon*, quotes an almost identical line: *tentes et tres et paveillons*, with the commentary "voilà 3 substantifs qui désignent le même objet." Cf. also 5079-83, where Guivret's *pavellon* is clearly referred to as *la tante* 4 lines later.

3908-12. For a discussion of this passage, see Roques, ed., 224-25; cf. Louis, 103.

3911. The expression *le gringalet* is used here and in the *Conte del Graal* to refer to Gawain's horse; unfortunately the precise meaning of the term is unclear. See Foerster, *Anm.* (3955); Paris (1890): 149-50; Loomis (1949): 156-59; Louis (gl.).

3975-76. *fame : sane* (also printed by F, 4019-20; cf. *Anm*) is another of Guiot's "rimes approximatives"; see Roques, xxxvii. Other manuscripts: *B = C*; *fenne : senne H*; *fene : sene P*; *feme : sene V*; *feme : senne A*; *fanme : sene E*. Cf. 1875-76 and note.

3976-77. Proverb; cf. Morawski 1575 and 2499: *(Ou) volentiers ou a enviz ve(i)t li prestres au sane.*

3979-80. These lines provide a necessary justification for Kay's negative prediction in 3978 (contrasting with the fine reception he had earlier announced, 3952-64). Cf. Roques, n. to 4002, and Louis, viii. F (1909) printed *n'an* in the first of these lines (his 4025), but recognized in his variants that all manuscripts have *an*.

3991-92. The rhyming of *molt* with *estout* is likely indicative of the vocalization of the pre-consonantal *l*, in which case no difference in sound would have been intended. Guiot consistently wrote *ml't*. I have followed Roques' usage in expanding this to *molt*; Foerster prints *mout.* Cf. Roques: xl, who says that *molt* may be read "*ad libitum,* molt, mout, *etc.*"

3996. For *arpant,* see note to 865.

4001. For the interpretation of *desarmez,* cf. 239 and note.

4041. For *gringalet,* cf. 3911 and note.

4085. The noun *aubagu* clearly refers to Arthur's horse, but like *gringalet,* noted above, the exact meaning of the term is mysterious. Godefroy: "épithète de cheval, p.-ê. blanc clair"; F (1909, *Anm* 4131): 'White point'; F, *W* (1933): 'Arthur's horse'; T.- L.: 'a kind of horse'; Louis (Gl.) follows Godefroy's speculation that the term may relate to the horse's white color. Though neither Godefroy nor T.-L. gives any other occurrences, and F (*Anm,* 4129) says he has not encountered the word elsewhere, Paris (1891): 150 says it occurs in the *Roman des Franceis* by André de Coutances. F adopted *C*'s reading (shared by *E,* according to Godefroy), and gave as variants *lambagu H, l'abagu A, le bagit V, labatu B, Tot maintenant P.*

4135-36. The rhyming of *molt* with *vout* is likely indicative of the vocalization of the pre-consonantal *l,* in which case no difference in sound would have been intended. Cf. 3991-92 and note. These are the only occurrences of *molt* as a rhyme-word in *EE.*

4150. F and R both print *vos* in this line, but F indicates *nos CBP* in his variants. Some uncertainty is often possible in such cases, but here *C* clearly reads *uos,* i.e. *vos* , as do *BA;* cf. *u⁹ H, v⁹ P, vos V.*

4156. Following this line F adds two lines from *HA* (missing *CBPV*):

F4201 La reïne et tuit s'esjoïssent,
F4202 Et qui einz einz des tantes issent.

These are numbered 4203-04 in his 1896 and 1909 editions, with the spelling *ainz ainz*; in the second line *A* omits *Et* and inserts *fors* before *des.*

4170. *C*'s line is totally at variance with the readings of the other manuscripts, and seems to make no sense in the context.

4183-84. For the order of terms, cf. 5087-88.

4213-14. *C*'s version of these lines stands in marked contrast to that of the other manuscripts, since it has Erec giving orders to the king. Roques, in a note to his 4233-36, argues that these lines "peuvent être compris comme une manifestation plaisante de la brusquerie un peu agacé d'Erec." I agree with Williams (1954): 460, who says this reading is forced and that R4236 (our 4216) "cannot be part of Erec's speech." See also Reid (1976): 13.

4257. For the form *Dé*, see 1637 and note.

4285-86. As F (*Anm* 4332-33) remarks, all the manuscripts are at variance with one another in these lines. *C* alone has *s'aloit tirant / et* (making the verb of 4285 reflexive and giving only one noun in 4286, the object of the verb that ends that line). *C*'s text does make sense, but is so different from the other manuscripts that it seems doubtful that it represents Chrétien's original. Given that *detirant* goes with *crins* and that *desirant* goes with both *dras* and *face*, the order of *VA* appears preferable to that of *B*, avoiding the interruption mentioned by F (1909, *Anm* 4333). Louis' translation unfortunately omits 4285-90 (R4305-10), no doubt the result of eye-skip (*La pucele*, 4285 and 4291).

4302. It may be noted that *Or est Erec an grant peril* would be an exact repetition of 3392.

4343. A 273-line fragment, in the form of a single detached folio, is preserved in Mons (Archives de l'Etat). The text corresponds to our lines 4343-4617; it includes ten lines not in R, our 4469-78, and omits our 4537-38. See Introduction, page xxvii.

4388-89. Proverb; cf. Morawski 2243: *Se les nubz cheent, les aloes sont toutes prises*. The following line also seems proverbial in tone and appears in R's index, p. 282.

4440. 'Had you not intervened' or 'without your help' is implied.

4465-66, the last two lines on folio 17^v, are both preceded by the sign //. (F mentions this indication in his notes but mistakenly assigns it to his lines 4513-14 instead of to 4511-12; R does not refer to it.) This may be an indication that these two lines were to be deleted, an operation that would result in our lines 4452-64, 67-68, and 79-97 (*C*'s 17^{v}c30-18^{r}a21, less 17^{v}c43-44; R4472-84 and 4487-4507) all being spoken by Erec. This would still be slightly unsatisfactory, since it would have Erec, in 4467, speaking of the knight's wanting to know his name as though the matter had already been mentioned, when in fact it had not. This would, however, be less perplexing than *C*'s text with lines 4465-66 included, which has the knight agreeing to give his name and then not doing so.

4488. The line below the *l* of *qu'il* may have been interpreted by R as related to the first word of the next line, which he printed as *revit*. My own study of the manuscripts indicates that *C* has *Recut*, as do *HBV* = F (Recus P).

4582-83. Although this version does not appear in Morawski, other similar proverbs oppose *parler* and *teisir*, e.g. 1254, *Mieus vaut bons taires que fous parlers*, and 2428 (with var.), *Trop parler nuit plus que trop taire.*

4641. One would expect *L'une et l'autre* (cf. *dit l'une a l'autre*, 5463), but *C* clearly reads *l un* as do *BPVE*; *H*'s reading is completely different for this and most of the following line.

4680. R4690 has *nos*; F4726 has *vos* and gives no variants. My own examination of most of the manuscripts is inconclusive: only *V* is unambiguously *vos*; *B* is probably *uos = vos*; *HP* look more like *nos*; I am unable to decide about *CA*.

4737. A faldstool (OF *fal-* or *faudestuel*) was a portable, folding, backless chair, often covered by a cushion, and used for persons of distinction.

4767. *C*'s *sire* is probably a repetition from the preceding line.

4807. Cf. Woledge (1979): 42: 'one might be tempted to read *home*, since the line is one syllable too short; it is preferable to read *li hom*, which according to Foerster is the reading of all the other manuscripts' (my translation).

4815. This line has been variously interpreted. I hold with Paul Imbs (1970): 431, n. 7, and Barbara Sargent-Baur (1980): 376, n. 8, that this is Erec's love for his wife (*avoit* as personal verb, with Erec as subject), rather than Enide's love for him (*avoit* as impersonal verb; cf. Louis 127, "l'amour dont sa femme faisait preuve"). Imbs affirms the same motivation in 915 and 5810-12.

4827-28. *eslais* : *palés* could be added to the list of "approximate rhymes" (Roques: xxxvii). Both *eslais* and *eslés* occur in *C*, twice each, and always in rhyme position, including *palés* : *eslés* in 6785-86, which may indicate that there was no difference in sound between *eslais* and *eslés*. The word *palés* occurs 13 times, three of them in rhyme position, with no variation in spelling.

4840. Woledge (1970): 51, n. 10, observes that this line (R4850) "might just mean 'he takes the lance from Enid' but is more likely to mean 'Enid takes the lance'." Louis 128 chooses the latter interpretation.

4867. I interpret *vangier* as an infinitive preceded by the pronoun *le* referring to the count, but it could just as well be understood as a nominalized infinitive. See Woledge (1979): 151.

329

TEXTUAL NOTES

4898. F4944 (4946 in 1909 ed.) presents a significantly different version
of this line: *Qu'Iseuz sanblast estre s'ancele*, based on *BP* (*sanbloit, H*).
His variants indicate that *VAE* do not mention Iseult here.

4925-26. Roques listed *retena(i)l* : *cheval* among the "rimes approximatives"
(p. xxxvii), but he printed *retenal* in his 4935, which is the reading in
C. Neither form occurs elsewhere in *EE*.

4985. I.e., 'you cannot give a reason that would justify this attack.'

5055-58. Foerster felt that these lines (F5101-04) could be part of the original (*Anm*). There are three recapitulations of the events involving
the Count of Limors. The first two are parallel, and tell of the *novele*
that made its way to Guivret: first Chrétien's narration, 4895-4904,
and then Guivret's account of what he heard, 5022-27. This third
recapitulation, 5046-58, told from Erec's point of view, takes up
where the other two left off and so completes them. Line 5055
adds a detail not previously given (*contre val*) while 5056-57 echo
4857-61.

5090-92. These lines have been variously interpreted. My translation is
taken, with minor modifications, from Z. P. Zaddy (1973): 12-14
and 184-89. She maintains that *esprover* in 5091 is used in the sense
of "assessing or recognising someone's character or worth" rather
than with its other meaning of subjecting someone or something to
a deliberate test, and that to argue from this line "that Erec set out
to test his wife is to mistake result for cause."

5127-29. One cannot be absolutely positive, but Chrétien certainly *seems* to
have been indulging in word play in these lines—an effect which,
unfortunately, does not come through in translation.

5129-30. Roques listed *mule* : *cure* among the "rimes approximatives" (p.
xxxvii), but he printed *mure* in his 5136, which is the reading in *C*.
The form *mule* occurs in 5134 (R5140).

5177. According to F, *BA* begin the line with *Que*, and share *C*'s reading
bien lor an sot. The singular *sot*, presumably with Erec as implied
subject, does not seem logical, given the conjunction *car* or *que* linking this clause to the preceding.

5179. This passage clearly shows that *robe* was used for both men's and
women's clothing. Cf. 1980 and note.

5190-5201. Given the parallel structure of so many lines in this passage, it
is easy to see how a scribe could skip from 5193 to 5201. Foerster
initially printed the entire text as given here, but because of the
similarity between 5193-94 (F5239-40) and 5201-02 (F5247-48) he

330

placed the former couplet in brackets in his 1890 edition and eliminated it from his later editions. See his *Anm* for a discussion of the passage (which he describes as 'hopelessly confused').

5236. Other manuscripts read *robais* (*H*), *rohais* (*P*; according to F5282, *BVE* share *P*'s reading, whereas *A* has *roal*). On the basis of these forms, Loomis: 490 speculated it might be identical to Roadan, the castle Erec gave to Enide's father (1323, 1846) which he identifies as Rudlan in North Wales. The second is the setting for the opening of *Yvain*, where its location is specified as *Carduel en Gales* (Wales) and is identified as the modern Carlisle in Cumberland (Loomis: 481). See West for additional forms and references.

5262. The abbreviation *.e.* is used exclusively for Erec; Enide's name is always spelled out in full, and that is clearly what the context requires here.

5282. A green line on a horse is both surprising and puzzling. Were it not for the comparison to a vine-leaf, this might be interpreted as a variant of *vair/veir*, referring perhaps to a shimmering or varicolored region where the black and white met. Furthermore, other manuscripts agree: *PV vert, B uert*, though *H* has *uers*. Foerster speculated that the term referred to some shade or tone ("Farbennüance", *Anm* 5328). Burgess (1984: 77-78) and Buckbee (1985: 74-75) see in this an allusion to the description of Camille's palfrey in the Old French *Eneas*, an even more extraordinary animal, combining not only a dazzling array of colors but also physical features of several different animals (*Eneas*, 4047-68).

5306. This interpretation and the reading on which it is based are defended by Reid (1976): 14.

5313. A fragment containing 86 complete and two partial lines, another detached folio, is preserved in the Bibliothèque Sainte-Geneviève, Paris. It begins with the *e* of *monte* and includes our lines 5314-34, 5335 through the *s* of *son*, 5339-60, 5366-86, and 5390-5411. See Introduction, page xxvi.

5316-17. Cf. note to 352-54.

5324. The brattice (OF *bretesche*) was a defensive structure, part of castle architecture; also called 'hoarding', it was "a wooden gallery which, in time of war, [was] erected outside crenellations to cover dead ground at foot of the walls and towers" (Bottomley, 1979: 85). According to Delort (1972: 196, *bretèche*, illus.), this term could be applied to a stone structure as well. Allen (trans. of Delort, 1983: 198) uses 'bretesse', but I have not found this form elsewhere. In this passage, Chrétien seems merely to be referring to the outermost fortifications of the town, without any particular implication that the place is or has been under attack; cf. lines 5346-68.

5349-50. Roques listed *vies* : *liues* among the "rimes approximatives" (p. xxxvii), but he printed *lies* in his 5348, which is the reading in *C*. The predominant form in *C* is *liue(s)*, as in 5323 (six occurrences in *EE*).

5359. Besides the ideas of peace and tranquillity, *an quiteé* also refers to legal status, meaning without obligation, in a condition of free possession (cf. OF *quite*).

5373. The text corresponding to our lines 5373-5680 is preserved in a portion of the fragmented Annonay manuscript. As printed by Pauphilet (1937), it contains 302 lines, though he omitted, without commentary, the line corresponding to F5616 (= R5568, our 5570). If one assumes this line to be present in the manuscript, the total would be 303. The text omits 5467-70 and includes four lines not in *C*, two of them after our 5634 (R5632), shared only with *E*, according to F and Pauphilet, and our 5653-54. Portions of some lines, as printed by Pauphilet, are missing; they range from a single letter up to several words. See Introduction, page xxvi.

5401. The verb in this line (OF *ot*) is ambiguous, since it could be either the simple past (preterite) of *avoir*, or the present indicative of *oïr*. Louis 143 chose the former interpretation ("Erec tient"); I find the latter preferable, given the context.

5431. As in other similar cases, it is difficult to be absolutely positive whether some manuscripts have *uos = vos* or *nos*. F printed *nos* and listed the variant *uos* for the other six manuscripts. My own examination of the manuscripts reveals that *V* is unambiguously *vos* (with a v), while *P* clearly has *nos*. For the others I am about 90% sure: *CB* have *vos* (*uos* and u^9, respectively) and *H* has $n^9 = nos$. (I was unable to verify this portion of *E*.)

5441. More literally, 'however dearly each of them holds himself', and may even mean 'on pain of death.'

5451. *tropeiax* must be read as a trisyllabic form. Woledge (1979): 725 sees in this a possible regionalism, since the Annonay fragment (Pauphilet: 314) presents the same spelling. Cf. Roques: 228-29, n. to 5449.

5521. A person's *sanblant* is basically what one shows, one's external appearance, bearing, mien; by extension, the way one acts, and hence, in this specific situation, the way King Evrain welcomed Erec and company.

5529. This is another case of an erroneous identical rhyme caused by "careless anticipation" (Reid 1976: 5 and 7; Hunt 1979: 262).

5590. F printed *qui*, but remarked (*Anm* 5636) that *H*'s *que* was better, and adopted that reading for his later editions.

5606. F (*Anm* 5652) specifically affirmed that the image was that of the plug of the barrel, and that the line (which he printed with *est* instead of *soit* in his editions) should be understood as meaning 'the matter is decided and I cannot go back on it'. T.-L. disagree as to the source of the expression, relating this proverbial usage to *broche* meaning pointed object, spear, or pike, rather than plug or bung, but agree as to the interpretation; explanations given by Roques, gl., and Louis, tr., are similar. Altieri (1976) does not include this expression in her discussion of the proverbial content of *EE*.

5653-54. Though the text of *C* is acceptable, with an implied antecedent for *qui* in 5655, the enumeration of 5653-54 seems very usual and in keeping with the style of similar passages. Cf. 1250, 2516, 3601, 6325.

5710. *C* must be emended because the line is one syllable too short. None of the manuscripts seems entirely satisfactory in this passage, though I find *P*'s wording preferable to that of *H* and *B* (which *VA* share, according to F).

5731-32. The order of lines and the peculiar wordings presented by *C* have the disadvantage of interrupting the enumeration of legendary heroes and appearing to separate *Tiebauz* from the group of *ces que or savons*, which seems illogical. All three names have been identified as characters from epic poetry. See Roques, Index; West; Foerster.

5847. The personal reference *sa* seems much more appropriate than the absolute negations given by *CP*. F chose *P*'s reading for his 1890 edition, but adopted *H* for his later editions. See his *Anm*, 5893.

5878-79. Proverb; cf. Morawski 2347: *Teus cuide gaingnier qui pert*.

5882. Proverb; cf. Morawski 2270: *Soit qui fuie, asez est que enchace*; 1953: *Qui fuit il treuve qui le chace*.

5884. This reading of the OF text and the resulting translation are based on Reid (1976): 14.

5918. The reference is presumably to the city on the Rhône, south of Lyon. Cf. *Roland* 997: *Ceignent espees del ac(i)er vianeis*.

TEXTUAL NOTES

5929. The nasal was "a piece depending from the front of a helmet to protect the nose of the wearer" (Stone). See also Hindley: 24; Koch: 62; *AHD* (illus.).

5953. One of the canonical hours, nones (OF *none*) was roughly three o'clock in the afternoon. See note to 2214.

5979. Roques (ed.: 214) indicates he read *et tel te* in this line (R5975), but *C* has *iel*, not *tel*.

6006-35. Frappier (1969): 11-13 discusses this passage (R6002-31) as the second example of the "rash boon" motif in Chrétien.

6059. A condition, on the order of 'had he faced me in combat', is implied.

6082. Literally, *fesniee* means 'enchanted', and is related to 'fascinated.'

6086. Guiot's spelling elsewhere (three other occurrences) is *-grain(s)*. F uniformly printed *Mabonagrain(s)*, the spelling of *H*. As is usual with proper names, there is considerable variation among the manuscripts. See Introduction, pages xxxiii-xxxiv.

6093. I agree with Woledge (1979: 53) that this apparent replacement of *cas régime* by *cas sujet* is probably inadvertent, and that Guiot simply anticipated the *-ez* of *savez*.

6105. This is another case of an erroneous identical rhyme caused by "careless anticipation" (Reid 1976): 5 and 7.

6117-18. Hunt (1979): 262 speculates that this omission resulted from eye-skip ("*saut du même au même*") on the part of Guiot or his model.

6173. As Reid (1976): 15 points out, this line "says the direct opposite of what the context requires."

6180. After this line *BP* insert *Contre les dames en estant* and omit 6182.

6224. Reid (1976): 11-12 discusses this passage, and speculates that the original may have had *soudoier* as a verb, as in *Que avuec aus soudoier vint* (n. 24).

6272. *peresce* had a much broader range of meanings than MF *paresse*: cf. Foulet (1955). In this line it could be variously interpreted, e.g. 'I shall not be at all reluctant about telling you (anything).'

6285. The pronoun *l'* could also refer to the lady.

6337-38. For 'psaltery' (OF *sautier*), see Note to 2006; both *sinphonies* and *armonies*, according to Roques, referred to stringed instruments capable of producing several sounds simultaneously. "In France from the twelfth century onwards, *symphonia* (or *symphonie, sinfonie, chifonie* and so on) meant organistrum or Hurdy-Gurdy" (*New Grove*, 18: 428). The organistrum was a large hurdy-gurdy; the name "was probably derived from 'organum', meaning in its broadest sense an instrument on which several parts could be rendered simultaneously" (*New Grove*, 8: 814-16).

6372. The substitution of *ot* for *tant* is somewhat conjectural, but is supported by *H*'s *not* (which would, however, normally be joined to *que* preceding the element on which the restriction bore. *C*'s *tant* leaves the clause without a verb. Cf. *Anm* F6418-19.

6399. *C*'s reading makes little sense, in the context of making preparations for lodging (6402).

6410. Rhyming a word with itself is uncharacteristic of Chrétien. Cf. *Anm* 6455-56.

6416-21. *C* alone omits these lines, a probable case of eye-skip from *d'Erec et d'Enyde* in 6415 to the same phrase in 6421.

6422. This puzzling line has provoked much commentary on the part of editors and critics, succinctly summarized by Imbs (1970): 427.

6436. F 6482 prints this same reading (shared by *B* and *C*); in his *Anm* he postulates 'a small anacoluthon', or break in grammatical structure, in which the poet mistakenly wrote *la*, referring to *la verité*, whereas he had in fact written *le voir* in 6480. Cf. *H*: *La uerite uos ai enclose*; *P*: *Ensi conme ie lai deuise* (defective rhyme).

6492-93. The cope, OF *chape*, is "A long ecclesiastical vestment worn over the alb or surplice" (*AHD*, illus.); the pelisse, OF *pelice* or *peliçon*, was usually fur-lined, was worn by both sexes, and was variously worn as an outer garment, a dress, or an under-dress. See Goddard: 187-93.

6495. The usual relative pronoun is *qui* as subject of the relative clause. Cf. Raynaud de Lage: 68.

6496. The *setier* or *sestier* was a measure of volume for liquids and grains, and of area for land. Holmes (1964: 196) gives ".96 pint (modern)" as the equivalent of the sestier in dry measure; Reid (1942: 257) says "about 4 bushels." The value of all measures varied extraordinarily from one region to another and depending on what was being measured. For some examples of this variation, see Delort (1972:

73; tr. Allen, 1983: 71-72). For *deniers*, see 1854.

6504. F 6550 notes this line as hypometric (-1) in *C*, but *fame* can be read as disyllabic.

6506. F 6552 has *nos* in 1890 and 1896, *vos* in 1909, indicating *CH* as sources for the former and *BPVAE* for the latter. As elsewhere in similar situations involving these pronouns, absolute certainty is not possible; my own examination of the manuscripts reveals an unambiguous v in *P*, and fairly certain confirmation of F's readings for *B* and *C*; *H*, however, is quite ambiguous, since the first letter appears joined at both top and bottom.

6508. I agree with Reid (1976): 15-16: "there is no possible justification for the third person plural *porteront* [Roques] 6496, where all other manuscripts have the expected second person *porteroiz* (Foerster 6554)."

6541-44. Although Guiot's text is adequate, it seems probable that the missing lines (6541 and 6543), present in other manuscripts, were part of the original text.

6570. One leaf has been torn out of *V*, corresponding to our lines 6570-683.

6574. Proverb; cf. Morawski 1886: *Qui de bons est soef fleire.*

6600. For this emendation and that of 6604, see Reid (1976): 16.

6605. Though the syntax of the latter part of this sentence, 6605-09, may appear somewhat confused, the version presented by *C* is in fact acceptable. For purposes of translation, as elsewhere in similar cases, I have chosen affirmative phrasing to replace the accumulation of negations.

6620. The adjective *miaudre* (*attribut*) seems to make more sense than the adverb.

6633. The *DMA* explains *dit* as "a short thirteenth-century verse narrative, without musical accompaniment, treating daily life" (4: 221, s.v. *Dit*). This occurrence in Chrétien indicates that the term was in use somewhat earlier. Zumthor (1972: 159) says it is one of several terms referring to non-sung narrative poetry, but that what they designate escapes all definition. According to Jauss (1964: 119-20), during a short period around 1200 the new terms *estoire* and *dit* were contrasted with *conte* and *fable*, the former claiming greater veracity than the latter. After having first been reserved for religious works in allegorical form, by 1240 or so *dit* was used in reference to the works of Chrétien.

6645. The *mui* (MF *muid*) was a measure of capacity, used for liquids, grains, and salt. Like all such, its value varied to an extraordinary degree; cf. note to 6496. Holmes (1964: 196) indicates that the *mui* was the equivalent of 16 *sestiers*. Foerster (*W*) translates *Scheffel* ("bushel"), but this seems too small. The word *esterlin* is simply a Gallicized form of *sterling*.

6664. *C*'s reading seems in direct contradiction to the narrator's immediately preceding remarks (6656-62).

6685. *Seisine* was the payment due to a feudal lord for taking possession of an inheritance dependent on him.

6692. For a discussion of this passage, including numerous references to earlier studies, see Kelly (1983), particularly 14-15, and Uitti (1983), especially 101-03.

6694. I agree with Reid (1976: 12), that "... there is little doubt that Guiot's *lantendie* is simply a blunder, under the influence of *antante* [6693], for the *lannedie* of the other manuscripts, and that the correct reading is that of Foerster 6740...."

6696. Kelly (1983: 15) makes the very valid point that Chrétien is not saying he found a description of this particular robe in Macrobius, but rather that he learned the *art* of description from M.

6726. F printed his own 'invention', *sons*, in 1890 and 1896; in 1909 he adopted *H*'s *son*. His variants indicate that *A* also has *son* and that *VE* have *sanz*, but I have not been able to confirm these.

6741. The plural forms (*consoillent, les*) seem to fit the context better than *C*'s singulars, given the mention of stars, moon, and sun in 6736-37.

6751. Given the mention of other colors for the back, belly, and tail in the following lines, *cors* seems inconsistent.

6756. For a discussion of this line, see Reid (1976): 12. According to F, *VE* share the reading of *HB*.

6761. Chrysolite is a transparent green gem, also called 'olivene' because of its color.

6761-62. *crisolites : ametistes* is another case of "approximate rhyme"; cf. Roques: xxxvii.

6834-93. Very little remains of this portion of the text in *V*, part of the folio having been torn off. See variants to F6880-6910 [sic, for 6909] and 6910-39 for more details.

TEXTUAL NOTES

6855. R6839 emended *C* to *textre*, but this form is found in no manuscript, nor does it occur in any of the numerous examples given by Godefroy and T.-L.

6882. I agree with F (*Anm* 6928) that *palés* refers to the great hall of the
palace, and not to the whole building; the following line makes this
clear.

6888. The remainder of the text in *A* consists of the equivalent of 6709-52,
and these concluding lines:

Bien les sot crestiens descrire
Qui ensi les escrist el liure
Et bien les i sot deuiser
Ci volons no roumant finer
Et ci doit finer par raison
Dius uos doist sa beneicon.

6896. The ending in *CBVA* is abrupt and unsatisfying. One feels the need
for some sort of conclusion, as found in *HPE*. Cf. F *Anm* 6943-end;
Niemeyer: 291. For a defense of the ending presented by Guiot,
see Maddox: 212, n. 73. Following 6896, *V* has

Et por ce uoel ie che laisier
De mangier ne quier plus plaidier
Quant orent mangie a plaisir
Les napes fist on requeillir
Por le [*sic*] feste plus engrangier
A fait li rois tantost drechier
Une quintaine en mi la pree

There is no more text of *Erec et Enide* beyond this in *V*.

338

INDEX TO OLD FRENCH TERMS EXPLAINED IN TEXTUAL NOTES

APPENDIX A: LINE-NUMBER COMPARISONS
WITH FOERSTER'S AND ROQUES' EDITIONS

Foerster [*]	Roques	Carroll
1-902	1-902	1-902
903-906	omits	903-906
907-1194	903-1190	907-1194
1195-1196	omits	omits
1197-1306	1191-1300	1195-1304
1307-1312	omits	omits
1313-1314	1301-1302	1305-1306
1315-1319	omits	omits
1320	1303	1307
omits	1304	1308
1321-1358	1305-1342	1309-1346
1359-1362	omits	1347-1350
1363-1704	1343-1684	1351-1692
1705-1706	omits	omits
1707-1708	1685-1686	1693-1694
1709-1712	omits	omits
1713-1714	1687-1688	1695-1696
1715-1718	omits	omits
1719-1726	1689-1696	1697-1704
1727-1728	omits	omits
1729-1738	1697-1706	1705-1714
1739-1750	omits	omits
1751-1830	1707-1786	1715-1794
1831-1834	omits	1795-1798
1835-1886	1787-1838	1799-1850
1887-1888	omits	1851-1852
1889-1960	1839-1910	1853-1924
1961-1962	omits	omits
1963-2042	1911-1990	1925-2004
2043-2044	omits	2005-2006
2045-2128	1991-2074	2007-2090
2129-2130	2077-2078	2091-2092
2131-2132	2075-2076	2093-2094
2133-2206	2079-2152	2095-2168
2207-2208	omits	2169-2170
2209-2378	2153-2322	2171-2340
omits	2323-2346	omits
2379-2380	2347-2348	2341-2342
omits	2349-2376	omits

[*] Line numbers are identical in all Foerster editions for lines 1-3814 and
5241-6958.

Foerster *	Roques	Carroll
2381-3062	2377-3058	2343-3024
3063-3064	omits	3025-3026
3065-3128	3059-3122	3027-3090
3129-3130	omits	3091-3092
3131-3458	3123-3450	3093-3420
omits	3451-3452	3421-3422
3459-3508	3453-3502	3423-3472
3509-3510	omits	3473-3474
3511-3541	3503-3533	3475-3505
3542-3543	omits	3506-3507
3544-3664	3534-3654	3508-3628
3665-3668	omits	omits
3669-3784	3655-3770	3629-3744
3785-3788	omits	omits
3789-3795	3771-3777	3745-3751
3796	omits	3752
3797	3778	3753
3798	omits	3754
3799-3814	3779-3794	3755-3770

Foerster[1]	Foerster[2]	Roques	Carroll
omits	3815-3816	omits	omits
3815-4022	3817-4024	3795-4002	3771-3978
4023-4024	4025-4026	omits	3979-3980
4025-4200	4027-4202	4003-4178	3981-4156
4201-4202	4203-4204	omits	omits
4203-4256	4205-4258	4179-4232	4157-4210
4257-4258	4259-4260	omits	4211-4212
4259-4514	4261-4516	4233-4488	4213-4468
4515-4524	4517-4526	omits	4469-4478
4525-5100	4527-5102	4489-5064	4479-5054
5101-5104	5103-5106	omits	5055-5058
5105-5238	5107-5240	5065-5198	5059-5192
5239-5240	omits	omits	5193-5194

Foerster *	Roques	Carroll
5241-5246	omits	5195-5200
5247-5698	5199-5650	5201-5652
5699-5700	omits	5653-5654

* Line numbers are identical in all Foerster editions for lines 1-3814 and 5241-6958.
[1] 1890 edition.
[2] 1896, 1909, and 1934 editions.

Foerster [*]	Roques	Carroll
5701-6162	5651-6112	5655-6116
6163-6164	omits	6117-6118
6165-6461	6113-6409	6119-6415
6462-6467	omits	6416-6421
6468-6586	6410-6528	6422-6540
6587	omits	6541
6588	6529	6542
6589	omits	6543
6590-6656	6530-6596	6544-6610
6657-6658	omits	6611-6612
6659-6923	6597-6861	6613-6877
6924	omits	6878
6925	6862	6879
6926	omits	6880
6927-6942	6863-6878	6881-6896
6943-6958	omits	6897-6912

[*] Line numbers are identical in all Foerster editions for lines 1-3814 and
5241-6958.

APPENDIX B: LINES ADDED TO GUIOT'S TEXT

903-06
1347-50
1795-98
1851-52
2005-06
2169-70
3025-26
3091-92
3473-74
3506-07
3752, 3754
3979-80
4211-12
4469-78
5055-58
5193-5200
5653-54
6117-18
6416-21
6541, 6543
6611-12
6878, 6880
6897-6912

Total: 86 lines (23 passages)

APPENDIX C: NON-EMENDATION CHANGES TO ROQUES' TEXT

In addition to many emendations (all indicated in the footnotes to the Old French text), the present edition differs from Roques' text in the following cases, where it conforms more closely to Guiot's manuscript. Many of the discrepancies between Roques and Guiot may have been printing errors introduced at the time Roques' text was set up, and were pointed out by Williams (1956: 459). In a few cases a genuine misreading seems to have been involved, and the difference is more substantive, as in our 4489, 6210, and 6518 (R4499, 6204, and 6506, respectively). I have also included below changes in spelling involving the expansion of Guiot's abbreviations. For the cases of alteration between *com* and *con*, *dom* and *don*, see Woledge (1980). Finally, in a few cases (marked with an asterisk), the letters are the same but I have divided the words differently. Capitalization and punctuation differences are not listed, nor are instances of numerals not written out by Roques but expanded in the present edition.

Roques		Carroll	
line	reading	line	reading (form in Guiot)
0139	quant	0139	qant
0154	isnelement	0154	isnelemant[1]
0171	de pute ere	0171	de put'ere
0308	Gauvains	0308	Gauvain (.G.)
0634	a tot	0634	atot *
0732	vavasor	0732	vavasors
0763	chevalier	0763	chevaliers (chr[s], *s* added above line)
0864	gens	0864	genz
0890	Andui	0890	Andeus (An.ii.)
0962	escus	0966	escuz
1014	grant	1018	Granz
1184	hon	1188	hom
1347	povrement	1355	povremant[1]
1445	leur	1453	les (le[s])
1450	grant	1458	granz (g[a]nz)
1595	fut	1603	fu
1617	cheinse	1625	chainse
1663	quant	1671	qant
1679	Sage	1687	Sages
1699	un	1707	uns
1707	Quant	1715	Qant
1708	au	1716	an
1785	Quant	1793	Qant
1832	la	1844	sa
1866	terme	1880	termes

[1] Adverbs regularly end in -*mant* when they are spelled out in full.

APPENDIX C

Roques		Carroll	
line	reading	line	reading (form in Guiot)
1936	mainz	1950	mains
1973	Quant	1987	Qant
2115	prandre	2131	prendre
2561	querrez	2527	querez (querez)
2687	chascun	2653	chascuns
2922	quant	2888	qant
2960	tot	2926	toz
3202	com	3172	con (con)
3337	commance	3307	comance (comance)
3479	ocire	3449	ocirre
3486	comença	3456	comança (comanca)
3509	à	3481	a
3580	com	3554	con (con)
3587	gens	3561	genz
3648	on	3622	ont
3652	einsi	3626	Ensi
3830	saras	3806	seras
3882	si	3858	s'i *
3944	sor	3920	soz
4018	champ	3996	chanp
4102	voie	4080	veie (ueie)
4163	tel	4141	tex
4280	A	4260	An
4387	vilainemant	4367	vilainnemant (-ainne-)[1]
4397	quant	4377	qant
4418	primerain	4398	premerain (premerain)
4480	lui	4460	li
4492	mout	4482	molt (ml't)
4499	revit	4489	reçut
4571	quant	4561	qant
4632	a trait	4622	atrait *
4690	nos	4680	vos
4695	si	4685	s'i *
4821	entandi	4811	antandi
4833	entr'ax	4823	antr'ax
4837	püent	4827	pueent
4841	grant	4831	granz
4856	dedans	4846	dedanz
4857	s'anfuient	4847	s'an fuient *
4960	es vos	4950	ez vos
5070	si	5064	s'i *
5070	vos	5064	voz (uoz)
5382	ge	5384	je (ie)

[1] Adverbs regularly end in -mant when they are spelled out in full.

348

Roques		Carroll	
line	reading	line	reading (form in Guiot)
5390	si	5392	s'i *
5424	Rien	5426	Riens
5707	desduire	5711	deduire
5762	autre	5766	autres
5880	a tant	5884	atant *
5983	de tot	5987	del tot
5994	dois	5998	doiz
6003	enfance	6007	anfance
6083	mes	6087	nes
6097	comencera	6101	comancera
6165	con	6171	com ("9")
6192	dom	6198	don (don)
6204	faut	6210	saut
6221	ans	6227	anz
6225	deux	6231	deus (.ii.)
6227	que	6233	qu'a (qᵃ)
6319	haus	6325	haut
6327	jusqu'à	6333	jusqu'a (iusqᵃ)
6329	semonnent	6335	semonent (semonent)
6396	apareillier	6402	aparellier
6444	ans	6456	anz
6485	Quant	6497	Qant
6502	roiz	6514	rois
6506	comanda	6518	remanda
6512	qui qui	6524	qui qu'i *

The Garland Library
of Medieval Literature